Women and the Equality Deficit:
The Impact of Restructuring
Canada's Social Programs

Shelagh Day
Gwen Brodsky

The research and publication of this study were funded by Status of Women Canada's Policy Research Fund. This document expresses the views and opinions of the authors and does not necessarily represent the official policy or opinion of Status of Women Canada or the Government of Canada.

March 1998

Status of Women Canada is committed to ensuring that all research produced through the Policy Research Fund adheres to high methodological, ethical, and professional standards. The research must also make a unique, value-added contribution to current policy debates, and be useful to policy-makers, researchers, women's organizations, communities, and others interested in the policy process. Each paper is anonymously reviewed by specialists in the field, and comments are solicited on:

- the accuracy, completeness and timeliness of the information presented;
- the extent to which the analysis and recommendations are supported by the methodology used and the data collected;
- the original contribution that the report would make to existing work on this subject, and its usefulness to equality-seeking organizations, advocacy communities, government policy-makers, researchers and other target audiences.

Status of Women Canada thanks those who contributed to this peer review process.

Canadian Cataloguing in Publication Data

Day, Shelagh

Women and the equality deficit: the impact of restructuring
Canada's social programs

Issued also in French under title: Les femmes et le déficit
en matière d'égalité.
Includes bibliographical references.
Issued also in electronic format through the Internet computer network.
ISBN 0-662-26767-2
Cat. no. SW21-32/1998E

1. Women -- Canada -- Social conditions.
2. Social security -- Canada.
3. Budget deficit -- Canada.
4. Women's rights -- Canada.
I. Brodsky, Gwen.
II. Canada. Status of Women Canada.
III. Title.
IV. Title: The impact of restructuring Canada's social programs.

HV1448.C3D29 1998   362.83'0971   C96-980161-6

Project Manager: Sarah Bélanger, Status of Women Canada
Publishing Coordinator: Angela McLaughlin, Status of Women Canada
Editing: 575 Productions Ltd.
Translation: Société Gamma Inc. and 575 Productions Ltd.

For more information contact:

Research Directorate
Status of Women Canada
360 Albert Street, Suite 700
Ottawa, ON K1A 1C3
telephone: (613) 995-7835
facsimile: (613) 957-3359
TDD: (613) 996-1322
Email: research@swc-cfc.gc.ca

This document is also available for download on the
Status of Women Canada Web site at:
http://www.swc-cfc.gc.ca/.

PREFACE

Status of Women Canada's Policy Research Fund was instituted in 1996 to support independent, nationally relevant policy research on gender equality issues. In order to determine the structure and priorities of the Policy Research Fund, Status of Women Canada held consultations from March to May 1996 with a range of national, regional and local women's organizations, researchers and research organizations, community, social service and professional groups, other levels of government, and individuals interested in women's equality. Consultation participants indicated their support for the Fund to address both long-term emerging policy issues as well as urgent issues, and recommended that a small, non-governmental external committee would play a key role in identifying priorities, selecting research proposals for funding, and exercising quality control over the final research papers.

As an interim measure during the fiscal year 1996-1997, consulation participants agreed that short-term research projects addressing immediate needs should be undertaken while the external committee was being established to develop longer-term priorities. In this context, policy research on issues surrounding the Canada Health and Social Transfer (CHST) and access to justice were identified as priorities.

On June 21, 1996, a call for research proposals on the impact of the CHST on women was issued. The proposals were assessed by Status of Women Canada and external reviewers. The research projects selected for funding in this area focus on women receiving social assistance, economic security for families with children, women with disabilities, the availability and affordability of child care services, women and health care, and women's human rights.

The call for research proposals on access to justice was issued on July 18, 1996. Also assessed by Status of Women Canada and external reviewers, the selected policy research projects in this area include a study of abused immigrant women, lesbians, women and civil legal aid, family mediation, and the implications for victims of sexual harassment of the Supreme Court ruling in *Béliveau-St. Jacques*.

The objective of Status of Women Canada's Policy Research Fund is to enhance public debate on gender equality issues and contribute to the ability of individuals and organizations to participate more effectively in the policy development process. We believe that good policy is based on good policy research. We thank all the authors for their contribution to this objective.

A complete listing of the research projects funded by Status of Women Canada on issues surrounding the Canada Health and Social Transfer and access to justice is provided at the end of this report.

TABLE OF CONTENTS

ACKNOWLEDGEMENTS

We thank Nitya Iyer, Martha Jackman, Lee Lakeman, Yvonne Peters, Lisa Philipps, Monica Townson, and Margot Young for their intellectual and political companionship, their excellent suggestions and criticisms, their generosity with ideas and materials, and their support throughout this project. Bruce Porter, Vince Calderhead, and Katherine Hardie also provided key materials, shared research and ideas, and offered encouragement. We have benefited from the support of the Charter Committee on Poverty Issues, the Centre for Equality Rights in Accommodation, and the B.C. Public Interest Advocacy Centre.

We are grateful to Sandra Goundry, Gillian Calder, and Kim Brooks for their excellent research assistance and for their friendship. Gillian Calder also generously shared with us her research on mechanisms for enforcing international human rights treaties. We also thank Susan Boyd, who provided us with access to her bibliographical work on feminist scholarship.

We appreciate Gayla Reid's careful editing and generous expenditure of time, and the excellent work of Marthe Lépine, Geneviève Gagnon, Maraya Raduha and Lucille Béland on translation, copy-editing and production.

Finally, we thank Status of Women Canada. Without the financial support of Status of Women Canada, we could not have undertaken this study. In particular, we thank Zeynep Karman and Sarah Bélanger for their encouragement and practical assistance.

ABBREVIATIONS

BIA	*Budget Implementation Act*
CAP	Canada Assistance Plan
CCPI	Charter Committee on Poverty Issues
CEDAW	*Convention on the Elimination of All Forms of Discrimination Against Women*
CHA	*Canada Health Act*
CHST	Canada Health and Social Transfer
ECLAC	Economic Commission for Latin America and the Caribbean
EPF	Established Programs Financing
GNP	Gross National Product
ICCPR	*International Covenant on Civil and Political Rights*
ICESCR	*International Covenant on Economic, Social and Cultural Rights*
ITA	*Income Tax Act*
LEAF	Women's Legal Education and Action Fund
NAC	National Action Committee on the Status of Women
NAPO	National Anti-Poverty Organization
UDHR	*Universal Declaration of Human Rights (1948)*
NAWL	National Association of Women and the Law
UNDP	United Nations Development Programme

INTRODUCTION

In February 1995, in legislation to implement the budget entitled the *Budget Implementation Act* (*BIA*),[1] the Government of Canada repealed the Canada Assistance Plan (CAP)[2] and introduced the Canada Health and Social Transfer (CHST).[3] This book is about the profound alteration to social policy in Canada that the *BIA* represents. It is also a book about women's right to equality. The two are linked.

Before the *BIA* was introduced, CAP provided that Canadians have a right to social assistance when in need, a right to an amount of social assistance that takes into account basic requirements, and a right to appeal when assistance is denied. Provinces were required to honour these conditions in order to qualify under CAP for 50:50 cost sharing with the federal government of social assistance and important social services.

In place of CAP, the *BIA* creates the CHST, a new vehicle for transferring federal funds to the provinces. The *BIA* eliminates the conditions formerly attached to social assistance spending. It removes the separate designation of funds for social assistance, combines those funds with block funds for health and post-secondary education, and permits the provinces to spend the funds in any way they wish. It continues the general trend of reducing federal contributions to social programs. By doing so, it increases the likelihood that the federal government will not be able to maintain national standards for any of Canada's social programs because of its reduced spending, and because of the demands of the provinces for control over the programs that they are increasingly responsible for funding.

For women, who are poorer than men, more vulnerable to domestic violence, and more likely to be caregivers for children and older people, the diminished commitment to social programs and services, and to national standards, has significant immediate and long-term consequences. For single mothers, elderly women, Aboriginal women, immigrant women, women of colour, and women with disabilities — who are among the very poorest Canadians — the impact is more drastic.

The *BIA* marks a profound change in the social and political life of Canada. It affects the role of the federal government in the provision of social programs; Canada's ability to create and maintain coherent and equitable standards for social programs; the distribution of power and responsibility between federal, provincial, and territorial governments; and, consequently, the shape of the Canadian state.

Because of this profound change, this is a historic moment for the meaning of women's rights in Canada. It is a moment no less significant than was the introduction of statutory prohibitions of sex discrimination in the 1970s, or the constitutionalization of equality guarantees in the 1980s. At stake now is not just the repeal of the general entitlement to social assistance, further cuts to federal funding, the loss of national standards, and the threat of a race to the bottom in social programs — all of which will affect Canadian women, and especially Canada's poorest women. Also at stake is the ability of women's human rights to be a vital, responding, alternative discourse in a time of global and national restructuring.

There is a danger that the human rights of Canadian women may slide into irrelevance unless they are understood by women, and interpreted by both governments and courts, to have content that can address the threats to women's advancement that neo-liberal economic policies currently pose in the Canadian context.

Unfortunately, at the same time as the federal government divests itself of responsibility for social programs and makes budgetary decisions that have significant negative effects on women, Canadian courts are selectively sidestepping rights challenges brought by disadvantaged groups that raise issues of material conditions. Too often, courts are acceding to government claims that it is not the role of the courts to judicially review economic policy decisions.

We are concerned about the direction of Canadian equality rights jurisprudence, the positions being advanced by governments in equality rights litigation, and the apparent unwillingness of the courts to be a counterbalancing influence when governments ignore women's interests and voices. How courts treat the relationship between the right to equality and economic policy is important because of its potential impact on women. What courts say about rights also influences the understanding people have of their relations to others, and how governments view their roles and responsibilities.

But we are not interested only in what courts say about rights. What governments, political parties, the media, and women say about rights influences what they come to mean, both in and out of court. Public talk about what women's right to equality means in relation to economic and social policy does matter — whether that talk is in the courts, in the media, in meetings, in legislatures, or in government corridors.

Although the *BIA* is of historic importance for Canada, we are not interested in it just for itself, but also as a paradigm, an example of an economic policy whose negative implications for women are not acknowledged or taken into account by policy makers. The *BIA*, unfortunately, is part of a pattern of national and international economic policy making that is deepening women's inequality.

In this book our broad interest, then, is the disturbing disconnection between the economic and social policy decisions that are affecting women's lives and the commitments that have been made over the last five decades, both domestically and internationally, to the equality of all women. Our specific concern is to set the *BIA* in an equality framework and to explore the ways in which, if women are to advance, economic and social policy must connect with women's right to equality.

Economic policy and women's equality rights do not belong in watertight compartments; they cannot be treated as though they have nothing to do with each other, as though they are different and unrelated discourses. They are integrally connected.

This book advances two propositions: (1) that women's persistent economic inequality violates Canada's domestic and international commitments to equality for all women, and (2) that because social programs — and social and economic policy more broadly — are a central means of realizing equality commitments and redressing women's economic disadvantage, they must be designed with the goal of advancing women's equality at their heart.

We believe in Canada's commitments to equality for women, and we believe that those commitments speak directly to the social and economic dimensions of women's inequality. We also believe that the *BIA* violates those commitments. This book explains why.

Chapter 1 examines the implications for women of Canada's most major social policy decision of the last 40 years: the introduction of the *BIA*. Chapter 2 describes the equality commitments that Canada has made internationally and domestically. Chapter 3 examines the arguments that are offered by courts and governments for narrowing the interpretation and application of equality rights when economic policies are challenged in the courts. Chapter 4 explores more closely the content of the rights instruments that women have available to them, and sets out interpretations of equality guarantees that can be responsive to women's material inequality and that draw on the richness and complexity of Canada's equality commitments. In Chapter 5 we consider the work that women must do to ensure that both social programs and equality guarantees can be responsive to women's needs and aspirations in this time of change. We suggest future directions for women's activism, institutional reform, and government policy.

Endnotes

[1] *Budget Implementation Act, 1995*, S.C. 1995, c. 17 [hereinafter *BIA*]. Section 31 of the *BIA* provided that no payment would be made under the Canada Assistance Plan for any fiscal year commencing after 1 April 1996, and no payment would be made to a province under CAP after 1 April 2000. Section 32 of the *BIA* provided that CAP would be repealed on 31 March 2000. The four-year delay between 1 April 1996 and 1 April 2000 merely permits payouts to be made to reimburse provinces for the federal share of CAP costs incurred before 1 April 1996.

[2] R.S.C. 1985, c. C-1 [hereinafter CAP].

[3] The CHST was established by means of an amendment to the *Federal-Provincial Fiscal Arrangements Act*, R.S.C. 1985, c. F-8.

CHAPTER 1

From CAP to the CHST: The Losses

Introduction

Women all over the world are struggling with increasing economic inequality and with the impact of restructuring, whose elements include reducing the size of government, deregulating markets, privatizing services, and cutting social programs. In Canada there is another element in the restructuring dynamic: the push for increased devolution of responsibility to the provinces, with a concomitant weakening of the capacity of the federal government to play a constructive role in creating and maintaining a Canadian social safety net.

The future of social programs and arrangements between levels of government for allocating resources and responsibilities is inextricably intertwined. Because of this, the *Budget Implementation Act (BIA)* represents both the most significant change in social policy and the most significant change in relations among Canadian governments since the 1950s. It has implications for Canada's ability to maintain coherent and equitable standards for social programs, for the distribution of power and responsibility between federal and provincial governments, and consequently for the shape of the Canadian state.

Many Canadian women now fear that the "social union" or the "social Canada"[1] that they believe in, and have relied on, is disappearing. The spectre arises of a diminishing patchwork of social programs, different in different provinces and territories, inconsistent in goals, form, and adequacy, and vulnerable to changing political temper.

In this chapter we ask: What was in the Canada Assistance Plan (CAP)? What does the *BIA* take away? What is the history of national standards for social programs and the federal government's role in setting them? We ask further: Is the federal government's role as national standard setter essential? If it is essential, how should the federal government as standard setter relate to Quebec, and how does this affect the national unity debate?

The Larger Frame

The Material Inequality of Women

The *BIA* is important to women because of their high rate of poverty and general economic inequality. This legislation fits into a larger pattern of government decision making that ignores, and consequently threatens to exacerbate, women's economic inequality.[2]

There is a tendency for discussions about poverty and social programs to become divorced from a critique of underlying unequal power relations and of social institutions. The gendered dimensions of poverty are rarely acknowledged. Poverty is seen as an indication of individual weakness, as individual tragedy, as an abstract social ill, or, currently, as a problem of children but not of their mothers, grandmothers, and aunts. For its effects to be fully understood, the *BIA* must be seen in the larger context of women's economic inequality.

Women in Canada are poorer than men and face a higher risk of poverty.[3] In 1995, 57 percent of all persons living in low-income situations in Canada were women: 2.059 million women.[4] At all ages and stages of their lives but one, the rates of poverty are higher for women than for men; however, the differences between the sexes are most pronounced in the youngest and oldest groups.[5] In 1995, 18.2 percent of women, compared to 14.3 percent of men, were living in poverty.[6]

Single mothers and other "unattached women" are most likely to be poor, with poverty rates for these groups reaching as high as 57.2 percent for single mothers under 65, and 43.4 percent for unattached women over 65.[7] The poverty rates for single mothers are much worse when the figures are disaggregated by their ages and the ages of their children. Single mothers with children under seven had poverty rates as high as 82.8 percent in 1995, and single mothers under age 25 had a poverty rate of 83 percent.[8] Poor single mothers under 65 are also living in the deepest poverty, with incomes $8,851 below the poverty line in 1995.[9]

Poor mothers have poor children. In 1995, 20.5 percent of all Canadian children under 18 were poor,[10] the highest rate in 16 years. The poverty rate among children with single mothers was 62.2 percent.[11]

Aboriginal women, immigrant women, visible minority women, and women with disabilities are more vulnerable to poverty than other women. In 1990, 33 percent of Aboriginal women, 28 percent of visible minority women, and 21 percent of immigrant women were living below the low-income cut-off, compared to 16 percent of other women.[12] Also, at all ages, women with disabilities have lower incomes than women without disabilities or men with disabilities.[13]

While national data on welfare recipients[14] is not disaggregated by sex, extrapolating from statistics on "family type" it is reasonable to estimate that more adult women than men receive social assistance.[15] Children are the largest group that receives social assistance in Canada.[16]

Women have a higher incidence of poverty. But even when their incomes are above the poverty level, they are not economically equal to men. Though women have moved into the paid labour force in ever-increasing numbers over the last two decades,[17] they do not enjoy equality in earnings, or in access to non-traditional jobs and managerial positions,[18] or in benefits.[19] The gap between men's and women's full-time, full-year wages is, in part, owing to occupational segregation in the workforce that remains entrenched and to the lower pay that is accorded to traditionally female jobs. Though the wage gap has decreased in recent years, with women employed on a full-time, full-year basis now earning about 72 percent of the amount earned by men in comparable jobs, part of this narrowing of the gap is due to a decline in men's earnings as a result of restructuring, not to an increase in women's earnings.[20]

The average annual income of women from all sources is about 58 percent of men's income,[21] and there is an equivalent gap in pension benefits, with women receiving only 58.8 percent of the Canada Pension Plan/Quebec Pension Plan (CPP/QPP) pension benefits that men receive.[22] This significant gap in annual income is due, in part, to the wage gap, but also to the fact that women work fewer hours in the paid labour force than men. They work fewer hours because they cannot obtain full-time work,[23] and because they carry more responsibility for unpaid care-giving duties.[24] As of 1994, 40 percent of women, compared to 27 percent of men, held non-standard jobs,[25] that is, they were self-employed, had multiple jobs, or jobs that are temporary or part-time. These jobs are unlikely to be unionized and unlikely to provide pensions or benefits.[26]

Visible minority women, Aboriginal women, and women with disabilities earn less than their male counterparts, and less than other women in most age groups.[27]

Although women's earnings are substantially lower than men's, women play a significant role in keeping their families out of poverty through their earnings. Without women's earnings, poverty rates would rise dramatically and the number of poor families would more than double.[28]

In addition to diminished rewards for their labour, women do not enjoy an equal share of wealth, including property, savings, and other resources. This means that their opportunities to make autonomous choices regarding relationships, education and work are restricted.[29]

It is clear that female sex, motherhood, and single status are significant determinants of poverty. Being a woman of colour, an Aboriginal woman, or a woman with a disability further increases the risk of poverty. It is also clear that women generally are economically unequal to men, and that race and disability complicate and deepen that inequality.

Women's persistent economic inequality is caused by a number of interlocking factors: the social assignment to women of the unpaid role of caregiver and nurturer for children, men, and old people;[30] the fact that in the paid labour force women perform the majority of work in the "caring" occupations and that this "women's work" is lower paid than "men's work";[31] the lack of affordable, safe child care;[32] the lack of adequate recognition and support for child care and parenting responsibilities that either constrains women's participation in the labour force or doubles the burden they carry; the fact that women are more likely than men to have non-standard jobs with no job security, union protection, or benefits;[33] the entrenched devaluation of the labour of women of colour, Aboriginal women, and women with disabilities; and the economic penalties that women incur when they are unattached to men, or have children alone. In general, women as a group are economically unequal because they bear and raise children and have been assigned the role of caregiver. Secondary status and income go with these roles.

To eliminate this inequality requires removing the economic penalty from doing "women's work"; valuing caregiving and nurturing work, both socially and economically; spreading the responsibility for it more evenly across society; compensating for the insecurities inherent in non-standard work; and eliminating economic insecurity as a means of keeping women attached to men.[34] Economic autonomy for women requires access to stable, decent-paying jobs with benefits, or access to other sources of incomes, such as adequate social assistance and pensions. It also requires that women can have children *and* adequate incomes. Without these opportunities, women, too often, have no choice but dependence on men, or poverty. Neither is a formula for equality.

The fact that the incidence of poverty is high and persistent among women and children makes it obvious that poverty cannot be dealt with unless the particular nature of women's poverty is addressed. Social policy has been unsuccessful at diminishing the substantial differences in the risk of poverty between single mothers and other unattached women, on the one hand, and couples, single fathers, and unattached men on the other.[35] Nor has it succeeded so far in putting women, economically, on an equal footing with men, and in changing the economic imbalance of power in most women's individual relationships with men, or between women and men as groups.

Women are not poor for the same reasons that men are poor; and women, as a group, experience economic inequality with all its ramifications. The lack of success in eliminating these conditions is directly attributable to an unwillingness on the part of policy makers to acknowledge that poverty and economic inequality have a gendered character that is further complicated by racism, and discrimination based on disability.

Restructuring

The *BIA* must also be situated in the context of global restructuring. Restructuring has been presented to women as a natural force over which governments have no control.[36] Isabella Bakker describes it this way:

> In the last few years, the term restructuring has been used as a "buzzword" referring to a necessary but painful process of change for Canadians. In general, restructuring is presented as a response to the inevitable pressures of global liberalization. The new global economy, we have been told, requires increased international competition between countries for investment and production, a greater emphasis on trade, and less government spending and regulation of the economy. In other words, governments have no choice but to adapt their domestic economies, particularly the fiscal side, to the new demands of an increasingly global economy. Treaties and international trade agreements such as NAFTA reflect governments' intentions to create a favourable investment climate for foreign capital. Firms, industries, and workers are also being challenged to be more "flexible" and "competitive" in an effort to stem the outflow of manufacturing operations to countries of the South.

The internationalization of production is the most obvious manifestation of the forces driving restructuring. Broadly referred to as globalization, what it signals is a transformation of the methods and locations of production. Technological and managerial changes are taking place that allow firms to divide the different aspects of their operations globally in order to take advantage of the lowest-cost raw materials, the best research and development, the highest-quality assembly, and the most effective marketing. ...

Nation states' responses to transnational production are increasingly circumscribed by a neo-liberal consensus that imposes the same demands on all governments: the need to reduce state spending and regulation, maximize exports, and enable market forces to restructure national economies as part of transnational or regional trading blocs. The economic becomes self-regulating and depoliticized in the sense that the imperatives of efficiency and competition become inevitable, imposed by some external force over which people have no control. ... Its presentation as a universal force makes "restructuring" appear apolitical and, in conjuction with this, gender, race, and class neutral.[37]

The neo-liberal economic agenda also dictates a particular approach to government. The private sphere — the home, the market — is considered worthy of enlargement and sanctification, and the public sphere, including the institution of government itself, is considered dangerous and best kept small. When governments follow this agenda, they treat their capacity to impose limits on the market, in the name of collective values, as suspect, and permit the unqualified assertion of market-oriented values, such as self-reliance and competition.[38] The citizenry becomes individualized. The emphasis is not on understanding and addressing the "social and structural foundations of dependency"[39] but on "individual solutions to what are perceived to be individually determined problems."[40]

The *BIA* is a prominent Canadian example of restructuring. It both reduces social spending and privatizes dependency, as programs and services formerly considered to be public are eliminated, and people are enjoined to turn to the private sphere of the family and the market to have their needs met.

The reduction in social spending and the dismantling of social safety nets have been justified worldwide as necessary to deal with deficits. In Canada, it is telling that the *Budget Implementation Act* is the official name of the statute that brings restructuring to social programs. Before the introduction of the *BIA*, the federal government had been engaged in a public review of social security programs. This was pre-empted by the February 1995 budget announcement. Government documents issued prior to the 1995 budget are replete with comments that blame the deficit on rising social program costs. A 1994 federal government publication *Improving Social Security in Canada: The Context of Reform, A Supplementary Paper*, states: "Our ability to pay for social programs is stretched to the limit. ... These trends toward ever greater expenditure cannot be sustained. Economic well-being and a healthy labour market are being jeopardized by the size of the deficit. Reducing the federal deficit will inevitably require lower spending on many governmental activities, including social security."[41]

However, many critics point out that increases in social spending have contributed very little to creating deficits and debt.[42] Economists Mimoto and Cross argue that government spending on social programs did not increase between 1975 and 1990, and accordingly that the deficit cannot be due to government social spending.[43] Lisa Philipps states that,

> The notion that excessive social spending was somehow responsible for the deterioration of Canada's fiscal condition has now been thoroughly discredited. Looking back on the last two decades, numerous analysts have concluded that an extraordinarily high interest rate policy, combined with the lower employment and economic growth that high interest rates helped to engender, are overwhelmingly responsible for the dramatic rise in the debt burden. Nor are social spending cuts primarily responsible for the recent success of some governments in shrinking or even eliminating their deficits. Rather, the explanation lies in the increased revenues they are enjoying in a period of stronger economic growth, helped along by lower interest rates. It is interesting to note that the same economic factors were responsible for diminishing the massive levels of public debt accumulated during the war years. These facts cast grave doubt on whether the degree of social spending cuts was ever warranted or needed to balance government budgets.[44]

There are other reasons for scepticism about the legitimacy of invoking the deficit as a rationale for current directions. As progressive Canadian scholars and activists have persuasively argued, it is an inadequate analysis of costs and benefits that chooses to focus only on the costs associated with social spending, without taking account of the costs of *not* engaging in adequate social spending. Social spending is not just an expense; it is a necessary social investment, the lack of which also has costs.[45] One significant cost of *not* spending on social programs is that women's inequality is reinforced. Not spending is not gender-neutral.[46]

However, governments do not admit this fact. Rather, they have pursued a course of persuading Canadians that social expectations must be reduced, and that social programs, as we know them, are beyond our means. This choice of political direction is a significant move away from the redistributive values that are key to women achieving equality. It also means that women are taken for granted. It is assumed, when social programs are cut, that women will provide unpaid care for children, husbands, elderly parents, and others. Numerous studies now show that the demands on women to play this role have serious consequences for their health, their incomes, and their autonomy.[47]

It is clear that, in the name of deficit reduction and restructuring, both the current federal Liberal government, and the Conservative government before it, have used the cover of economic policy to depoliticize highly value-laden decisions. These decisions have been characterized as urgent fiscal decisions that serve the common interests of all Canadians, in order to block critics from debating their ideological content and their social impact. Deficit rhetoric relies on quantification and a mathematical version of reality, but the choices made are not neutral. Lisa Philipps argues that,

> technical discourses have worked to depoliticize one of the most pressing social conflicts of our time, translating it into a matter of expert knowledge and shrinking the space for popular resistance to the harmful effects of such policies on many citizens. At the same time, they have helped to legitimate the way restraint policies exploit and deepen class, gender and other social inequalities, by promoting an ideological vision of society in which market power is minimally constrained, and individuals are held personally responsible for their own economic difficulties.[48]

In Canada, blocking debate over the ideological content and the social impact of restructuring is further assisted by the shift of power and responsibility to the provinces to design and pay for social programs and services. The impact of the restructuring of social programs and services is thrust out of public debate, both by being characterized as a neutral economic issue, and by being driven into a fragmented sphere of provincial and territorial jurisdictions, where there is no identifiable venue for discussion of the overall impact on Canada and on its most disadvantaged people.

National Social Programs and Fiscal Federalism

There can be no doubt that the repeal of the CAP, combined with the shift to the CHST, represents an extremely serious threat to the social security system in Canada. In one fell swoop the federal government has eliminated the regulatory underpinnings and the funding framework for crucial components of a national safety net, including social assistance, counselling and referral services, child care, child welfare programs, community development services, legal aid, and services for persons with disabilities. The shifts effected by the *BIA* have been referred to as "a fundamental watershed in the evolution of Canadian social assistance policy,"[49] and as "the most important social policy changes in Canada in almost thirty years."[50] To understand these shifts, it is essential to look more closely at how social programs in the areas of health, post-secondary education, and welfare developed in Canada, the fiscal arrangements that have supported these social programs, the content of national standards, and the role of the federal government.

Health

For the last 30 years, Canada has had national standards for health and social assistance. These standards were set out in federal legislation in the *Medicare Care Act*, the *Canada Health Act* (*CHA*), and the CAP, even though health and social assistance (as well as post-secondary education) fall into provincial jurisdiction under the division of powers in Canada's constitution. The national medicare and welfare programs were created and their standards were enforced through the use of the federal spending power. The story of their development is the story of fiscal federalism.

In 1948[51] the federal government first used the power of its treasury in the field of health by providing grants to the provinces for hospital construction, cancer control programs, and other specific health care services. Gradually, grants for other services were added. In 1953, after four provinces had initiated some form of public hospital insurance, the federal government introduced the *Hospital Insurance and Diagnostic Services Act*. Under this *Act* the federal government reimbursed 50 percent of the provinces' costs of providing specified hospital services under their insurance plans. By 1961 all provinces had joined this scheme.

In 1968 the *Medicare Care Act* came into effect. This provided medical care insurance similar to the hospital insurance that was already in place. Under this *Act*, "[t]he federal contribution to each province was 50% of the average national per capita cost multiplied by the province's population. Provincial expenditure levels were not taken into account directly, and no ceiling was imposed on the amount of the grant. Initially provinces were required to meet four conditions to be eligible for reimbursement: the provincial plans had to provide universal coverage, be comprehensive in the range of services covered, be administered by the province or an agency of the province, and be portable between provinces."[52] Although medicare was invented in Saskatchewan, the federal government converted it into a national program by offering, on certain conditions, to share its costs. By 1971 all provinces were a part of the national medicare program.

In 1977 the financial arrangements were changed and the separate grants that the federal government provided for hospital insurance, medicare insurance, and post-secondary education were rolled into Established Programs Financing (EPF). Under this arrangement, the federal government transferred more "tax points" to the provinces; that is, it reduced its share of corporate and personal income tax and allowed the provinces to raise theirs proportionately.

Although both federal and provincial governments have constitutional powers to impose income taxes on individuals and corporations, in practice, the two levels of government coordinate and rationalize income taxes for the practical reason that they both look to the same tax base, that is, to the same taxpayers and the same income. At various times, one or the other level of government has agreed to cede some of its "tax room" to the other. In other words, one level agrees to reduce its income tax rate on the understanding that there will be a corresponding rise in the taxes collected by the other level. The amount of "tax room" ceded in this fashion is often expressed as a certain number of "tax points," referring to the percentage points by which one level of government reduces tax rates in order to leave "room" for the other.[53]

In 1967 the federal government began ceding tax points to the provinces to replace part of its cash commitment for post-secondary education. In 1977, with the new EPF, the federal government gave up an additional chunk of tax points as part of a permanent arrangement for funding post-secondary education and health. It also provided block cash transfers to support both health and education, which gave an equal per capita payment to each province. This cash transfer was set at the level of 50 percent of the federal contribution to hospital, medicare, and post-secondary education programs in 1975–76. The cash transfer would grow from year to year to reflect changes in provincial population and growth in Gross National Product (GNP).[54] The 1977 EPF was an agreement through which the provinces agreed to provide post-secondary education and health services with the cash and tax points transferred by the federal government.

The National Council on Welfare explains how the EPF arrangement works on an ongoing basis in this way:

> Each year, the federal government calculates its total commitments under EPF to each province and territory. It then calculates the revenue raised that year by the tax points that were transferred to each province and territory [in 1977], and it subtracts the tax revenue from total EPF entitlements. The amount left over is paid in cash by Ottawa.[55]

This change from cost sharing to block funding for health and post-secondary education was a result of unease at both federal and provincial levels. At the federal level, there was increasing concern about the open-endedness of the funding formula and the lack of control it afforded as health costs rose. As long as the federal government paid 50 percent of provincial health-care costs with no ceiling, its expenditures were dictated by provincial levels of spending. At the provincial level, there was resentment because of the extent of federal intrusion into the province's constitutional jurisdiction over health and education.[56] The shift to the block funding of the EPF meant that the amount of the federal government's cash transfer was no longer determined solely by the provinces. For the provinces, it meant that they were freer to allocate the funds between health and education according to their priorities and with fewer conditions.[57]

In 1984, at the time when federal cash transfers were at their highest level, the *Canada Health Act* (*CHA*) was enacted to replace the legislation that dealt separately with hospital insurance and medical care insurance. The *CHA* sets out the five standards that provinces must meet in order to receive the full EPF cash transfer:

- accessibility: provide reasonable access to health care without financial or other barriers;

- comprehensiveness: cover all medically necessary hospital and medical services;

- universality: cover all legal residents of a province (after a three-month residency);

- portability: entitle residents to coverage when temporarily absent from their province or when moving between provinces; and

- public administration: administer health plans by an agency of the province on a non-profit basis.[58]

The *CHA* outlines the federal government's authority to enforce the standard of accessibility by reducing the cash transfer dollar for dollar if a province allows doctors to bill their patients or hospitals to charge user fees. It also allows the federal government to reduce the cash transfer if other standards are violated.[59]

Though the *CHA* articulates the standards and recognizes the federal role in the health field, legislation is not the key here. Both the existence of the national medicare program, and the enforcement of the five national standards flow from the federal government's (1) spending on a matter that constitutionally falls within provincial jurisdiction, and (2) conditioning the transfer of funds to the provinces on their adherence to the standards that it sets.

Social Assistance and Social Services

As with health, national standards regarding welfare have been developed through the federal government's sharing the costs of social assistance and social services with the provinces and setting conditions on its contribution.

In the 1950s, the federal government passed the *Old Age Assistance Act*, the *Blind Persons Act*, the *Disabled Persons Act*, and the *Unemployment Assistance Act*. This legislation permitted the federal and provincial governments to share the costs of assisting low-income seniors, blind and severely disabled adults, and some unemployed people.[60] At the time, provincial and local governments provided allowances for single mothers and relief programs for others who were needy.[61]

In the 1960s, there were two major advances. The federal government introduced the Guaranteed Income Supplement (GIS) for low-income Canadians over 65. The GIS was simply added to the Old Age Security Pension for those who passed an income test. It has changed markedly the rates of poverty among seniors in Canada.[62]

For people under 65, the CAP in 1966 overtook the scatter of programs operated and funded by both levels of government, replacing it with a scheme that meant "for the first time ever, welfare was available everywhere in Canada to all people who were unable to provide for their own needs."[63]

Since that time, the CAP, a federal statute, has been the vehicle for federal-provincial cost sharing for social assistance, and for national standard setting in the welfare field. Peter Hogg says: "Without the federal initiative, and the federal sharing of costs, it is certain that at least some of these services would have come later, at standards which varied from province to province, and not at all in some provinces."[64]

The CAP was adopted by Parliament in order to encourage provinces to develop social assistance programs that met national standards. In its preamble the CAP stated:

> WHEREAS the Parliament of Canada, recognizing the provision of adequate

assistance to and in respect of persons in need and the prevention and removal of the causes of poverty and dependence on social assistance are the concern of all Canadians, is desirous of encouraging the further development and extension of assistance and welfare services programs throughout Canada by cost-sharing more fully with the provinces in the cost thereof.

The CAP authorized the federal government to make payments to provincial governments, to enable them to finance and administer social assistance programs and other welfare-related services, subject to contractual conditions,[65] or in other words, standards. The standards included:

- accessibility: provide financial aid or other assistance to any person in need;[66]

- adequacy: provide an amount that is consistent with a person's basic requirements.

   (The CAP defined basic requirements as "food, shelter, clothing, fuel, utilities, household supplies and personal requirements."[67] In other words, the CAP established a minimum national standard of substantive adequacy for provincial social assistance programs.)[68]

- universality: impose no residency requirement as a condition of eligibility to receive or to continue to receive assistance;[69]

- right of appeal: provide a procedure for appeals for applicants for assistance from decisions of welfare agencies;[70] and

- right to refuse work: impose no requirement that recipients of assistance provide labour in a federal-provincial cost-shared work project.

The importance of the standards set out by the CAP cannot be overemphasized. Although, in our view, they were significantly incomplete, they provided basic entitlements. Because of these standards, residents anywhere in Canada were entitled to social assistance. Since the 1960s, Canadians have not been required to have a particular status, such as widowed mother, or to have a particular condition, such as blindness, to qualify for social assistance, but only to show that they meet an income test for eligibility.[71] Also, applicants were entitled to appeal decisions of the welfare-granting agency. Finally, the CAP, while not barring it completely, put a definite chill on workfare. Each one of these standards was essential to the dignity of those who found themselves without means.

Collectively, the CAP protections constituted crucial elements of a social safety net for people living in poverty. They were useful because they represented a kind of commitment by governments that they do not usually ignore lightly. Under the CAP, any provincial government that violated a funding agreement knew it was vulnerable to involvement in expensive litigation. An individual could sue the federal government, as Jim Finlay did in the early 1980s, for failing to require a province to meet the conditions of the CAP.[72] Provinces were also vulnerable to a withdrawal of federal funding.[73] Thus, the CAP gave social assistance beneficiaries a reasonable expectation that the CAP standards would be enforced by the federal government and respected by provincial governments.

As well as providing 50:50 cost sharing for social assistance, the CAP also provided 50:50 cost sharing of important welfare-related social services, including:

- homemaker services for the elderly, to assist them with shopping, cooking, cleaning;

- attendant services for people with disabilities, to allow them to live independently;

- child care services to assist parents with the care of young children while they completed their education, got training, or worked;

- services to unemployed people to assist them to enter or re-enter the workforce, by paying for start-up costs, such as transportation and clothing, or tools;

- child welfare services to assist children who are neglected or abused;

- services for women fleeing male violence and abusive relationships, such as shelters and transition homes;

- counselling services for individuals, couples, families, and children, to assist them with personal, health-related, or employment problems;

- information and referral services to direct people in need to counselling, training, shelters, or emergency support;

- respite services to assist parents caring at home for children with severe disabilities; and

- assistance in covering the costs of medically prescribed diets, wheelchairs, special eyeglasses, and prostheses for people unable to purchase these necessities on their own.[74]

There was an incentive under the CAP for provincial governments to provide the services that were eligible for 50:50 cost sharing because for every 50 cents they spent, they could provide a dollar's worth of services for the residents of their province.

The CAP also committed the federal government to pay 50 percent of the real costs of social assistance and CAP-funded services in each province.[75] In other words, the CAP contemplated that the amount of money contributed by the federal government would vary in proportion to the levels of need experienced in a province.

Additionally, the CAP regulations required that funds contributed by the federal government under the CAP were available only as reimbursement to the provinces for actual expenditures on social assistance and social services;[76] that is, federal funds designated for social assistance programs and welfare services were not available for provinces to spend on other initiatives that might be more popular among the less needy residents of a province.

The National Council of Welfare estimates that in March 1994 there were about 3.1 million people on welfare, or about 11 percent of Canada's population, with one of the largest groups being single mothers and their children.[77] Two-thirds of CAP dollars have gone directly into social assistance and to legal aid for family and other non-criminal cases; the other third has been directed to administration and to CAP-funded services.[78] The National Council concludes that CAP-funded programs have, over 30 years, helped many millions of Canadians.[79]

The Impact of the *Budget Implementation Act*

Under the *BIA*, four things are lost:

1. The CAP standards are gone. The requirement that social assistance programs adhere to substantive and procedural standards is eliminated, along with the reasonable expectation that the federal government will enforce those standards.[80] Canadians no longer have an entitlement in every jurisdiction to social assistance, to an adequate standard of social assistance, to appeal decisions made by welfare agencies,[81] or to challenge in the courts transfers that do not meet the CAP conditions. And it is clear that provinces have been given the "flexibility" to require work for welfare. The only condition that survives in the CHST is that no residency requirement can be imposed on applicants for welfare.

    By contrast, in the *BIA*, the *Canada Health Act* is retained with its five standards. This provides a clear indication that while the federal government considers medicare standards national icons, not to be vandalized overtly, the CAP standards do not have the same status and can be abolished without political penalty.

2. The 50:50 cost sharing for social assistance and social services is gone. Funds for social assistance are now part of a block fund for health, post-secondary education, and social assistance, and each province receives funds in the same proportion as the 1995–96 transfers under the EPF and CAP.

    The loss of 50:50 cost sharing for social assistance and social services is significant. Block funding does not reimburse for 50 percent of actual expenditures. It does not allow for the fact that welfare is a more volatile social program than health care or post-secondary education, and that funds required to adequately support it fluctuate with economic cycles and with rises and falls in the rate of unemployment.[82] Also, the loss of cost sharing means that an important incentive to provide the CAP-funded social services is gone, because now provincial governments have to pay the whole cost of those services.

3.	The specific allocation of funds for social assistance and social services, which the CAP provided, is gone. Now, funds for social assistance and social services are rolled in with those for health and post-secondary education to provide to the provinces one comprehensive Canadian Health and Social Transfer. Further, despite its name, there is no condition requiring the provinces to spend *any* of the Transfer funds on health, post-secondary education, or social assistance. Consequently, provinces can allocate the transfer monies to health, post-secondary education, and welfare in whatever way they wish, or they can allocate the monies to none of these. Only if they spend some CHST money on health do they have to conform to the *CHA* standards, and only if they spend some CHST money on social assistance do they have to respect the no-residency-requirement rule for social assistance.

4.	Finally, the amounts transferred to the provinces under the CHST are cut. Thomas Courchene notes that,

> ... the 1995 budget ... imposed two substantial cuts on the overall CHST entitlement — first a $2.5 billion cut in 1996/97 from what the overall funding levels would otherwise have been (that is, beyond the previous cuts announced in the 1994 federal budget), and then a further $1.8 billion cut in the overall CHST entitlements between 1996/97 and 1997/98. The result is a level for the CHST entitlement ceiling in 1997/98 of $25.1 billion.[83]

Under the terms of the 1995 budget, the cash portion of the transfer was to be $6.6 billion less in 1997–98 than in 1994–95, bringing the cash payments under the CHST to about $11 billion for 1997–98.[84] As an election promise, the Liberal government cancelled the planned 1997–98 cut in April 1997, leaving the cash floor for the CHST at $12.5 billion.[85,86]

The Controversy Over Financial Arrangements

The 1995 budget cuts are not the federal government's first unilateral cuts to transfer payments for social programs, but rather the latest in a series. As Courchene points out, the federal government has been an unreliable and unpredictable partner in the financing of social programs for some time.[87]

In particular, after the initial financial formula was set in 1977 for the EPF transfers for health and post-secondary education, a steady string of financial restraints was imposed on provincial entitlements between 1983 and 1995, with the result that federal cash transfers for health fell from paying for 36.5 percent of provincial health expenditures in 1980 to 21.1 percent in 1995.[88]

Also, the 50:50 cost-sharing formula of the CAP was changed abruptly in 1990 when, in the federal budget speech, without any prior notice, Finance Minister Michael Wilson announced a "cap on CAP" for the three wealthiest provinces: Alberta, British Columbia, and Ontario. Ottawa indicated that it would no longer be bound by the 50:50 formula; in these provinces it would limit any increase in its CAP contribution to 5 percent a year.

The CHST entrenches these cuts and adds to them. One of the problematic elements of the financial arrangements has been that the cash portion of the transfer is vanishing. The CHST is an extension of the EPF model, so it too is a combination of tax points and cash. Because under this formula the federal government calculates the current value of the tax points that were transferred in 1977 and subtracts this amount from the current value of the entitlements, the amount of the cash transfer is reduced as the value of the tax points rises. The combination of restraints on the overall amount of the entitlements and the rising value of the 1977 tax points means that the federal government has been gradually reducing the amount of the cash transfer. The cuts that were part of the 1995 budget made this reduction in the cash transfer dramatic. Without change, the cash transfers to the provinces would run out in about another decade.[89]

The provinces argue that only the cash transfers are felt as direct federal contributions to social programs, because the provinces consider the tax room transferred in 1977 to be a permanent part of their revenue base now.[90] As far as they are concerned, only the cash portion of the transfer matters. And, as the federal government's cash contribution diminishes, so does its ability to set or enforce any standards, including those in the area of health. The federal government has little leverage as its contribution declines. This is evident, for example, from the statement of the Western Premiers in November 1995: "All provinces agreed that it is unacceptable for the federal government to unilaterally prescribe structure and standards for social policy while abandoning their commitment to support social programs with adequate, stable and predictable funding."[91]

There is, in fact, no reason for the CHST cash transfer to run out. Taking the deficit agenda at face value, the provinces have made a big contribution to reducing the federal deficit, and, as the federal government contemplates impending surpluses, there is no fiscal argument to support continuing reductions.[92] In fact, after the 1995 budget, the federal government indicated that it may not allow the cash portion of the transfer to decline to zero. As noted, during the 1997 election campaign, the Liberals promised to keep the floor for cash payments at $12.5 billion.

One of the results of the history and the changing structure of fiscal federalism is that currently there is an intense, sometimes acrimonious, federal-provincial and interprovincial struggle under way over fairness. Because of the combination of the original 50:50 cost-sharing formula, the series of freezes and cuts to EPF, the cap on CAP, and the CHST allocation of payments to the provinces based on their 1995–96 level of EPF and CAP funds, the provinces do not receive equal per capita grants under the CHST. Added to other reasons for tension, levels of payments are a hot issue, with vying claims of unfair treatment. How the CHST funds should be allocated after 1997–98 is an issue of nation-wide dispute.

There are many signs of this ongoing disagreement. For example, because of the effects of the cap on CAP,[93] the British Columbia government claimed that it had been treated unfairly by the federal government. It unsuccessfully challenged the cap on CAP in court. Subsequently it imposed a three-month waiting period on applicants for social assistance, contrary to the one CAP rule that survives in the CHST. The federal government held back $47 million in payments as a penalty. British Columbia explained its actions by stating that it supports equalization payments, but it does not support the federal government taking funds from British Columbia in every program to redistribute to the poorer provinces. It complained that "Ottawa discriminates against the trio of prosperous provinces by failing to provide equal levels of funding for health, post-secondary education and welfare programs. ... Under the CHST, British Columbia is receiving $472 per capita compared to Newfoundland's $594."[94]

In August 1996, writing for the Ontario government, Thomas Courchene developed a new model for an interprovincial economic and social union and a new structuring of transfer payments. He proposed that there should be a complete federal withdrawal from the funding of social programs by converting the CHST cash transfers into "additional equalized tax-point transfers."[95] This was greeted with outrage by the Premiers of the poorer provinces, and it led Premier John Savage, of Nova Scotia, to make an impassioned speech to the Empire Club in October 1996 entitled "Two Canadas: The Have Canada and The Have-Not Canada." He reported that in August 1996 at the First Ministers' Meeting,

> Courchene was thrown from the train. ... Thomas Courchene's controversial paper on re-balancing federal-provincial social responsibilities gave us a defining moment. For the first time Nova Scotia and five other have-not provinces voiced a resounding and harmonious "no" to an option which obviously has some appeal to Canada's rich provinces. We said "no" to the Courchene scenario in which Ottawa would completely get out of social programs like health care and turn its cash transfers into equalized tax points for the provinces.
>
> ... The plain truth is Nova Scotia can't afford to let Ottawa vacate the social welfare field because, on its own, our province doesn't have the money to bankroll a takeover. Ontario, Alberta and British Columbia do. ...
>
> It should be remembered that if every have-not province paid full fare for its social programs, this country's existing disparities would be greatly magnified. ... As our east-west economic links slacken to take advantage of the continental north-south pull, it's generally agreed we must maintain social bonds, like medicare, which Canadians recognize as national family traits — as entitlements of citizenship and unifying features of this country.
>
> ... Canadians in richer provinces should not have substantially better social programs than those in poorer provinces.

It is important to note here that not only have contributions to social programs been cut, and national standards for social assistance repealed, with the exception of the no-residency-requirement rule, but the federal government also has imposed limits on its own use of the spending power with respect to any new programs. In the 1996 Throne Speech, the federal government announced:

> The Government of Canada will not use its spending power to create new cost-shared programs in areas of exclusive [provincial] jurisdiction without the consent of the majority of the provinces. Any new program will be designed so that non-participating provinces will be compensated, provided they establish equivalent or comparable initiatives.

The federal government is backing away from using its spending power to create and set standards for social programs in spite of the fact that this practice is supported by the *Constitution Act, 1867*. Provincial programs for health, welfare, and post-secondary education fall within provincial jurisdiction. However, the federal government is permitted to spend in these areas, and to attach conditions to its expenditures in the form of national standards that bind the provinces. This issue has been squarely addressed by the courts.

In the case of *Winterhaven Stables Ltd.* v. *Canada (A.G.)*,[96] an Alberta taxpayer challenged the constitutional validity of various government spending statutes, including the CAP, on the grounds that they impinged on the legislative authority of the provinces. The taxpayer argued that by the power of its purse, the federal government unconstitutionally coerced the provinces into participating in certain programs in the fields of health, welfare, and post-secondary education.

The challenge was rejected in its entirety by the Alberta Court of Appeal, which held that the federal government has the constitutional authority to spend on social programs and to attach conditions to those expenditures. Moreover, the constitutional validity of the challenged spending statutes, including the CAP, was specifically upheld. The Court recognized that "… Canada, over many years, has established a robust posture in negotiating with provinces towards establishing these cost-shared programs which are intended to provide Canadians with common national standards of services."[97] The Court even went so far as to acknowledge that the consequence is to "impose considerable pressure on the provinces to pass complementary legislation or otherwise comply with the conditions,"[98] and nevertheless upheld the federal government's standard-setting authority, commenting on the potential harm of federal retreat from cost sharing. The Court said: "To hold that conditions cannot be imposed would be an invitation to discontinue federal assistance to any region or province, destroying an important feature of Canadian federalism."[99]

In short, *Winterhaven Stables* accords judicial recognition to the spending power of the federal government. Leave to appeal in *Winterhaven Stables* was denied by the Supreme Court of Canada.[100]

What conclusions should we come to? First of all, the federal government's authority to set and enforce national standards is based on money. Historically, it has converted provincial programs into national ones by the use of its spending power, and also used this power to set and enforce national standards. Its right to do this has been constitutionally confirmed. However, if its contributions decrease, its power to shape or maintain a Canadian social union also diminishes. Many commentators have concluded that "[n]o federal cash means no enforceable conditions, no national standards, no realizable objectives for medicare or an income safety net."[101]

The Liberal government acknowledged this problem, in part, during the 1997 election by promising that the cash portion of the transfer will not disappear and that a floor of $12.5 billion for the cash payments will be maintained. It stated that while other federal parties have called for elimination of cash transfers to the provinces in favour of a transfer system based on tax points alone, "this would amount to an abandonment of the federal government's authority to uphold the fundamental principles of medicare. By continuing to provide significant cash transfers to the provinces, we will be able to retain this authority under the *Canada Health Act*."[102] This statement is significant. While the Liberal government seems to concede that the federal spending power is an essential tool for maintaining and enforcing national standards, only national standards for health care now exist and only these receive attention.

With respect to other standards, the CHST directs the Minister of Human Resources to invite representatives of all the provinces to consult and work together to develop, through mutual consent, a set of shared principles and objectives for social programs.[103] This apparently envisions federal-provincial agreement on "principles and objectives" as a substitute for national standards for social assistance and social services. The federal government and the provinces have formed a Ministerial Council on Social Policy and Renewal. The provinces appear to believe that they can develop pan-Canadian standards that can be implemented effectively without the federal government using its spending power to enforce them. The provinces' resistance to the use of the federal spending power to enforce standards was demonstrated again at the December 1997 meeting of First Ministers on the social union. At that time, First Ministers, with the exception of Premier Lucien Bouchard, appeared to be in agreement about first steps for developing a new framework for Canada's social union. However, in reporting the results of the meeting, it became apparent that they disagreed over how the national standards in the *Canada Health Act* will be enforced in future. The Premiers thought it was a question open for negotiation; the Prime Minister responded that the federal government would continue to enforce the *Act* through the use of the spending power as before.[104]

There are many reasons to be sceptical about the provinces' ability to develop pan-Canadian standards that can be effectively implemented in the absence of federal enforcement through spending power. As Michael Mendelson points out, the track record on interprovincial agreement is poor, and provincial governments are not likely to agree to national standards that are meaningful and substantial. If consensus is required, this is likely to block agreement on standards that are more than mere platitudes. If they did agree on standards with substance, it is not clear how those standards would be enforced since the provinces would not have the ability to impose financial penalties on each other as the federal government has.[105] It is difficult not to conclude that there is no simple, effective alternative to the federal spending power to turn to for establishing and enforcing national standards for social programs.

Secondly, social values have become lost in the fiscal struggle. Whereas fiscal arrangements were originally the vehicle for creating a comprehensive and equitable social safety net for Canada, they are now the main concern. There is no new social vision here, and what governments (although not the people) are most concerned about is whether they are, relative to each other, carrying a fair share of the cost of social programs. Governments are now arguing about "equality." But the subject is not the "equality" of Canadian residents; rather it is the "equal treatment" of governments.

Keith Banting notes: "In most Western nations, debate focuses primarily on the role of social policy in redistributing income between high and low income groups. However, in Canada, the political intensity of linguistic and regional divisions ensures that social policy debate is also concerned with interregional distribution."[106] He concludes that the 1995 budget is concerned principally with interregional, not interpersonal distribution, even though "Canadians ... have obligations to each other that go well beyond an interregional laundering of money."[107]

Finally, there is a very strong decentralizing thrust to the CHST. Canadians may be left with 12 very different health and welfare programs and a federal government that, in the field of social policy, is only an instrument for some interregional equalization.

Why Should Standards Be National?

Clearly, if we believe that social programs and social services are vital to women, and that standards are necessary to ensure the availability and adequacy of those programs and services, it follows that those standards should apply to all programs for all women. However, this brings us to the "national unity debate."

Women's organizations have had more comfort than other groups with the idea that there could be differences among the powers allocated to different provincial governments. The National Action Committee on the Status of Women (NAC) and some other women's organizations have supported a "three-nations" position since the Charlottetown Round of Constitutional Talks, recognizing that Canada can be thought of, and governed as, three nations, with Quebec and Aboriginal peoples enjoying levels of sovereignty that would not be enjoyed by other provincial and territorial governments.[108] In February 1994, NAC described the perspectives of these "three nations" in its brief to the Standing Committee on Human Resource Development in this way:

Social programs are valued by all Canadians. At the same time, Canada's constitutional debates have demonstrated that English-speaking Canadians, aboriginal peoples and the people of Quebec have distinct perspectives on the role of particular governments in the management and delivery of social programs. A restructuring of social programs must respect these differences and not attempt to impose a formula which meets the needs of one national community onto the others. With respect to English-speaking Canada, this means respecting the desire of most Canadians outside of Quebec to have the Canadian government play a strong role in social programs. With respect to Quebec, this means recognizing that the majority of Quebecers look to the Quebec government for the management and delivery of their social programs. With respect to aboriginal peoples, this means respecting their desire for self-government which includes control of social services. Furthermore, the multi-racial and multi-cultural makeup of Quebec and the rest of Canada must be recognized in the design and delivery of anti-racist and culturally appropriate social services.

Accepting these different perspectives, it is important to permit Quebec to develop social programs suited to its distinct cultural and social needs, and it is just as important to permit the rest of Canada to retain and improve "national" standards for its social programs, rather than abandoning them and blaming Quebec for their loss. Barbara Cameron points out that "there is a conflict inherent in existing Canadian federalism between the social rights of English Canadians and the national rights of Quebec."[109] At present, Canadians in Quebec and the rest of Canada are being offered solutions that satisfy neither interest — too little provincial autonomy for Quebec and too much provincial autonomy for the rest of Canada.

In the rest of Canada, women experience the current shove towards decentralization, not as a new opportunity to increase the powers of the government nearest to them, but as the triumph of territorial interests over those of disadvantaged Canadians. Many women harbour a deep suspicion of the commitment of male-dominated provincial governments in the rest of Canada to values or policies that will assist women in the long term. Provincial governments do not advocate for more powers for themselves on the grounds that this power will enable them to provide more progressive social programs or advances for women. In fact, they do not try to persuade residents that decentralization is best for them on the terrain of values at all. Instead, they argue that further decentralization will eliminate duplication and "confusion," or that they are defending the honour of their province by not allowing any other province to get more (money, or powers). Women see the need for national standards as a way to speak across regional interests, which, in the rest of Canada, often seem petty, parochial, and male.[110] They care about a strong role for the federal government not because they believe that the federal government will necessarily have women's interests closer to its heart, but because, by definition, its role is to cut across territorial interests. This provides an opening for some other values to be asserted.

Because women are so directly affected by social programs and social services, and by cuts to them, women need coherence, certainty, and adequacy. These cannot be provided without standards that provide parameters and guarantees for all women. While women in Quebec are likely to remain in Quebec in order to live and work in French, women in the rest of Canada move from one province to another, often not because of their own choice, but because of the dictates of family members or a spouse's work requirements.[111] This means that security for women in the rest of Canada requires that social programs are adequate in all the provinces and territories. The spectre that is raised for women, if there are no national standards, is of trying to lobby effectively nine provincial (not counting Quebec) governments, two territorial governments, and an increasing plethora of regional and community boards to whom responsibility for health care and social programs is being devolved. Far from bringing democracy closer to the people, this dispersion of responsibility makes it increasingly difficult for politically marginalized groups to have any impact.

Also, it is not the experience of women that the geographical proximity of a seat of government translates into greater government responsiveness. The gulf between women and governments is a gulf created by a lack of adequate mechanisms for women's democratic participation, and a lack of willingness on the part of government to create them.

The irony of the current impasse is that women in Quebec and women in the rest of Canada want the same thing from governments — practical realization of commitments to eradicating their inequality. Yet women in the rest of Canada are being told that they cannot have national standards for social programs that might ensure that practical realization, while women in Quebec are being told that they cannot have the national powers for their government that might ensure it. Any solution that actually satisfies the interests of Quebec and the rest of Canada will have to have two characteristics: (1) real content that expresses shared values and a commitment to addressing disadvantage, and (2) asymmetry with respect to powers in order to recognize the sovereignty of Quebec in the area of social programs, the desire of Aboriginal peoples to control social services in their own communities, and a central role for the federal government in social programs for the rest of Canada.[112]

At the time of the Charlottetown Round of Constitutional Talks, women argued against the principle of same treatment for the provinces as an unworkable version of equality to apply in a complex nation. Since that time, however, it has become more accepted, and in the 1997 elections the Reform Party presented its divisive version of it under the rallying cry of "equality of provinces and citizens."

Slogan to the contrary, Preston Manning's vision of a new Canada is profoundly anti-egalitarian. To Preston Manning, "equality" simply means "same treatment," and therefore, in his mouth, equality stands for a blatant refusal to deal with cultural difference, regional disparities, or disadvantage. "Equality of provinces and citizens" is a code for a form of devolution that elevates identical treatment for provincial governments to the status of a core social value, while abandoning a collective sense of responsibility for the well-being or equality of Canadians.

Central to the reasons that many women opposed the Charlottetown Accord was that it did not satisfy the demands of Quebec; it proposed to make new social programs more difficult to initiate by requiring that they have the support of seven provinces and 50 percent of the population; and it proposed to devolve powers to the provinces in the rest of Canada without speaking to the issue of maintaining standards for health, education, social assistance, or the environment. Though the Charlottetown Accord was defeated, it seems clear that the Accord is being implemented nonetheless through administrative decisions and budgets.

The Premiers' Principles and Executive Federalism

The CHST has spawned the Ministerial Council on Social Policy Reform and Renewal. Established by the federal government and the provincial Premiers in 1995, all provinces and territories, except Quebec, appointed a Minister to this Council. The Premiers, who have taken the lead role so far in this configuration, asked the Council to "formulate common positions on national social policy issues" and "draft a set of guiding principles and underlying values for social policy reform and renewal." The Council produced a report in December 1995, which was adopted by the Premiers in March 1996.

In the *Report* adopted by the Premiers, 15 "Principles" are offered to guide social policy reform and renewal. These principles are vague and sometimes contradictory. It is not clear in what way they can "guide" social policy reform and renewal.

The obfuscation of the gendered character of poverty and economic inequality is a feature of the *Report to Premiers*. Women appear in the last of the 15 Principles, but the language is reminiscent of the references in *The Federal Plan for Gender Equality* to the need for "gender-based analysis."[48] Ironically, the need for gender-based analysis was acknowledged by the federal government at just about the same time as the CAP was repealed. The analysis of the impact of social policies on women is essential,[49] but we already know a lot about the inequality of women. Gender-based analysis will not be valuable if, rather than being a vehicle for making women's advancement a central goal of policy formulation now, it is used to provide backward-gazing reflections on the reasons for lack of progress.

With the exception of this fifteenth Principle, women appear in the remainder of the *Report to Premiers* as an unnamed social phenomenon. The *Report to Premiers* cites as one of the reasons for social policy reform the fact that "the family's role and the structure of society itself are changing." To illustrate this, the *Report to Premiers* indicates that "the number of children per family is decreasing and the number of families headed by single parents has increased dramatically in the past few decades. As well, the percentage of two parent families with both parents working outside the home has increased significantly."[50]

The fact that these changes in the "family's role" and the "structure of society" are principally a reflection of the changes in the lives of women over this period is obscured. The number of families headed by single parents has increased dramatically, and over 82 percent of these families are headed by single mothers.[51] The percentage of two-parent families with both parents working outside the home has increased significantly because women have gone out to work in the paid labour

The Premiers' Principles

1. Social policy must assure reasonable access to health, education and training, income support and social services that meet Canadians' basic needs.

2. Social policy must support and protect Canadians most in need.

3. Social policy must promote social and economic conditions which enhance self-sufficiency and well-being, to assist all Canadians to actively participate in economic and social life.

4. Social policy must promote active development of individuals' skills and capabilities as the foundation for social and economic development.

5. Social policy must promote the well-being of children and families, as children are our future. It must ensure the protection and development of children and youth in a healthy, safe and nurturing environment.

6. Social policy must reflect our individual and collective responsibility for health, education and social security, and reinforce the commitment of Canadians to the dignity and independence of the individual.

7. Partnerships among governments, communities, social organizations, business, labour, families and individuals are essential to the continued strength of our social system.

8. There is a continuing and important role, to be defined, for both orders of government in the establishment, maintenance and interpretation of national principles for social programs.

9. The ability to fund social programs must be protected. Social programs must be affordable, sustainable, and designed to achieve intended and measurable results.

10. The long-term benefits of prevention and early intervention must be reflected in the design of social programs.

11. Federal constitutional, fiduciary, treaty and other historic responsibilities for assurance of Aboriginal health, income support, social services, housing, training and educational opportunities must be fulfilled. The federal government must recognize its financial responsibilities for Aboriginal Canadians, both on and off reserve.

12. Governments must coordinate and integrate social programming and funding in order to ensure efficient and effective program delivery, and to reduce waste and duplication.

13. Social policy must be flexible and responsive to changing social and economic conditions, regional/local priorities and individual circumstances.

14. Governments must ensure that all Canadians have access to reasonably comparable basic social programming throughout Canada, and ensure that Canadians are treated with fairness and equity.

15. Social policy must recognize and take into account the differential impact social programming can have on men and women.

force in growing numbers. Governments are unlikely to devise social programs that will lead to equality for women when they do not identify women separately from "family" or from "the structure of society."

The *Report to Premiers* also states that the Council is building a framework that "increases appreciation for the strength of families and communities, and the role which they can play with other partners, such as business and labour."

In practice, women know that "families and communities" means them; that "increasing appreciation for the strength of families and communities" is a way of saying that governments, after an all too brief period of relieving women of some of their burden of caregiving through public social programs, are in the business of downloading caregiving to women once more. "Social policy reform" seem to be code words that mean women will be expected to do more, not less, unpaid caregiving in their families and in their communities. Apparently lost in these Principles is the comprehension that social programs and services are essential to women's equality.[117]

The weakness of the Premiers' Principles is very disturbing, as is the fact that principles are what is on offer. The message is that national standards, as Canadians have known them, are not a part of the future, as far as the provinces are concerned.[118] The provinces state that the use of the federal spending power should not allow the federal government "to unilaterally dictate program design." Instead, both orders of government will have a role, to be defined, in the "establishment, maintenance and interpretation of principles for social programs." This statement is no substitute for standards that must be met as a condition of funding.

The *Report to Premiers* is now the basis for dialogue with the Prime Minister on the future of Canada's social safety net, and the basis for establishing a national framework for the reform process in areas of provincial/territorial responsibility. The key elements of this framework are: (1) the principles; (2) the agenda for reform being developed by the Ministerial Council with input from sectoral Ministerial Committees;[119,120] and (3) a mechanism for settling differences and monitoring national progress on social policy reform and renewal. The dialogue between the Prime Minister and the provinces apparently began in earnest in December 1997 when Prime Minister Chrétien and the Premiers of all provinces, except Quebec, agreed to start negotiating a new framework agreement for Canada's social union.

Unfortunately, this dialogue is premised on a report that, in its content, is disturbingly weak. Also, the *Report to Premiers* takes for granted a form of decision making that is disturbingly private.[121]

Decision making by the Ministerial Council on Social Policy Reform and Renewal, in combination with the First Ministers, constitutes a form of governance reminiscent of the Council of the Federation, an institution that was proposed by the federal government in 1991 during the Charlottetown Round of Constitutional Talks. The Council of the Federation was to be given the power to decide on issues of intergovernmental coordination and collaboration, including on the use of the federal spending power on new Canada-wide shared-cost programs and conditional transfers in areas of exclusive provincial jurisdiction. It was rejected by many at the time because it would be an institution of governance that lacked transparency and accountability, while being given authority over crucial decisions.

In the Ministerial Council on Social Policy Reform and Renewal and the Premiers' and First Ministers' Conferences that follow its work, executive federalism is being established as the vehicle for making decisions about social policy, the financing of social programs, and the distribution of responsibilities between levels of government. These are decisions that are central to women and to all Canadians. The problem with executive federalism is that the decision-making process is opaque; those who are affected have no access to participation; and decisions are not reviewed or confirmed by the Parliament and the legislatures.

This form of executive federalism is all too familiar, but the situation is worse. Women were sceptical of the proposed Council of the Federation at the time of the Charlottetown Round of Constitutional Talks because of the way in which constitutional talks had taken place in the 1980s. Women were excluded then, and women are being excluded now, when unprecedented shifts in social policy are taking place.

Ministers are, once again, dealing with vital questions behind closed doors; weak principles are proposed as a substitute for abandoned national standards; the federal government's clout has diminished; and groups affected by the decisions have no access.

This means that the federal government has stepped back, and the provinces have stepped into the centre of the social policy arena. While the provinces have an essential role to play, they are not capable of setting and maintaining enforceable standards for social programs for the rest of Canada. They lack the will to enforce against each other binding, meaningful standards, and they have no tangible and effective tool, such as the spending power, with which to do so.

This decentralization is not inevitable; the federal government could continue to play a strong role. But that would require an open and strong commitment to all social programs, not just health care, a willingness to provide secure long-term funding, the determination to develop and enforce meaningful standards, and the courage to make an asymmetrical arrangement with Quebec.

Conclusion

Although the full implications of the CHST and the *BIA* have not yet made their way into social programs and services, the impact on women of this restructuring is already clear: It increases women's social and economic vulnerability.

Women's rates of poverty are disproportionately high. And women's vulnerability to poverty is higher than men's. Single mothers, Aboriginal women, women of colour, women with disabilities, and older single women are particularly likely to live their lives in poverty. Many women are only one beating, one marriage breakdown, or one non-standard job away from needing welfare. Many women count on the social services that have been funded under the CAP, such as child care, home care services, counselling, and job re-entry costs, to fill in essential gaps, to keep themselves and their families afloat. Also, access to legal aid for family law matters and to shelters and transition houses are a *sine qua non* of women's equality.

The cuts to caregiving services that are taking place across the country both eliminate paid jobs that are mainly held by women, and push more unpaid caregiving onto women. This increases women's workload, constrains their participation in paid work, and makes them more economically dependent. It is clear that women's equality depends on the willingness of governments to counterbalance the powerful dynamics of patriarchy that keep women poorer, dependent, and marginal to decision making. Social programs and social services are a central means of assisting women to contend with conditions of social and economic inequality.

What is most disturbing of all, then, in light of the tight connection between social programs and services and women's equality, is that the most drastic changes to social programs of the last 40 years have been presented as a purely budgetary matter, unrelated to the rights of women.

Endnotes for Chapter 1

[1] These are terms used by different commentators. "Social Canada" is the term used by Thomas Courchene to refer to the social compact that Canadians will take care of each other and share resources in order to do so: "The Federal Provincial Dimension of the Budget: Two Cheers for the CHST" in Thomas J. Courchene and Thomas A. Wilson, eds., *The 1995 Federal Budget: Retrospect and Prospect* (Kingston, Ont.: John Deutsch Institute for the Study of Economic Policy, Queen's University, 1995) 107 at 108.

[2] Another recent decision of this kind is the introduction of family income testing, rather than individual income testing, for eligibility for Old Age Security. Monica Townson points out in *Independent Means: A Canadian Woman's Guide to Pensions and a Secure Financial Future* (Toronto: Macmillan, 1997) [hereinafter *Independent Means*] at 60 that "[f]or women, a family-income test for OAS is a major step backwards because it denies them economic autonomy. It also assumes that women have equal access to family income, which is not always the case — especially in families where there is wife abuse. A married woman's right to OAS, in most cases, will now depend on her husband's income, whether or not she works outside the home before retirement. That's because the average income of husbands usually far exceeds that of wives — even in retirement. So when you add a husband's income to a wife's, generally the husband's income will determine if either spouse gets OAS. The family-income test means that a woman who has spent most of her life as a full-time homemaker will no longer be able to count on an OAS benefit in her own name at 65. But it also means that women who spend most of their lives in the paid work force will not be able to count on an OAS benefit to meet part of their needs for replacement income in retirement."

[3] Following the practice of the National Council of Welfare, we use "poverty" and "low income" interchangeably here, and references are to those living below Statistics Canada's low-income cut-offs, or LICOs.

There has been some debate recently about the use of Statistics Canada's low-income cut-offs as measures of poverty in Canada. Ivan Fellegi, Canada's Chief Statistician, in a recent op-ed piece indicated that the low-income cut-offs are not "official" poverty lines because they are not set by government. Fellegi indicated that defining poverty is political, "intrinsically a question of social consensus [about what constitutes 'poverty'], at a point in time and in the context of a given country." According to Fellegi, Statistics Canada takes no position on how it should be defined in Canada now. Statistics Canada's low-income cut-offs measure who is "substantially worse off than the average" in Canada, and provide a way of keeping track of the characteristics of this worst-off group. See Ivan Fellegi, "StatsCan measures income, not 'poverty'" *The [Montreal] Gazette* (17 September 1997) at B3.

However, we note that the National Council of Welfare in its most recent report states:

> The National Council of Welfare, like many other social policy groups, regards the low income cut-offs as poverty lines and uses the term poor and low-income interchangeably.
>
> Statistics Canada takes pains to avoid references to poverty. It says the cut-offs have no official status, and it does not promote their use as poverty lines.
>
> Regardless of the terminology, the cut-offs are a useful tool for defining and analyzing the significantly large portion of the Canadian population with low incomes. They are not the only measures of poverty used in Canada, but they are the most widely accepted and are roughly comparable to most alternative measures.

National Council of Welfare, *Poverty Profile, 1995: A Report by the National Council of Welfare* (Ottawa: Supply and Services Canada, 1997) [hereinafter *Poverty Profile 1995*] at 5–6.

[4] *Ibid.* at 84.

[5] When calculated by age and sex, women had a higher rate of poverty than men in all categories but one in 1995. The age categories are 18–24; 25–34; 35–44; 45–54; 55–64; 65–74; 75–84; and 85+. Only for women and men between the ages of 45 and 54 was the rate of poverty about the same. *Ibid.* at 34.

[6] *Ibid.* at 84.

[7] *Ibid.* at 85. The National Council of Welfare states that "most of the differences between the sexes can be explained by the high poverty rates of three family types: unattached women under 65, unattached women 65 and older, and single-parent mothers under 65 with children under 18." Poverty rates for these "family types" are: single mothers under 65 — 57.2 percent; unattached women over 65 — 43.4 percent; unattached women under 65 — 38.7 percent. By comparison unattached men under 65 have a poverty rate of 33.2 percent and unattached men over 65 have a poverty rate of 21.3 percent.

[8] *Ibid.* at 2.

[9] *Ibid.* at 52.

[10] *Ibid.* at 75. Canada's record on child poverty has been commented on critically by a number of United Nations bodies, including the Committee that oversees the *International Covenant on Economic, Social and Cultural Rights* in 1993, the Committee on the Rights of the Child in 1995, and UNICEF in its *Progress of Nations Report* in 1996. UNICEF found that Canada has the second-highest number of poor children of 18 industrialized nations. Only the United States is worse.

[11] *Ibid.* at 76.

[12] *Women in Canada: A Statistical Report*, 3d ed. (Ottawa: Industry, 1995) [hereinafter *Women in Canada*] at 153, 123, and 138. The 16 percent figure given here is the figure for the rate of poverty among women overall given in this study. It is not as current a figure as that given in *Poverty Profile 1995*, *supra* note 3.

[13] *Ibid.* at 166.

[14] The inadequacy of data on welfare recipients in Canada is shocking. What we do not know far outstrips what we do know. The numbers of welfare recipients estimated for 1994 and 1995 are 3,100,200 and 3,070,900: National Council of Welfare, *Welfare Income 1995* (Ottawa: Supply and Services Canada, 1997) at 44. But because statistics on welfare recipients are kept differently by different provinces, there is no satisfactory national profile. There are no national statistics showing the representation among welfare recipients of women, or of immigrant women, visible minority women, Aboriginal women, and women with disabilities. There is information about "family types."

[15] In *The 1995 Budget and Block Funding* (Ottawa: Supply and Services Canada, 1995) at 4–5, the National Council of Welfare reports that in 1994 children receiving assistance through their parents were 38 percent of welfare recipients, 15 percent were single parents, mostly single mothers, 12 percent were married parents, 5 percent were couples with no children, and 31 percent were single people. Frances Woolley in *Women and the Canada Assistance Plan* (Ottawa: Status of Women Canada, 1995) at 5 notes that women disproportionately make up the group of single parents on welfare by an estimated ratio of 9 to 1 in Canada, while men disproportionately make up the group of single people on welfare by an estimated ratio of 2 to 1. Woolley concludes that more than half the people supported through social assistance are women. This conclusion is also endorsed by academic literature on the feminization of poverty in Canada. See, for example, Martha Jackman, "Women and the Canada Health and Social Transfer: Ensuring Gender Equality in Federal Welfare Reform" (1995) 8:2 *Canadian Journal of Women and the Law* 371 at 373; Isabella Bakker and Janine Brodie, *The New Canada Health and Social Transfer (CHST): The Implications for*

Women (Ottawa: Status of Women Canada, 1995) at 11 and 38; and Frances Woolley, *ibid.* at 1. As well, statistical information forwarded to us by the province of Saskatchewan shows one province's statistics for one recent month. In December 1996, 78,821 persons were welfare recipients. Of this number, 21,070 were women, and 40,732 were children. This means that more adult women than men were social assistance recipients. Saskatchewan Social Services: *Saskatchewan Assistance Plan: Distribution by Age Range, Sex of Head and Type of Case, for the Month of December 1996.*

[16] The largest single group of persons on welfare is children: *The 1995 Budget and Block Funding, ibid.* at 4–5. The National Council of Welfare notes that children are poor because their parents are poor. It also notes that while most poor children are living in two-parent families, the proportion of poor children living with single mothers has grown substantially in recent years. In 1980, 33 percent of poor children lived in families headed by single mothers. In 1995, 40 percent of poor children lived in families headed by single mothers. *Poverty Profile 1995, supra* note 3 at 75–77.

[17] *Women in Canada, supra* note 12 at 64.

[18] *Ibid.* at 65. This Statistics Canada report notes: "In 1994, 70% of all employed women were working in either teaching, nursing and health-related occupations, clerical positions, or sales and service occupations. ... Women also account for a large share of total employment in each of these occupational groups. In 1994 86% of nurses and health-related therapists, 80% of clerks, 63% of teachers, 56% of service personnel, and 46% of salespersons were women." While women increased their representation in managerial and administrative positions between 1982 and 1994 from 26 percent to 43 percent, the statistics on this increase are not reliable because as much as 40 percent of this reported increase may be attributable to changes in occupational definitions. *Ibid.* at 67 and 70.

[19] Forty-four percent of women, compared to 51 percent of men are now covered by employer-sponsored pension plans. *Ibid.* at 89. However, since benefits are tied to earnings, women's benefits from these plans are lower than men's. Monica Townson also notes in *Independent Means, supra* note 2 at 98–100, that pension rules that discriminated against women in the 1970s and 1980s, by requiring women to work longer to be eligible for a pension or to retire earlier than men, still have a lingering effect on the amount of women's pension benefits or on access to a pension because when the rules were changed, those changes were not retroactive.

[20] See Isabella Bakker, "Introduction: The Gendered Foundations of Restructuring in Canada" in Isabella Bakker, ed., *Rethinking Restructuring: Gender and Change in Canada* (Toronto: University of Toronto Press, 1996) at 13–14 [hereinafter "The Gendered Foundations of Restructuring in Canada"]; Pat Armstrong, "The Feminization of the Labour Force: Harmonizing Down in a Global Economy" in Isabella Bakker, ed., *Rethinking Restructuring: Gender and Change in Canada, ibid.* 29; *Women in Canada, supra* note 12 at 86. See also "Canadian women closing wage gap" *The [Toronto] Globe and Mail* (23 July 1997) A6. Despite its misleading headline, this article, reporting on a new study released by the Canadian Council on Social Development, states that though Canadian women appear to be closing the wage gap, this advance "is threatened by cuts to job fields such as health and education that have boosted their earning power ... The narrowing of the wage gap 'is limited' and could be jeopardized by Canada's changing economy, including cuts to the public sector ... Also, the wage improvements that have been made are not flowing through to the younger generation."

Katherine Scott and Clarence Lochhead state: "Preliminary analysis shows that the women who made wage gains over the last decade were the beneficiaries of a pool of good jobs in the health, education and social service sectors. However, as the structure of the economy continues to change, with the continuing polarization of job opportunities, there is a real danger that women's economic advances will be halted. And such a situation would herald greater economic insecurity for all Canadians." See Katherine Scott and Clarence Lochhead, *Are Women Catching Up in the Earnings Race?* (Ottawa: Canadian Council on Social Development, 1997) at 2.

[21] *Women in Canada, supra* note 12 at 84.

[22] Canadian Advisory Council on the Status of Women, *Work in Progress: Tracking Women's Equality in Canada* (Ottawa: Canadian Advisory Council on the Status of Women, 1994) at 44.

[23] Many women work part-time because they cannot find full-time employment. In 1994, 34 percent of all female part-time workers indicated that they wanted full-time employment, but could not find it. See *Women in Canada*, *supra* note 12 at 66.

[24] Two indicators that women's care of children affects their participation in employment, and consequently their incomes, are that women with pre-school-aged children are less likely than those with school-aged children to be employed, and that single mothers are considerably less likely than women in two-parent families to be employed. See *Women in Canada*, ibid., at 64 and 65; and Nancy Z. Ghalam, *Women in the Workplace*, 2d ed. (Ottawa: Statistics Canada, 1993), cat. no. 71-534E, at 22.

[25] Monica Townson, "Non-Standard Work: The Implications For Pension Policy and Retirement Readiness" (unpublished paper prepared for Women's Bureau, Human Resources Development Canada, 1996) at 11.

[26] *Ibid.* at 1 and 3.

[27] *Women in Canada*, *supra* note 12 at 138, 153, and 166.

[28] *Poverty Profile 1995*, *supra* note 3 at 85–86.

[29] "The Gendered Foundations of Restructuring in Canada," *supra* note 20 at 18–19; Lisa Philipps, "Tax Policy and the Gendered Distribution of Wealth" in Isabella Bakker, ed., *Rethinking Restructuring: Gender and Change in Canada*, *supra* note 20 141 [hereinafter "Tax Policy and the Gendered Distribution of Wealth"].

[30] Judith L. MacBride-King in *Work and Family: Employment Challenge of the '90s* (Ottawa: Conference Board of Canada, 1990) reports at 12–13 that 60 percent of women, compared with 26 percent of men, indicate that they are primarily responsible for the care of dependent relatives; Statistics Canada (in its *General Social Survey, Initial Data Release from the 1992 General Social Survey on Time Use* (March 1993), Table 1; Tabulation from Statistics Canada, 1990 General Social Survey, Cycle 7: Time Use, unpublished data) reports that mothers spend more time on primary child-care activities than fathers.

[31] According to the 1991 Census, child care workers are the lowest paid occupational group, with an average employment income of $13,518. This statistic is drawn from Statistics Canada, *The Daily* (13 April 1993), cat. no. 11-001E, and is cited in Donna S. Lero and Karen L. Johnson, *110 Canadian Statistics on Work and Family* (Ottawa: Canadian Advisory Council on the Status of Women, 1994) [hereinafter *110 Canadian Statistics*] at 38.

[32] For statistical information on child care in Canada, see *110 Canadian Statistics*, *ibid.* at 31–38.

[33] See *ibid.* at 6; see also "Non-Standard Work: The Implications For Pension Policy and Retirement Readiness," *supra* note 25. Townson defines non-standard jobs as anything that does not fit the definition of a standard job, that is, a full-time, full-year job with a single employer on a permanent long-term basis.

[34] Marital breakdown has a different impact on women's incomes than on men's incomes. In *Family Income After Separation*, a study by Diane Galarneau and Jim Sturrock cited in *Crossing the Low Income Line: Survey of Labour and Income Dynamics* (Ottawa: Statistics Canada, 1997), cat. no. 97-11, the authors report at 22–23 that "[a]fter separation, women experience losses in adjusted family income of approximately 23% between the year before and the year following separation. Men experience a 10% increase in adjusted family income. Five years after separation, women still record a 5% income shortfall, whereas men have made gains of approximately 15%. Women heading single-parent families experience the greatest losses."

[35] Martin D. Dooley, "Women, Children and Poverty in Canada" in *Economic Equality Workshop: Summary of Proceedings* (Ottawa: Status of Women Canada, 1993) at 41.

[36] "The Gendered Foundations of Restructuring in Canada," *supra* note 20 at 4. Bakker is quoting from Marjorie Cohen, "Democracy and Trade Agreements: Challenges for Disadvantaged Women, Minorities and States" in R. Boyer and D. Drache, eds., *Markets Against States: The Limits of Globalization* (London: Routledge, 1996) at 274.

[37] *Ibid.* at 3 and 4.

[38] *Ibid.* at 4.

[39] *Ibid.*

[40] *Ibid.* at 5.

[41] Canada, *Improving Social Security in Canada: The Context of Reform, A Supplementary Paper* (Ottawa: Queen's Printer, 1994) at 8. See also Canada, *Reforming the Canada Assistance Plan: A Supplementary Paper* (Ottawa: Queen's Printer, 1994); and Canada, *Creating a Healthy Fiscal Climate: An Economic and Fiscal Update* (Ottawa: Queen's Printer, 1994).

[42] "The Gendered Foundations of Restructuring in Canada," *supra* note 20 at 5.

[43] H. Mimoto and P. Cross, "The Growth of the Federal Debt" (1991) 3:1 *Canadian Economic Observer*. See also Gideon Rosenbluth, who argues that "[c]onservative deficit-phobia continues to be a convenient excuse for cutting social spending and following procyclical fiscal policies." He suggests that an appropriate policy for keeping deficits under control would rely on low real interest rates, and public investment in physical and human capital, to ensure that the interest burden does not rise more quickly than the tax base. Gideon Rosenbluth, "The Political Economy of Deficit-Phobia" in Gideon Rosenbluth and Robert Allen, eds., *False Promises: The Failure of Conservative Economics* (Vancouver: New Star Books, 1992) at 74. See also David Wolfe, "The Politics of the Deficit" in Bruce Doern, ed., *The Politics of Economic Policy* (Toronto: University of Toronto Press, 1985) 111.

[44] Lisa C. Philipps, "The Rise of Balanced Budget Laws in Canada: Legislating Fiscal (Ir)responsibility" (1996) 34:4 *Osgoode Hall Law Journal* 681 at 724. It is also worth noting that economists disagree about how the debt and deficit should be measured. Marilyn Waring and other feminist economists have argued there are severe deficiencies in the way that classical economics engages in accounting: Marilyn Waring, *If Women Counted: A New Feminist Economics* (San Francisco: Harper & Row, 1988). One conclusion that flows from the work of Marilyn Waring is that the failure to include women's unpaid labour in the Gross Domestic Product (GDP), results in an exaggeration of debt. The extent of the debt is calculated by comparing the size of the deficit with the size of a country's GDP. However, if women's labour were included in the GDP, it is estimated that the GDP would rise between 15 percent and 50 percent. This would reduce the ratio of the deficit in comparison. See also Julie Nelson, *Feminism, Objectivity and Economics* (New York: Routledge, 1996).

[45] See, for example, Canadian Council on Social Development, *Roundtables on the Canada Health and Social Transfer: Final Report* (Ottawa: Canadian Council on Social Development, 1996), and from that report, in particular, Michael Mendelson, "Establishing a Social Investment Framework" 129; David Cameron, "Comments" 137; Marcia Rioux, "The CHST: From Pathology to Social Investment" 141; Michael Wolfson, "Comments" 151.

[46] In this book, though sometimes we use the word "gender," generally we prefer to talk about women. References to "gender equality," "gender neutrality," and "gender analysis" are common in Canadian discourse, but we believe it is important to continue to point out that the topic is women, and it is women who are unequal in Canadian society.

[47] These studies are catalogued by Lero and Johnson in *110 Canadian Statistics*, *supra* note 31 at 4–8.

[48] Lisa Philipps, "Discursive Deficits: A Feminist Perspective on the Power of Technical Knowledge in Fiscal Law and Policy" (1996) 11:1 *Canadian Journal of Law and Society* 141 at 155.

[49] Isabella Bakker and Janine Brodie, *The New Canada Health and Social Transfer (CHST): The Implications for Women*, *supra* note 15 at 1.

[50] Martha Jackman, "Women and the Canada Health and Social Transfer: Ensuring Gender Equality in Federal Welfare Reform," *supra* note 15 at 372.

[51] The following historical account relies heavily on Allan M. Maslove, *National Goals and the Federal Role in Health Care* (Ottawa: National Forum on Health, 1995), Appendix A at 32–41.

[52] *Ibid.* at 33.

[53] A debt of gratitude is owed to Lisa Philipps for providing this explanation of tax room and tax points. Lisa Philipps, "Tax Points" memorandum to Gwen Brodsky and Shelagh Day, 2 May 1997, on file with the authors.

[54] Maslove, *National Goals and the Federal Role in Health Care*, *supra* note 51 at 35.

[55] *The 1995 Budget and Block Funding*, *supra* note 15 at 9.

[56] *National Goals and the Federal Role in Health Care*, *supra* note 51 at 35.

[57] *Ibid.* at 36.

[58] *Ibid.* at 37–38.

[59] *Ibid.* at 38.

[60] *The 1995 Budget and Block Funding*, *supra* note 15 at 2.

[61] *Ibid.*

[62] See Jillian Oderkirk, "Old Age Security" (Spring 1996) *Canadian Social Trends* 3, cat. no. 11-008E.

[63] *The 1995 Budget and Block Funding*, *supra* note 15 at 3.

[64] Peter Hogg, *Constitutional Law of Canada*, 3d ed. (Toronto: Carswell, 1993) at 146.

[65] We note that Sherri Torjman and Ken Battle in *Can We Have National Standards?* (Ottawa: Caledon Institute of Social Policy, 1995) at 5–10 make a distinction between conditions and standards. The requirements that provinces had to meet to receive CAP funds, they call conditions, while we call them standards. They consider standards to be "benchmarks by which to judge the adequacy of programs or services." We believe that the CAP conditions did set important standards, as they define that term, for social assistance. Most clearly, they set a standard for availability. We agree, however, that CAP's specification that social assistance meet "basic requirements" does not set a clear enough standard for the adequacy of the social assistance provided.

[66] See the CAP, s. 6(2)(a). In the case of *Alden* v. *Gagliardi et al,* [1973] S.C.R. 199, [1973] 2 W.W.R. 92, 30 D.L.R. (3d) 760, the Supreme Court of Canada held that it is the test established by the provincial legislation which must be taken as the measure of a "person in need."

[67] See the CAP, s. 2(a).

[68] The CAP stated that the provincial plan must "take into account" the "basic requirements of the person." These words have been interpreted by the Supreme Court of Canada as indicating actual provision of an amount that is "compatible or consistent with" an individual's basic requirements, not mere "consideration" of basic requirements. *Finlay* v. *Canada (Minister of Finance),* [1993], 1 S.C.R. 1080, 101 D.L.R. (4th) 567, 150 N.R. 81, 63 F.T.R. 99 (note), 2 D.M.P.L. 203.

[69] See the CAP, s. 6(2)(c).

[70] See the CAP, s. 6(2)(e).

[71] *Can We Have National Standards?, supra* note 65 at 5.

[72] In effect, the CAP also created for persons in need a right of access to the courts to obtain review of the substantive adequacy of welfare payments made by a province. This was established by the Court in the case of *Finlay* v. *Canada (Minister of Finance)* [1986], 2 S.C.R. 607, which arose in Manitoba. The Supreme Court of Canada held that possible violations of the CAP were reviewable by the courts at the behest of welfare beneficiaries. Although the Court was not prepared to grant standing to Jim Finlay as a matter of right, he was nonetheless granted standing, on the basis of the public interest in compliance with the CAP standards. Moreover, the Court explicitly recognized that welfare recipients have a direct, personal interest in provincial compliance with CAP standards.

However, this CAP enforcement mechanism was cumbersome in that it did not, in itself, confer on welfare beneficiaries rights and remedies against provincial governments. Where a provincial government was alleged to be in non-compliance with CAP funding conditions, the welfare beneficiary's cause of action lay against the federal government for having made an unauthorized payment to the province. The shortcoming of this approach is that the welfare recipient was in a funding relationship, not with the federal government, but rather with the provincial government. It is the provincial government that actually controls the funds that go to social assistance recipients. And yet, the CAP did not give welfare recipients the ability to go to court to compel provincial governments to make payments in accordance with the CAP. Awkward and indirect as the CAP enforcement mechanism was, it nonetheless gave the beneficiaries of social assistance programs an avenue of legal redress, when CAP protections were or may have been violated.

To clarify, the *Finlay* avenue of redress arose directly out of the CAP, and related to the terms and conditions of funding agreements between the federal government and the provinces. It must not be confused with provincial welfare appeal mechanisms that the CAP obligated provincial governments to provide, and that give welfare recipients an avenue of redress against provincial government officials who do not properly interpret and apply provincial welfare legislation.

[73] Over the period that the CAP was in place, at least three provincial governments (Saskatchewan, Quebec, and Manitoba) had to change their programs in order to qualify for federal cost sharing. In each case, it was the "needs" requirement that was in issue. For example, in 1974 Saskatchewan introduced a family income plan to supplement the incomes of the working poor with dependent children. However, the federal government objected to sharing 50 percent of the cost because recipients were not required to pass a means test. Similar programs introduced in Quebec in 1979 and Manitoba in 1981 were also ineligible under the CAP. See Richard Bird, "Federal-Provincial Fiscal Transfers in Canada: Retrospect and Prospect" (1987) 35 *Canadian Tax Journal* 118 at 132.

[74] See Sherri Torjman, *The Let-Them-Eat-Cake Law* (Ottawa: Caledon Institute of Social Policy, 1995).

[75] This does not mean that the federal government was precluded from placing a ceiling on its contribution. In *Reference Re: Canada Assistance Plan (B.C.)*, [1991] 2 S.C.R. 525, 58 B.C.L.R. (2d) 1, 1 Admin. L.R. (2d) 1, 6 W.W.R. 1 [hereinafter *Re: CAP* cited to S.C.R.], the Supreme Court of Canada held that CAP could be unilaterally amended by the Parliament of Canada, and that the federal government of the day could not bind Parliament so as to preclude it from making such a legislative amendment in the future. The effect of this decision was to allow the federal government to depart from the 50:50 cost-sharing formula, which it did by capping its contributions to certain provinces in 1990.

[76] *Canada Assistance Plan Regulations*, C.R.C. 1978, c. 382, s. 13.

[77] *The 1995 Budget and Block Funding*, *supra* note 15 at 4.

[78] *Ibid.* at 5.

[79] *Ibid.* at 6.

[80] The one exception is the residency requirement. The British Columbia government failed to comply with this requirement for a number of years and has only recently, with some federal government incentives, removed their provincial residency requirement. See Craig McInnes, "B.C. to Abolish Welfare Rule: Ottawa Agrees to Pay Sixty Million for Dropping of Controversial Residency Requirement" *The [Toronto] Globe and Mail* (6 March 1997) A1.

[81] Most provinces are likely to retain at least some elements of the appeal procedures they have in place; but there is no requirement under the CHST for them to do so. Section 7 of the *Canadian Charter of Rights and Freedoms*, Part I of the *Constitution Act, 1982*, being Schedule B to the *Canada Act 1982* (U.K.), 1982, c. 11 [hereinafter the *Charter*] may be relevant here since it states that "everyone has the right to life, liberty and security of the person and the right not to be deprived thereof except in accordance with the principles of fundamental justice." If "security of the person" includes economic security, then an appeal process may be necessary when a person is refused welfare. However, this has not been established yet.

[82] These arguments are made by Ken Battle and Sherri Torjman in *How Finance Re-Formed Social Policy* (Ottawa: Caledon Institute of Social Policy, 1995) at 10.

[83] Thomas Courchene, *Redistributing Money and Power: A Guide to the Canada Health and Social Transfer* (Toronto: C.D. Howe Institute, 1995) at 56 [hereinafter *Redistributing Money and Power*]. Michael Mendelson gives similar figures in *Looking for Mr. Good-Transfer: A Guide to the CHST Negotiations* (Ottawa: Caledon Institute of Social Policy, 1995) at 3 [hereinafter *Looking for Mr. Good-Transfer*].

[84] *Looking for Mr. Good-Transfer*, *ibid.* at 4.

[85] See "Liberals Will Strengthen Health Care Funding" Press Release, Liberal Party of Canada, (28 April 1997).

[86] In Canada's Third Report to the Economic, Social and Cultural Rights Committee on its compliance with the *International Covenant on Economic, Social and Cultural Rights*, the current funding arrangement is described this way: "In 1996, the Budget of the Government of Canada set out a five-year funding arrangement through which transfers are maintained and then grow. CHST entitlements are set at 26.9 billion in 1996–97 and 25.1 billion in 1997–98, and will be maintained at the 1997–98 level of 25.1 billion in 1998–99 and 1999–2000. For 2000–01, entitlements will grow at two percent less than the growth rate of GDP. The rate of entitlement growth will then accelerate in 2001–02, when growth will be at the GDP rate minus 1.5 percent, and in 2002–03 when growth will be at one percent less than the growth rate of GDP. The resumption of entitlements growth is projected to first

stabilize, and then restore growth in the CHST cash component. To provide additional security against unexpected economic fluctuations, a legislated cash floor will ensure that the CHST cash component will total at least 11 billion a year throughout the five-year fiscal arrangement." See *The International Covenant on Economic, Social and Cultural Rights: Third Report of Canada* (Ottawa: Public Works and Government Services, 1997) at paragraph 83.

[87] *Redistributing Money and Power*, *supra* note 83 at 57.

[88] *National Goals and the Federal Role in Health Care*, *supra* note 51, Table 4 at 41.

[89] See Robin Boadway, "The Implications of the Budget for Fiscal Federalism" in Thomas J. Courchene and Thomas A. Wilson, eds., *The 1995 Federal Budget: Retrospect and Prospect*, *supra* note 1 at 95. Ken Battle and Sherri Torjman calculated this would occur by 2011–12 in *How Finance Re-Formed Social Policy*, *supra* note 82 at 7. Courchene estimated that they will fall to zero for the three "have" provinces by 2009–10 in "The Federal Provincial Dimension of the Budget," *supra* note 1 at 115. See Courchene also in *Redistributing Money and Power*, *supra* note 83 at 32–33.

[90] *Redistributing Money and Power*, *supra* note 83 at 12-13.

[91] Western Premiers' Conference, Premiers' Statement, November 1995 at 13.

[92] Mendelson in *Looking for Mr. Good-Transfer*, *supra* note 83 at 5–6, and Courchene in *Redistributing Money and Power*, *supra* note 83 at 59, both make this argument.

[93] The British Columbia government appealed the imposition of this cap unsuccessfully in *Re: CAP*, *supra* note 75.

[94] Barbara Yaffe, "Financially-strapped Ottawa views B.C. as a cash cow" *The [Vancouver] Sun* (22 June 1996) A3. This dispute was resolved in March 1997 when Ottawa and British Columbia made a deal. The federal government gave British Columbia $60 million over three years to cope with the costs of settling immigrants, and in return, British Columbia agreed to drop its residency requirement for welfare and its $47 million lawsuit against the federal government. The federal government also agreed to give back to British Columbia $26.6 million of the $47 million that it withheld. The difference between the $47 million penalty and the $26.6 million payback is the amount that British Columbia saved by not providing welfare to persons not resident for three months. See "Chrétien, Clark warming to each other" *The [Toronto] Globe and Mail* (7 March 1997) A7; "B.C. to abolish welfare rule" *The [Toronto] Globe and Mail* (6 March 1997) at A1, A4; "Election-minded Chrétien comes to B.C. bearing gifts," *The [Vancouver] Sun* (7 March 1997) at A1, A14.

[95] See Thomas J. Courchene, *ACCESS: A Convention on the Canadian Economic and Social Systems* (Toronto: Government of Ontario, 1996) at 17–18.

[96] (1988), 53 D.L.R. (4th) 413 (Alta C.A.)

[97] *Ibid.* at 432.

[98] *Ibid.* at 433.

[99] *Ibid.*

[100] Leave application dismissed, with costs, April 13, 1989.

[101] *Can We Have National Standards?*, *supra* note 65 at 1. It is important to note, however, that Lisa Philipps in "Tax Points," *supra* note 53, finds that it is not inconceivable that the federal government could "take back" tax revenue from a province that was not honouring the agreement by which a tax point transfer had been established. To date, tax points have not been understood as a mechanism for enforcing compliance with national standards. However, tax points are not much different from cash transfers; both have an ascertainable dollar value and both are integral to federal/provincial revenue sharing. According to Professor Philipps, it is only the invisibility of tax points as a component of the federal contribution to social programming that prevents the full federal leverage from being explored.

[102] See "Liberals Will Strengthen Health Care Funding," *supra* note 85.

[103] Section 13(3) of the *Budget Implementation Act*, 1995, S.C. 1995, c. 17.

[104] See *The [Toronto] Globe and Mail*, "9 Provinces to talk social policy" (13 December 1997) A1, A10; "Discord dominates message coming out of conference," (13 December 1997) A10.

[105] Michael Mendelson, *The Provinces' Position: A Second Chance For the Social Security Review?* (Ottawa: Caledon Institute of Social Policy, 1996) at 11–12.

[106] Keith Banting, "Who 'R' Us?" in Thomas J. Courchene and Thomas A. Wilson, eds., *The 1995 Federal Budget: Retrospect and Prospect*, *supra* note 81 at 176.

[107] *Ibid.* at 179.

[108] In "Constitutional Reform: Canada's Equality Crisis" in David Schneiderman, ed., *Conversations Among Friends: Women and Constitutional Reform* (Edmonton: University of Alberta, Centre for Constitutional Studies, 1991), Shelagh Day argued that Quebec and Aboriginal peoples present Canada with equality issues that cannot be resolved by applying a same treatment formula. Quebec and Aboriginal peoples ask for, and deserve to be given, asymmetrical treatment from other provinces and from non-Aboriginal individuals because of their histories, and their cultural and linguistic needs.

[109] Barbara Cameron, "Social Citizenship In A Multinational State: The Social Charter Revisited" (Paper presented to Federal Constitutions in Comparative Perspective: A Conference in Honour of Douglas V. Verney, May 1996, York University, Toronto) at 24.

[110] Glen Clark, British Columbia's N.D.P. Premier, provides an illustrative example. *The [Toronto] Globe and Mail* reported that "freshly elected Mr. Clark seemed to bask in his unremitting British-Columbia-First persona. He boasted to several people that he had been east of the Ottawa River only twice in his life, once to change planes at Mirabel and once at a finance ministers' meeting in Quebec City in the early 1990s. That was fine with him. He likened his limited experience of the rest of the country with that of his average constituent in Vancouver." See "Chrétien, Clark warming to each other," *supra* note 94.

[111] Jill Vickers, "Why Should Women Care About Federalism?" in Douglas M. Brown and Janet Hiebert, eds., *Canada: The State of the Federation 1994* (Ottawa: Institute of Intergovernmental Relations, 1994) at 139.

[112] Barbara Cameron, *supra* note 109 at 24.

[113] Status of Women Canada, *Setting the Stage for the Next Century: The Federal Plan for Gender Equality* (Ottawa: Status of Women Canada, 1995) at 16.

[114] See *Can We Have National Standards?*, *supra* note 65 at 6; and Isabella Bakker and Janine Brodie, *The New Canada Health and Social Transfer (CHST): The Implications for Women*, *supra* note 15 at 11 regarding the failure to keep statistics, disaggregated by sex, on recipients of welfare.

[115] Ministerial Council on Social Policy Reform and Renewal, *Report to Premiers* (Ottawa: December 1995) at 3 [hereinafter *Report to Premiers*].

[116] See Statistics Canada, *Families: Number, Type and Structure* (Ottawa: 1992), cat. no. 93-312, Table 2; Donna S. Lero, Alan R. Pence, Margot Shields, Lois M. Brockman, and Hillel Goelman, *Canadian National Child Care Study: Introductory Report* (Ottawa: Statistics Canada; Health and Welfare Canada, 1992), cat. no. 89-526E, at 44. These reports use data from the 1991 census, and indicate that women are 82 percent of all lone-parent families with unmarried children of any age. In 1988 women were 92 percent of lone-parent families with children under age 13.

[117] The argument of this book is that economic policy should take women's inequality into account because women have a right to equality that has been socially agreed upon. Ours is an argument based on justice and is a fully adequate justification for requiring that economic policy further the aspirations of women to overcome their inequality. Others may wish to add a different argument. For example, it is also arguable that greater social and economic equality for women has additional social benefits because it results in a better educated and more skilled labour force, and ensures that more women individually, and more families, can withstand economic shocks, preventing larger-scale dependencies and economic depression. While such arguments may be empirically valid and rhetorically powerful, we do not believe that proof of additional social benefits is a precondition to implementing economic policy that is good for women.

[118] Note Principle 8.

[119] We presume this means Ministers responsible for related areas — youth, status of women, health, education, and others.

[120] The two major items on this agenda currently are a new National Child Benefit System, and a federal/provincial framework to improve supports for persons with disabilities.

The National Child Benefit System, according to Ken Battle of the Caledon Institute, "is intended to provide a common child income benefit to all low-income families regardless of the source(s) of income." The federal child benefits are being provided to working poor families in 1997, and will be extended to all low-income families, including those receiving welfare, in 1998. However, he also notes welfare families will not be allowed to keep the benefit. It will be deducted from their welfare payments. "[P]rovinces will deduct the increases in federal child benefits from welfare payments on behalf of children, but they must 're-invest' these savings in other programs for low-income families with children, such as income-tested benefits, wage supplements, in-kind benefits (e.g. supplementary health care) and social services."

Battle describes the re-investment agreement as a sort of "back-door, softly-softly form of conditional cost-sharing. The provinces agree to spend their federally-enabled savings on welfare benefits for children on other programs for low-income families ... [however] ... [i]t is hard to imagine the provinces, flush with their freedom of action in the new era of the Canada Health and Social Transfer, agreeing to any process which tried to develop and apply conditions or standards to their various programs and services for low-income families with children." See Ken Battle, *The National Child Benefit: Best Thing Since Medicare or New Poor Law?* (Ottawa: Caledon Institute of Social Policy, 1997) at 3–15.

While Battle is cautiously supportive of this new program, Jane Pulkingham, Gordon Ternowetsky, and David Hay are much more critical. In "The New Canada Child Tax Benefit: Eradicating Poverty or Victimizing the Poorest?" (1997) 4:1 *The Monitor*, they state: "[F]amilies who receive income assistance will be no better off than they are under the current system. Although there is no explicit 'work test' attached to the new federal CCTB, recipients of income assistance are nonetheless penalized by the provinces, in collusion with the federal government, because of the source of their income (welfare)." They also note that "[i]t is a mistake ... to treat this $600 million [that will go into the program in 1998] as new money. Rather, it constitutes nothing more than a small repayment of funds that have been siphoned from federal transfer payments to the provinces for social assistance since the 1995–96 Liberal budget."

[121] The exclusion of the public and the media from the First Ministers' meetings where the future of Canada's social union is being decided is highlighted in a press story by Scott Feschuk entitled "A day in the life of the Almighty Microphone," *The [Toronto] Globe and Mail* (13 December 1997) A10. Feschuk describes the media waiting by the one "almighty" microphone for politicians to emerge from the meetings to make statements. Neither the public nor the media has any other access to information about the decisions being made.

CHAPTER 2

Women's Equality: The Normative Commitment

Introduction

The commitment of Canadians to equality values has been made express in various human rights instruments — international, constitutional, and statutory. These commitments to equality for women must be understood to encompass the goal of redressing the social and economic inequality of women, not just inequality in the form of laws.

At some level this seems an incredibly obvious claim. Why is it even necessary to argue that the commitment to women's equality includes the social and economic dimensions of women's inequality? The answer to this lies, in part at least, in the relative newness of the acknowledgement that inequality has systemic, group dimensions, and in the persistence of formal equality thinking.

Formal equality is an old idea, rooted in the notion of the rule of law, an early incarnation of equality rights. The rule of law, which holds simply that everyone shall be subject to law, was a reaction against a hierarchical social order in which laws did not apply to everyone. Some people, like kings, were above the law; others, like women, were below it. Formal equality and the rule of law are closely linked. The rule of law requires that everyone should be equally subject to the law, and formal equality requires that the law treat all like persons alike. When French and U.S. revolutionaries proclaimed that "all men [*sic*] are born equal" and are "free and equal in respect of rights," they were endorsing the ideas inherent in the rule of law.

Although contemporary understandings of equality have far surpassed this early version, key tenets of formal equality thinking live on as ideology in the political memory of the culture. Because of its lingering hold, it is important to examine the elements of formal equality theory.

In formal equality theory it is assumed that equality is achieved if the law treats likes alike. An absence of different treatment of men and women in the form of the law (gender neutrality), together with neutral application of the law, is thought to make men and women equal. Certainly, there are times when like treatment is exactly what women want. The fights for the vote and for admission to professions were fights by women to be treated the same as men. In circumstances where women and men are identically situated with respect to the opportunity or right sought, the model of formal equality works. However, when women and men are not identically situated, which is most of the time, the formal equality model is no help; in fact, it perpetuates discrimination, because it cannot address real inequality in conditions.

There are problems for women at the heart of formal equality. To begin with, equality is considered a matter of sameness and difference, and there is an insistence on narrow comparability. This can be seen in the test that is applied in formal equality theory, the "similarly situated test." This test holds that an equality violation consists of different treatment of similarly situated individuals. To satisfy this test a woman is required to show that she is just like men who are treated more favourably by a given law, policy, or practice. Advantaged groups establish the norms for comparison. Women can fail the similarly situated test by having a characteristic that is unique, or by being designated as "different" simply because they are relatively disadvantaged. To the extent that women are not like men, because they are biologically different from men or because society has assigned them a subordinate status, they cannot achieve equality through the application of formal equality. The persistent social and economic inequality of women is obscured when equality is defined as a matter of difference in the form of the law. Disadvantage in real conditions is made invisible.

Also, formal equality does not compel an inquiry into the discriminatory effects that a seemingly neutral rule may have. For example, if equality analysis of the *Budget Implementation Act (BIA)* that created the CHST were restricted solely to the language of the legislation, ignoring its effects on women, the sex equality issue would disappear.

Closer examination of the formal equality model reveals that it is a package of interlocking components, which function to both conceal and legitimate the oppression of marginalized groups in the society. Formal equality is characterized by:

- acceptance of the highly formalistic similarly situated test, which derives from the Aristotelian formulation that things that are alike should be treated alike, while things that are unalike should be treated unalike in proportion to their unalikeness;

- a refusal to see that inequality is a question of dominance and subordination between groups in the society;

- a refusal to see that relations of inequality between groups are sustained by government inaction as well as by government action;

- a propensity to place many forms of inequality in a realm, such as the family or the market, that is categorized as "private," beyond the reach and responsibility of government;

- a policy of blindness to personal characteristics thought to be out of the control of the individual, such as genitalia and skin colour;

- resistance to dealing with discrimination relating to a category of stigmatization concerning which there may be a significant element of choice, such as being lesbian, or which, like poverty, is not readily reduced to personal characteristics analogous to skin colour;

- an incapacity to appreciate the adverse effects of facially neutral laws;

- an understanding of discrimination, not as systemic, but rather as consisting of individualized, intentional differential treatment;

- a tendency to individualize everything so that patterns of group-based oppression and subordination are rendered invisible;

- a conception of government as always a threat to individual liberty, and not as a significant actor in creating the conditions necessary for human flourishing; and

- a false polarization of liberty and equality.

The neo-liberal restructuring agenda has recently given some renewed life to formal equality, because formal equality tends to idealize market freedom and demonize state intervention to ameliorate extreme disparities in wealth and social power. It supports social Darwinism by asserting that as long as laws and policies are facially neutral, everyone has the same opportunities, and those who flourish do so because of their fitness. Formal equality is thus an ideological underpinning of the restructuring agenda of recent years, and it is therefore popular within governments and the media.

However, formal equality can never solve the real problems of inequality. To embrace it as a sole model is, in effect, to refuse to fulfil social commitments to equality. This highly individualistic version of equality, which refuses to deal with the disadvantage of groups, which also accepts that the right to equality applies only to the form of laws, and not to social and economic inequality, and which precludes a role for the state in promoting equality among groups, cannot adequately serve the interests of women. It also provides an inadequate theoretical base upon which to build interpretations of legal equality rights guarantees.

Fortunately, equality thinking has moved well beyond this narrow interpretation over the last 50 years. The meaning of equality has changed and expanded dramatically. There is wide acknowledgement now that inequality affects groups, and that it has historic roots and structural dimensions. The "normal" functioning of central institutions causes and perpetuates the inequality of some groups, and remedying that inequality requires changing how those institutions function. The trend in analysis is away from an approach that sees only the individual and only an individual remedy, and towards a more broadly focused, socially comprehensive one that recognizes there are complex, historically engendered hierarchies of relationships among groups, and that some groups experience compounded forms of disadvantage and multiple violations of human rights. It is widely understood now that women as a group are disadvantaged, and that equality measures must address the economic, social, legal, and political dimensions of that group disadvantage.

In legal literature, this newer and broader understanding is referred to as substantive equality, to reflect its concern about content, rather than form. Substantive equality, by contrast to formal equality, posits that:

- equality is not a matter of sameness and difference, but rather a matter of dominance, subordination, and material disparities between groups;

- the effects of laws, policies, and practices, not the absence or presence of facial neutrality, determine whether laws or actions are discriminatory;

- remedying inequality between groups requires government action;

- the so-called "private" realms of the family and the marketplace cannot be set outside the boundaries of equality inquiry or obligation, because they are key sites of inequality;

- neither liberty nor equality for individuals can be achieved unless equality is achieved for disadvantaged groups;

- it is essential to be conscious of patterns of advantage and disadvantage associated with group membership; and

- the test of equality is not whether an individual is like the members of a group that is treated more favourably by a law, policy, or practice; rather, the test is whether the members of a group that has historically been disadvantaged enjoy equality in real conditions, including economic conditions.

Substantive equality thinking has fundamentally altered social, political, and legal understandings of what discrimination is and how it occurs. It has made the equality framework both more expansive and more attuned to the need for legislation and legal reasoning grounded in the social realities of disadvantaged groups. The history of international human rights commitments, Canadian human rights law, and the Constitution all reveal an enlarged post–World War II understanding of equality that is concerned with redressing group disadvantage, including the economic dimensions of group disadvantage, and that acknowledges that government action is essential to creating equality of condition.

International Human Rights Commitments

The Covenants

Canada is a signatory to all of the central international human rights treaties. Together they form a body of international human rights law by which Canada has agreed to be bound. In these treaties, Canada has made commitments to substantive equality for women.

The 1948 *Universal Declaration of Human Rights (UDHR)*, the *International Covenant on Civil and Political Rights (ICCPR)*, the International Covenant on Economic, Social and Cultural Rights (*ICESCR*), and the *Convention on the Elimination of All Forms of Discrimination Against Women (CEDAW)*, all commit governments to taking positive steps to promote legal, social, and economic equality.

The *UDHR* laid the foundation for post–World War II thinking on human rights. It is a declaration — not a binding treaty to which governments agree to become signatories.

46

However, the *UDHR* has great moral authority, setting out a common standard of achievement for all peoples and all nations,[1] and it is the root document from which the international human rights treaties have grown.

The *UDHR* presents an integrated vision of what is necessary to make human beings secure and free. It declares that everyone has civil and political rights, such as the right to life, liberty, and security of the person; to freedom from slavery; to freedom from torture or cruel, inhuman, or degrading treatment; and to freedom from arbitrary arrest, detention, or exile. It also declares the right of everyone to freedom of thought, conscience, and religion, and freedom of expression, peaceful assembly, and association with others. It sets out the democratic rights to take part in the conduct of public affairs, to vote, and to be elected at genuine periodic elections. These are the kinds of civil and political rights commonly associated with eighteenth and nineteenth century understandings of human rights.

The *UDHR* also recognizes social and economic rights, rights more typical of later stages of human rights development. Notably, it declares that everyone has a right to an adequate standard of living,[2] to social security, to realization of the economic, social, and cultural rights indispensable to dignity,[3] and to a social and international order in which these rights can be fully implemented.[4] Thus, the *UDHR* embodies in one scheme an integrated conception of human rights, including both civil and political rights and social and economic rights.

The two central Covenants, the *International Covenant on Civil and Political Rights* and the *International Covenant on Economic, Social and Cultural Rights,* which are binding international treaties for the governments that have ratified them,[5] grew out of this Declaration. The *ICCPR* obliges States Parties to guarantee in law the same civil and political rights that appear in the *UDHR* and to provide the means of fully enforcing them. The *ICESCR* obliges States Parties to progressively realize social and economic rights, including the right of everyone to gain a living by work that is freely chosen;[6] to social security, including social insurance;[7] to an adequate standard of living, including adequate food, clothing, and housing, and to the continuous improvement of living conditions;[8] to the enjoyment of the highest attainable standard of physical and mental health;[9] and to education.[10] Canada ratified both Covenants, with the consent of the provinces, in 1976.

While the rights that appear together in the *UDHR* were divided into the two Covenants, the Preamble to the *ICCPR* expressly asserts the indivisibility of civil and political freedoms from economic, social, and cultural rights. The Preamble to the *ICCPR* states: "... the ideal of free human beings enjoying civil and political freedom and freedom from fear and want can only be achieved if conditions are created whereby everyone may enjoy ... economic, social and cultural rights."

In the lived experience of women and men, economic, social, and cultural rights cannot be easily separated from civil and political rights. People who are hungry will not be active participants in the political life of their societies. Likewise, people who do not enjoy freedom

47

of expression cannot effectively struggle for social and economic fairness.[11] The Economic Commission for Latin America and the Caribbean (ECLAC) describes the interaction between economic, social and cultural rights, and civil and political rights in this way:

> Without progress in economic and social rights, civil and political rights … tend to become a dead letter for the sectors with least resources and lowest levels of education and information. Today it is abundantly clear that these sectors have much greater difficulty in gaining access to justice and opportunities for defending themselves against abuse by third parties or the State. Poverty and the non-exercise of citizenship very often go hand in hand. Changing this situation is a fundamental necessity in order to … achieve genuinely universal citizenship.[12]

Recently Canada reaffirmed its commitment to the indivisibility of civil, political, economic, social, and cultural rights by supporting a 1997 resolution of the United Nations General Assembly which states: "All human rights and fundamental freedoms are indivisible and interdependent." The resolution also recognizes that the "full realization of civil and political rights without the enjoyment of economic, social and cultural rights is impossible."[13] Canada voted in favour of the resolution, notwithstanding that the United Kingdom, the United States, and several other industrial democracies abstained. The resolution was adopted by the United Nations General Assembly.

When thinking about the indivisibility of rights, it is important to understand that the international instruments recognize an integral relationship between civil and political rights, social and economic rights, and equality rights. Indeed, it is useful to think of equality as the bridge between these two sets of rights. Both the *ICCPR* and the *ICESCR* guarantee that the rights in each Covenant will be available to all without discrimination based on race, colour, sex, language, religion, political or other opinion, national or social origin, property, birth, or other status.[14] Further, in Article 3 of both Covenants, "States Parties undertake to ensure the equal right of men and women to the enjoyment of all … rights set forth in the … Covenant."[15] Article 26 of the *ICCPR* makes an additional guarantee of equality that goes beyond the four corners of that Covenant. Article 26 requires States Parties to make broad guarantees of equality in law and to provide effective protection against discrimination wherever it arises.[16]

The Covenants guarantee the right of everyone to enjoy equally civil and political rights, and economic, social, and cultural rights. But there is more. Together, the *ICESCR* and the *ICCPR* delineate the multiple dimensions of equality. To enjoy equality, a woman must be able to enjoy fully all her rights. Equality is a bridging and an encompassing value, whose realization requires the full realization of both civil and political rights, and economic, social, and cultural rights.

It is also important to note that the *ICESCR* requires positive action by governments to realize economic, social, and cultural rights. The *ICCPR* projects a more classical liberal conception of the relationship between the individual and the state, with the state envisioned principally as the main perpetrator of rights violations,[17] and liberty, defined as freedom from government interference, as the dominant value. The *ICESCR*, however, views governments as key implementers of rights, actors who can give rights practical meaning. The general obligation of each State Party to this Covenant[18] is "to take steps, … to the maximum of its available resources, with a view to achieving progressively the full realization of the rights recognized in the present Covenant by all appropriate means, including … the adoption of legislative measures."[19]

The *ICESCR* is important to women's equality because its subject matter is practical, material conditions, and because it articulates the responsibility of governments for making those conditions adequate. As Barbara Stark points out, it recognizes "the right of every human being to be nurtured — to be housed, fed, clothed, healed and educated."[20] These rights, she argues, describe women's work. Caregiving work is constructed as female and therefore as undeserving of adequate compensation; and this is a major factor in women's poverty. Stark says the importance of the *ICESCR* lies in the fact that it "shifts the responsibility from women to the State for some nurturing work." [21]

Convention on the Elimination of All Forms of Discrimination Against Women (CEDAW)

CEDAW[22] was developed as a new treaty in 1979 after the *ICCPR* and the *ICESCR* had already come into force. It contains elements of both civil and political rights, and economic, social, and cultural rights, knitting the two together in a women's rights instrument.

CEDAW is significant precisely because it is a convention about women, and a convention that commits signatories to eliminating *all* forms of discrimination against women. It recognizes that women are a subordinated group in all societies, and that governments must make conscious, concerted efforts to change this fact.

Various provisions of *CEDAW* make it clear that this is a document concerned with women's substantive right to equality. At the outset, the Preamble to the Convention recognizes that formal guarantees of equality are not enough. It recognizes that despite the existence of various treaties guaranteeing equal rights to women, "extensive discrimination against women continues to exist."[23] The explicit purpose of the Convention is to ensure that measures are adopted that will "[eliminate] such discrimination in all its forms and manifestations."[24]

CEDAW requires States Parties, or signatories to the Convention, to enact legal guarantees of equality and to provide the means of fully enforcing them. It also requires much more. First, the Convention obliges States Parties to guarantee women the "exercise and enjoyment" of these legal rights.[25] "Exercise of the rights" connotes access to the use of them, by making adjudicative procedures for vindicating rights accessible, affordable, and known. "Enjoyment of the rights" means actually experiencing the benefit of the right, having the content of the right made real in one's life.[26]

The Convention's definition of discrimination reinforces this concern with women's enjoyment of their rights. According to the Convention, discrimination includes "any distinction, exclusion or restriction ... which has the purpose or effect of impairing or nullifying the ... enjoyment ... by women ... of human rights and fundamental freedoms. ..." The Convention, then, prohibits both acts and omissions that impair women's ability to enjoy, in their actual conditions, the substantive content of human rights and fundamental freedoms.

The Convention also requires States Parties not just to state, in legal documents, that they are committed to the principle of equality for women, but also to "ensure, through law and other appropriate means, the practical realization of this principle."

Thus, the scope of *CEDAW*'s concerns is broad. The goal of the Convention is the elimination of all forms of discrimination against women "in all fields, including the political, economic, social, and cultural fields."[27] This language precludes a reading of *CEDAW* that would permit signatories to address only the forms of discrimination which appear on the face of laws or policies, and thus to ignore the structural subordination of women. It also indicates that the Convention's application is not limited in any way, and that economic, social, and cultural forms of inequality are of particular concern. This concern with social and economic inequality is reinforced by the detailed Articles of Part III of *CEDAW* which require specific measures to overcome inequality in women's economic conditions, and in relation to access to work, remuneration for work, social security, pregnancy and maternity, education, health care, and living conditions.[28]

CEDAW obliges States Parties to pursue the goals of the treaty by "all appropriate means" or by taking "all appropriate measures." Most of the specific Articles in the Convention state that States Parties shall "take all appropriate measures" (to eliminate discrimination against women in education, public life, etc.). Legislation may be required, but legislation is not the complete solution. All appropriate measures are required and those may include designing and implementing programs, or allocating resources. The obligation is a positive one. Governments are required to act, not just to refrain from discriminating.

CEDAW also repudiates the split between public and private spheres, and the tendency of formal equality to designate the family and the market as private and therefore off limits. It does so by obliging States Parties to eliminate discrimination against women by "any person, or organization or enterprise." This distinction is crucial for women, because if discrimination in the "private" spheres of the family and the marketplace are not matters of state obligation, significant sites of women's subordination are set outside the boundary of equality commitments. Acknowledging this fact, *CEDAW* places obligations on States Parties to eliminate discrimination against women not just in the acts of government, but also in the conduct of non-governmental actors, whether they are individuals, organizations, or enterprises.[29]

CEDAW explicitly addresses two different ways in which women as a group are subordinated: through the social construction of stereotyped and subservient roles[30] and through the commodification of their sexuality.[31] These provisions demonstrate that the Convention's vision is not a rigidly individualistic one. Rather, it comprehends systemic, structural, and group-based forms of oppression.

The Convention also recognizes the need for governments and other actors to implement affirmative measures to overcome the historical disadvantage of women.[32] This reveals the underlying principle of the Convention, and clarifies that its goal is *de facto* equality. The general rule of the Convention is that women should be treated in a way that will bring the subordination of women to an end and produce equality in the real conditions of women's lives, regardless of whether that treatment is the same as, or different from, the treatment of men. The affirmative action clause reinforces the Convention's interest in real, material equality for women by repudiating a formal version of equality that would automatically deem measures discriminatory if they involve treating women differently from men.

Report of the Fourth World Conference on Women

The Beijing *Platform for Action*[33] provides further evidence that Canada has committed itself to substantive equality for women. The *Platform for Action* was adopted by participating governments, including Canada, in September 1995 at the Fourth World Conference on Women. It is the newest statement on the conditions of women's inequality around the world. It is also the latest effort by governments, negotiating together, to articulate in detail the concrete steps that are necessary if women are to advance. Notably, the *Platform* does not confine its focus to the forms of laws, or to the "public" sphere. Rather, the *Platform* is wide-ranging, dealing with the multiple facets of women's inequality, and setting out a long list of corrective actions that governments need to take.

The *Platform for Action* is not just important in itself. It is also an aid to understanding the meaning of *CEDAW*. The *Platform for Action* and *CEDAW* are complementary documents. Since 1975 there have been four United Nations-sponsored women's conferences, an International Women's Year (1975), and a Decade for Women (1976–1985). Through these events, strategies for advancing the equality of women have been developed, including the *Forward-looking Strategies* adopted in 1985 at the Third World Conference on Women, and the *Declaration on Violence Against Women* adopted in 1993.[34] These documents and the *Platform for Action* should be regarded as basic interpretive aids to *CEDAW*. *CEDAW* cannot be given a static, or time-fixed, reading. The *Platform for Action* provides a 1995 statement of the specific commitments of participating governments to advancing the equality of women. It is also, therefore, the most up-to-date guide to interpreting what *CEDAW* commitments mean now.

There are two parts of the *Platform for Action* that deal directly with economic issues: one addresses the issue of poverty; the other addresses the issues of women's inequality in economic structures and policies, in particular those related to remunerated and unremunerated work.

The *Platform* recognizes that "[i]n the past decade the number of women living in poverty has increased disproportionately to the number of men";[35] that there is "a persistent and increasing burden of poverty on women";[36] and that women's poverty has been deepened by globalization, economic restructuring, and structural adjustment programs.[37] The *Platform* commits governments to reviewing and modifying macro-economic and social policies that impede the advancement of women, or reinforce their inequality.

The actions to be taken by governments to eliminate women's poverty include the following:[38]

- Review and modify, with the full and equal participation of women, macro-economic and social policies with a view to achieving the objectives of the *Platform for Action*;

- Analyze, from a gender perspective, policies and programs — including those related to macro-economic stability, structural adjustment, external debt problems, taxation, investments, employment, markets and all relevant sectors of the economy — with respect to their impact on poverty, on inequality and particularly on women; assess their impact on family well-being and conditions, and adjust them, as appropriate, to promote more equitable distribution of productive assets, wealth, opportunities, income and services;

- Pursue and implement sound and stable macro-economic and sectoral policies that are designed and monitored with the full and equal participation of women, encourage broad-based sustained economic growth, address the structural causes of poverty and are geared towards eradicating poverty and reducing gender-based inequality within the overall framework of achieving people-centred sustainable development;

- Restructure and target the allocation of public expenditures to promote women's economic opportunities and equal access to productive resources and to address the basic social, educational and health needs of women, particularly those living in poverty;

- Provide adequate safety nets and strengthen state-based and community-based support systems, as an integral part of social policy, in order to enable women living in poverty to withstand adverse economic environments and preserve their livelihood, assets and revenues in times of crisis;

- Formulate and implement, when necessary, specific economic, social, agricultural and related policies in support of female-headed households;

- Introduce measures for the empowerment of women migrants and internally displaced women through the easing of stringent and restrictive migration policies, recognition of qualifications and skills of documented immigrants and their full integration into the labour force, and the undertaking of other measures necessary for the full realization of the human rights of internally displaced persons;

- Enable women to obtain affordable housing and access to land by, among other things, removing all obstacles to access, with special emphasis on meeting the needs of women, especially those living in poverty and female heads of households;

- Create social security systems wherever they do not exist, or review them with a view to placing individual women and men on an equal footing, at every stage of their lives;

- Ensure access to free or low-cost legal services, including legal literacy, especially designed to reach women living in poverty;

- Take particular measures to promote and strengthen policies and programs for indigenous women with their full participation and respect for their cultural diversity, so that they have opportunities and the possibility of choice in the development process in order to eradicate the poverty that affects them.

The *Platform for Action* also addresses women's "inequality in economic structures and policies, in all forms of productive activities and in access to resources."[39] The *Platform* is targeted at women's lack of economic autonomy, the disparity between their incomes and wealth and those of men, and the ways in which discrimination in employment, and the devaluation of women's paid and unpaid work contribute to this inequality.[40]

To address the negative impact on women of economic structures and policies, the actions to be taken by governments include the following:

- Enact and enforce legislation to guarantee the rights of women and men to equal pay for ... work of equal value;

- Devise mechanisms and take positive action to enable women to gain access to full and equal participation in the formulation of policies and definition of structures through such bodies as ministries of finance and trade, national economic commissions, economic research institutes and other key agencies, as well as through their participation in appropriate international bodies;

- Conduct reviews of national income and inheritance tax and social security systems to eliminate any existing bias against women;

- Seek to ensure that national policies related to international and regional trade agreements do not adversely impact women's new and traditional economic activities;

- Ensure that all corporations, including transnational corporations, comply with national laws and codes, social security regulations, applicable international agreements, instruments and conventions, including those related to the environment, and other relevant laws;

- Enact and enforce equal opportunity laws, take positive action and ensure compliance by the public and private sectors through various means;

- Use gender-impact analysis in the development of macro- and micro-economic and social policies in order to monitor such impact and restructure policies in cases where harmful impact occurs ...[41]

The fact that Canada is a signatory to *CEDAW*, and that it has indicated it fully intends to satisfy the terms of the *Platform for Action*, confirms that Canada's commitment to the equality of women includes a commitment to eradicating women's economic inequality.

Taken together, the international treaties to which Canada is a signatory, as well as other UN declarations and documents, make it clear that substantive equality for women is part of the explicit commitment of our nation.

Domestic Human Rights Commitments

Canada's Human Rights Statutes

The commitment of Canadians to equality is also expressed in domestic human rights legislation at the federal, provincial, and territorial levels.

Some early anti-discrimination initiatives in Canada included British Columbia's 1931 *Unemployment Relief Act*, Ontario's 1932 *Insurance Act*, Manitoba's 1934 *Libel Act*, British Columbia's 1945 *Social Assistance Act*, and Saskatchewan's 1947 *Bill of Rights*.[42]

However, Canada's domestic human rights legislation, like the international human rights treaties, really developed during the post–World War II period. After World War II, there was a dramatic increase in human rights activity. In Canada the lesson of the Holocaust led to the gradual repeal of discriminatory laws and a reduction in blatantly racist practices. Restrictive covenants forbidding the sale of property in certain areas to "Jews and persons of other objectionable nationality" were revoked. Segregated schools for Blacks and Aboriginal peoples gradually disappeared, as did segregated swimming pools and separate sections in theatres and restaurants for non-whites. Bars on the entry of Jews and non-whites into certain professions were dropped. Japanese-Canadians, Inuit, Indo-Canadians, Doukhobours, and finally status Indians were given the vote for the first time in Canada during this post-war period.

Human rights legislation appeared, prohibiting discrimination in employment and accommodation and public services. More complex human rights laws have since been developed in every jurisdiction. These laws are administered by human rights commissions, with specialized tribunals to hear and decide on allegations of discrimination brought before them.

The history of human rights legislation in Canada is a history of growing commitment to advancing the equality of disadvantaged groups in the society. At first human rights legislation prohibited discrimination only on the grounds of race, religion, colour, ethnic, or national origin. But in response to an expanding understanding of discrimination and to the demands of other groups, including women, other grounds of discrimination have been added gradually, extending coverage to include sex, physical and mental disability, marital status, family status, age, and, in some jurisdictions, political belief, criminal record, and sexual orientation.[43] A few human rights statutes now recognize social assistance recipients as a group entitled to protection from discrimination,[44] reflecting a commitment to dealing with economic inequality as a human rights issue.

As well, faced with new laws and with the particularities and complexities of real discrimination cases, tribunals and courts have been required to consider the status of human rights law in relation to other laws, and to expand and deepen their conception of discrimination.

Since 1982 the Supreme Court of Canada has made a number of pronouncements about the nature of human rights law and its place in the hierarchy of laws. The Court has concluded that human rights legislation is of a special nature because of the importance of the values it endeavours to buttress and protect. It is quasi-constitutional; that is, not quite constitutional, but more important than all other laws. No one can contract out of human rights legislation, nor can it be suspended, repealed, or altered except by clear legislative pronouncement.[45] Because of its important purpose and because it is remedial in nature, the Court has said that human rights legislation should not be interpreted restrictively, but rather in such a way as to give the rights their full recognition and effect.[46]

These conclusions reached about the nature of human rights legislation have led logically to the development of other human rights principles. One of these principles is that discrimination must be identified by its effects on the victim, not by the intent of the perpetrator. In 1985 the Supreme Court of Canada ruled in the case of *Ontario (Human Rights Commission) and O'Malley* v. *Simpsons Sears*[47] that discrimination need not be intentional to violate human rights protections. Theresa O'Malley disputed a requirement that all employees of Simpsons Sears work Friday evenings and Saturdays on a rotation basis. Ms. O'Malley was a Seventh Day Adventist and her religion required strict observance of the Sabbath from sundown Friday to sundown Saturday. Clearly this employment requirement was not imposed with the intention of discriminating against Ms. O'Malley as a Seventh Day Adventist. Nonetheless, the rule had a discriminatory effect, forcing her to choose between her employment and her religion.

Although the discrimination was unintentional, the Supreme Court of Canada found that Ms.

O'Malley was discriminated against. Further, the Court ruled that policies or practices that appear neutral on their face, but which have an adverse effect on a protected group, contravene the law. Because human rights legislation is remedial in nature and must be given an interpretation that will fulfil the broad aim of eliminating discrimination, the Court concluded that it is not necessary to prove intent in order to establish that discrimination has occurred, and that discrimination must be identified by its effects.

When discrimination is identified by its effects, it is also clear that treatment is not determinative. In some cases, as in *O'Malley,* identical treatment causes discrimination, and asymmetrical treatment may be necessary to create equality. The assumption, inherent in a formal equality approach, that same treatment is good and different treatment is bad, has exploded when tribunals and courts have had to apply the law to the realities of discrimination in Canada. The repudiation of same treatment as a formula for equality began early in human rights adjudication. In cases such as *Tharp* v. *Lornex Mining Corp. Ltd.,*[48] *Singh* v. *Security and Investigation Services Ltd.,*[49] and *Colfer* v. *Ottawa Police Commission,*[50] Boards of Inquiry found that same treatment caused discrimination. In *Tharp,* a British Columbia Board of Inquiry ruled that Jean Tharp was denied company-provided room and board at a mining site because of her sex, contrary to her right to be free from discrimination. The Board of Inquiry rejected the company's argument that it had offered her the "equality" of sharing the men's bunk house, shower, and washroom facilities.[51] In *Singh,* the Board of Inquiry found that the complainant was discriminated against by a rule that required all employees to be clean-shaven and to wear caps. Mr. Singh was a practising Sikh, and the tenets of his religion forbade him from shaving and required him to wear a turban. In *Colfer,* the Board of Inquiry found that Ann Colfer was discriminated against by a rule that required all Ottawa police officers to meet standard height and weight requirements. Because the standards were based on a male norm, they had the effect of screening out a disproportionate number of women. Had the adjudicators in these cases applied a same treatment model of equality, findings of discrimination could not have been made.

The issue of the adequacy of same treatment as the formula for equality reached the higher courts in the 1980s. In 1985 the Saskatchewan Court of Appeal handed down its decision in *Huck* v. *Canadian Odeon Theatres.*[52] (A subsequent application for leave to appeal to the Supreme Court of Canada was refused.) In this case, the Court was called upon to decide whether Canadian Odeon Theatres had discriminated against Michael Huck because of his physical disability. Mr. Huck, who had muscular dystrophy and used a motorized wheelchair, was refused service at the new Canadian Odeon Theatre in Regina unless he agreed to sit in front of the front row of seats. The theatre argued that Mr. Huck had been offered the same service as every other patron: a ticket for the movie and a seat to watch it from. If Mr. Huck could not enjoy the service in the same way as everyone else, the problem was caused by his disability, not by the theatre, it was contended. The Saskatchewan Court of Appeal rejected this analysis in forceful terms:

> If that interpretation of the meaning of discrimination ... is correct then the right not to be discriminated for physical disability ... is meaningless. If that

interpretation is correct, I can conceive of no situation in which a disabled person could be discriminated against in the use of accommodation, services or facilities which are offered to the public. If that interpretation is correct, the owner of a public facility, who offers washroom facilities of the same kind offered to the public generally to a disabled person or offers any other service notwithstanding that it can't be used by a wheelchair reliant person, will then be found to have discharged his obligation under the Code. A physically reliant person does not, in my opinion, acquire an equal opportunity to utilize facilities or services which are of no use to him or her. Identical treatment does not necessarily mean equal treatment or lack of discrimination.[53]

The Court further stated:

The treatment of a person differently from others may or may not amount to discrimination just as treating people equally is not determinative of the issue. If the effect of the treatment has adverse consequences which are incompatible with the objects of the legislation by restricting or excluding a right of full and equal recognition and exercise of those rights it will be discriminatory.[54]

The Supreme Court of Canada's decision in *Brooks* v. *Canada Safeway*[55] also added important nuances to the understanding of equality. In this decision, the Supreme Court of Canada ruled that Canada Safeway's disability plan discriminated against pregnant employees, and that discrimination because of pregnancy is discrimination because of sex within the meaning of the *Manitoba Human Rights Act*.[56] The Canada Safeway disability plan provided 26 weeks of benefits to any worker who had worked for Safeway for three months and who had to be absent from work for health reasons. However, it denied benefits to pregnant employees during a 17-week period commencing 10 weeks before childbirth and extending six weeks after it. Benefits were denied during this period no matter whether women were unable to work because of pregnancy-related complications or non-pregnancy-related illnesses. Unemployment Insurance maternity benefits provided an imperfect substitute for the disability benefits because they provided less money for a shorter time. The Court's decision in *Brooks* repudiated *Bliss* v. *Canada (A.G.)*,[57] a ruling made 10 years earlier under the *Canadian Bill of Rights*.

In *Bliss*, the Supreme Court of Canada ruled in 1979 that the *Unemployment Insurance Act*, which had a provision similar to the Canada Safeway disability plan, did not discriminate on the basis of sex. Stella Bliss challenged the *Act* when she was denied unemployment insurance benefits because she was pregnant. Even though she had worked the requisite number of weeks to qualify for them, Ms. Bliss could not claim regular unemployment benefits because the *Act* barred a pregnant woman from claiming regular unemployment insurance benefits in the 15 weeks immediately surrounding the birth of her child.

Denied regular benefits, Ms. Bliss could not qualify for unemployment insurance pregnancy benefits either. The *Unemployment Insurance Act* required a woman to have been employed for a longer period to be eligible for these benefits. Because she was not eligible under this rule, Bliss could not get any benefits. She was refused pregnancy benefits because she did not qualify and refused regular benefits because she was pregnant. In both ways, Ms. Bliss was discriminated against because of her sex.

However, the Court ruled that there was no discrimination based on sex, "since the distinction being made is not between male and female persons, but between pregnant and non-pregnant persons."[58] The Court adopted the view that because not all women become pregnant, the distinction is not one based on sex. It overlooked the fact that only women become pregnant and that laws that discriminate against those who are pregnant discriminate against women exclusively.

The Court expressed agreement with Justice Pratte of the Federal Court of Appeal who said:

> Assuming the respondent to have been "discriminated against," it would not have been by reason of her sex. Section 46 applies to women, and has no application to women who are not pregnant, and it has no application, of course to men. If section 46 treats unemployed pregnant women differently from other unemployed persons, be they male or female, it is, it seems to me, because they are pregnant not because they are women.[59]

In other words, by treating all non-pregnant persons the same (whether male or female), the *Act* satisfied the requirement of neutrality, that is, of treating likes alike.

The *Bliss* Court also distinguished penalties from benefits, contending that there should be a difference in the way that equality analysis thinks about penalizing legislation, such as a criminal law provision, that treats one section of the population more harshly than others, and legislation providing "additional benefits to one class of women." Contrasting the case of *Drybones*, which dealt with a *Criminal Code* provision that made it an offence for an Indian to be intoxicated, the Court said:

> There is a wide difference between legislation which treats one section of the population more harshly than all others by reason of race as in the case of *Regina v. Drybones*, and legislation providing additional benefits to one class of women, specifying conditions which entitle a claimant to such benefits and defining a period during which no benefits are available.[60]

Looking back at *Bliss*, it can be seen as an early blueprint for derailing challenges to laws and policies that contribute to the economic inequality of women. In *Bliss* the Court shifted responsibility for the inequality complained of by Stella Bliss away from the legislative scheme, finding the cause of the inequality did not reside in the legislation but rather was created by nature. The Court said that "[these provisions] are concerned with conditions from which men are excluded. Any inequality between the sexes in this area is not created by legislation but by nature."[61]

Because of that reasoning, it was important that 10 years later in *Brooks*, the Court repudiated *Bliss*. Unlike *Bliss*, which made the social disadvantage associated with pregnancy disappear, the *Brooks* decision makes disadvantage visible. In *Brooks* the Court found that burdening women with a disproportionate share of the cost of procreation is discriminatory. The Court anchored its analysis in the purpose of human rights legislation, saying:

> … one of the purposes of anti-discrimination legislation … is the removal of unfair disadvantages which have been imposed on individuals or groups in society. Such an unfair disadvantage may result when the costs of an activity from which all of society benefits are placed upon a single group of persons. This is the effect of the Safeway plan. It cannot be disputed that everyone in society benefits from procreation. The Safeway plan, however, places one of the major costs of procreation entirely upon one group in society: pregnant women. … Removal of such unfair impositions upon women and other groups in society is a key purpose of anti-discrimination legislation.[62]

Women experience a tangible and serious disadvantage when they are penalized because of childbearing or childbearing capacity. This is a social consequence of biology that men will never experience. Unlike *Bliss*, the *Brooks* decision makes women's disadvantage visible precisely because it admits that women are negatively affected by pregnancy-related discrimination in a way that men are not. In *Brooks* the Court found that the social disadvantages that are uniquely linked to women's gender are issues of sex discrimination.

It is notable in the *Brooks* decision that the Court pays attention to a larger social context of childbearing and the inequality of women. The Court does not focus solely on the narrow question of the legitimacy of the Safeway disability plan, but considers also the broader question of what is necessary for women to be able to function equally in society. The pervasiveness of discrimination based on pregnancy and the unfair disadvantage to women created by this are recognized and taken into account in determining that discrimination has occurred.

As in the decision in *Brooks*, in *Janzen* v. *Platy Enterprises Ltd.*[63] the Supreme Court of Canada adopted an inclusive, effects-based approach to the ground of sex discrimination that prioritizes the perspective of women, and assesses the significance of the challenged law or practice in the context of the social, historical, economic, and political realities of discrimination. In this case, this approach led the Supreme Court of Canada to conclude that sexual harassment is sex discrimination. Had the Court followed the reasoning of *Bliss*, or the reasoning of the lower courts, sexual harassment would have been dismissed as a matter of an individual man's sexual attraction to a particular woman. Instead, the Court recognized that sexual harassment is experienced by women predominantly, and that sexual harassment is an acting out of power relations between dominant men and subordinate women. As such, it is a form of sex discrimination.

The acceptance of effects as the test of discrimination has led not only to an expanded and more complicated understanding of how discrimination occurs, but also to the recognition of systemic discrimination. In addition to the fact that systemic discrimination can be recognized by its effects, it can also be recognized by the fact that it affects whole groups of people. Canadian adjudicators have moved beyond the notion that discrimination is a smattering of isolated events, unconnected to history or social context, which occur between individuals. Although individual instances of discrimination occur and require individual remedies, there is also discrimination that affects whole groups of people because of their sex, race, disability, or sexual orientation. That a rule or practice has an impact on a whole group is a key element of what is meant by systemic discrimination.

Systemic discrimination was identified in *Action Travail des Femmes*,[64] a case initiated and carried forward by Action Travail des Femmes, a Montreal women's organization. In that case, the Supreme Court said that "[t]he complaint was not that of a single complainant or even of a series of individual complainants; it was a complaint of systemic discrimination practised against an identifiable group."[65] The Court held that, in a case of systemic discrimination, a systemic remedy is appropriate.

The evidence in the case of *Action Travail des Femmes* revealed that women were being systematically discriminated against with respect to employment in blue-collar jobs with the Canadian National Railway. Women were discriminated against at the time they applied for jobs. They were also required to take discriminatory tests, required to have unnecessary qualifications, and harassed on the job if they were hired. Some of the discrimination was overt in form; for example, there was sex-based harassment on the job. Some of it occurred through the discriminatory operation of seemingly neutral requirements; for example, tests were used that screened out a disproportionate number of women and were not job related. The result was a pattern of exclusion of women from blue-collar jobs. At the end of 1981, there were only 57 women in blue-collar jobs in the St. Lawrence region of Canadian National Railway. These 57 women were 0.7 percent of Canadian National's blue-collar labour force in the region.

In the circumstances, the Tribunal that originally heard the complaint considered it necessary to order that a number of steps be taken to rectify the situation. It ordered Canadian National to cease using discriminatory tests and requiring women to take physical tests that were not given to men; to change its recruitment and interviewing practices; to stop its supervisory personnel from discriminating when hiring; and to take steps to prevent women from being sexually harassed on the job. In addition, it ordered Canadian National to hire one woman in every four new hires until the representation of women in blue-collar jobs in the St. Lawrence region reached 13 percent.

Canadian National disputed the part of the remedial order that set the hiring quota. At the Supreme Court level the question was whether the Tribunal had erred in fashioning such a remedy. The Court concluded that it had not, and described the operation of the remedy in this way:

An employment equity programme … is designed to work in three ways. First, by countering the cumulative effects of systemic discrimination, such a programme renders further discrimination pointless. To the extent that some intentional discrimination may be present, for example in the case of a foreman who controls hiring and who simply does not want women in the unit, a mandatory employment equity scheme places women in the unit despite the discriminatory intent of the foreman. His battle is lost.

Secondly, by placing members of the group that had previously been excluded into the heart of the work place and by allowing them to prove ability on the job, the employment equity scheme addresses the attitudinal problem of stereotyping. For example, if women are seen to be doing the job of "brakeman" or heavy cleaner or signaller at Canadian National, it is no longer possible to see women as capable of fulfilling only certain traditional occupational roles. It will become more and more difficult to ascribe characteristics to an individual by reference to the stereotypical characteristics ascribed to all women.

Thirdly, an employment equity programme helps to create what has been termed a "critical mass" of the previously excluded group in the work place. This "critical mass" has important effects. The presence of a significant number of individuals from the targeted group eliminates the problems of "tokenism"; it is no longer the case that one or two women, for example, will be seen to "represent" all women. … Moreover, women will not be so easily placed on the periphery of management concern. The "critical mass" also effectively remedies systemic inequities in the process of hiring … once a "critical mass" of the previously excluded group has been created in the work force, there is a significant chance for the continuing self-correction of the system.[66]

The Court concluded:

To render future discrimination pointless, to destroy discriminatory stereotyping and to create the required "critical mass" of target group participation in the work force, it is essential to combat the effects of past systemic discrimination. In so doing, possibilities are created for the continuing amelioration of employment opportunities for the previously excluded group. The dominant purpose of employment equity programmes is always to improve the situation of the target group in the future. … Systemic remedies must be built upon the experience of the past so as to prevent discrimination in the future. Specific hiring goals … are a rational attempt to impose a systemic remedy on a systemic problem.[67]

At virtually the same time as the Supreme Court of Canada's decision in *Action Travail des Femmes*, the Court issued another decision underlining its position on the remedial character of human rights legislation. In *Canada (Treasury Board)* v. *Robichaud*,[68] the Court was asked to decide whether the Department of National Defence (DND) was liable for an employee's sexual harassment by her supervisor, Dennis Brennan. Drawing on its earlier decisions, the Supreme Court of Canada found that DND was liable for the harassment because only the employer could provide an effective remedy.

The Court stated:

> Since the Act is essentially concerned with the removal of discrimination, as opposed to punishing anti-social behaviour, it follows that the motives or intention of those who discriminate are not central to its concerns. Rather the Act is directed to redressing socially undesirable conditions quite apart from the reasons for their existence.[69]

> ... the Act is not aimed at determining fault or punishing conduct. It is remedial. Its aim is to identify and eliminate discrimination. If this is to be done, then the remedies must be effective, consistent with the "almost constitutional" nature of the rights protected.[70]

> ... if the Act is concerned with the *effects* of discrimination rather than its *causes* (or motivations), it must be admitted that only an employer can remedy undesirable effects; only an employer can provide the most important remedy — a healthy work environment. The legislative emphasis on prevention and elimination of undesirable conditions, rather than on fault, moral responsibility and punishment, argues for making the Act's carefully crafted remedies effective. ... if the Act is to achieve its purpose, the Commission must be empowered to strike at the heart of the problem, to prevent its recurrence and to require that steps be taken to enhance the work environment.[71]

All these decisions, taken together, mean that in the 1990s there is a much more complex foundation for equality analysis. Neither sameness nor difference of treatment is determinative. Discrimination has a group-based dimension; identifying and eliminating it requires focusing on the broader social context and on the conditions of the group in question. Effects of discrimination, not intentions, are the concern of human rights protections; the goal is not to punish the perpetrator but to change the circumstances of the victims.

Charter Equality Rights Guarantees

In 1982, when Canada's Constitution was repatriated from Britain, a *Charter of Rights and Freedoms* that includes equality guarantees was added. Those constitutional guarantees of equality, now in section 15 of the *Charter,* are part of the trend of the past several decades in Canada to enact and expand human rights protections that will reduce inequality. However, it was because of the danger posed by decisions such as *Bliss,* which were rendered by courts under the *Canadian Bill of Rights*, that women mounted a massive lobby to influence the wording of the *Charter.* Important amendments to the text of the *Charter* were made, which can be directly traced to representations by women's organizations concerning the inadequacy of *Bill of Rights* jurisprudence.

Section 15 underwent a transformation from a clause guaranteeing "equality before the law" and "equal protection of the law" to a guarantee of these rights together with "equality under the law" and "equal benefit of the law." The additions were intended to give s. 15 substantive content and to ensure that the guarantee is applied to benefits, not just penalties. Section 28, a specific sex equality guarantee, was added to ensure that women would receive the equal benefit of all the rights guaranteed in the *Charter*.

One of the strongest supports for the view that s. 15 is intended to promote conditions of equality for historically disadvantaged groups is provided by s. 15(2) of the *Charter*. Section 15(2) authorizes laws, programs, or activities designed to ameliorate "conditions" of disadvantage for members of disadvantaged groups. Section 15(2) clarifies the meaning of *Charter* equality rights by ruling out the idea that treating someone differently is, by definition, discriminatory.[72]

It was a logical next step in the evolution of equality law when the Supreme Court of Canada in *Andrews* v. *Law Society (British Columbia)*,[73] its first decision interpreting the equality guarantees, swept into s. 15 the human rights principles that it had shaped over the previous decade. "In general," the Court said, "the principles which have been applied under the Human Rights Acts are equally applicable in considering questions of discrimination under s. 15(1)."[74]

Viewed against the backdrop of *Bliss* and other *Bill of Rights* equality cases,[75] the 1989 decision of the Supreme Court of Canada in *Andrews* was a watershed development.[76] The facts of the case — a challenge by a British subject to a citizenship requirement for practising law in British Columbia — were not particularly important to women, but because it was the first *Charter* equality rights case to reach the Supreme Court of Canada, the interpretive issues were critical. The question at the time of *Andrews* was whether the Court would simply entrench formal equality or begin to develop a contemporary Canadian theory of constitutional equality rights that could address the persistent, substantive inequality of women, people of colour, Aboriginal people, and people with disabilities.

In *Andrews* the Court endorsed a concept of discrimination that focused on adverse effects, made group disadvantage central to its analysis, and jettisoned any requirement for proof of intent to discriminate.

Regarding the content of s. 15, the Court said:

> The principle of equality before the law has long been recognized as a feature of our constitutional tradition and found statutory recognition in the *Canadian Bill of Rights*. However, unlike the *Canadian Bill of Rights*, which spoke only of equality before the law, s. 15 (1) of the *Charter* provides much broader protection. Section 15 spells out four basic rights (1) the right to equality before the law; (2) the right to equality under the law; (3) the right to equal protection of the law; and (4) the right to equal benefit of the law. The inclusion of these additional rights

in s. 15 of the *Charter* was an attempt to remedy some of the shortcomings of the right to equality under the *Canadian Bill of Rights*.[77]

Concerning *Bill of Rights* case law such as *Bliss*, the Court said: "It is readily apparent that the language of s. 15 was chosen to remedy some of the perceived defects under the *Canadian Bill of Rights*."[78]

In *Turpin*,[79] a subsequent *Charter* equality rights decision, the Supreme Court of Canada elaborated further on the approach articulated in *Andrews*, emphasizing the importance of a finding of disadvantage that exists apart from the particular legal distinction being challenged. On behalf of a unanimous Court, Wilson J. recognized that a purpose of s. 15 is "remedying or preventing discrimination against groups suffering social, political and legal disadvantage in our society."[80] The Court's holding in *Turpin* was consistent with a conception of s. 15 as primarily concerned with the remediation of the inequality of disadvantaged groups.

Since *Andrews*, various members of the Court have at various times confirmed their agreement with its overall approach.[81] They have also repudiated the similarly situated test;[82] acknowledged the inadequacies of a same treatment theory of equality;[83] recognized the importance of discriminatory effects and adverse effects analysis;[84] affirmed that discrimination may be unintentional;[85] emphasized the crucial role of context;[86] endorsed a purposive interpretive approach to s. 15;[87] and identified as purposes of s. 15 the protection of human dignity and the prevention of distinctions that may worsen the circumstances of those who have already suffered marginalization or historical disadvantage in our society.[88]

The Supreme Court of Canada has expressly recognized that *Charter* equality rights have positive content. In *Schachter* v. *Canada*, a case concerning the right of fathers to parental leave, Lamer C.J. stated:

> The right which was determined to be violated here is a positive right: the right to equal *benefit* of the law. ... Other rights will be more in the nature of "negative rights" which merely restrict government ... the equality right is a hybrid of sorts since it is neither purely positive nor purely negative. In some contexts it will be proper to characterize s. 15 as providing positive benefits.[89]

Schachter was applied by the Ontario Court of Appeal in the case of *Haig* v. *Canada*, wherein it was held that s. 15 requires the extension of human rights protections to gays and lesbians. Adopting a purposive approach that places disadvantaged groups at the forefront of the analysis, Krever J.A. stated:

> [T]he remedy chosen must not only respect the role of the legislature but it must also promote the purposes of the *Charter*. In choosing the remedy one must look to the values and objectives of the *Charter*, because an appreciation of the

Charter's deeper social purposes is central to the determination of remedy, especially when the impugned legislation confers a benefit on disadvantaged groups.[90]

These interpretive developments all reflect Canada's commitments to substantive equality.

Social Programs and Other Domestic Legislation

Canada's commitment to equality is expressed not just in those instruments that declare human rights as their subject matter. It is expressed in other laws and in social programs as well. In particular, it can be found in the laws and programs that constitute Canada's social safety net, including unemployment insurance (now employment insurance), social assistance, public pensions, and health care. These programs involve government in redistribution, regulation, and planning. Canada's social safety net, along with workers' compensation schemes, labour standards legislation, health and safety regulations, environmental laws, and other such interventions, all reflect a recognition of the inability of nineteenth century laissez-faire capitalism or formal equality to provide fairness and equality.

Family law reforms, equal pay laws, employment equity legislation, and workplace anti-harassment policies also reflect a trend in Canadian law and policy to dismantle social hierarchies that are premised on the economic and social subordination of women.

Section 36 of the Constitution

Also significant, as evidence that the normative content of equality is not necessarily fulfilled by the absence of government intervention, is s. 36 of the Constitution which commits the federal government and the provinces together to "promoting equal opportunities for the well-being of all Canadians"; "furthering economic development to reduce disparities in opportunities"; and "providing essential public services of reasonable quality to all Canadians."

The history of constitutional debates leading up to the enactment of s. 36 discloses a sensitivity to the reality that the goal of individual equality is inextricably linked to the availability of an adequate social safety net, and to the capacity of government to redistribute income in favour of disadvantaged groups and regions. Moreover, it is clear that successive generations of Canadian political leaders have recognized that the goals of economic equality and basic security for all Canadians are so fundamental as to surpass regional interests.

These fundamental objectives were recognized by former Prime Minister Lester Pearson, who asserted in a paper presented to the Federal/Provincial First Ministers' Conference held in Ottawa, on 5–7 February 1968:

> The economic prospects of Canadians of certain regions remain more limited than those of people in other regions. ... Only through that sense of equality — equality in the opportunities open to all Canadians, whatever their language or

cultural heritage, and wherever they may choose to live or move — can we give a purpose to Canada that will meet the proper expectations of our people. And only through measures that will carry this conviction — that we intend to make equality of opportunity an achievement as well as a goal — can we preserve the unity of the country. ... Caring for the less privileged, and the disadvantaged, no longer is a matter for the local community alone; for haphazard municipal or charitable relief. ... [A] loose association of political units ... would jeopardize the ability of the federal government to contribute to rising living standards for the people of Canada. ... We believe that the Government of Canada must have the power to redistribute income, between persons and between provinces, if it is to equalize opportunity across the country. This would involve, as it does now, the rights to make payments to individuals, for the purpose of supporting their income levels — old age security pensions, unemployment insurance, family allowances — and the right to make payments to provinces, for the purpose of equalizing the level of provincial government services. It must involve, too, the powers of taxation which would enable the federal government to tax those best able to contribute to those equalization measures. Only in this way can the national government contribute to the equalization of opportunity in Canada, and thus supplement and support provincial measures to this end.[91]

Similarly, former Prime Minister Pierre Trudeau wrote:

There is no room in our society for great or widening disparities — disparities as between the opportunities available to individual Canadians, or disparities in the opportunities or the public services available in the several regions of the country. ... [The federal government] must have the power to redistribute income and to maintain reasonable levels of livelihood for individual Canadians, if the effects of regional disparities on individual citizens are to be minimized. The provincial governments ... must be able to provide an adequate standard of public services to their citizens and to support the incomes of those who are in need.[92]

Conclusion

Canada has made commitments to equality at every level — internationally, constitutionally, in quasi-constitutional human rights statutes in every jurisdiction, and through related laws, social programs, and other forms of social regulation. These various levels of commitments are not disconnected from each other; they are components of a larger equality framework. Each instrument can be given its full meaning only when it is seen as part of this framework, and not in isolation.

There is widespread consensus in Canada that equality is a central and fundamental value, and that women are entitled to it. Although the idea of formal equality still has power and is being reasserted now by corporate and political forces, it is clear that Canada's human rights treaty commitments, domestic human rights legislation, the *Charter*'s equality guarantees, the social safety net and related legislation, as well as s. 36 of the Constitution, are commitments to a vision of social equality that goes well beyond what is offered by formal equality.

There can be no question, looking at the larger framework of Canada's equality commitments and all its components, that it encompasses a commitment to the elimination of women's social and economic inequality. The question now is: Will Canada live up to this commitment?

Endnotes for Chapter 2

[1] See Preamble to the *Universal Declaration of Human Rights*, adopted 10 December 1948, GA Res. 217A (III), UN Doc. A/810 (1948) [hereinafter *UDHR*].

[2] *Ibid.* Article 25.

[3] *Ibid.* Article 22.

[4] *Ibid.* Article 28.

[5] These countries are referred to as States Parties to a particular Covenant or Convention.

[6] *International Covenant on Economic, Social and Cultural Rights* (adopted 16 December 1966, entered into force 3 January 1976), GA Res. 2200A (XXI), UN Doc. A/6316 (1966), Article 6, 993 U.N.T.S. 3, reprinted in 6 I.L.M. 360 (1967) [hereinafter *ICESCR*].

[7] *Ibid.* Article 9.

[8] *Ibid.* Article 11.

[9] *Ibid.* Article 12.

[10] *Ibid.* Article 13.

[11] For a discussion of the indivisibility of rights in the *UDHR, supra* note 1, and their subsequent division in the drafting of the two Covenants, see Craig Scott and Patrick Macklem, "Constitutional Ropes of Sand or Justiciable Guarantees? Social Rights in a New South African Constitution" (1992) 141:1 *University of Pennsylvania Law Review* 1 at 85–114.

[12] Economic Commission for Latin America and the Caribbean, "Human Rights in Latin America and the Caribbean: Growth with Equity" in Richard Reoch, ed., *Human Rights: The New Consensus* (London: Regency House (Humanity) 1994) at 143–44.

[13] GA Res. 32/130 (1997), supported by Canada; see also the decision of MacGuigan J. of the Federal Court of Appeal in *International Fund for Animal Welfare* v. *Canada*, [1989] 1 F.C. 335, (1988), 83 N.R. 303, 45 C.C.C. (3d) 457, 35 C.R.R. 359. In this decision, which is discussed in H. Echenberg and B. Porter, "Poverty Stops Equality, Equality Stops Poverty: The Case for Social and Economic Rights" in Ryszard Cholewinsky, ed., *Human Rights in Canada: Into the 1990s and Beyond* (Ottawa: Human Rights Research and Education Centre, 1990) 1, MacGuigan J. cites international rights provisions and decides that civil rights entrenched in the *Charter* cannot be considered apart from social and economic rights as set out in the *ICESCR*.

[14] See the *International Covenant on Civil and Political Rights*, GA Res. 2200A (XXI), 21 UN GAOR, (Supp. No. 16) 52, UN Doc. A/6316 (1966), Article 2(1) [hereinafter *ICCPR*], and *ICESCR, supra* note 6 Article 2(2).

[15] See *ICCPR, ibid.* Article 3, and *ICESCR, ibid.* Article 3.

[16] Article 26 of the *ICCPR* states:

> All persons are equal before the law and are entitled without any discrimination to the equal

protection of the law. In this respect, the law shall prohibit any discrimination and guarantee to all persons equal and effective protection against discrimination on any ground such as race, colour, sex, language, religion, political or other opinion, national or social origin, property, birth or other status.

This Article, in our view, does not permit Canada, or any jurisdiction in Canada, to treat the enactment of human rights legislation as though it were a matter of government choice, as the Alberta and Ontario governments argued recently in the Supreme Court of Canada in the appeal of *Vriend* v. *Alberta (A.G.)* (1996), 132 D.L.R. (4th) 595, 5 W.W.R. 617, 37 Alta. L.R. (3d) 364, 181 A.R. 16, 18 C.C.E.L. (2d) 1 (Alta C.A.). In this case, Delwin Vriend and others argued that the omission of sexual orientation from the list of protected grounds in Alberta human rights legislation contravenes their right to equality guaranteed in s. 15 of the *Charter*. The Attorneys General of Alberta and Ontario argued that they are not required to have human rights legislation at all, or to legislate the inclusion of any particular ground. Considering the commitment Canada has made in Article 26 of the *ICCPR*, this argument appears to be wrong. We are confirmed in this interpretation by a recent address entitled "International Standards on Non-Discrimination" given by Elizabeth Evatt, Rapporteur of the UN Human Rights Committee at the Conference on Hong Kong Equal Opportunities Law in International and Comparative Perspective, 10 November 1997. Elizabeth Evatt stated clearly that Hong Kong, as a signatory to the *ICCPR*, is required to have anti-discrimination legislation that protects residents effectively from the forms of discrimination that they are actually experiencing.

[17] Craig Scott and Patrick Macklem, *supra* note 11, point out, however, that the characterization of civil and political rights as "negative" rights, which prevent government from interfering in the lives of citizens, does not accurately describe the requirements that Canadian and European courts have placed on governments in response to actual claims. In a number of cases adjudicating what are considered to be "negative" rights claims, courts have required governments to make costly programmatic changes. Where civil and political rights have been at issue, the judicial response is not always to order the government to cease an offending act; sometimes court orders require the state to take corrective action, including actions that have implications for government expenditure. For example in *R.* v. *Askov,* [1990] 2 S.C.R. 1199, 75 O.R. (2d) 673, 74 D.L.R. (4th) 355, 113 N.R. 241, 42 O.A.C. 81, 59 C.C.C. (3d) 449, 79 C.R. (3d) 273, 49 C.R.R. 1, and *Singh* v. *Canada (Minister of Employment and Immigration),* [1985] 1 S.C.R. 177, 17 D.L.R. (4th) 422, 58 N.R. 1, 12 Admin. L.R. 137, 14 C.R.R. 13, two cases dealing with procedural fairness and undue delay, Canadian courts made orders that required a costly reorganization of adjudicative procedures. In *Askov* the issue was a delay of two years between the committal date for trial and the trial itself; this delay was found to violate Askov's right to be tried within a reasonable time pursuant to s. 10 of the *Charter.* The Supreme Court of Canada ruling resulted in a major review of the court system, and in many other cases being thrown out because they were already older than the two-year limit set by the Court. In *Singh,* the Supreme Court of Canada found that immigration hearings did not comply with the requirements of procedural fairness; this required the government to adopt new administrative procedures to correct the problem. In both cases, governments were required to act, and in both cases there were significant financial implications. Indeed, in these cases, the Court made orders that required governments to actively undertake major reorganizing in Canada's justice system.

[18] *ICESCR, supra* note 6 Article 2(1).

[19] *Ibid.*

[20] Barbara Stark, "International Human Rights Law, Feminist Jurisprudence, and Neitzsche's 'Eternal Return': Turning the Wheel" (1996) *Harvard Women's Law Journal* 169 at 178–79.

[21] *Ibid.* at 179.

[22] *Convention on the Elimination of All Forms of Discrimination Against Women*, GA Res. 34/180, UN GAOR, 34th Sess. (Supp. No. 46), 19 I.L.M. 33, Can. T.S. 1982 No. 31, (concluded 18 December 1979; in force for Canada 9 January 1982) [hereinafter *CEDAW*].

[23] The preamble refers to the *Charter of the United Nations*, the *Universal Declaration of Human Rights*, the two International Covenants, and the international Conventions concluded under the auspices of the United Nations and the specialized agencies promoting equality for women and in preambular paragraph 5 expresses concern that "despite these various instruments extensive discrimination continues to exist."

[24] See *CEDAW*, *supra* note 22 preambular paragraph 14.

[25] Article 3 is one of six central Articles in Part I of *CEDAW* which provide the general core commitments and general interpretive aids to reading the whole Convention. They are these:

Article 1
For the purpose of the present Convention, the term "discrimination against women" shall mean any distinction, exclusion or restriction made on the basis of sex which has the effect or purpose of impairing or nullifying the recognition, enjoyment or exercise by women, irrespective of their marital status, on a basis of equality of men and women, of human rights and fundamental freedoms in the political, economic, social, cultural, civil or any other field.

Article 2
States Parties condemn discrimination against women in all its forms, agree to pursue by all appropriate means and without delay a policy of eliminating discrimination against women and, to this end, undertake:

(a) To embody the principle of the equality of men and women in their national constitutions or other appropriate legislation if not yet incorporated therein and to ensure, through law and other appropriate means, the practical realization of this principle;
(b) To adopt appropriate legislative and other measures, including sanctions where appropriate, prohibiting all discrimination against women;
(c) To establish legal protection of the rights of women on an equal basis with men and to ensure through competent national tribunals and other public institutions the effective protection of women against any act of discrimination;
(d) To refrain from engaging in any act or practice of discrimination against women and to ensure that public authorities and institutions shall act in conformity with this obligation;
(e) To take all appropriate measures to eliminate discrimination against women by any person, organization or enterprise;
(f) To take all appropriate measures, including legislation, to modify or abolish existing laws, regulations, customs and practices which constitute discrimination against women;
(g) To repeal all national penal provisions which constitute discrimination against women.

Article 3
States Parties shall take in all fields, in particular in the political, social, economic and cultural fields, all appropriate measures, including legislation, to ensure the full development and advancement of women, for the purpose of guaranteeing them the exercise and enjoyment of human rights and fundamental freedoms on a basis of equality with men.

Article 4
1) Adoption by States Parties of temporary special measures aimed at accelerating *de facto* equality between men and women shall not be considered discrimination as defined in the present Convention, but shall in no way entail as a consequence the maintenance of unequal or separate

standards; these measures shall be discontinued when the objectives of equality of opportunity and treatment have been achieved.

2) Adoption by States Parties of special measures, including those measures contained in the present Convention aimed at protecting maternity shall not be considered discriminatory.

Article 5
States Parties shall take all appropriate measures:

a) To modify the social and cultural patterns of conduct of men and women, with a view to achieving the elimination of prejudices and customary and all other practices which are based on the idea of the inferiority or the superiority of either of the sexes or on stereotyped roles for men and women; ...

Article 6
States Parties shall take all appropriate measures, including legislation, to suppress all forms of traffic in women and exploitation of prostitution of women.

[26] For a discussion of this point and related developments in international human rights case law, see Rebecca J. Cook, "State Accountability Under the Convention on the Elimination of All Forms of Discrimination Against Women" in Rebecca J. Cook, ed., *Human Rights of Women: National and International Perspectives* (Philadelphia: University of Pennsylvania Press, 1994) at 230–39.

[27] See *CEDAW*, *supra* note 22, Article 3.

[28] Part III provides that States Parties shall "take all appropriate measures":

Article 10
... to eliminate discrimination against women in order to ensure to them equal rights with men in the field of education ...

Article 11
... to eliminate discrimination against women in the field of employment in order to ensure ... in particular:

(a) The right to work as an inalienable right of all human beings;

(b) The right to the same employment opportunities, ...;

(c) The right to free choice of profession and employment, the right to promotion, job security and all benefits and conditions of service and the right to receive vocational training and ... recurrent training;

(d) The right to equal remuneration, including benefits, and to equal treatment in respect of work of equal value, ...;

(e) The right to social security, particularly in cases of retirement, unemployment, sickness, invalidity and old age and other incapacity to work, as well as the right to paid leave;

(f) The right to protection of health and to safety in working conditions, including the safeguarding of the function of reproduction.

... and [protection from] discrimination ... on the grounds of marriage and maternity ...

Article 12
... to eliminate discrimination against women in the field of health care ...

Article 13
... to eliminate discrimination against women in other areas of economic and social life ...

[29] That the Convention applies to non-governmental action has also been confirmed by the *CEDAW* Committee. In General Recommendation No. 19 on gender-based violence, the Committee states that the Convention applies to violence perpetrated by public authorities, but that States Parties "may also be responsible for private acts if they fail to act with due diligence to prevent violations of rights or to investigate and punish acts of violence, and for providing compensation." See General Recommendation No. 19, UN Doc. A/47/38 (1992) paragraph 19. The Recommendation describes in detail the forms of public and private-actor violence that States Parties should prevent, and concludes by recommending "that States Parties should take appropriate and effective measures to overcome all forms of gender-based violence, whether by public or private act." See *ibid.* paragraph 24(a).

[30] *CEDAW, supra* note 22 Article 5(a).

[31] *Ibid.* Article 6.

[32] *Ibid.* Article 4.

[33] *Report of the Fourth World Conference on Women*, Beijing, China, 4–15 September 1995, A/CONF.177/20, 17 October 1995 [hereinafter *Platform for Action*].

[34] This history is cited in the *Platform for Action, ibid.* at Chapter II paragraph 26.

[35] See *ibid.* at Chapter IV, section A paragraph 50.

[36] *Ibid.*

[37] *Ibid.* at Chapter IV, section A paragraph 47. Further, the *Platform for Action* states:

> Poverty has various manifestations, including lack of income and productive resources sufficient to ensure a sustainable livelihood; hunger and malnutrition; ill health; limited or lack of access to education and other basic services; increasing morbidity and mortality from illness; homelessness and inadequate housing; unsafe environments; and social discrimination and exclusion. It is also characterized by lack of participation in decision-making and in civil, social and cultural life. It occurs in all countries — as mass poverty in many developing countries and as pockets of poverty amidst wealth in developed countries. Poverty may be caused by an economic recession that results in loss of livelihood or by disaster or conflict. There is also the poverty of low-wage workers and the utter destitution of people who fall outside family support systems, social institutions and safety nets ... In order to eradicate poverty and achieve sustainable development, women and men must participate fully and equally in the formulation of macro-economic and social policies and strategies for the eradication of poverty. The eradication of poverty cannot be accomplished through anti-poverty programs alone but will require democratic participation and changes in economic structures in order to ensure access for all women to resources, opportunities and public services.

[38] *Ibid.* paragraph 58.

[39] *Ibid.* at Chapter IV, section F.

[40] *Ibid.* at Chapter IV, section F paragraph 157. The *Platform for Action* notes that:

> Discrimination in education and training, hiring and remuneration, promotion and horizontal mobility practices, as well as inflexible working conditions, lack of access to productive resources and inadequate sharing of family responsibilities, combined with a lack of or insufficient services such as child care, continue to restrict employment, economic, professional and other opportunities and mobility for women and make their involvement stressful. *Ibid.* at Chapter IV, section F paragraph 152.

> [W]omen have been particularly affected by the economic situation and restructuring processes, which have changed the nature of employment and, in some cases, have led to a loss of jobs, even for professional and skilled women. In addition, many women have entered the informal sector due to the lack of other opportunities. *Ibid.* at Chapter IV, section F paragraph 151.

> [W]omen still also perform the great majority of unremunerated domestic work and community work, such as caring for children and older persons, preparing food for the family, protecting the environment and providing voluntary assistance to vulnerable and disadvantaged individuals and groups. *Ibid.* at Chapter IV, section F paragraph 156.

> Insufficient attention to gender analysis has meant that women's contributions and concerns remain too often ignored in economic structures, such as financial markets and institutions, labour markets, economics as an academic discipline, economic and social infrastructure, taxation and social security systems, as well as in families and households. *Ibid.* at Chapter IV, section F paragraph 155.

[41] These are excerpts from *Platform for Action*, *ibid.* at Chapter IV section F paragraph 167.

[42] These statutes are: *An Act Respecting Unemployment Relief*, S.B.C. 1931, c. 65, schedule A, s. 8; *An Act to Amend the Libel Act*, S.M. 1934, c. 23, s. 1; *An Act to Protect Certain Civil Rights*, S.S. 1947, c. 35; *An Act to Provide Social Assistance*, R.S.B.C. 1948, c. 310, s. 8; *The Insurance Act*, S.O. 1932, c. 24, s. 4.

[43] Discrimination is prohibited based on "political convictions" in Quebec, (R.S.Q. 1977, c. C-12, s. 10); on "political belief" in Prince Edward Island and Nova Scotia, (R.S.P.E.I. 1988, c. H-12, s. 1(1)(d) and R.S.N.S. 1989, c. 214, s. 5(1)(u)); and on "political opinion" in Newfoundland, (R.S.N. 1990, c H-14, ss. 6(1), 7(1), 8, 9(1), (2), (3), (4), 12, 13). Discrimination based on sexual orientation is prohibited in federal jurisdiction (R.S.C. 1985, c. H-6, s. 3(1)); New Brunswick (R.S.N.B. 1973, c. H-11, ss. 3(1),(2),(3),(4), 4(1),(2),(3), 5(1), 6(1), 7(1); Nova Scotia (R.S.N.S. 1989, c. 214, s. 5(1)(n); Quebec (R.S.Q. 1977, c. C-12, s.10; Ontario (R.S.O. 1990, c. H.19, ss. 1, 2(1), 3, 6; Manitoba (C.C.S.M., c. H175, s. 9(2)(h); Saskatchewan (S.S. 1979, c. S-24.1, ss. 9, 10(1), 11(1), 12(1), 13(1), 14(1), 15(1); British Columbia (R.S.B.C. 1996, c. 210, ss. 7(1), 8(1), 9, 10(1), 11, 13(1), 14; and Yukon Territory (R.S.Y. 1986 (Suppl.), c. 11, s. 6(g)). Discrimination is prohibited based on a criminal conviction for which a pardon has been granted in federal jurisdiction (R.S.C. 1985, c. H-6, s. 3(1)) and in the Northwest Territories (R.S.N.W.T. 1988, c. F-2, s. 3(1), (3), 4(1), 4(2), 5(1). In British Columbia, discrimination in employment is prohibited because of a "criminal or summary conviction offence that is unrelated to the employment or intended employment of a person," (R.S.B.C. 1996, c. 210, ss. 13(1), 14. Quebec also prohibits discrimination based on language (R.S.Q. 1977, c. C-12, s.10).

[44] See *Human Rights, Citizenship and Multiculturalism Act*, R.S.A. 1980, c. H-11.7, s.7(1) ("source of income"); *Human Rights Code*, C.C.S.M., c. H175, s.9(2)(j) ("source of income"); *Human Rights Code*, R.S.O. 1990, c. H.19, s. 2(1) ("receipt of social assistance"); *Charter of Human Rights and Freedoms*, R.S.Q. 1977, c. C-12, s. 10 ("social condition"); *Human Rights Act*, R.S.N.S. 1989, c. 214, s. 16(1) ("receipt of assistance"); *The*

Human Rights Code, R.S.N. 1990, c. H-14, ss. 6(1), 7(1), 8, 9(1), (2), (3), (4), 10(3), 14(1) ("social origin").

[45] *Winnipeg School Division No. 1* v. *Craton*, [1985] 2 S.C.R. 150, 21 D.L.R. (4th) 1, 61 N.R. 241, 6 W.W.R. 166, 38 Man.R. (2d) 1, 15 Admin. L.R. 177, 8 C.C.E.L. 105, 85 C.L.L.C. 17,020, 6 C.H.R.R. D/3104.

[46] *Canadian National Railway Co.* v. *Canada (Human Rights Commission)*, [1987] 1 S.C.R. 1114 at 1134, 40 D.L.R. (4th) 193, 76 N.R. 161, 27 Admin. L.R. 172, 87 C.L.L.C. 17,022 [hereinafter *Action Travail des Femmes* cited to S.C.R.].

[47] [1985] 2 S.C.R. 536, 23 D.L.R. (4th) 321, 9 C.C.E.L. 185, 52 O.R. (2d) 799, 17 Admin. L.R. 89, 86 C.L.L.C. 17,002, 64 N.R. 161, 7 C.H.R.R. D/3102,12 O.A.C. 241 [hereinafter *O'Malley*].

[48] *Tharp* v. *Lornex Mining Corp. Ltd.* (1975), Dec. No. 57 (B.C. Bd. of Inq.) [unreported] [hereinafter *Tharp*].

[49] *Singh* v. *Security and Investigation Services Ltd. (1977)*, (Ont. Bd. of Inq.) [unreported] [hereinafter *Singh*].

[50] *Colfer* v. *Ottawa Police Commission* (1979), (Ont. Bd. of Inq.) [unreported] [hereinafter *Colfer*].

[51] The Board of Inquiry in *Tharp*, *supra* note 48, wrote:

> The position of Lornex from the outset was that it could not be discriminating against Jean Tharp because it was offering her precisely the same accommodation that it offered every other employee at the campsite. In other words it was contended that there can be no discrimination where everyone receives identical treatment. We reject that contention. It is a fundamentally important notion that identical treatment does not necessarily mean equal treatment or the absence of discrimination. We would add only that the circumstances of this complaint graphically illustrate the truth of this important notion.

[52] *Huck* v. *Canadian Odeon Theatres Ltd.*, (1985), 18 D.L.R. (4th) 93, [1985] 3 W.W.R. 717, 39 Sask. R. 81 6 C.H.R.R. D/2682 (Sask. C.A.); leave to appeal to S.C.C. refused (1985), 18 D.L.R. (4th) 93 (note).

[53] *Ibid.*(1985) 6 C.H.R.R. D/2682 at D/2688.

[54] *Ibid.* at D/2689.

[55] *Brooks* v. *Canada Safeway*, [1989] 1 S.C.R. 1219, C.E.B. & P.G.R. 8126, 26 C.C.E.L. 1, 4 W.W.R. 93, 89 C.L.L.C. 17,012, 94 N.R. 373, 58 Man. R. (2d) 161, 10 C.H.R.R. D/6183, 59 D.L.R. (4th) 321, 45 C.R.R. 115 [hereinafter *Brooks* cited to S.C.R.].

[56] Some human rights statutes, for example, the *Ontario Human Rights Code*, now state that the right to freedom from discrimination based on sex includes the right to freedom from discrimination based on pregnancy or the capacity to become pregnant. The *Manitoba Human Rights Act* at the time of *Brooks* contained no explicit reference to pregnancy; it simply prohibited discrimination based on sex.

[57] *Bliss* v. *Canada (A.G.)*, [1979] 1 S.C.R. 183 at 191, [1978] 6 W.W.R. 711, 92 D.L.R. (3d) 417, 23 N.R. 527, 78 C.L.L.C. 14,175 [hereinafter *Bliss* cited to S.C.R.].

[58] *Ibid.* at 190–91.

[59] *Ibid.*

[60] *Ibid.*

[61] *Ibid.* at 190.

[62] *Brooks, supra* note 55 at 1238.

[63] *Janzen* v. *Platy Enterprises Ltd.*, [1989] 1 S.C.R. 1252, 59 D.L.R. (4th) 352, 25 C.C.E.L. 1, [1989] 4 W.W.R. 39, 10 C.H.R.R. D/6205, 58 Man. R. (2d) 1, 47 C.R.R. 274 [hereinafter *Janzen* cited to S.C.R.].

[64] *Action Travail des Femmes, supra* note 46.

[65] *Ibid.* at 1118.

[66] *Ibid.* at 1143–44.

[67] *Ibid.* at 1145.

[68] [1987] 2 S.C.R. 84, 40 D.L.R. (4th) 577, 75 N.R. 303, 8 C.H.R.R. D/4326, 87 C.L.L.C. 17,025.

[69] *Ibid.* at 90.

[70] *Ibid.* at 92.

[71] *Ibid.* at 94.

[72] Additional support for the observation that the *Charter* supports group aspirations to equality can be found in ss. 2 and 29, which accord rights to religious minorities; ss. 14, 16, and 23, which entrench language rights and require the use of public funds for minority language educational facilities; ss. 14 and 27, which recognize Canada's multicultural make-up; ss. 25 and 35 of the *Constitution Act, 1982*, which recognize the constitutional rights of Aboriginal people.

[73] *Andrews* v. *Law Society (British Columbia)*, [1989] 1 S.C.R. 143, [1989] 2 W.W.R. 289, 25 C.C.E.L. 255, 91 N.R. 255, 34 B.C.L.R. (2d) 273, 10 C.H.R.R. D/5719, 36 C.R.R. 193, 56 D.L.R. (4th) 1 [hereinafter *Andrews* cited to S.C.R.].

[74] *Ibid.* at 175.

[75] *Canada (A.G.)* v. *Lavell*, [1974] S.C.R. 1349, (1973) 38 D.L.R. (3d) 481, 7 C.N.L.C. 236, 23 C.R.N.S. 197, 11 R.F.L. 333 was another notorious women's equality case decided under the *Bill of Rights*. The Court upheld s. 12(1)(b) of the *Indian Act*, which deprived women, but not men, of their membership in Indian Bands if they married non-Indians. The provision was held not to violate equality before the law although it might, the Court said, violate equality under the law if such were protected.

[76] *Andrews, supra* note 73.

[77] *Ibid.* at 170.

[78] *Ibid.*

[79] *R.* v. *Turpin*, [1989] 1 S.C.R. 1296, 69 C.R. (3d) 97, 48 C.C.C. (3d) 8, 96 N.R. 115, 34 O.A.C. 115, 39 C.R.R. 306 [hereinafter *Turpin* cited to S.C.R.].

[80] *Ibid.* at 1333.

[81] See *R. v. Nguyen (sub nom R. v. Hess)*, [1990] 2 S.C.R. 906 at 944, [1990] 6 W.W.R. 289, 59 C.C.C. (3d) 161, 50 C.R.R. 71, 119 N.R. 353, 73 Man. R. (2d) 1, 46 O.A.C. 13, 79 C.R. (3d) 332 [hereinafter *Hess* cited to S.C.R.] where McLachlin J. writes, "[i]n my view, the essential requirements for discrimination under s. 15 remain as set forth in *Andrews*." This opinion is concurred in by Sopinka and Gonthier JJ. The majority opinion, authored by Wilson J., also purports to apply *Andrews* [See *Hess, ibid.* at 927–28]. See also, *R. v. Swain*, [1991] 1 S.C.R. 933 at 990–91, 63 C.C.C. (3d) 481, 5 C.R. (4th) 253, 125 N.R. 1, 3 C.R.R. (2d) 1, 47 O.A.C. 81 [hereinafter *Swain* cited to S.C.R.] where Lamer C.J. reviews, with apparent approval, the Court's equality doctrine as set out in *Andrews* and *Turpin*. In fact, Lamer C.J. notes that the approach to section 15(1) described by McIntyre J. in *Andrews* was expanded in *Turpin*. Lamer C.J. quotes Justice Wilson on behalf of the court in *Turpin* as stating that "[t]he internal qualification in s. 15 that the differential treatment be 'without discrimination' is determinative of whether or not there has been a violation of the section. It is only when one of the four equality rights has been denied with discrimination that the values protected by s. 15 are threatened and the court's legitimate role as the protector of such values comes into play." As well, in *Miron v. Trudel*, [1995] 2 S.C.R. 418 at 484, 10 M.V.R. (3d) 151, 23 O.R. (3d) 160 (note) [1995] 1 L.R. 1-3185, 13 R.F.L. (4th) 1, 181 N.R. 253, 124 D.L.R. (4th) 693, 81 O.A.C. 253 [hereinafter *Miron* cited to S.C.R.] McLachlin J., writing for the majority, L'Heureux-Dubé J. in a separate concurring opinion, and Gonthier J. in dissent, all acknowledge *Andrews* as supplying the analytical framework for the s. 15 analysis.

[82] La Forest J., writing for the majority in *McKinney v. University of Guelph*, [1990] 3 S.C.R. 229 at 279, 91 C.L.L.C. 17,004, 76 D.L.R. (4th) 545, 118 N.R. 1, 13 C.H.R.R. D/171, 45 O.A.C. 1, 2 O.R. (3d) 319 (note) 2 C.R.R. (2d) 1 [hereinafter *McKinney* cited to S.C.R.], repudiated the similarly situated test as mechanical and stated, "I do not believe that the similarly situated test can be applied other than mechanically, and I do not believe that it survived *Andrews* v. *Law Society of British Columbia*."

In *Symes v. Canada*, [1993] 4 S.C.R. 695 at 754, 94 D.T.C. 6001, 161 N.R. 243, [1994] 1 C.T.C. 40, 19 C.R.R. (2d) 1, 110 D.L.R. (4th) 470, [1994] W.D.F.L. 171 [hereinafter *Symes* cited to S.C.R.] Iacobucci J., writing for the majority, reaffirmed the Court's discarding of the similarly situated test. Iacobucci J. also noted that in *Andrews* the Court had rejected the view that s. 15 analysis should be governed by the comparison of similarly situated persons.

In *Miron, supra* note 81 at 466, L'Heureux-Dubé J. noted that the similarly situated test "was rejected by this Court on the basis that it contemplated only formal, Aristotelian equality, and because it excluded any consideration of the nature of the impugned law itself ..." In asserting that the similarly situated test had been rejected, L'Heureux-Dubé J. pointed to *Andrews, supra* note 73 at 165–68.

[83] In *Symes, ibid.* at 754, the same treatment model of equality was discarded by Iacobucci J., writing for the majority. In that case, Iacobucci J. recognized that s. 15 is more concerned with the impact of an impugned law than its form. He stated that "Section 15(1) guarantees more than formal equality; it guarantees that equality will be mainly concerned with the 'impact of the law on the individual or group concerned.'"

[84] In *McKinney, supra* note 82 at 279, La Forest J., writing for the majority, acknowledged that s. 15 protects against adverse effects discrimination. He states that, "not only does the *Charter* protect from direct or intentional discrimination, it also protects from adverse impact discrimination." The same acknowledgement was made in *Symes, supra* note 82 at 755, by Iacobucci J. who stated that "it is clear that a law may be discriminatory even if it is not directly or expressly discriminatory. In other words, adverse effects discrimination is comprehended by s. 15(1)." Iacobucci J. also referred to the opinion of McIntyre in *O'Malley, supra* note 47, holding that discrimination may result from the adverse effects of a facially neutral rule, and a finding of discrimination may be made even if there is no intention to discriminate.

[85] In *Swain*, *supra* note 81 at 990, Lamer C.J. clearly notes that discrimination may be unintentional when he cites the *Andrews* definition of discrimination as: "[A] distinction, whether intentional or not but based on grounds relating to personal characteristics of the individual or group, which has the effect of imposing burdens, obligations, or disadvantages on such individual or group not imposed upon others, or which withholds or limits access to opportunities, benefits, and advantages available to other members of society". Lamer C.J. also notes that this definition of "discrimination" was affirmed in *McKinney*.

[86] In *Swain*, *ibid.* at 991, Lamer C.J. looks to Wilson J.'s judgment in *Turpin* and reaffirms the correctness of the view that in determining whether the requirement of discrimination is present in a particular case, it is important to look not only at the impugned legislation which has created a distinction, but also to the "larger social, political and legal context." Thus, Lamer C.J. opines that, "in determining whether an individual or group falls into a category analogous to those specifically enumerated in s. 15, courts must examine 'the place of the group in the entire social, political and legal fabric of our society.'"

The need to contextualize is also underlined by Iacobucci J. in *Symes*, *supra* note 82 at 756. Iacobucci J. also looks to Wilson J.'s decision in *Turpin* for the proposition that in determining whether there is discrimination, it is important to look not only at the impugned legislation but also to the larger social, political, and legal context. He notes that "[w]hat is recognized by both *Andrews* and *Turpin* is that the working definition of 'discrimination' is not self-applying. Instead, within the analytical parameters established by that definition, this Court must 'search for indicia of discrimination.'" (See *Turpin*, *supra* note 79 at 1333 and *Symes*, *ibid.* at 757.)

In her dissent in *Symes*, *ibid.* at 826, L'Heureux-Dubé J. also notes the importance of context. She states: "I believe that it is important to recall the context in which the determination of *Charter* issues must be considered, as was set out by my colleague in reference to Wilson J.'s statement in *R. v. Turpin*, [1989] 1 S.C.R. 1296, and as I wrote in *R. v. Seaboyer*, [1991] 2 S.C.R. 577 at 647: 'It is my view that the constitutional questions must be examined in their broader political, social and historical context in order to attempt any kind of meaningful constitutional analysis.'"

In a dissenting opinion in *Miron*, *supra* note 81 at 438, Gonthier J. also acknowledges the importance of context. He states that "[t]he larger context importantly informs all stages of the analysis and ensures that it is not narrowly restricted to the 'four corners of the impugned legislation'"; Gonthier J. quotes from Wilson J. in *Turpin*, *supra* note 79 at 1332.

[87] In *Egan* v. *Canada*, [1995] 2 S.C.R. 513, 95 C.L.L.C. 210-025, [1995] W.D.F.L. 981, C.E.B. & P.G.R. 8216, 12 R.F.L. (4th) 201, 124 D.L.R. (4th) 609, 182 N.R. 161, 29 C.R.R. (2d) 79, 96 F.T.R 80 (note) [hereinafter *Egan* cited to S.C.R.], an opinion in which there are three major divisions, the interpretive mantra is repeated, with La Forest J. writing for himself and three other members of the Court, emphasizing the importance of contextual analysis. La Forest J. cites Gonthier J. and Wilson J. in *Turpin*, *supra* note 79 at 1331–32, for the proposition that "[the s. 15 analysis] must be linked to an examination of the larger context, and in particular with an understanding that the *Charter* was, in Dickson C.J.'s words, 'not enacted in a vacuum,' but must 'be placed in its proper linguistic, philosophic and historical contexts' if we are to avoid mechanical and sterile categorization." See *Egan*, *ibid.* at 532. Also in *Egan*, Sopinka J. opines, using a quote from La Forest J. in *McKinney* (see *McKinney*, *supra* note 82 at 318–19) that "[t]he courts should adopt a stance that encourages legislative advances in the protection of human rights." See *Egan*, *ibid.* at 574. As will be discussed in the text, Sopinka J. finds that discrimination based on sexual orientation in this case is a reasonable limit on equality rights, pursuant to s. 1 of the *Charter*. However, the point here is to highlight the apparent agreement among the judges as to the goal of s. 15 and the framework for interpreting it.

[88] In *Egan*, *ibid.* at 544, an extended exposition on the purpose of s. 15, written by L'Heureux-Dubé J., in dissent, characterizes s. 15 as both an individual rights guarantee that protects fundamental human dignity and a protection for vulnerable groups against systemic discrimination. She reminds the Court of its previous holdings

in *Andrews* and *Turpin* which have held that "an important, though not necessarily exclusive, purpose of s. 15 is the prevention or reduction of distinctions that may worsen the circumstances of those who have already suffered marginalization or historical disadvantage in our society." Cory and Iacobucci JJ. also highlight the s. 15 goal of protecting human dignity. Cory J. writes on behalf of himself and Iacobucci J. that "[s]ection 15(1) of the *Charter* is of fundamental importance to Canadian society. The praiseworthy object of the section is the prevention of discrimination and the promotion of a 'society in which all are secure in the knowledge that they are recognized at law as human beings equally deserving of concern, respect and consideration. It has a large remedial component': *Andrews* v. *Law Society of British Columbia*, [1989] 1 S.C.R. 143, at p. 171. It has been recognized that the purpose of s. 15(1) is 'to advance the value that all persons be subject to the equal demands and burdens of the law and not suffer any greater disability in the substance and application of the law than others.': *R.* v. *Turpin*, [1989] 1 S.C.R. 1296, at p. 1329. It is this section of the *Charter*, more than any other, which recognizes and cherishes the innate human dignity of every individual. It is this section which recognizes that no legislation should treat individuals unfairly simply on the basis of personal characteristics which bear no relationship to their merit, capacity or need." See *Egan, ibid.* at 583–84.

In *Thibaudeau* v. *Canada (M.N.R.)*, [1995] 2 S.C.R. 627 at 701, [1995] W.D.F.L. 957, [1995] 1 C.T.C. 382, 95 D.T.C. 5273, 12 R.F.L. (4th) 1, 124 D.L.R. (4th) 449, 182 N.R. 1, 29 C.R.R. (2d) 1, Cory and Iacobucci JJ. indicate that the purpose of s. 15(1) is to protect human dignity by ensuring that all individuals are recognized at law as being equally deserving of concern, respect and consideration. This leads them to the conclusion that it is the effect that an impugned distinction has upon a claimant which is the prime concern under s. 15(1).

[89] *Schachter* v. *Canada (Employment & Immigration Commission)*, [1992] 2 S.C.R. 679 at 721, 93 D.L.R. (4th) 1, 139 N.R. 1, 92 C.L.L.C. 14,036, 10 C.R.R. (2d).

[90] *Haig* v. *Canada* (1992) 9 O.R. (3d) 495 at 505, 94 D.L.R. (4th) 1, 57 O.A.C. 272, 92 C.L.L.C. 17,034, 10 C.R.R. (2d) 287.

[91] The Right Honourable Lester B. Pearson, Prime Minister of Canada, *Federalism for the Future: A Statement of Policy by the Government of Canada* (Ottawa: Government of Canada, 1968) at 4, 12, 16, 38.

[92] The Right Honourable Pierre Elliott Trudeau, Prime Minister of Canada, *The Constitution and the People of Canada: An Approach to the Objectives of Confederation, the Rights of People and the Institutions of Government* (Ottawa: Government of Canada, 1969) at 8, 10.

CHAPTER 3

The Arguments of the Opposition[*]

Introduction

What are the rationalizations offered for not giving full effect to Canada's equality commitments? This chapter is concerned with the rhetorical moves that are used to push the social and economic dimensions of inequality outside the equality rights frame. The equality rights guarantees that are intended to give effect to equality commitments are always in danger of being marginalized and diminished so that less powerful groups do not receive the full benefit of them. Because of this, it is essential to understand the rationalizations given for escaping from the equality commitments that are so important to women, and the form those rationalizations take in standard argumentation.

We draw on decisions of the courts to illustrate the rhetorical moves, noting, however, that the same arguments are made by governments outside the courts and by the media. They infect public debate.

Five *Charter* equality cases are drawn upon: *Egan* v. *Canada*,[1] a gay rights challenge to a public pension plan; *Masse* v. *Ontario (Ministry of Community and Social Services)*,[2] a challenge to cuts in social assistance programs, brought by welfare recipients; *Eldridge* v. *British Columbia*,[3] which challenges the lack of interpreter services for people who are deaf; *Symes* v. *Canada*,[4] and *Thibaudeau* v. *Canada*,[5] which are women's claims of sex discrimination in the income tax system. These cases have been chosen because they illuminate a range of problems in the way that courts have been dealing with *Charter* challenges in areas that are thought to engage social and/or economic policy considerations.[6] They also reveal what arguments government lawyers have been advancing in such cases.

The cases tell a story about how equality rights can get divorced from the social and economic dimensions of inequality and be rendered ineffectual. They also tell a story about a judiciary that is not yet reconciled to the task of responding to the equality rights claims of groups, and the discriminatory effects that certain taxation and expenditure choices may have on such groups. And some decisions reveal a judiciary that is divided, and — particularly at the level of the Supreme Court of Canada — divided along gender lines.

However, the obstacles that confronted the rights claimants in these cases are not necessarily confined to *Charter* litigation, because they are obstacles that can be traced back to the enduring influence of formal equality thinking. It follows that similar problems can be

---

[*] Gwen Brodsky is the sole author of this chapter.

anticipated in connection with efforts to enforce Canada's human rights treaty commitments, notwithstanding that the treaties speak to issues of social and economic inequality explicitly, concretely, and unambiguously.

It also bears underscoring that *Charter* equality rights law is not only a source of information about what judges think. The cases also reveal a lot about what governments consider their equality obligations to be. In particular, the cases reveal government ambivalence about having rights claims enforced against them, even though enforceability is essential to the definition of a right.

It appears that governments are especially reluctant to submit to adjudication of rights claims that are brought by women or other disadvantaged groups that raise questions about how government funds are raised and spent (or not spent) on social programs such as pensions, health care, and social assistance. Governments are not quite as reluctant to have their criminal laws subjected to review by a court, because judicial review of criminal laws and practices accords with an older recognition that in their police role governments threaten the liberty of some individuals. Governments are more or less resigned to the courts having a role as protectors of "the individual." However, when it comes to the more recently acknowledged and developed role of the state as regulator of the economy and provider of social programs, and to the insight that human rights violations have group dimensions, governments are ambivalent about giving up power to any independent oversight body. This ambivalence places Canada in a contradictory position. On the one hand, Canada wants to, and does, hold itself out as a world leader in its commitments to equality and social justice, pointing to the *Charter* and human rights statutes as evidence of those commitments. On the other hand, governments want to be free to abandon and minimize their commitments at will, as though they were merely policy objectives, and not real rights.

The goal of achieving equality for women cannot be served by interpretive approaches that either place issues of economic inequality outside the purview of equality rights or that allow governments to deny responsibility for legislated social and economic inequality.

Overview of the Cases

Egan v. Canada

The appellants Egan and Nesbit, two gay men who had lived together since 1948, challenged the spousal allowance provisions of the *Old Age Security Act*. When Mr. Egan became 65 years old in 1968, he began to receive old age security and guaranteed annual income supplements under the *Old Age Security Act*. On reaching age 60, Mr. Nesbit applied for spousal allowance under s. 19(1) of the *Act*, which is available to spouses between the ages of 60 to 65 whose combined income falls below a fixed level.

Mr. Nesbit's application was rejected on the basis that his relationship with Mr. Egan did not fall within the definition of "spouse" in the *Act*, which includes a person of the opposite sex who is living with the pensioner, if the two persons have publicly represented themselves as husband and wife. Messrs. Nesbit and Egan brought an action in the Federal Court seeking a declaration that the definition should be extended to include "partners in same-sex relationships otherwise akin to a conjugal relationship." The Trial Division dismissed the action. The Federal Court of Appeal upheld the judgment. In the Supreme Court of Canada a majority of five judges held that the *Act* was discriminatory. However, Sopinka J. held that the equality rights violation was justified pursuant to s. 1 of the *Charter*. The four remaining judges held that the *Act* was not discriminatory, and in the alternative that s. 1 of the *Charter* provided a justification.

Masse v. Ontario (Ministry of Community and Social Services)

In the *Masse* case, multiple plaintiffs joined together to challenge the welfare cuts of Ontario's Harris government. Their claim was that the cuts were discriminatory in that they imposed a disproportionate responsibility for fiscal austerity measures on welfare recipients, contrary to s. 15 of the *Charter*, and that the cuts pushed welfare recipients below an irreducible minimum standard without fundamental justice, contrary to s. 7 of the *Charter*. The applicants filed extensive evidence attesting to the fact that the government had targeted welfare recipients for prejudicial treatment, and that reduced rates were creating extreme hardship including hunger and loss of shelter. A Court of three judges, Corbett, O'Driscoll, and O'Brien JJ., dismissed the claim.[7]

Eldridge v. British Columbia

In *Eldridge (B.C.C.A.)*,[8] the appellants, Robin Eldridge and Linda and John Warren, challenged the *Medical and Health Care Services Act* and the *Hospital Insurance Act* because of a failure to provide medical interpreting services for the deaf as a benefit, effectively denying to the deaf medical services that are available to the hearing.

A medical interpreting service was previously provided to deaf people in the Lower Mainland of British Columbia by an organization known as the Western Institute for the Deaf and Hard of Hearing. The Institute had stopped the service because it no longer had sufficient monies to pay for it.

Robin Eldridge and the Warrens brought suit in the British Columbia Supreme Court against the provincial government. They sought relief under s. 15 of the *Charter*, which guarantees equal benefit of the law without discrimination based on disability.[9] The British Columbia Supreme Court dismissed the application. The British Columbia Court of Appeal also rejected the claim. Hollinrake and Cumming JJ.A. found that there was no discrimination. Lambert J.A. found that there was discrimination but that it was justified under s. 1 of the *Charter*.

Thibaudeau v. Canada

Suzanne Thibaudeau challenged s. 56(1)(b) of the *Income Tax Act (ITA)* pursuant to which she was required to pay income tax on child support received from her ex-husband. Section 56(1)(b) of the *ITA* required a separated or divorced parent to include in income any amounts received as child support, while s. 60(b) allowed the non-custodial parent who has paid child support to deduct those payments from his income. For Ms. Thibaudeau the inclusion of the children's support payments in her taxable income increased her tax burden by $3,705 in 1989, whereas the divorce decree provided only $1,200 for this additional burden. The Federal Court of Appeal in a 2 to 1 decision held that the deduction/inclusion scheme penalizes the custodial parent by imposing a proportionately higher tax burden on her than on the non-custodial parent who benefits from a 100 percent deduction for the amounts he pays towards the support of his children. On appeal to the Supreme Court of Canada, a majority found that there was no discrimination.

Symes v. *Canada*

Beth Symes, a self-employed lawyer, sought the right to deduct child care expenses from her income pursuant to the principle that expenses related to the cost of earning business income are deductible expenses. She argued that child care is vital to women's ability to earn an income, and that to exclude child care expenses from the concept of "business expense" is contrary to the basic principles of s. 15 of the *Charter*. Revenue Canada initially allowed the deductions claimed by Ms. Symes, but subsequently disallowed them on the basis that child care expenses were not incurred for the purpose of producing income, but rather were personal or living expenses. Ms. Symes appealed.

The Federal Court Trial Division agreed with Ms. Symes; however, the Federal Court of Appeal affirmed Revenue Canada's refusal to recognize the claimed expenses. In the Supreme Court of Canada, a majority of the Court ruled against Ms. Symes. McLachlin and L'Heureux-Dubé JJ. dissented.

Pushing the Social and Economic Dimensions of Inequality Outside the Equality Frame

The standard oppositional moves that are made to counter claims of discrimination in government economic policy involve pushing the subject matter of the claim outside the boundary of law and into the realm of the social and economic, and conducting the discrimination analysis in such a way as to break the cause and effect linkage between the inequality complained of and the *Charter*'s equality guarantees.

The first move and the second move are closely related. In some decisions, such as *Masse*, several things happen at once: a judge says both that the case is about social and economic policy that the court should not interfere with, and that there is no discrimination. The moves are unified by underlying premises. One underlying premise is that social and economic inequality are within the control of the affected individual. A related premise is that because individuals can achieve equality as a matter of personal choice and merit, there is no obligation on government to reduce *de facto* disparities between groups and provide a social safety net. Governments may choose to do these things, but the choice and the criteria for establishing program parameters and entitlements are within the sole discretion of the government. However, for the sake of analytical clarity, we focus separately, first, on the characterization of socio-economic policy as a special species of legislation, and second, on the question of how discrimination analysis is conducted.

The Separation of Equality Rights from Social and Economic Policy

There is a line of government and judicial commentary contending that legislation concerning social or economic policy questions should either be immune from judicial review, or subject to a lower standard of scrutiny. The usual candidates for the socio-economic legislation category are income tax legislation and social program legislation providing such benefits as health care, pensions, and social assistance.

It would appear that this line of commentary finds its roots in two ideas. One idea is that economic legislation is value neutral. The other idea is that it is not institutionally legitimate for courts to intrude on government decision making that involves the allocation of resources between groups. Judges can and should do law. Law is concerned with a contest between the individual and the state, and not with group interests, which are really policy issues. Policy issues should be left to legislatures.

Economics as Value Neutral

Governments have argued that some legislation is only based on economic realities and not on political choices about how resources are to be distributed among groups. The idea is to elevate economic considerations to a plane that transcends both law and politics, and excludes discriminatory motives. In *Thibaudeau (F.C.A.)* such a characterization of the *ITA* found a supporter in Létourneau J.A. He said: "The *Income Tax Act* is essentially economic legislation, which may even be described as amoral ... its purpose being to trace income and tax it on the basis of the social and economic needs of the community, taking into account the reality of the taxpayer's situation ... numerous provisions of the *Act* ... impose different burdens based on different economic realities."[10]

Létourneau J.A.'s portrayal of the *ITA* as "essentially economic legislation, which may even be described as amoral" serves, though perhaps unconsciously, to establish authority for the *ITA* that places it outside the norm of equality, and in turn to shelter the judge's decision from scrutiny. The inference to be drawn is that ordinary people are in no position to judge the *ITA* because it is driven by unchallengeable, unknowable, value free, economic factors that should not be second guessed.

The income tax system is commonly portrayed by lawyers, economists, and others as amoral, that is, neutral or value free. Lisa Philipps and Margot Young describe the problem this way:

> There has been tremendous resistance to seeing the *Income Tax Act* for what it is: a social policy document, influenced by notions of just distribution and ideologically-specific understandings of ideal forms of social ordering. Instead, the

ITA is often viewed as a politically and morally neutral document, structured by the dictates of financial accounting, economic theory and tax principles that permit no political shades or shaping.[11]

An additional problem with an approach to equality rights that concedes that certain legislation has neutral goals is that it draws attention away from the more important question, which is the effects of the legislation. Even if income tax legislation were value neutral in its goals or intentions, which it is not, equality rights analysis should be concerned with disparate effects.

The decision of the Federal Court of Appeal in *Thibaudeau (F.C.A.)* was appealed to the Supreme Court of Canada.[12] A majority of the Court rejected the view that the socio-economic label can operate so as to completely immunize a certain category of legislation from review. On behalf of the majority, Iacobucci J. said: "As must any other legislation, the *Income Tax Act* is subject to *Charter* scrutiny. The *scope* of the s. 15 right is not dependent upon the legislation which is being challenged."[13]

However, Gonthier J. contended in *Thibaudeau* that the "special nature" of the *ITA* is "a significant factor that must be taken into account" in defining the scope of the right to equal benefit of the law. Gonthier J. said:

> It is the very essence of the ITA to make distinctions, so as to generate revenue for government while equitably reconciling a range of divergent interests. In view of this, the right to equal benefit of the law cannot mean that each taxpayer has an equal right to receive the same amounts, deductions or benefits, but merely the right to be *equally governed* by the law.[14]

The decisions in *Thibaudeau* indicate a continuing reluctance on the part of some members of the judiciary to subject tax law to the same equality standards as other legislation.[15]

Discrimination and the Democratic Legitimacy of the Courts

The first s. 15 case in which the issue of institutional legitimacy arises is *Andrews*, wherein La Forest J. of the Supreme Court of Canada said: "Much economic and social policy-making is simply beyond the institutional competence of courts: their role is to protect against incursions on fundamental values, not to second guess policy decisions."[16] He also cautioned against judicial intervention in areas "beyond the traditionally established and analogous policies against discrimination."[17] Initially, in *Andrews*, these statements were made in *obiter*, as cautionary notes.

However, the argument about institutional legitimacy has been repeatedly articulated by La Forest J. Recently, in *RJR MacDonald Inc.* v. *Canada (A.G.)* he stated:

> In drawing a distinction between legislation aimed at "mediating between groups"

where a higher standard of s. 1 justification may be appropriate, and legislation where the state acts as the "singular antagonist of the individual", where a higher standard of justification is necessary, the Court in *Irwin Toy* was drawing upon the more fundamental institutional distinction between the legislative and judicial functions that lies at the very heart of our political and constitutional system. Courts are specialists in the protection of liberty and the interpretation of legislation and are, accordingly, well-placed to subject criminal legislation to careful scrutiny. However, courts are not specialists in the realm of policy-making, nor should they be. This is a role properly assigned to the elected representatives of the people, who have at their disposal the necessary institutional resources to enable them to compile and assess social science evidence, to mediate between competing social interests and reach out and protect vulnerable groups. In according a greater degree of deference to social legislation than to legislation in the criminal justice context, this Court has recognized these important institutional differences between legislatures and the judiciary.[18]

A similar point was made by Décary J.A. in *Symes (F.C.A.)*, although somewhat more succinctly and less elegantly. Regarding Beth Symes's s. 15 challenge to the *ITA*, he expressed the view that courts ought not to "fish" in "troubled economic waters" but rather defer to Parliament in the social and economic domain.[19]

The idea that courts should defer to governments because of the superior capacity of governments to deal with complex problems and protect vulnerable groups might be appealing but for the fact that in numerous s. 15 cases, the language of judicial deference has been used not to uphold legislation that protects vulnerable groups, but rather to justify discrimination against them. In other words, judges' anxieties about second guessing policy decisions translate into defeat for equality rights claimants.

The opinion of Lambert J.A. in *Eldridge (B.C.C.A.)* is illustrative. Lambert J.A. found that refusing to provide interpreter services for people who are deaf is discriminatory. But then he observed that there are competing demands on medical services and concluded that the discrimination should be rectified, "if at all" by legislative or administrative action, but not by judicial action. He ruled that discrimination against deaf people in the allocation of medical services is justified pursuant to s. 1 of the *Charter*.[20]

Lambert J.A.'s deferential approach in *Eldridge (B.C.C.A.)* is particularly disturbing, given that he clearly understood and agreed that the denial complained of was discriminatory, that the harm to the disadvantaged group was great, and that the cost to government of rectifying the problem was small. Lambert J.A. completely abandoned established frameworks for s. 1 analysis, including the requirement that the respondent bear the burden of proving that the rights violation is justified in a free and democratic society, substituting a policy of judicial non-responsibility. In essence, Lambert J.A.'s hands-off approach to s. 1 is just a variation on the idea that there are certain kinds of legislation to which s. 15 simply does not apply, a proposition that the Supreme Court of Canada has rejected.

The British Columbia Court of Appeal decision in *Eldridge (B.C.C.A.)* was overturned by the Supreme Court of Canada on 9 October 1997.[21] In a unanimous decision the Supreme Court of Canada held that where sign language interpreters are necessary for effective communication in the delivery of medical services, the failure to provide them constitutes a violation of s. 15 of the *Charter*, and is not a reasonable limit on equality under s. 1. This outcome is a clear reversal of the Court of Appeal's holding. However, it would be premature to say that the issue of judicial deference in relation to social benefit schemes has gone away. In *Eldridge* the Supreme Court of Canada was at pains to acknowledge that there is a lack of consensus in the Court about whether or not a deferential approach should be adopted in such cases. The Court found its way around the issue by holding that the challenged lack of interpreter services could not be upheld under s. 1, *even on a deferential approach*.[22]

The dissenting opinion of Sopinka J. in *Egan*[23] is also illustrative of the correlation between expressed concern about the role of the courts and defeat for disadvantaged groups. Sopinka J. formed part of the majority that held that the *Old Age Security Act* discriminates against gays, contrary to s. 15 of the *Charter*. However, relying on the notion that government should not second guess Parliament on social policy questions involving competing interests between groups, he finds the discrimination to be justified under s. 1 of the *Charter*.[24]

The following passage from the opinion of Sopinka J. in *Egan* confirms that the core image of rights that animates his approach is that of the individual against the state. He states:

> [T]he legislation in question represents the kind of socio-economic question in respect of which the government is required to mediate between competing groups rather than being the protagonist [sic] of an individual. In these circumstances the Court will be more reluctant to second-guess the choice which Parliament has made.[25]

The opinion of Sopinka J. in *Egan* has been subject to much criticism[26] and was roundly rejected by four of his colleagues on the Bench.[27] It was not even entirely endorsed by any of the other judges. Nonetheless, it determined the outcome of the case. Had Sopinka J. not ruled against the plaintiffs under s. 1, they would have won their case by 5 to 4.

Similarly, in *Egan*, La Forest J. uses the language of judicial deference, not to support the equality aspirations of gays, but rather to defeat them. Unlike Sopinka J., La Forest J. does not even find it necessary to resort to s. 1. He finds that preferential treatment of heterosexual couples is simply not discriminatory. Drawing on his earlier opinion in *Andrews*, La Forest J. says:

> It would bring the legitimate work of our legislative bodies to a standstill if courts were to question every distinction that had a disadvantageous effect on an enumerated or analogous group. This would open up a s. 1 inquiry in every case involving a protected group. [I]t was never intended in enacting s. 15 that it become a tool for the whole-sale subjection to judicial scrutiny of variegated

legislative choices in no way infringing on values fundamental to a free and democratic society.[28]

The striking thing about La Forest J.'s opinion in *Egan* is that it shows very clearly that talk of judicial deference, while purportedly about refraining from making a value judgement, can actually be a cover or reinforcement for the judge's values. In *Egan*, La Forest J. does not decide to defer to Parliament based on the notions of institutional role articulated in *RJR MacDonald*.[29] He decides to defer to Parliament because he agrees with the values that are promoted by the legislation. He does not attempt to hide this. He says, with approval, "[The singling out of legally married and common law couples for benefits] is deeply rooted in our fundamental values and traditions that could not have been lost on the framers of the *Charter*."[30] He says further that "Parliament may quite properly give special support to the institution of marriage" and to common law couples.[31] Thus, at the same time as clearly supporting the substantive content of the government's policy of favouritism towards the "traditional" couple, the opinion of La Forest J. derives support from the language of judicial restraint.

The approach of La Forest J. in *Egan*, although supported by three other judges on the Supreme Court, is not the majority opinion; it is in fact a dissenting opinion. Similarly, the opinion of Sopinka J. in *Egan* regarding the interpretation and application of s. 1 of the *Charter* is not the opinion of the majority.[32] However, in thinking about what is going wrong in the equality jurisprudence, these opinions cannot be entirely discounted because the themes are repeated in lower court decisions such as *Masse*.[33]

What is most striking about the *Masse* decision is how closely connected the legal category of socio-economic policy is to the exclusion of poor people from rights. Poor people's issues, by definition, are seen as issues for socio-economic policy and not as rights issues. Indeed, rights for people living in poverty are seen as an oxymoron. The lawyers representing the Government of Ontario in *Masse* argued that "while poverty is a deeply troubling *social* problem it is not unconstitutional,"[34] and predictably, that the challenge to deep cuts in the welfare system "involves matters of *economic and social policy* beyond the competence and jurisdiction of the courts."[35] [Emphasis added.] Clearly, this theme had resonance for at least two members of the Ontario Divisional Court. O'Brien J., who dismissed the claim in its entirety, begins his opinion by saying:

> I approach the arguments on these issues bearing in mind the statements made by Sopinka J. in *Egan*: "It is not realistic for the Court to assume that there are unlimited funds to address the needs of all. A judicial approach on this basis would tend to make a government reluctant to create any new social benefit scheme because their limits would depend on an accurate prediction of the outcome of court proceedings under 15(1) of the *Charter*."[36]

O'Brien J.'s approach, he indicates, is also informed by the following statement made by La Forest J. in *McKinney* and approved by Sopinka J. in *Egan*:

But generally, courts should not lightly second-guess legislative judgment as to just how quickly it should proceed in moving forward towards the ideal of equality.[37]

And he closes his opinion by saying, "I believe that the comments of La Forest J. in *Andrews* are particularly appropriate to the applicants argument on the s. 15 issue."[38] He quotes La Forest J. stating:

> [I]t was never intended in enacting s. 15 that it become a tool for the wholesale subjection to judicial scrutiny of variegated legislative choices in no way infringing values fundamental to a free and democratic society. Like my colleague, I am not prepared to accept that *all* [emphasis in the original] legislative classifications must be rationally supportable before the courts. Much economic and social policy-making is simply beyond the institutional competence of the courts. Their role is to protect against incursions on fundamental values, not to second-guess policy decisions.[39]

In a separate opinion, O'Driscoll J., like O'Brien J., also dismisses all aspects of the *Masse* claim. O'Driscoll J. also quotes extensively from the opinions of both Sopinka and La Forest JJ. in *Egan*, calling for judicial deference. He invokes the same passages as O'Brien J., and adds the following statement of Sopinka J. made in *Egan*:

> This Court has recognized that it is legitimate for the government to make choices between disadvantaged groups and that it must be provided with some leeway to do so.[40]

However, at the conclusion of his opinion, O'Driscoll J. says:

> The applicants will appreciate that the court has no jurisdiction or desire to second-guess policy/political decisions. ... The matter cannot be summed up any better than was done by the United States Supreme Court in *Dandridge* v. *Williams* at p. 1162-1163: "The intractable economic, social and even philosophical problems presented by welfare assistance programs are not the business of this Court."[41]

This statement indicates that O'Driscoll J.'s position goes far beyond the proposition that governments should have some leeway to make choices between disadvantaged groups. His comments strongly suggest that O'Driscoll J. wholeheartedly supports the government's argument that given the socio-economic character of poverty, the courts simply have no responsibility to hear the equality rights claims of people on income assistance.

As the cases show, the explicit separation of law from social and economic policy operates as a kind of trump. It makes individual freedom from government interference the dominant constitutional right, and it blocks equality analysis. The socio-economic policy trump may shape the court's entire approach to the claim, to legitimate a refusal to make a finding of discrimination, as in *Masse*. Or, as in *Eldridge (B.C.C.A.)*, it may in itself relieve the respondent of the burden of making out a s. 1 defence.

Breaking the Linkage between Inequality and Equality Rights

To fully understand the mechanics of how equality rights can be drained of their capacity to address real equality problems, consideration must also be given to some of the ways in which the linkage between *de facto* inequality and a legal finding of discrimination gets broken.

The Supreme Court of Canada has held that the analysis under s. 15 involves two steps. First, the claimant must show that there has been a denial of equal protection or benefit of the law. Second, the claimant must show that the denial constitutes discrimination. In order for discrimination to be made out, the claimant must show that the denial rests on one of the grounds enumerated in s. 15, such as race or sex, or on analogous grounds such as marital status or sexual orientation, and that the unequal treatment is based on the stereotypical application of presumed group or personal characteristics.[42] In short, discrimination is understood to be detrimental treatment based on personal characteristics.

Courts have also recognized repeatedly that discrimination is primarily a question of adverse effects, rather than treatment or intention. However, the usefulness of this theoretical development will be uncertain if judges are too easily swayed by defences calculated to attribute the causes of discrimination to factors other than a challenged law, and to discount adverse effects.

Shifting Blame

When courts do not want to hold governments responsible for addressing certain forms of inequality, the tendency is to revert to a blame and punishment model of responsibility, ignoring that the key goal of human rights protections is not to find fault, but rather to remedy discriminatory effects. Among the eligible targets for blame are nature, the equality rights claimant, or some other legislation. Blaming nature is a very familiar defensive move. This is what the Supreme Court of Canada did in *Bliss* v. *Canada (A.G.)*[43] when it attributed the harm of pregnancy discrimination to nature, and not to the legislation.

The pattern of blaming nature is repeated in the decision of the majority of the British Columbia Court of Appeal in *Eldridge*.[44] Hollinrake and Cumming JJ.A. reasoned that the lack of access to medical services complained of by the plaintiffs was not caused by the *Medical Services Act* — which treats everyone the same, without regard to deafness — but rather by the fact of deafness itself. They said: "This inequality exists independently of the legislation and cannot be said to be in any way an effect of the legislation."[45]

The theme of attributing the cause of the alleged discrimination to nature is also repeated in La Forest J.'s opinion in *Egan,* when he finds that marriage is by nature heterosexual.

The *Thibaudeau* decision provides an illustration of responsibility being shifted away from a challenged legislative scheme and on to another scheme or to an extraneous social cause. In *Thibaudeau*, the evidence was clear that the deduction/inclusion system under the *ITA* had adverse effects on Suzanne Thibaudeau as well as many other women because women are the vast majority of separated custodial parents. However, the majority was prepared to dismiss those effects as the fault of another system of legislation, the family law system. In a concurring opinion, Gonthier J. adds that the inequality in the income tax system complained of by Ms. Thibaudeau is not caused by the *ITA* but rather is attributable to social causes such as the failure of non-custodial parents to fulfil their obligations to their children adequately. Along with his male colleagues, he also finds that the real cause of the problems complained of by Ms. Thibaudeau is the provincial family law system.

Alternatively, the rights claimant can be blamed for having been complicit in a "family decision." This occurred in the case of *Symes*, at the level of the Supreme Court of Canada.[46] A majority of the Court rejected Beth Symes's claim, because she was seen to have chosen to assume child care expenses that her husband could have assumed or shared. Her choice was seen as atypical, and therefore her own fault. On behalf of the majority, Iacobucci J. said:

> [T]he appellant and her husband made a "family decision" to the effect that the appellant alone was to bear the financial burden of having children. ... [T]he "family decision" is not mandated by law and public policy.[47]

Iacobucci J. points out that at law, parents are viewed as having "joint" legal responsibilities. He concludes with a warning that adverse effects analysis requires that the effects complained of be caused by the impugned legislation, not by independent factors. He writes:

> If the adverse effects analysis is to be coherent, it must not assume that a statutory provision has an effect which is not proved. We must take care to distinguish between effects which are wholly caused, or are contributed to, by an impugned provision, and those social circumstances which exist independently of such a provision.[48]

In *Symes*, as in *Thibaudeau*, L'Heureux-Dubé and McLachlin JJ. dissented and would have ruled in favour of the rights claimant.

The *Thibaudeau* and *Symes* decisions illustrate a point that goes to the heart of the discussion about how courts are thinking about what discrimination is, and what the responsibility of governments is for dealing with it. An implication of these decisions seems to be that there is no discrimination unless the harm complained of can be shown to be caused exclusively by the challenged law, as evidenced by a comparison that is conducted within the four corners of the legislation. This interpretation is disturbing because the character of discrimination often precludes rights claimants from being able to prove that a given law is the sole cause of the inequality complained of.[49] It will almost always be possible to point to the claimant's group membership as a factor in a claim of discrimination. Discrimination is often a matter of a dynamic between a given practice and a wider context of inequality experienced by the group. The more disadvantaged the group, the easier it becomes to attribute a given instance of discrimination to pre-existing disadvantage.

A different example may help to clarify the point. If one thinks about cuts in funding for rape crisis centres, a crucial factor that makes such cuts an issue of sex discrimination is that overwhelmingly women are the victims of sexual violence and the users of rape crisis centre services. But to see this, it is necessary to take the situation of the group into account. A logical though ludicrous implication of a mono-causal approach to discrimination is that governments could be absolved of responsibility for the consequences of women's decreased access to rape crisis centres, on the basis that the harm does not flow only from the government cuts but also from the fact that women are raped. The conclusion to be drawn from some of the cases is that judges are asking the wrong question.

In keeping with the remedial goal of human rights protections, the question that should be asked is not, "Is there someone or something else that could be blamed?" but rather, "Who has the capacity to make a difference to the conditions of inequality experienced by this group?" If a government policy contributes to or worsens women's disadvantaged position, this should be sufficient to establish a causal connection between the policy and the disadvantage for the purposes of equality analysis.

Discounting Adverse Effects

The principle that discrimination is a question of adverse effects is well established in case law. However, adverse effects can be discounted if the court can be persuaded to focus on legislative purpose or treatment rather than adverse effects. Also, adverse effects may be discounted if not everyone in the group is adversely affected, or if people not in the group are also having problems.

The first two moves are illustrated by the Supreme Court of Canada decision in *Thibaudeau*. The majority finds that the most important effect of the legislation is to benefit post-divorce couples. The Court focuses on the legislative goal of assisting divorced couples, and then deals with the "post-divorce family unit" as though it can be taken for granted that a tax benefit to the husband trickles down to the wife.[50] The fact that Suzanne Thibaudeau and many other women were penalized by the legislation, while their husbands benefited, is ignored.

On this point, Madam Justice McLachlin and Madam Justice L'Heureux-Dubé explicitly dissent from their male colleagues. McLachlin J. recognizes that the legislation had the "laudable aim of ameliorating the position of all members of the broken family,"[51] but finds that Parliament failed to consider the impact of the scheme on custodial parents, the great majority of whom are women. McLachlin J. finds that on its face, the *ITA* demonstrates adverse unequal treatment of custodial parents in that it artificially inflates the custodial parent's taxable income.[52]

Similarly, L'Heureux-Dubé J. concedes that the purpose of the impugned distinction may be to confer tax savings upon "couples," but she finds that it does not follow that its effect is experienced equally by both members of the couple. L'Heureux Dubé J. finds also that the fact that some isolated individuals within the group may not be adversely affected does not alter the general validity of this conclusion.

The British Columbia Court of Appeal decision in *Eldridge* is another example of purpose or treatment being permitted to eclipse discriminatory effects. A majority of the Court found that there is no discrimination because the *Medical Services Act* treats deaf and non-hearing people alike. There is coverage for everyone for medical services. The Court makes this finding notwithstanding that the effect of the no-interpreter policy is to deny to deaf people the equal benefit of paid medical services. As previously mentioned, the Court attributes the fact that deaf people are required to pay for translators in order to receive medical services, to nature rather than to the legislation. As for the legislation, the Court says: "Both purposively and effectively the legislation provides its benefit of making payment for medical services equally to the hearing and the deaf."[53]

As previously mentioned, the decision of the British Columbia Court of Appeal in *Eldridge* was overturned by the Supreme Court of Canada.[54] The Supreme Court of Canada rejected argument to the effect that s. 15 requires only that people be treated the same and does not oblige the state to ensure that disadvantaged members of the society can take advantage of public benefit programs. The Court affirmed its commitment to the idea that discrimination can arise from the adverse effects of facially neutral rules, and held that the failure to provide sign language interpreters necessary for effective communication in the delivery of medical services is a violation of the *Charter*. Although the Supreme Court of Canada decision in *Eldridge* is an advance over the impoverished analysis of the Court of Appeal, it does not disprove the thesis that judges are vulnerable to arguments designed to shut down adverse effects analysis.

The s. 15 dissent in *Egan*[55] provides a further illustration of the problem. In the decision of La Forest J. in *Egan*, the effects complained of by the two gay men are ignored. It is recognized that the *ITA* favours heterosexual couples, a goal which La Forest J. regards as constitutionally permissible. However, the *ITA* is understood to treat homosexual couples the same as other non-spousal "couples."[56]

A variation on the theme of discounting adverse effects involves diffusing the effects so either the effects or the group are forced outside the bounds of a protected ground. The jurisprudence requires s. 15 rights claimants to show that the alleged discrimination is *based on* personal characteristics. The decision of Hugessen J. in *Thibaudeau (F.C.A.)* illustrates the judicial view that harmful effects are not based on personal characteristics, unless those harmful effects are proven to be confined to one, and only one, group.[57]

Hugessen J. recognized that within the group negatively affected by the challenged provision of the *ITA*, women were overwhelmingly represented. However, because 2 percent of the negatively affected group were custodial fathers, the claim of sex discrimination was not borne out, he found. In particular, the distinction could not be said to be based on the shared characteristic of femaleness, held Hugessen J. It is clear that Hugessen J.'s conception of what constitutes femaleness excludes a range of social, legal, and economic factors that define women as an unequal group in the society. He also overlooks the fact that, in a social context of inequality and stigmatization in which single mothers raise their children, the imposition of an income tax penalty on custodial parents does have a qualitatively disproportionate impact on women, as well as a numerically disproportionate one.

Hugessen J.'s approach to the ground of sex discrimination is a narrow, socially decontextualized, biological, and defeating one. Philipps and Young have described the problem this way:

> Hugessen J.A.'s notion of sex difference works ... for ... only a few characteristics we associate with sex. Pregnancy is the most obvious and — apart from other aspects of women's reproductive physiology, perhaps breast feeding — may be the only gender dimension along which discrimination occurs that fits with Hugessen J.A.'s analysis. ... All other characteristics that one associates with one sex or the other point, potentially, to at least some members of the "opposite" sex. What Hugessen J.A. fails to realize ... is that categorization (how we demarcate the female and the male) is only a theoretical device; its relationship with the real world is necessarily a complicated one.[58]

Significant consolation can be taken from the fact that on appeal, the Supreme Court of Canada did not fasten on the Hugessen J. approach. Nonetheless, Hugessen J.'s opinion stands as a demonstration of an archetypal problem that confronts women when equality is constructed as a question of sameness and difference. Women are required to show that they are the same as men for the purpose of establishing the entitlement to equality, and simultaneously that they are different from men for the purpose of establishing the rights violation. This is the impossibility of the sameness-difference model of sex equality.

Resisting the Disconnection of Equality Rights from *De Facto* Social and Economic Inequality

The cases referred to here show that there are many ways to couch a refusal to deal with adverse effects. Whereas the invocation of the socio-economic policy category functions to divorce social conditions of inequality from the ambit of equality rights, breaking the linkage between *de facto* inequality and a legal finding of discrimination depends on conducting the discrimination analysis in such a way as to either shift responsibility away from the government or to discount the harm complained of by the rights claimant.

To review, these are the basic moves:

- create a special hands-off category for socio-economic issues;

- shift responsibility away from the government by blaming nature or the claimant herself or some other legislative system;

- discount adverse effects by focusing instead on legislative appearances or intentions;

- discount adverse effects by redrawing the boundaries of the group and observing that not everyone in the group is adversely affected, thus diluting the adverse effects;

- discount adverse effects by observing that people outside the group are also negatively affected, thereby diffusing the adverse effects.

Categorizing an equality rights claim as a question of social or economic policy is a means of invalidating the claim. Although the idea of allowing governments sufficient room to implement equality-promoting measures is appealing, the reality is that in the s. 15 cases where judges have decided to "defer" to governments to give them "room to manoeuvre" in the "socio-economic sphere," that room has functioned to allow discriminatory legislation to stand.

The purported distinction between social and economic policy on the one hand, and real law, on the other, is not sustainable. At the heart of this categorical distinction is a problematic view of what rights are supposed to do and not supposed to do. The view is that rights are supposed to protect the individual's liberty from incursions by the state. Rights are not supposed to address disparities between groups. Rights are supposed to be individualistic and negative. They are not supposed to be group-based and positive.

However, founding equality rights interpretation on a core idea of rights as individualistic and negative cannot serve women's interests. Although the inequality problems of women are experienced by individual women and in this sense are individual, they also have a larger context of social, economic, political, and legal inequality. Deprived of their group context, women's equality problems can be rendered invisible, but not eliminated.

The assumption that rights are injunctions *not* to do something rather than to do something is detrimental to women because women need governments to act positively, to provide benefit schemes, to provide protection from domestic violence, and to reverse historical patterns of discrimination.

For women, a division between rights to economic security and rights to personal liberty is purely artificial. In the circumstances of women who have violent or psychologically abusive male partners, for example, the indivisibility of economic issues from violence issues is clear. As a result of the Conservative government's cuts to social assistance and social programs, the Ontario Association of Interval and Transition Houses reports that "a significant number of women in Ontario are now making decisions to remain in or return to abusive situations."[59] A woman who has inadequate economic supports is more vulnerable to threats to her physical security and less able to escape. Thus, a woman's right to physical security is intimately linked to her economic conditions.

For women, even the assumption that liberty is a negative right that can be adequately respected by restraining government action is fictitious. Liberty from domestic violence, for example, is contingent on the willingness of governments to actively fulfil their policing responsibilities.

Economic inequality also has profound effects on women's enjoyment of all other rights. It not only increases women's vulnerability to violence, sexual exploitation, coercion, and imprisonment, it also deprives women of equal status and decision-making authority in their domestic relationships with men, and it affects their ability to care for their children. It limits women's access to justice, to expression of their ideas, and to participation in political life. It affects not only women's individual opportunities, but also the ability of women as a group to improve their status and conditions.

It is simply not the case, then, that liberty rights can be understood as separate from other rights when women are concerned. Women's inequality manifests itself in multiple ways — spanning the range of civil and political, economic, social, and cultural rights.

The situation of meritorious equality claims being rejected based on their perceived socio-economic character is all the more troubling in light of the unevenness with which the concept is applied. Some cases trigger judges' concerns about overstepping the judicial role. Others do not. It is notable that challenges by doctors[60] and lawyers to government regulatory schemes are not met with anything like the kind of resistance engendered by welfare rights challenges.

Andrews, the first equality rights case to be decided by the Supreme Court of Canada, stands in stark contrast to cases in which courts have adopted a policy of deference towards government policies affecting disadvantaged groups. Mark Andrews, a white, male lawyer was allowed to succeed in his challenge to legislation designed to regulate the legal profession. And, as previously mentioned, although La Forest J. warned of the dangers of questioning legislative decisions in areas that go beyond traditional human rights coverage, he did not argue that government should be given room to mediate between different groups of lawyers. Rather, La Forest J.'s opinion reveals his sympathy towards Mr. Andrews's goal of pursuing his economic goals. He says:

> By and large, the use in legislation of citizenship as a basis for distinguishing between persons, here for the purpose of conditioning access to the practice of a profession, harbours the potential for undermining the essential or underlying values of a free and democratic society that are embodied in s. 15.[61]

Even from a very narrow legal perspective, according a higher level of constitutional protection to traditional criminal law liberty rights is problematic because it rests on an inadequate conception of what criminal law is. McLachlin J. put it this way:

> [It] has been suggested that greater deference to Parliament or the Legislature may be appropriate if the law is concerned with competing rights between different sectors of society than if it is a contest between the individual and the state. ... However, such distinctions may not always be easy to apply. For example, criminal law is seen as involving a contest between the state and the accused, but it also involves an allocation of priorities between the accused and the victim, actual or potential.[62]

The superficial attractiveness of the idea that courts should allow governments to make legislation that addresses social problems does not dictate that equality rights should have nothing to say about the relationship between the effects of given legislative action or inaction, and social and economic inequality. Nor does the fact that the solutions to some equality problems are difficult mean that they are not real equality rights problems.

The notion that judicial activism threatens democracy rests on a conception of democracy that is too thin and too process oriented. The ideal of democracy must be understood to be big enough to include the goal of equality. There is judicial support for this perspective. In *R.* v. *Oakes*, Dickson C.J. of the Supreme Court of Canada said:

> [C]ourt[s] must be guided by the values and principles essential to a free and democratic society which I believe embody, to name but a few, respect for the inherent dignity of the human person, commitment to social justice and equality, accommodation of a wide variety of beliefs, respect for cultural and group identity, and faith in social and political institutions which enhance the participation of individuals and groups in society.[63]

The legitimacy of judicial intervention to uphold *Charter* rights does not reside in the kind of line drawing that seeks to differentiate this kind of legislation from that, or to separate legal issues from socio-economic issues, but rather in the values that the *Charter* embodies. When democracy and equality are understood to be consistent rather than oppositional concepts, it may be recognized that judicial interventions to promote the social and economic equality of women are not a threat to democracy, but rather a potential enhancement of it.

The notion that courts lack the democratic legitimacy to address certain issues rings hollow for groups that are not adequately represented within legislatures.[64] Women are not equally represented in either the legislatures or the judiciary. However, courts sometimes provide an alternative venue when elected officials are not listening.[65]

It is all very well to have debates about whether courts should leave some tasks to governments. However, establishing categories that sort cases according to the type of legislation or type of issue will never lead to satisfactory results. As particular cases come along, judges will continually be forced to redefine the categories so that an appearance of consistency is maintained. Yesterday's legal issue will be tomorrow's social policy issue because a judge either feels moved by the facts of a particular case or does not feel so moved.

Great care must be taken to ensure that judges do not recoil from issues simply on the basis that they are the issues of disadvantaged groups in the society. Social and economic equality are, by definition, the issues of disadvantaged groups. There cannot be one standard of rights protection for dominant groups in the society, with a lower standard of protection being accorded to the rights of disadvantaged groups. To have a legal right to equality means that there is an institution of enforcement whose job it is to judge laws, policies, and practices for their conformity with the protected value. It is not legitimate for judges to abdicate this responsibility, especially for groups that are not adequately represented within government.

When judges say that courts should not "second guess" governments in the realm of social and economic policy making, the damaging public message is that there is no obligation on anyone to take positive steps to address inequality of conditions, and governments can make laws that perpetuate inequality, with impunity. The message might come across differently if there were some other institution, apart from the courts, that was charged with the responsibility for enforcing equality rights, but there is no other such institution. In this circumstance, judicial deference translates into permission for government complacency about the persistent social and economic inequality of women and other disadvantaged groups.

Just as it is unacceptable for judges to decide that they do not deal with cases involving challenges to structures that create social and economic inequality, so, too, it is highly problematic for discrimination analysis to revert to a blame and punishment model of liability. The point of discrimination analysis should not be to look for ways of allowing government to minimize its responsibility to promote the equality of disadvantaged groups, but rather to ensure that the *Charter* goal of assisting disadvantaged groups to overcome their inequality is advanced.

Associated with the various linkage-breaking moves identified in this chapter is an unhelpful framework for s. 15 analysis which has been developed by the Supreme Court of Canada. Although it is not impossible to use the "different treatment based on personal characteristics" framework to illuminate the adverse effects that government decisions have on women, the framework is not particularly helpful because it has a tilt in favour of equality as same treatment of individuals. Its starting place for understanding whether discrimination has occurred is treatment rather than effects. The capacity of the decision maker to perceive adverse effects on the group is undermined when the starting place for the analysis is the treatment of the individual claimant.

The prioritization of treatment over effects must be rejected. Quite simply, the goal of achieving equality for disadvantaged groups cannot be served by understandings of inequality that are indifferent to the effects of government choices on disadvantaged groups.

Fundamentally, the different treatment/same treatment formulation version of equality is concerned with abstract difference rather than with subordination. Its normative goal is neutral treatment. It does not comprehend that a seemingly neutral rule may not be neutral for women because it rests on sexist social structures. Many seemingly neutral rules retain their appearance of neutrality only as long as they are viewed in isolation from social patterns of inequality. The very idea of neutral rules should be suspect, especially given that many rules are made without the participation and influence of women.

Finally, the "different treatment based on personal characteristics" formulation is apt to reinforce an understanding of sex as a matter of biological characteristics rather than as the socially constructed consequences of being female. Being a woman is not simply a biological fact. It is a social, economic, and legal construction. Moreover, a dominant social and economic expectation is that caretaking will be poorly paid, if at all, and performed by women who will be economically dependent on men.[66]

However, the Supreme Court's framework for s. 15 analysis is not the core problem in the jurisprudence. The core problem is resistance to the insight that discrimination is a question of adverse effects on disadvantaged groups. Equality jurisprudence has recognized that equality may sometimes require different treatment, but this insight is too superficial. It does not necessarily translate into an awareness that same treatment is a mischaracterization of the normative goal of equality. It does not represent a clear understanding that inequality is not a question of different treatment but rather of subordination, marginalization, exclusion, and group disadvantage. As long as equality rights law continues to revolve around a conception of equality as sameness and difference, more problems can be anticipated.

Conclusion

This chapter has examined techniques of legal argument that have been used to push the social and economic dimensions of group-based inequality outside the equality framework: creating a hands-off category for socio-economic issues; shifting responsibility away from government by blaming nature, the rights claimant, or another legislative scheme; discounting adverse effects by focusing on legislative appearances or intentions; and diluting or dispersing adverse effects.

It is readily apparent that our claim that the *BIA* violates women's *Charter* equality rights can be summarily dismissed if equality rights are understood to have nothing to say about economic inequality or if s. 15 analysis is reduced to a small and highly predictable repertoire of mechanical and legalistic comparisons. However, we argue these approaches to equality rights cannot be sustained.

The judicial opinions discussed — in the cases of *Egan, Masse, Eldridge (B.C.C.A.)*,[67] *Thibaudeau*, and *Symes* — fall back on the very kind of discredited reasoning that resulted in the defeat of Stella Bliss's claim more than a decade ago.[68] As such, they go against the main current of the major jurisprudential developments in human rights and *Charter* equality rights law of the past decade, a central feature of which is the recognition that discrimination is a question of effects on disadvantaged groups. It has been explicitly recognized that s. 15 confers more than formal equality. And regarding *Bill of Rights* decisions such as *Bliss*, the Supreme Court of Canada acknowledged in *Andrews* that "[i]t is readily apparent that the language of s. 15 was deliberately chosen in order to remedy some of the perceived defects under the *Canadian Bill of Rights*.[69]

Having come this far in equality rights case law, for the judges to revert to formal equality reasoning of the very kind that resulted in the systematic defeat of equality claims under the *Canadian Bill of Rights* risks creating a real crisis in the legitimacy of the courts.

Viewed against the backdrop of Canadian political history, many of the judicial opinions discussed in this chapter are also historically anomalous. They are a throwback to a nineteenth century version of equality as same treatment. They are consistent with a classical liberal image of the autonomous, self-defining individual in need only of protection from state interference. This imagery leads to an impoverished conception of what the norm of equality requires. However, the extreme individualism and sexism of nineteenth century rights is inconsistent with more than 50 years of Canadian government commitments to social and economic equality for women, and concerted government efforts within the same time period to construct a social safety net that ameliorates conditions of people in need (many of whom are women) and simultaneously reduces disparities between groups.

The cases discussed here point to the necessity of continually recalling courts and governments to the contemporary values, analytical insights, and group aspirations that underlie equality rights. They also provide some indication of the challenges that women face in their ongoing efforts to replace outdated conceptions of rights with contemporary understandings that can serve women's interests in achieving true social and economic equality.

Endnotes for Chapter 3

[1] *Egan* v. *Canada*, [1995] 2 S.C.R. 513, 124 D.L.R. (4th) 609, 95 C.L.L.C. 210-025, [1995] W.D.F.L. 981, C.E.B. & P.G.R. 8216, 12 R.F.L. (4th) 201, 182 N.R. 161, 29 C.R.R. (2d) 79, 96 F.T.R 80 (note) [hereinafter *Egan* cited to S.C.R.].

[2] *Masse* v. *Ontario (Ministry of Community and Social Services)* (1996), 134 D.L.R. (4th) 20, 35 C.R.R. (2d) 44, 89 O.A.C. 81, 40 Admin L.R. (2d) 87 (Ont. Ct. (Gen. Div.)) [hereinafter *Masse* cited to D.L.R.]. Application for leave to appeal to the Ontario Court of Appeal refused on 30 April 1996; leave to appeal to the Supreme Court of Canada refused 5 December 1996.

[3] *Eldridge* v. *British Columbia (A.G.)* (1995), 125 D.L.R. (4th) 323 (1995) 59 B.C.A.C. 254, 7 B.C.L.R. (3d) 156, [1995] 1 W.W.R. 50, 96 B.C.A.C. 254, reversed [1997] 3 S.C.R. 624, 151 D.L.R. (4th) 577, 218 N.R. 161, 624, [1998] 1 W.W.R. 50 96 B.C.A.C. 81, 38 B.C.L.R. (3d) 1.

[4] *Symes* v. *Canada*, [1989] 3 F.C. 59, 25 T.T.R. 306, 40 C.R.R. 278, 1 C.T.C 476 (F.C.T.D.; reversed [1991] 3 F.C 507, 127 N.R. 348, 7 C.R.R. (2D) 333, 2 C.T.C. 1, 91 D.T.C. 5386 (F.C.A.) [hereinafter *Symes (F.C.A.)* cited to F.C.]; affirmed [1993] 4 S.C.R. 695, [1994] 1 C.T.C. 40, 19 C.R.R. (2d) 1, 110 D.L.R. (4th) 470, [1994] W.D.F.L. 171 [hereinafter *Symes* cited to S.C.R.].

[5] *Thibaudeau* v. *Canada*, [1994] 2 F.C. 189, [1994] 2 C.T.C. 4, 3 R.F.L. (4th) 153, 167 N.R. 161, 114 D.L.R. (4th) 261, 21 C.R.R. (2d) 35, [1994] W.D.F.L. 812 [hereinafter *Thibaudeau (F.C.A.)* cited to D.L.R.], affirmed, [1995] 2 S.C.R. 627 at 675–76, [1995] W.D.F.L. 957, [1995] 1 C.T.C. 382, 95 D.T.C. 5273, 12 R.F.L. (4th) 1, 124 D.L.R. (4th) 449, 182 N.R. 1, 29 C.R.R. (2d) 1 [hereinafter *Thibaudeau* cited to S.C.R.].

[6] There are two clarifying points to be made about the cases. First, the cases should not be taken to represent the definitive statement on the law in particular fields. Second, it may be objected that not all the cases were "good cases." Some people have questioned whether the *Symes* case was a good case, in light of the fact that the situation of many women is much worse than that of professional women such as Beth Symes. Exception could also be taken to the *Egan* case on the basis that it can be understood to perpetuate coupleism in pension benefit allocation while ignoring the serious problem of poverty among single elderly women. Legitimate as such concerns may be, they do not amount to legal principles for deciding these cases. It must be granted that a tendency of *Charter* litigation is to present a rather narrow picture of any given problem. The plaintiff may come forward with one concern. However, the problem may be bigger than this. For example, if the situation of Ms. Symes is placed in a bigger frame, it may be understood as symptomatic of the concerns that most women have about socially constructed conflicts between the world of paid work and the world in which children are cared for. Similarly, the *Egan* situation may be understood to present a narrow slice of the larger problem of preferential treatment for heterosexual couples. This is one of the reasons that interventions by community organizations can be useful. They can help to fill out the picture. However, the important point for our discussion is that a court can both grant relief *and* comment on the broader implications of a case.The fact that a particular claim is not representative or not "the best" (or "the worst") case should not lead a court to reject it.

[7] Corbett J. would have allowed one aspect of the claim, but he is in dissent from the other two judges on this point.

[8] See *Eldridge (B.C.C.A.)*, *supra* note 3.

[9] Robin Eldridge and the Warrens testified about difficulties they had in communicating effectively with doctors who do not use sign language. Those difficulties included, in the case of Linda Warren who had a difficult childbirth, an inability to obtain information from hospital staff about the condition of her newly born twin girls. Eldridge's physician testified that he was unsure about the accuracy of information he was receiving by means of handwritten

notes passed back and forth between himself and Robin Eldridge.

[10] *Thibaudeau (F.C.A.)*, *supra* note 5 at 289, Létourneau J.A. in dissent.

[11] Lisa Philipps and Margot Young, "Sex, Tax and the *Charter*: A Review of *Thibaudeau* v. *Canada*" (1995) 2 *Review of Constitutional Studies* 221 at 222. See also Claire Young, "It's All in the Family: Child Support, Tax, and *Thibaudeau*" (1995) 6 *Constitutional Forum* 107 at 110 where she similarly states that at least some of the justices at the Supreme Court of Canada seemed reluctant to apply the *Charter* as rigorously to the *Income Tax Act* as to other types of legislation.

[12] *Supra* note 5.

[13] *Thibaudeau (S.C.C.)*, *supra* note 5. The position of the majority of the Supreme Court in *Thibaudeau* is consistent with its earlier decision in *Symes* (S.C.C.), *supra* note 4, wherein Iacobucci J. said on behalf of the majority at 753:

> A preliminary "debate" took place before this Court which questioned the propriety of using the *Charter* to challenge the scheme of deductibility created by the Act. With respect to this debate, I have two brief comments.
>
> First, it has been suggested that to subject the Act to the *Charter* would risk "overshooting" the purposes of the *Charter*. However, the danger of "overshooting" relates not to the kinds of legislation which are subject to the *Charter*, but to the proper interpretive approach which courts should adopt as they imbue *Charter* rights and freedoms with meaning: see *R.* v. *Big M Drug Mart Ltd*, [1985] 1 S.C.R. 295, at p. 344. Second, it has been said that courts should defer to legislatures with respect to difficult economic questions. However, support for this proposition is said to come from cases in which a degree of deference has been exhibited as part of a s. 1 *Charter* analysis: see, e.g., *PSAC* v. *Canada*, [1987] 1 S.C.R. 424, at p. 442. Such cases do not advocate a deferential approach at any earlier stage of *Charter* analysis.
>
> Since neither of the two propositions upon which this preliminary "debate" was founded can withstand even brief critical analysis, I consider it unnecessary to comment further in this regard. The Act is certainly not insulated against all forms of *Charter* review.

[14] *Thibaudeau (S.C.C.)*, *supra* note 5 at 676.

[15] Lisa Philipps assesses the judgments in *Thibaudeau* (S.C.C.) this way:

> "Despite their explicit rejection of Gonthier J.'s methodology, Iacobucci and Cory JJ. sent very mixed signals on this issue. On the one hand they asserted in direct contrast to Gonthier J. that "[t]he scope of the section 15 right is *not* dependent upon the nature of the legislation which is being challenged." On the other, they agreed with him that "courts should be sensitive to the fact that intrinsic to taxation policy is the creation of distinctions which operate … to generate fiscal revenue while equitably reconciling what are often divergent, if not competing, interests." Though more ambivalent than Gonthier J.'s, these remarks will be perceived to support some form of diminished *Charter* protection in the tax area. Sopinka and La Forest JJ. added no comments of their own on this question.

See "Tax Law: Equality Rights" (1995) 74 *Canadian Bar Review* 668 at 676.

[16] *Andrews* v. *Law Society (British Columbia)*, [1989] 1 S.C.R. 143 at 194, [1989] 2 W.W.R. 289, 25 C.C.E.L. 255, 91 N.R. 255, 34 B.C.L.R. (2d) 273, 10 C.H.R.R. D/5719, 36 C.R.R. 193, 56 D.L.R. (4th) 1 [hereinafter *Andrews* cited to S.C.R.].

[17] *Ibid.*

[18] *RJR MacDonald Inc.* v. *Canada (A.G.)*, [1995] 3 S.C.R. 199 at 277, 127 D.L.R. (4th) 1, 100 C.C.C. (3d) 449, 62 C.P.R. (3d) 417 [hereinafter *RJR MacDonald* cited to S.C.R.].

[19] Décary J. for a unanimous court, *supra* note 4 at 532. As indicated in note 13, *supra*, on further appeal a majority of the Supreme Court of Canada rejected this approach.

[20] In *Eldridge (B.C.C.A.)*, *supra* note 3 at 70–71, Lambert J.A. said:

> Some of the limits imposed under the *Medical and Health Care Services Act* and some of the financial allocation choices that I have mentioned have resulted and will result in adverse effects discrimination against people suffering from disabilities, including serious illness itself. But we do not have those cases before us. How can we say, in those circumstances, that expenditure of scarce resources on services that remedy infringed constitutional rights under s. 15, on the one hand, are more desirable than expenditures of scarce resources on things that cure people without affecting constitutional rights, on the other. And, indeed, how can we prefer the allocation of scarce resources to services that remedy the infringed constitutional rights of one disadvantaged group over the allocation of scarce resources to services that remedy the infringed constitutional rights of a different disadvantaged group.
>
> In my opinion the kind of adverse effects discrimination which I consider has occurred in this case should be rectified, if at all, by legislative or administrative action and not by judicial action.

[21] *Eldridge (S.C.C.)*, *supra* note 3.

[22] More particularly, the Court is referring to what is known as the minimal impairment branch of the *Oakes* test for s. 1 analysis. In *R. v. Oakes*, [1986] 1 S.C.R. 103, the Court established a framework for s. 1 analysis which includes a requirement that the impugned provision must "minimally impair" the *Charter* guarantee. However, subsequently, in *McKinney v. University of Guelph*, [1990] 3 S.C.R. 229, a majority of the Court held that a more deferential approach to the minimal impairment branch of the *Oakes* test may be adopted in cases that involve complex social problems, requiring a delicate balancing of competing rights and social interests, or attempts to distribute scarce resources. According to *McKinney*, in cases where such legislative balancing has occurred, the minimal impairment criterion may be satisfied by showing that the government had a "reasonable basis" for concluding that the legislation impaired the right as little as possible. The reasonable basis test also appeared in *Tétreault-Gadoury* v. *Canada (Employment and Immigration Commission)*, [1991] 2 S.C.R. 22. However, *Egan*, *supra* note 1, revealed divisions within the Court on the question of whether deference should be accorded to a legislature merely because an issue is identified as a social one or because a need for governmental incrementalism is shown. In *Eldridge*, the Court acknowledges this difference of opinion about the implications of the concept of judicial deference.

[23] *Egan*, *supra* note 1.

[24] Sopinka J. added three concepts to the obstacles confronting the equality rights claimant: scarce resources, the "new" social relationship, and incrementalism. In what has since become a frequently quoted passage, Sopinka J. said in *Egan*, *ibid.* at 572–73:

> I agree with the respondent the Attorney General of Canada that *government must be accorded*

some flexibility in extending social benefits and does not have to be proactive in recognizing new social relationships. It is not realistic for the Court to assume that there are unlimited funds to address the needs of all. A judicial approach on this basis would tend to make a government reluctant to create any new social benefit scheme because their limits would depend on an accurate prediction of the outcome of court proceedings under s. 15(1) of the *Charter*. [Emphasis added.]

Regarding incrementalism, Sopinka J. also cites La Forest J. in *McKinney* v. *University of Guelph*, [1990] 3 S.C.R. 229, 91 C.L.L.C. 17,004, 76 D.L.R. (4th) 545, 118 N.R. 1, 13 C.H.R.R. D/171, 45 O.A.C. 1, 2 O.R. (3d) 319 (note), 2 C.R.R. (2d) 1 [hereinafter *McKinney* cited to S.C.R.], a mandatory retirement case, for the proposition that,

> … generally, courts should not lightly second-guess legislative judgment as to just how quickly it should proceed in moving forward towards the ideal of equality. The courts should adopt a stance that encourages advances in the protection of human rights. Some of the steps adopted may well fall short of perfection, but as earlier mentioned, the recognition of human rights emerges slowly out of the human condition, and short or incremental steps may at times be a harbinger of a developing right, a further step in the long journey towards the full and ungrudging recognition of the dignity of the human person. (*Egan, ibid.* at 574.)

[25] *Egan, ibid.* at 575–76.

[26] For academic criticism of *Egan, ibid.*, see Diane Pothier, "M'Aider, Mayday: Section 15 of the *Charter* in Distress" (1996) 6 *National Journal of Constitutional Law* 295; Bruce Ryder, "*Egan* v. *Canada*: Equality Deferred, Again" (1996) 4 *Canadian Labour and Employment Journal* 101; and John Fisher, "The Impact of the Supreme Court Decision in *Egan* v. *Canada* Upon Claims for the Equal Recognition of Same-Sex Relationships" (1997) [unpublished article].

[27] Regarding the "new" social relationship, the comment of Iacobucci J. is particularly apt. He says on behalf of four members of the Court in *Egan, supra* note 1 at 618–19:

> A concern is my colleague's position that, because the prohibition of discrimination against gays and lesbians is "of recent origin" and "generally regarded as a novel concept," the government can be justified in discriminatorily denying same-sex couples a benefit enuring to opposite-sex couples. Another argument he raises is that government can take an incremental approach in providing state benefits.

> With respect, I find both of these approaches to be undesirable. Permitting discrimination to be justified on account of the "novelty" of its prohibition or on account of the need for government "incrementalism" introduces two unprecedented and potentially undefinable criteria into s. 1. It also permits s. 1 to be used in an unduly deferential manner well beyond anything found in the prior jurisprudence of this Court. The very real possibility emerges that the government will always be able to uphold legislation selectively and discriminatorily allocate resources. This would undercut the values of the *Charter* and belittle its purpose.

[28] *Egan, supra* note 1 at 529–30; *Andrews, supra* note 16 at 194.

[29] *Supra* note 18.

[30] *Egan, supra* note 1 at 535.

[31] *Ibid.* at 536 and 537.

[32] Regarding section 1, La Forest J. says: "Had I concluded that the impugned legislation infringed s. 15 of the *Charter*, I would still uphold it under s. 1 of the *Charter* for the reasons set forth ... which are referred to in the reasons of my colleague Justice Sopinka, as well as for those mentioned in my discussion of discrimination in the present case." See *Egan*, *supra* note 1 at 539–40.

[33] *Masse*, *supra* note 2.

[34] *Ibid.* at 49.

[35] *Ibid.*

[36] *Egan*, *supra* note 1 at 272–73.

[37] *Ibid.* at 574; *McKinney*, *supra* note 24 at 318–19.

[38] *Masse*, *supra* note 2 at 60; *Andrews*, *supra* note 16 at 194.

[39] *Ibid.* at 45–46.

[40] *Ibid.* at 46; *Egan*, *supra* note 1 at 573.

[41] *Masse*, *supra* note 2 at 46–47; and *Dandridge* v. *Williams*, 90 S. Ct. 1153 (1970) at 1162–63.

[42] The cases reveal a degree of variation in the way that the s. 15 test is articulated. The version we have provided is drawn from the majority opinion of McLachlin J. in *Miron* v. *Trudel*, [1995] 2 S.C.R. 418 at 485, 10 M.V.R. (3d) 151, 23 O.R. (3d) 160 (note), [1995] 1 L.R. 1-3185, 13 R.F.L. (4th) 1, 181 N.R. 253, 124 D.L.R. (4th) 693, 81 O.A.C. 253.

[43] [1979] 1 S.C.R. 183, 92 D.L.R. (3d) 417, [1978] 6 W.W.R. 711, 23 N.R. 527, 78 C.L.L.C. 14,175 [hereinafter *Bliss* cited to S.C.R.].

[44] For Hollinrake and Cumming JJ.A., the issue of the *Charter*'s application to legislative inaction, and the issue of how discrimination is defined, are connected to a deeper question, which is just how much equality disadvantaged groups are supposed to get. In a very revealing statement, Hollinrake J.A. says in *Eldridge (B.C.C.A.)*, *supra* note 3 at 341:

> [The Appellants] submit that s. 15 be interpreted in such a manner as to effectively impose on the government a positive duty to address all inequalities when legislating benefits in the area of medical services. That, in my opinion, is equivalent to imposing an obligation on the government of ensuring absolute equality ... I do not think that s. 15 imposes such an obligation.

[45] *Ibid.*

[46] *Symes* (S.C.C.), *supra* note 4.

[47] *Ibid.* at 763–64.

[48] *Ibid.* at 764–65.

[49] Further, in *Symes*, *ibid.*, the effects of the law are assessed without regard to the inequality of women. There is an unwillingness to allow the analysis of the effects of the law to be informed by the fact of the unequal cost of child care that women have traditionally born, the implications of such costs for the ability of women to participate in the paid labour force, or the impact of child care responsibilities on women's economic inequality.

Thus, even though Iacobucci J. acknowledges that s. 15 is supposed to be concerned with adverse effects, he is only focused on the challenged law. The possibility that the law may rest on sexist stereotype is not considered. Nor is the analysis focused on the tendency of the law to perpetuate and reinforce women's inequality, in the context of a web of child care and employment-related inequalities experienced by women.

Another way of putting this is to say that the law looks different when viewed from the perspective of the group experiencing discrimination. From the standpoint of Beth Symes and many other women, the question is not whether women disproportionately pay child care expenses, but rather: Is this a law which perpetuates or reinforces women's inequality by refusing to recognize a kind of responsibility that women are culturally expected to assume? L'Heureux-Dubé and McLachlin JJ. understand this. In *Symes*, *ibid.* at 786, L'Heureux-Dubé J. says:

> ... though ostensibly about the proper statutory interpretation of the Act, this case reflects a far more complex struggle over fundamental issues, the meaning of equality and the extent to which these values require that women's experience be considered when the interpretation of legal concepts is at issue.

[50] Central to the reasoning in the opinions upholding s. 56(1)(b) of the *ITA* is a refusal to recognize Suzanne Thibaudeau as a person in her own right separate from her husband. The Court decides that Ms. Thibaudeau should not be seen as either an individual woman or as a member of the group "women" but rather as a member of a "post-divorce family unit." The Court rejects the comparison that the rights claimant seeks to make between custodial parents and non-custodial parents. As the Court sees it, the entity that matters is the divorced or separated couple, and comparisons cannot be made between the custodial parent and the non-custodial parent. This makes the sex discrimination complained of by Ms. Thibaudeau invisible, and renders her invisible too. The majority does not explain why Ms. Thibaudeau cannot be recognized as a person, separate from her ex-husband. Neither McLachlin J. nor L'Heureux-Dubé J. has any difficulty in seeing the absurdity of treating Ms. Thibaudeau and Mr. Thibaudeau as though they were a unit. McLachlin J. acknowledges that the *ITA* treats the non-custodial parent as part of a single taxation unit, namely "the family." McLachlin J. refers to this as legislative fiction. She says in *Thibaudeau*, *supra* note 5 at 707–8:

> The deduction/inclusion scheme does not treat each taxpayer as a separate taxation unit, but treats the non-custodial parent as forming part of a single taxation unit, the family. By a legislative fiction, the deduction/inclusion scheme removes the amount of the support payments paid between former spouses from the non-custodial parent's taxable income, and transfers it to the custodial parent's taxable income.

L'Heureux-Dubé J. agrees with McLachlin J. that the appropriate unit of analysis is not the couple. Whereas McLachlin J. finds that the appropriate unit of comparison is the individual custodial parent who is divorced or separated, L'Heureux-Dubé J. focuses on custodial parents as a group, while acknowledging that the scheme makes many layers of distinctions, between those who receive or make payments pursuant to a court order or written agreement and those who do not; between parents who are separated or divorced and those who are not; and between those who pay and those who receive maintenance. The more important question for L'Heureux-Dubé J. is whether the combination of distinctions has the effect of imposing a benefit or burden unequally on the basis of one's membership in an identifiable group, in this case, women. She finds that it does.

[51] *Ibid.* at 709.

[52] *Ibid.* at 711.

[53] *Eldridge (B.C.C.A.)*, *supra* note 3 at 339.

[54] *Supra* note 20 and accompanying text.

[55] *Supra* note 1.

[56] *Egan*, *supra* note 1 at 539.

[57] The decision of the Ontario Divisional Court in *Masse* also exemplifies the requirement that the effects must be confined to one group. In this case an overflow of effects is taken as evidence that the group is not a protected s. 15 group. Corbett J. rejects the s. 15 claim that targeting social assistance recipients for spending cuts constitutes discrimination. Corbett J. notes that welfare recipients are not the only people who are subject to budgetary restraint or who suffer from inadequate incomes, and then, without weighing evidence presented by the applicants to the effect that welfare recipients are subject to an additional burden, concluded that the applicants had failed to establish "that any differentiation had been made based on the personal characteristics of social assistance recipients." *Masse*, *supra* note 2 at 71. And on this basis, Corbett J. finds that social assistance recipients are not a protected s. 15 group, or at least not in the context of this case.

Corbett J.'s approach is consistent with that of O'Driscoll and O'Brien JJ. Both judges advert to the fact that poverty is not confined to people on social assistance, and O'Driscoll J. says that the status of being on social assistance is not a personal characteristic within the meaning of s. 15. *Masse*, *ibid*. The question of whether poverty or the status of being on social assistance constitutes a protected ground has not yet been taken up by the Supreme Court of Canada. However, a number of lower courts, not including the Ontario Divisional Court, have viewed this issue differently. See, for example, *Dartmouth/Halifax County Regional Housing Authority* v. *Sparks* (1993), 101 D.L.R. (4th) 224, 30 R.P.R. (2d) 146, 119 N.S.R. (2d) 91, 330 A.P.R. 91, 1 D.R.P.L. 462 (N.S.C.A.) [the Nova Scotia Court of Appeal found discrimination on the basis of race, sex and income]; *Federated Anti-Poverty Groups of B.C.* v. *British Columbia (A.G.)* (1991), 70 B.C.L.R. (2d) 325, B.C.W.L.D. 1571, W.D.F.L. 710 (B.C.S.C.) [the British Columbia Supreme Court held that persons receiving income assistance constitute a discrete and insular minority within the meaning of section 15]; *R.* v. *Rehberg* (1994), 111 D.L.R. (4th) 336, 127 N.S.R. (2d) 331, 355 A.P.R. 331, 19 C.R.R. (2d) 242, W.D.F.L. 3787 (N.S.S.C.) [the Nova Scotia Supreme Court found that single mothers along with their children constitute a group likely to experience poverty, and that poverty is likely to be a personal characteristic of the group]; and *Schaff* v. *R.* (1993), 18 C.R.R. (2d) 143, 2 C.T.C. 2695 (T.C.C.) [the Tax Court of Canada held that poor, female, single custodial parents have historically suffered social, political, and legal disadvantage, and should be protected under s. 15].

[58] Philipps and Young, "Sex, Tax and the *Charter*: A Review of *Thibaudeau* v. *Canada*," *supra* note 11 at 254.

[59] Ontario Association of Interval and Transition Houses (OAITH), Submission to the UN Special Rapporteur on Violence Against Women, *Home Truth: Exposing the False Face of Equality and Security Rights For Abused Women in Canada*, November 1996, at 21.

[60] See, for example, *Mia* v. *British Columbia (Medical Services Commission)* (1985), 17 D.L.R. (4th) 385, 61 B.C.L.R. 273, 15 Admin. L.R. 265, 16 C.R.R. 233 (S.C.), in which the Court embraces the claim of a doctor to be free of geographic restrictions on her right to pursue her medical practice.

[61] *Andrews*, *supra* note 16 at 196–97.

[62] *RJR MacDonald*, *supra* note 18 at 332.

[63] *R.* v. *Oakes*, [1986] 1 S.C.R. 103 at 136, 26 D.L.R. (4th) 200, 65 N.R. 87, 14 O.A.C. 335, 24 C.C.C. (3d) 321, 50 C.R. (3d) 1, 19 C.R.R. 308.

[64] The Charter Committee on Poverty Issues put it this way in their submission to the Supreme Court of Canada in the *Symes* case: "Disadvantaged groups may rely on the *Charter* to provide them with a "voice" in the democratic process which they are otherwise denied. Judicial processes under the *Charter* may often be more respectful of disadvantaged groups than political processes, ensuring that they receive a full hearing." See *Symes* v. *Canada* (S.C.C.), *supra* note 4. Factum of the Intervenor, the Charter Committee on Poverty Issues, paragraph 32.

[65] As John Hart Ely wrote in *Democracy and Distrust: A Theory of Judicial Review* (Cambridge: Harvard University Press, 1980) at 151 regarding the term "discrete and insular minorities" adopted by the Supreme Court of Canada in *Andrews*, *supra* note 16 at 152, "The whole point of the approach is to identify those groups in society to whose needs and wishes elected officials have no apparent interest in attending."

[66] This rigid hierarchy of gender roles has implications not only for women who live with men, but also for lesbians and gay men who choose to bond with one another. In particular, from a morally conservative perspective, "family" and "spousal" benefit schemes are seen as the exclusive preserve of women and men whose relationships conform to traditional heterosexual norms. This view of sex roles also dictates that women who aspire to professional advancement should eschew childbearing.

Granted, the same treatment formula can be usefully deployed in some situations. Essentially, it is a call for gender blindness and individual assessment. This sometimes works well for individual women in job-hiring situations, for example, because it requires that each applicant be judged individually rather than being sorted according to group membership. However, when it comes to legislative schemes that reinforce the pre-existing social inequality of women, an equality analysis is required that looks not only to a relationship between a challenged law and an individual woman, but to the relationship between the challenged law, the inequality of the group in the society, and other layers of subordinating stereotypes, laws, and practices that, together, create the inequality of the group.

[67] As indicated, here, the reference is to the decision of the British Columbia Court of Appeal in *Eldridge*. On further appeal, that decision was reversed by the Supreme Court of Canada. See *supra* notes 3 and 20, as well as accompanying text.

[68] In summary, in *Bliss*, *supra* note 43 at 191, the Court made these moves:

1.   The *Bliss* Court distinguished penalties from benefits, insisting that there is a difference in the way that equality analysis should think about penalizing legislation, such as a criminal law provision, that treats one section of the population more harshly than others, and legislation providing "additional benefits" to a group of women. Contrasting the case of *Drybones*, which concerned the criminalization of drinking by Aboriginals, making it an offence for an Indian to be intoxicated, the Court said:

> There is a wide difference between legislation which treats one section of the population more harshly than all others by reason of race as in the case of *Regina* v. *Drybones*, and legislation providing additional benefits to one class of women, specifying conditions which entitle a claimant to such benefits and defining a period during which no benefits are available.

2.   The *Bliss* Court shifted responsibility for the inequality complained of by Stella Bliss away from the legislative scheme, finding the cause of the inequality did not reside in the legislation, but rather was created by nature. The Court said: "[these provisions] are concerned with conditions from which men are excluded. Any inequality between the sexes in this area is not created by legislation but by nature." *Ibid.* at 190.

3.   The *Bliss* Court broke the link between the ground of sex and the equality violation by insisting that all women be negatively affected, a criterion that the claim of Stella Bliss could not satisfy because the challenged provision did not affect all women negatively, only those who were pregnant. The Court failed

to take into account the fact that the adverse effects complained of were experienced exclusively by women. Because the challenged provision did not affect all women, and noting that the *Unemployment Insurance Act* treated all non-pregnant employees alike, the Court concluded that if the *Unemployment Insurance Act* treats pregnant women differently from other employed persons, it is because they are pregnant, not because they are women. The Court expressed agreement with Justice Pratte of the Federal Court of Appeal (1977), 16 N.R. 254) who said:

> Assuming the respondent to have been "discriminated against," it would not have been by reason of her sex. Section 46 applies to women, and has no application to women who are not pregnant, and it has no application, of course to men. If section 46 treats unemployed pregnant women differently from other unemployed persons, be they male or female, it is, it seems to me, because they are pregnant not because they are women. *Bliss*, (S.C.C.) *ibid.* at 190–1917.

In other words, by treating all non-pregnant persons the same (whether male or female), the *Unemployment Insurance Act* satisfied the requirement of neutrality, that is, of treating likes alike.

4.   The *Bliss* Court stated repeatedly that the challenged scheme was enacted for valid federal objectives, as though the validity of the government's objectives could in itself be dispositive, regardless of the discriminatory effects on women.

5.   The *Bliss* Court invoked a relevancy test for determining the legality of eligibility criteria based on pregnancy, holding that an extended eligibility period for pregnant women is a relevant distinction for determining entitlement to unemployment insurance benefits. The Court failed to recognize that a law may be relevant to a government objective, but nevertheless discriminatory in purpose or effect.

6.   The Court did not draw any analytical distinction between the plaintiff's claim and the government's defence.

[69] *Andrews, supra* note 16 at 170.

CHAPTER 4

The *Budget Implementation Act*, Canada's Treaty Obligations, and the *Charter*'s Equality Rights Guarantees

Introduction

Because the meaning of equality guarantees is always in danger of being diminished, it is important to examine fully the dimensions of an interpretive approach to equality rights that gives full effect to Canada's equality commitments — an approach that speaks to women's concerns about material inequality, that is grounded in the cultural understanding of equality, and that incorporates the content of Canada's international human rights commitments. It is important also to test the *BIA*[1] against this interpretation of equality. Our conclusion is that the *BIA* is not consonant with Canada's treaty obligations nor with the *Charter*.[2]

As we have noted, there is a stock of rhetorical arguments that are used to make rights less expansive than the commitments on which they are premised. However, we believe that the *Charter*'s equality guarantees require an interpretation that fully reflects the richness of their historical and philosophical context within Canada, and within the international human rights movement. We believe that the *BIA* is a violation of the *Charter*, but that claim is not premised on a naive conviction that the *Charter* is the answer to all of women's inequality problems. Neither is it our view that a court decision upholding the *BIA* would preclude Canadians from denouncing it as a violation of women's socially agreed upon entitlement to equality.[3] However, we do believe that equality jurisprudence must be pushed to reflect women's concerns. Decisions interpreting the *Charter* have legal, political, and cultural authority.

The Implications of Treaty Commitments

Canada's international human rights commitments work in two ways: (1) the treaties form a separate level of human rights obligations by which Canada is bound, and domestic legislation is understood to be an important means of fulfilling those obligations; and (2) the treaties are an aid to interpretation of the *Charter*.

What is the content of the treaties that is specifically pertinent to the problem of women's material inequality? The full meaning of the social and economic equality of women that is affirmed by international instruments can only be understood by considering the *ICESCR*[4] and *CEDAW*[5] together. These treaties must be given an intertwined reading that is also informed by the most recent internationally agreed upon pronouncement on the advancement of women's equality, the *Platform for Action*.[6]

CEDAW must encompass at least the rights that are included in the *ICESCR*. It cannot be understood to offer women less because that would contradict guarantees of equality in both the *ICCPR*[7] and the *ICESCR*.

This means that a same treatment, or formal equality, reading of *CEDAW* with respect to economic equality is inadequate. A formal equality reading could permit governments to conclude that they would meet the terms of *CEDAW* with respect to economic inequality by passing laws to prohibit differential treatment of women in workplaces. Such legislation, it could be argued, would satisfy the formal equality test by requiring neutrality in the law as it applies to economic matters.

Taking a formal equality approach, governments might not deal with the poverty of women at all since formal equality tends to make group-based economic disadvantage disappear from view. But if they did, governments might argue that the requirements of formal equality are met by ensuring that men and women experience the same incidence and depth of poverty. Equality could be achieved not by alleviating women's poverty, but by making men equally poor.[8]

This empty idea of equality confined to facial sameness means that equality has no bottom; it can be satisfied if men and women are equally destitute. It also means that equality cannot tell down from up; it can be brought about either by equalizing up or equalizing down.

However, the *ICESCR* does not permit reading *CEDAW* in this shallow fashion because to do so would diminish the substantive meaning of women's economic and social rights, as guaranteed by the *ICESCR*. The *ICESCR* guarantees women the right to an adequate standard of living and to the continuous improvement of living conditions. It guarantees everyone the right to work, to health, and to education. It does not guarantee to women the right to the same rate of poverty as men, but rather the right to the social and economic conditions that are consistent with the maximum available resources of the state. The *ICESCR* precludes equalizing downwards, that is, creating "equality" by making more men poor, because it entitles everyone to "the continuous improvement of living conditions." As the *ICESCR* Committee states in General Comment No. 3, because of the general obligation in the *ICESCR* to take steps "with a view to achieving progressively the full realization of the rights," there is a very strong presumption against "any deliberately retrogressive measures."[9] Equalizing downwards would be deliberately retrogressive.

While the *ICESCR* makes it clear that equality has a bottom, *CEDAW* builds on the *ICESCR*. In case the *ICESCR* is read as requiring governments only to ensure economic minimums for women, *CEDAW* shows that the commitment to women's equality goes further. Ensuring that the poorest women get to live above the poverty line, and that all women have an adequate standard of living, will not satisfy the requirement of equality, even though, considering the impoverished conditions of women around the world and the poverty of women in Canada, this would be a giant step forward.

However, it would not satisfy the commitments in *CEDAW*, because women's equality requires not just the eradication of women's poverty, but also the elimination of the economic disparity between women and men as groups. That economic imbalance, and women's economic dependence on men, is a key facet of women's subordination, and *CEDAW* is concerned with the subordination of women as a group.[10] Thus, the equality of women requires not only the eradication of poverty, but also an equitable distribution of wealth, income, and resources between women and men as groups.

Both the *ICESCR* and *CEDAW* speak to the issue of state obligations. Under the *ICESCR* governments have obligations to use their resources to satisfy the social and economic rights of their people. Although there is a current struggle being waged over how to make governments accountable in an effective way for realizing these rights, the obligations of governments have, nonetheless, been recognized repeatedly. Lucie Lamarche says that "economic rights have been built and designed against the state, not for its ability to violate them but for its capacity to protect the economic and social dimensions of human dignity."[11]

While the *ICESCR* reinforces the responsibility of governments to correct women's economic and social inequality, *CEDAW*'s commitment is different from the *ICESCR*'s commitment to the "progressive realization" of social and economic rights. *CEDAW*'s commitment is to the immediate implementation of "all appropriate measures to ensure the full development and advancement of women." In practice, equality is a right that can be immediately recognized in law and progressively realized through programs and other means. The *de facto* equality of women will not come about overnight, but this does not mean that the measures necessary to foster and support it can be delayed, or that governments can treat equality-promoting measures as ones to be implemented only when there are ample resources available.

Thus, a commitment to "progressively realize" the equality of blacks would be quickly understood as a mere cover for racism, if it meant that delay was an option. There is no credible commitment to equality, if it is acceptable for it to occur at some time in the future, unless all possible steps are being taken in the present and continuously. For this reason, the commitment in *CEDAW* is to take all appropriate measures "without delay" to ensure women's advancement. Because the social and economic dimensions of women's inequality are indivisible from the civil and political dimensions, *CEDAW* can only be understood as a commitment to take all appropriate measures immediately with respect to all manifestations of women's inequality, including their economic exclusion and subordination. *CEDAW* precludes treating "progressive realization" as an invitation to stall where women's social and economic social rights are concerned.

Neither the *ICESCR* nor *CEDAW* permits States Parties to rely on arguments about the impact of globalization, the demands of the market, or the requirements of international agencies to justify economic policies that do not conform to the standards set by international human rights law.[12] Human rights are not a sometimes thing, good for some times and not others, nor is any part of human activity exempt from their application. Philip Alston, Chair of the *ICESCR* Committee, points out that permitting economic justifications to trump social and economic rights simply amounts to a refusal to accept them as basic entitlements.[13] The *Platform for Action* adds the recognition that current macro-economic policies, such as globalization and structural adjustment programs, are deepening women's economic exclusion and subordination, and are themselves obstacles to women's advancement.[14]

Taken together, *CEDAW* and the *ICESCR*, reinforced by the *Platform for Action*, stand for these central propositions:

- Equality has a bottom, that is, it is not achieved merely when the incidence of poverty among women is the same as the incidence of poverty among men; rather, equality includes, as a part of its meaning, the social and economic rights of the *ICESCR*, including an adequate standard of living;

- Equality requires the elimination of economic disparities between women and men as groups;

- Governments have positive obligations to create conditions of social and economic equality for women;

- Those obligations do not permit governments to delay in taking the appropriate measures to meet them or to move backwards; and

- Economic policies violate women's right to equality if they permit or foster poverty among women, or if they perpetuate, and do not repair, the *status quo* of women's economic inequality.

Canada's Compliance with International Commitments

Does the *BIA* comply with the international obligations by which Canada has agreed to be bound? It is important to note when considering whether the *BIA* complies that Canada has cited the now repealed CAP, ss. 7 and 15 of the *Charter*, and s. 36 of the *Constitution Act, 1982*, Part III to demonstrate in its official reports that it is in compliance with the *ICESCR*, in particular Article 11 regarding the right to an adequate standard of living. Canada's statements are official acknowledgement of the specific positive obligations on it to provide social programs and services that will satisfy the right to an adequate standard of living.

The *1982 Report of Canada* cites the CAP as a means of implementing the right to an adequate standard of living. The *Report* states:

> The Canada Assistance Plan is the legal authority through which the federal government shares with the provinces the cost of providing social assistance and welfare services to individuals in need or likely to become in need ...[15]

The *Report* states further that:

> [u]nder Part I of the Canada Assistance Plan provision is made for the cost-sharing with provinces and territories of general social assistance payments to

112

persons in need. Assistance includes payment for food, shelter, clothing, fuel, utilities, household supplies, and personal requirements as well as prescribed welfare services ... [16]

In 1992, the *Second Report of Canada on Articles 10–15* states,

In Canada, the provinces have established programs for the payment of social allowances to persons in need. The federal government assists in the funding of these programs through the Canada Assistance Plan, which sets standards for the provinces to be eligible for this assistance ...[17]

Also in its 1982 *Report* on its progress in complying with the requirements of the *ICESCR*, Canada referred to s. 36 of the Constitution as a means of implementing Articles 10–12 of the Covenant.[18] In its 1987 *Report*, Canada cited s. 36(1) of the Constitution as a form of implementation of other *ICESCR* commitments.[19] In oral submissions to the Committee in 1992, the Canadian delegation characterized Canada's obligations under s. 36(1) of the Constitution in the following terms:

The 1982 *Constitution Act* made it a duty of the federal government and all provincial and territorial governments to ... provide essential services of reasonable quality to all Canadians.[20]

Moreover, Canada's 1992 *Report* highlights s. 15 of the *Charter* as a "very relevant provision" in relation to the question of Canada's compliance with Articles 10–15 of the *ICESCR*.[21] The *Report* states:

Section 15 applies to the full range of governmental action. Thus it serves to ensure that the rights enunciated by Articles 10–15 of the *International Covenant on Economic, Social and Cultural Rights* are guaranteed without discrimination in Canada, as required by Article 2(2) of the Covenant.[22]

In 1993 the *ICESCR* Committee reviewed the *Second Report of Canada on Articles 10–15*, and received representations from a coalition of non-governmental organizations including the Charter Committee on Poverty Issues (CCPI), and the National Anti-Poverty Organization (NAPO). The Committee expressed a number of serious concerns about Canada's failure to make any measurable progress in alleviating poverty over the previous decade, or in alleviating the severity of poverty among a number of particularly vulnerable groups. The Committee expressed particular concern that more than half the single mothers in Canada live in poverty; that there is no procedure to ensure that income under welfare programs is at or above the poverty line; and that there is hunger in Canada and widespread reliance on foodbanks.[23]

The contradiction of high rates of poverty among women and other vulnerable groups in a country as wealthy as Canada was not lost on the Committee. The Committee said:

In view of the obligation arising out of article 2 of the Covenant to apply the maximum of available resources to the progressive realization of the rights recognized in the treaty, and considering Canada's enviable situation with regard to such resources, the Committee expresses concern about the persistence of poverty in Canada.[24]

The Committee also expressed concern that in some court decisions and in constitutional discussions, social and economic rights had been described as mere "policy objectives" of government rather than as fundamental human rights.[25] The Committee recommended, in view of the important role played by courts in the enforcement of social and economic rights, that the Canadian judiciary be provided with training courses on Canada's obligations under the Covenant and on their effect on the interpretation and application of Canadian law.[26]

Since the Committee was concerned with Canada's compliance with the *ICESCR* before the introduction of the *BIA*, in May 1995 the same NGO coalition, now including the National Action Committee on the Status of Women, sought and obtained leave to make representations to the *ICESCR* Committee regarding the impact of the *BIA* on poor people in Canada. The coalition requested that Canada be called to account specially for its actions and to explain how the *BIA* is consistent with the terms of the *ICESCR*.

In November 1996, after the *BIA* came into force, the coalition, joined by the Canadian Association of Foodbanks, made a further submission to the *ICESCR* Committee.[27] In this most recent submission, the groups stated:

> [The *BIA*] represents, in the opinion of our organizations and many other experts in Canada, the most serious retrogressive measure ever taken in Canada with respect to legislative protection of the right to an adequate standard of living. On April 1, 1996, Canada was transformed from a country in which the right to adequate financial assistance for persons in need was a legal requirement, enforceable in court by individuals affected, to one in which there is no federal legislation recognizing this right or providing any means of enforcing it.[28]

The *ICESCR* Committee considered the representations of the community organizations, and called upon Canada to provide an accounting, first on 4 May 1995[29] and again in December 1996.[30] The Committee's communications with Canada are unprecedented initiatives for a Committee that normally confines itself to making observations upon receipt of a States Party's scheduled report.[31] Canada has now responded and defends the new CHST regime on the predictable grounds that it provides flexibility for the provinces to allocate resources where they believe that they are most needed, and that it was necessary for budgetary reasons.[32] The Committee will review this report in 1998.

The conclusions of the *ICESCR* Committee will be important. However, it is also important for Canadian women to reach their own conclusions about whether the *BIA* and the new CHST regime comply with Canada's international commitments to women's equality, taken as a whole. We conclude they do not, for the following reasons:

- CAP is gone. This means that women no longer have a legally recognized entitlement to social assistance. There is no national legislative framework for social assistance and social services.

- Federal funds have been cut and the CHST does not require provincial and territorial governments to spend any of the federal transfer on social programs and social services. This means that the existence and viability of social programs and social services are threatened.

- The federal government has withdrawn from its role as standard setter. This means that there is no mechanism for ensuring that women have access to adequate social supports.

- Women have a higher risk of poverty and a greater reliance on social programs and social services. This means that the *BIA* has the effect of increasing the social and economic vulnerability of women, and Canada's poorest women in particular.

Canada's actions cannot be considered to comply with the commitments it has undertaken to:

- refrain from engaging in any act or practice of discrimination against women, (*CEDAW*, Article 2(d));

- take all appropriate measures to eliminate discrimination against women by any person, or organization or enterprise, (*CEDAW*, Article 2(e);

- take in all fields, in particular in the ... social, economic ... fields, all appropriate measures, including legislation, to ensure the full development and advancement of women, for the purpose of guaranteeing them the exercise and enjoyment of human rights ... on a basis of equality with men, (*CEDAW*, Article 3).[33]

Nor is the *BIA* consonant with undertakings Canada agreed to in the *Platform for Action* to:

- pursue and implement sound and stable macro-economic ... policies that are designed to ... address the structural causes of poverty and are geared to eradicating poverty and reducing gender-based inequality ... ;[34] and

- provide adequate safety nets and strengthen State-based ... support systems, as an integral part of social policy ... .[35]

115

Further, the *BIA* does not comply with the *ICESCR*'s requirement that the right to an adequate standard of living and the continuous improvement of living conditions, which is guaranteed equally to women, be "progressively realized."[36] According to the Limburg Principles for implementing the *ICESCR*, which were adopted by the Commission on Human Rights at its 43rd session in 1987, a State Party violates the *ICESCR* if it "deliberately retards or halts the progressive realization of a right."[37] In its General Comment No. 3 the *ICESCR* Committee states that the *ICESCR* "imposes an obligation to move as expeditiously and effectively as possible towards [the full realization of the rights]" and warns that "any deliberately retrogressive measures" would need to be fully justified.[38]

Finally, we have concluded that when *CEDAW*, the *ICESCR*, and the *Platform for Action* are read together, it is clear that economic policies violate women's right to equality if they permit or foster poverty among women, or if they perpetuate, and do not repair, the *status quo* of women's economic inequality.

The *BIA* increases the vulnerability of women by removing the legislative framework for social assistance and social services, and by eliminating the basic entitlement. It permits poor women to live unaided. It permits the *status quo* of women's inequality to continue.

For all these reasons, we believe that the *BIA* violates Canada's international commitments to women's equality.

Interpreting Section 15 of the *Charter*

One can argue that non-compliance with treaty obligations is sufficient reason for a wholesale rejection of the *BIA*. However, non-compliance with the *Charter* makes the case against the *BIA* even stronger. Further, the *Charter* is an obvious vehicle through which an integrated reading of the *ICESCR* and *CEDAW* may be given practical effect.

Canadian courts to date have not been asked to consider a *Charter* case that squarely raises the issue of women's right to an adequate standard of living. However, the legal foundations are in place for a reading of s. 15 that furthers the goal of redressing group disadvantage and incorporating the specific content of Canada's treaty commitments. From the earliest days of the *Charter*, courts have embraced the view that *Charter* rights are to be interpreted generously and in light of their purpose. The elements of a purposive approach were articulated in *Andrews* v. *Law Society (British Columbia)*, wherein McIntyre J. wrote on behalf of a unanimous Supreme Court:

> [T]he provisions of the *Charter* must be given their full effect. In *R* v. *Big M Drug Mart Ltd.*, this Court emphasized this point at p. 344 where Dickson C.J. stated:
>
> This Court has already, in some measure, set out the basic approach to be taken in interpreting the *Charter*. In *Hunter* v. *Southam Inc.* [1984] 2 S.C.R. 145, this

Court expressed the view that the proper approach to the definition of the rights and freedoms guaranteed by the *Charter* was a purposive one. The meaning of a right or freedom guaranteed by the *Charter* was to be ascertained by an analysis of the purpose of such a guarantee; it was to be understood, in other words, in light of the interests it was meant to protect.

In my view this analysis is to be undertaken, and the purpose of the right or freedom in question is to be sought by reference to the character and the larger objects of the *Charter* itself, to the language chosen to articulate the specific right or freedom, to the historical origins of the concepts enshrined, and where applicable, to the meaning and purpose of the other specific rights and freedoms with which it is associated within the text of the *Charter*. The interpretation should be, as the judgement in *Southam* emphasizes, a generous rather than a legalistic one aimed at fulfilling the purpose of the guarantee and securing for individuals the full benefit of the *Charter*'s protections.[39]

In short, the purpose of a *Charter* right is to be ascertained by having regard to:

- the character and larger objects of the *Charter;*

- the historical origins and text of s.15; and

- the meaning and purpose of associated *Charter* rights and freedoms.

We argue that the character and larger objects of the *Charter,* the historical origins and text of s. 15, the status, history and text of s. 15, and the meaning and purpose of associated constitutional rights, including s. 36 of the Constitution and ss. 7 and 28 of the *Charter*, all point to the conclusion that a key purpose of s. 15 is to assist disadvantaged groups in overcoming inequality of conditions. Moreover, this has been recognized by the Supreme Court of Canada. In *Andrews*, Wilson J. said, "[Section] 15 is designed to protect those groups who suffer social, political and legal disadvantage in our society."[40] This sentiment was subsequently adopted by a unanimous Supreme Court in *Turpin*.[41]

Further, the *Charter* was introduced within a historical and philosophical context of broad public consensus that the federal government, as well as provincial governments, have an obligation to provide social programs to promote the equality and well-being of disadvantaged Canadians and regions.

What are the legal foundations for a reading of women's rights under s. 15 of the *Charter* that draws in international treaty commitments? Courts have held that domestic statutes should, whenever possible, be interpreted so as to be consistent with provisions of international instruments to which Canada is bound. This is on the assumption that Parliament and legislatures intend to legislate in conformity with them. The Supreme Court of Canada has held that this principle also applies to the interpretation of the *Charter*. In the case of *Slaight Communications*, Dickson C.J. speaking for the majority said:

> The content of Canada's international human rights obligations is, in my view, an important indicia of the meaning of "full benefit of the *Charter*'s protection." I believe that the *Charter* should generally be presumed to provide protection at least as great as that afforded by similar provisions in international human rights documents which Canada has ratified.[42]

The facts of *Slaight* provide an indication of the difference that it can make when *Charter* rights are interpreted in light of Canada's human rights treaty commitments. The case of *Slaight* concerned a wrongful dismissal under the *Canada Labour Code*. The adjudicator ordered the employer to give the employee a letter of recommendation attesting to the employee's positive record and acknowledging that the termination had been held to be unjust. In addition, by order of the adjudicator, the employer was precluded from responding to a request for information about the employee except by sending the letter of recommendation. The employer appealed, arguing that these orders constituted an infringement of s. 2(b) of the *Charter* that guarantees freedom of expression. The Supreme Court of Canada granted that the employer's freedom of expression had been infringed, but upheld the adjudicator's orders on the basis that they were a justifiable limit under s. 1 of the *Charter*.

One step in the s. 1 analysis consists of balancing the harmful effects of the challenged measure against the importance of the objective of the measure. In the course of concluding that the deleterious effects of the arbitrator's orders were not so great as to outweigh the importance of their objective, the majority in *Slaight* referred to Canada's obligations under the *ICESCR*, in particular to Canada's commitment to protect the right to work. Speaking for the majority, Dickson C.J. said:

> Especially in light of Canada's ratification of the International Covenant on Economic, Social and Cultural Rights ... and commitment therein to protect, *inter alia,* the right to work in its various dimensions found in Article 6 of that treaty, it cannot be doubted that the objective in this case is a very important one.[43]

Dickson C.J. said further that:

> ... Canada's international human rights obligations should inform not only the interpretation of the content of the rights guaranteed by the *Charter* but also the interpretation of what can constitute pressing and substantial s. 1 objectives which may justify restrictions on those rights. Furthermore, for purposes of this ... inquiry, the fact that a value has the status of an international human right, either in customary international law or under a treaty to which Canada is a State Party,

should generally be indicative of a high degree of importance attached to that objective. This is consistent with the importance that this Court has placed on the protection of employees as a vulnerable group in the society.[44]

Thus, *Slaight* stands for the proposition that Canada's international human rights obligations may have two roles to play as aids to the interpretation of *Charter* rights. First, they are relevant to defining the content of *Charter* rights. Second, they may be useful in defining the scope of the limits that can be imposed upon them under s. 1 of the *Charter*. More particularly, the fact that a value has the status of an international human right is to be taken as indicative of a high degree of importance attached to that objective, in the context of s. 1 analysis.

In another case, *R* v. *Brydges*,[45] the Supreme Court of Canada relied on an international treaty commitment under the *ICCPR* to interpret the *Charter* right to instruct and retain counsel as including the right to be informed of the existence and availability of duty counsel and legal aid plans. This is consistent with the principle that treaty commitments may supply content for *Charter* rights, which are expressed in relatively open-textured language.[46]

However, it is apparent that the rationale for applying international human rights norms is not restricted to the presumption of consistency between a State Party's legislation and its treaty commitments. The rationale is broader than this. As Matthew Craven has noted: "It is clear … that the Canadian courts do not take cognizance of international standards merely on the basis of the presumption that Parliament intended to legislate in conformity with its international obligations. … Rather, it appears that reference is made to international human rights standards in general because, in the words of Dickson C.J., they 'reflect the values and principles that underlie the *Charter* itself.'"[47]

In another case, *Reference Re Public Service Employee Relations Act*,[48] Dickson C.J. acknowledged, even more generally, the international human rights norms as part of the *Charter*'s interpretive backdrop. He said:

> A body of treaties … and customary norms now constitutes an international law of human rights under which the nations of the world have undertaken to adhere to the standards and principles necessary for ensuring freedom, dignity and social justice for their citizens. The *Charter* conforms to the spirit of this contemporary international human rights movement, and it incorporates many of the policies and prescriptions of the various international documents pertaining to human rights. The various sources of international human rights law — declarations, covenants, conventions, and *quasi*-judicial decisions of international tribunals, customary norms — must, in my opinion, be relevant and persuasive sources for interpretation of the *Charter*'s provisions.[49]

International human rights norms were a principal source of inspiration for the *Charter*. Anne Bayevsky explains:

[the legislative history of the *Charter*] contains frequent references to human rights law. Throughout the period from 1968 to 1982 when the *Charter* was being drafted, the proliferation of international norms was digested by Canadian constitutional framers. ... From the outset of the federal government's concerted efforts in 1968 to realize a constitutional Bill of Rights the architects were conscious of international human rights norms.[50]

Similarly, John Claydon states that:

Canada's international human rights obligations served as not only the necessary and pervasive context in which the *Charter of Rights* was introduced and adopted, but also the direct inspiration for amendments designed to strengthen the human rights protection provided.[51]

And Lynn Smith and William Black state that "s. 15 is a primary vehicle for implementing Canada's obligations under those [international] instruments."[52]

In many domestic and international contexts Canadian government officials have represented the *Charter* as implementing Canada's international human rights obligations. In 1983 the federal government presented a paper to a Federal-Provincial-Territorial Ministerial Conference on Human Rights, which states:

[I]t is no coincidence that the *Charter* happens to satisfy most of Canada's human rights obligations pursuant to the International Covenant on Civil and Political Rights, and many of those assumed under other international human rights instruments, since it was framed in light of their requirements. ... At an early point in the deliberations of the Special Joint Committee, the then Federal Minister of Justice, the Honourable Jean Chrétien, affirmed that "the rights that we have agreed upon in international agreements should be reflected in the laws or the *Charter of Rights* that we have in Canada."[53]

In February 1990, the Canadian delegation that appeared before the *CEDAW* Committee concerning the *Second Report of Canada, Convention on the Elimination of All Forms of Discrimination Against Women*, told the Committee that "the *Charter* was an important means of implementing the Convention in Canada."[54]

It is clear from this history and from pronouncements by the Supreme Court of Canada that *Charter* equality rights should be interpreted in light of their larger social context and goals, including the goal of realizing Canada's human rights treaty obligations, with a view to giving life to Canada's equality commitments, not trivializing or circumventing them.

The *BIA* Violates Women's Equality Rights under the *Charter*

When interpretation of s. 15 is informed by Canada's treaty obligations to take appropriate measures to realize the right to an adequate standard of living and Canada's compendious commitments to equality for women, it is unreasonable to understand s. 15 as conferring on women anything less than:

- a right to adequate social programs and services for women in need;

- a right to be equal beneficiaries of all social and economic policies; and

- a right to economic policies that will promote women's equality.

In turn, this interpretation of s. 15 must be understood to impose a positive obligation on all levels of government to provide adequate social programs and services, and to prefer economic policies that will promote social and economic equality for women. On this substantive interpretation of s. 15, the *BIA* constitutes an equality rights violation because it allows the federal government to wash its hands of responsibility for the adequacy of social assistance programs and related services. Seen in the larger frame of global restructuring, the *BIA* is also an element of macro-economic policy that hurts women.

It should be acknowledged that the Supreme Court of Canada has not yet considered the question of whether s. 15 imposes positive obligations on governments to tax and spend in ways that will reduce disparities between women and men. Nor has the Court considered whether the *Charter* imposes an obligation on governments to maintain adequate social programs. It is time that s. 15 jurisprudence recognized more explicitly than it has in the past that the norm of equality has a bottom, and that women have a right to share equally in all of the society's material resources.

However, it is not necessary to break this new jurisprudential ground in order to establish that the *BIA* is a violation of women's *Charter* equality rights. The *BIA* is so egregious that it does not stand up to even a relatively narrow form of s. 15 scrutiny.

Even on its face, the *BIA* is blatantly discriminatory[55] in its treatment of Canada's poorest Canadians. The affected interests — entitlements to social assistance — go to the very core of human needs for survival and well-being. With one hand, the *BIA* expressly reconfirms national standards for health care. With the other hand, the *BIA* virtually wipes out national standards for social assistance. Moreover, it is not just coincidental that health care standards are retained while social assistance standards are abandoned.

The *BIA* is rooted in prejudicial attitudes about the worth of single mothers and poor people generally. One need only recall the prevalence of negative stereotyping of welfare recipients as unworthy, lazy, and the author of their own misfortunes, to derive a sense of why it is that Parliament felt safe in singling out welfare recipients for prejudicial treatment.[56] On 17

February 1997, Edward Greenspon of *The [Toronto] Globe and Mail* offered this observation about public opinion:

> Whereas a generation ago, Canadians blamed society at large for the plight of the poor, today they are more likely to blame the poor. No longer are single mothers automatically viewed as victims; people are much more inclined today to question why the women allowed themselves to get pregnant.[57]

The same negative images of welfare recipients that are likely to lead to provincial governments favouring health care and post-secondary education over social assistance programs also underlie the federal government's decisions to defend health care standards and forego social assistance standards. People in need of social assistance are a stigmatized minority group, an easy target for the deficit-cutting agenda because they are unpopular and relatively lacking in political power.[58] In this regard, the comment of Parrett J. of the British Columbia Court of Appeal in the case of *Federated Anti-Poverty Groups of B.C. v. British Columbia (A.G.)*[59] is apt. In the course of rejecting a Crown motion to strike a s. 15 challenge brought by the Federated Anti-Poverty Groups, Parrett J. said that "recipients of public assistance generally lack substantial political influence, they comprise 'those groups in society to whose needs and wishes elected officials have no apparent interest in attending.'"[60]

The preferential treatment that the *BIA* accords to health care recipients over social assistance recipients results in a funding framework that, under well-established principles of equality rights analysis, is discriminatory. It is discriminatory in two senses of the term. First, stigmatizing attitudes about the beneficiaries underlie the removal of protective conditions for social assistance programs. Second, the *BIA* is discriminatory in that it is underinclusive; that is, it provides protections for one group while withholding them from another equally deserving group. Canadian courts have recognized that underinclusiveness in a legislative scheme of protections or benefits can constitute discrimination. The Ontario Court of Appeal held in the case of *Haig*[61] that the exclusion of gays and lesbians from the protection of a human rights statute is a violation of s. 15 of the *Charter*, which results from underinclusiveness. The denial of protective conditions to social assistance recipients under the *BIA* is very like the denial of statutory human rights protections to gays and lesbians under human rights legislation. Thus, the holding in *Haig* strongly supports the claim that the *BIA* is a violation of s. 15.

The Supreme Court of Canada has also recognized that discrimination may arise through underinclusiveness, and has granted remedies that have the effect of extending a benefit scheme to a wrongfully excluded group. For example, in the case of *Tétreault-Gadoury v. Canada (Employment and Immigration Commission)*,[62] an exclusion based on age was found to contravene the *Unemployment Insurance Act*. The effect of the declaratory order of the Court was to extend benefits to previously excluded claimants over the age of 65. There is no principled basis for thinking that the equality rights issues raised by the exclusion of poor women and social assistance programs from the equal protection of national standards should be accorded any less constitutional importance that the wrongful exclusion of a group from human rights legislation or unemployment insurance.

However, the claim that the *BIA* is discriminatory does not hinge exclusively on the fact that health care conditions are retained while social assistance conditions are abandoned.[63] The *BIA* is discriminatory in that it targets social assistance recipients for negative treatment, as compared with the treatment of the public at large. The fact that conditions for health care have been preserved lends support to this argument, but even absent this comparison, the *BIA* should be understood to be discriminatory because it targets disadvantaged groups in the society, not only by removing conditions for social assistance, but also by reducing federal government contributions for social assistance funding, and liberating provinces to spend on more popular priorities.

The claim that the *BIA* is discriminatory must meet the objection that the challenged treatment, no matter how offensive it may be, is not "based on personal characteristics." However, it is clear that the impact of the *BIA* falls on poor people, a great many of whom are single mothers with dependent children. The *BIA* is harmful to women in that it undermines their material security and equality interests. It also has the potential to reinforce negative images of poor women as sexually irresponsible and politically expendable. Further, notwithstanding certain difficulties that some judges are having in actually implementing adverse effects analysis, there is no question that equality rights jurisprudence dictates that the central focus of s. 15 analysis must be on adverse effects.

For women, poverty and lack of economic autonomy are personal characteristics of the group in the same way that vulnerability to pregnancy discrimination and vulnerability to harassment are characteristics of the group; that is, they are key indicators of the group's inequality and obstacles to the achievement of equality. The Supreme Court of Canada has recognized the connection between gender and material inequality. In *Moge* v. *Moge*, a case arising under the spousal maintenance provisions of the *Divorce Act,* L'Heureux-Dubé J., speaking for the majority said, "In Canada, the feminization of poverty is an entrenched social phenomenon."[64]

Any analysis of the *BIA* must take into account the intersection of adverse effects based on poverty, receipt of social assistance, gender, and the status of being a single mother, as well as race and disability. Courts have also specifically addressed the question of whether poverty is a personal characteristic for purposes of s. 15 analysis, and found that it is.

In the case of *Dartmouth/Halifax County Regional Housing Authority* v. *Sparks,*[65] the Nova Scotia Court of Appeal struck down provisions of the *Residential Tenancies Act* which excluded public housing tenants from the security of tenure afforded to other renters in the province. The appellant, Ms. Sparks, was a Black, single mother on social assistance. As a tenant of public housing, she could be evicted on one month's notice, without cause. Had she been a private sector tenant, she would have been entitled, by law, to security of tenure, meaning that she could not have been evicted except by order of a judge, based on default of specified obligations under the *Act*.

Initially, the Nova Scotia Supreme Court rejected Ms. Sparks's s. 15 challenge, saying that "[the appellant] would have to show that the legislation somehow exempted blacks, women, and recipients of social assistance from the protection of the statute by singling out a characteristic of being a black, female social assistance recipient."[66]

Reversing the lower court, the Nova Scotia Court of Appeal found that the effect of denying security of tenure to public housing tenants is to discriminate against public housing tenants as a group, on the basis of race, sex, and income. In reaching its decision that public housing tenants are an analogous group for purposes of s. 15 analysis, the Court found that low income is a characteristic shared by all residents of public housing, and that poverty is a condition experienced more frequently by Blacks, women, in particular single mothers, as well as by senior citizens. The Court said at 233–34:

> Low income, in most cases verging on or below poverty, is undeniably a characteristic shared by all residents of public housing; the principle criteria of eligibility for public housing are to have a low income and have a need for better housing. Poverty is, in addition, a condition more frequently experienced by members of the three groups identified by the appellant. The evidence before us supports this.

> Single mothers are now known to be the group in society most likely to experience poverty in the extreme. It is by virtue of being a single mother that this poverty is likely to affect the members of this group. This is no less a personal characteristic of such individuals than non-citizenship was in *Andrews*. To find otherwise would strain the interpretation of "personal characteristic" unduly.

> Similarly, senior citizens that are in public housing are there because they qualify by reason of their low-incomes and need for better housing. As a general proposition, persons who qualify for public housing are the economically disadvantaged and are so disadvantaged because of their age and correspondingly low incomes (seniors) or families with low-incomes, a majority of whom are disadvantaged because they are single female parents on social assistance, many of whom are black. The public housing tenants group as a whole is historically disadvantaged as a result of the combined effect of several personal characteristics listed in s. 15(1). As a result, they are a group analogous to those persons or groups specifically referred to by the characteristics set out in s. 15(1) of the *Charter* being characteristics that are most commonly the subject of discrimination.

Following the Court of Appeal ruling in *Sparks*, the Nova Scotia Supreme Court ruled in the case of *R. v. Rehberg*[67] that legislation that disentitles women who cohabit with men from receiving welfare has a discriminatory effect on single mothers, contrary to s. 15 of the *Charter*. In reaching this conclusion the Court adopted an approach to s. 15 which was informed by a recognition that poverty and gender are importantly connected. The Court stated at 361:

> I note that the Court in *Sparks* had no difficulty in finding that single mothers are a "group" in society most likely to experience poverty in the extreme, and that poverty is likely to be a personal characteristic of a single mother. I have no difficulty reaching the same conclusion from the evidence before me.

> We are therefore faced with a situation where the regulations specifically authorized under the Act provide that a special group, "single parents otherwise eligible for family benefits", can be determined ineligible to receive these benefits if they contravene the man in the house rule, however it is applied. Moreover, this "group" is overwhelmingly female single mothers who are, *with their children*, a group in society "most likely to experience poverty in the extreme". I find in these circumstances, as was found in *Sparks*, that poverty is likely a personal characteristic of this group, and in this instance poverty is analogous to the listed grounds in s. 15. As well, of course, the group encompasses a listed ground, "sex", as it is most likely that members of this group are female.

In another case, *Schaff* v. *R.*,[68] the Tax Court also found that poverty is a personal characteristic that can form the basis of discrimination. The appellant, a single mother living in poverty argued that s. 56(1)(b) of the *Income Tax Act* violated her rights under ss. 7 and 15 of the *Charter* because it required her to include in any computation of her income the child support payments she received. Although the Court did not find a violation of the *Charter*, it nonetheless found that the appellant was a member of a disadvantaged group that is entitled to *Charter* protection. The Court said at 158:

> The appellant, in my opinion, is part of a "discrete and insular minority" worthy of protection under s. 15 of the *Charter*. More specifically, poverty is a personal characteristic that can form the basis of discrimination.

And further at 158:

> In my opinion, the appellant is worthy of protection under s. 15 of the *Charter* in so far as poor, female, single custodial parents have historically suffered social, political and legal disadvantage.

Similarly, the Alberta Court of Queen's Bench ruled in the case of *M.(R.H.)* v. *H.(S.S.)*[69] that a law requiring corroboration of an unmarried mother's evidence discriminated on the basis of gender and marital status. In the course of reaching this conclusion, the Court made reference to the likelihood that single mothers would be poor. The Judge stated at 341:

Although I have already found s. 19(1) to be discriminatory for the above reasons, I make the following additional comments on the matter of what is now referred to as the feminization of poverty. ...

... I have no difficulty finding that single mothers are more likely to suffer the effects of poverty. ... In my view, this simply is another route through which discrimination against single mothers is established.

The recognition that the *Charter* should provide protection in cases involving the intersection of poverty, receipt of social assistance, gender, and the status of being a single mother, resonates with holdings of the Supreme Court of Canada recognizing that vulnerability to harassment and pregnancy-related discrimination are forms of sex discrimination to which human rights protections apply.

Conclusion

It might be argued that the *BIA* is not subject to the *Charter* because it is budgetary legislation arising from economic realities and difficult legislative choices with which courts should not interfere. However, the *Charter* does not exempt any class of legislation from the requirement of conforming with s. 15.

An overwhelming majority of the Supreme Court of Canada has held that no legislation is immune from s. 15 review.[70] Courts have also recognized that s. 15 is an all-encompassing right to freedom from discrimination which governs all legislative action.[71]

It is notable that s. 32 (1) of the *Charter* is very broad in its wording, making it clear that the *Charter* applies to all federal and provincial government legislation. It states:

> (a) The *Charter* applies to the Parliament and government of Canada in respect of all matters within the authority of Parliament including all matters relating to the Yukon Territory and Northwest Territories; and

> (b) to the legislature and government of each province in respect of all matters within the authority of the legislature of each province.

In addition to applying the *Charter* to income tax legislation, the Supreme Court of Canada has also applied it to legislation governing benefits such as unemployment insurance.[72] The Court has also been willing to order remedies with financial implications that are potentially substantial.[73] Thus, even on existing case law, an argument that the *BIA* is immune from *Charter* review is not sustainable.

In a court of law it might be argued that the infringements of equality rights occasioned by the *BIA* are justified, pursuant to s. 1 of the *Charter*. However, it is well established that government bears the burden of showing that the rights violation is demonstrably justified. As

Wilson J. recognized in *Andrews*, it is fitting that this burden be onerous. She said: "Given that s. 15 is designed to protect those groups who suffer social, political, and legal disadvantage in our society, the burden resting on government to justify the ... discrimination against such groups is appropriately an onerous one."[74]

The government must show the legislation addresses a pressing and substantial objective, that there is a rational connection between the legislative objective and the rights violation, that the challenged legislation impairs[75] the guaranteed right as little as possible, and that there is overall proportionality between the harmful effects of the legislation and importance of the objective.[76] This onerous burden, the federal government cannot discharge. The aspirations of provincial governments for increased autonomy can be respected. However, this does not justify cutting women and other vulnerable groups adrift in the way that the *BIA* does, wiping out protections and supports for social assistance programs and related services.

We conclude that the *BIA* contravenes Canada's treaty obligations under the *CEDAW* and the *ICESCR*, and violates women's *Charter* equality rights. The *BIA* should be rejected by Canadians, and the CHST should be revisited by governments as an urgent priority.

Endnotes for Chapter 4

[1] *The Budget Implementation Act, 1995*, S.C. 1995, c. 17 [hereinafter *BIA*].

[2] *Canadian Charter of Rights and Freedoms*, Part I of the *Constitution Act, 1982*, being schedule B to the *Canada Act 1982* (U.K.), 1982, c. 11 [hereinafter *Charter*].

[3] There are also other angles from which the *BIA* may be attacked. For example, it is strongly arguable that the *BIA* violates the right to security under s. 7 of the *Charter*, and places the federal government in breach of its obligations under s. 36 of the *Constitution Act*. Regarding arguments in favour of interpretations of s. 7 which extend to broader aspects of physical and social welfare, see: John D. Whyte, "Fundamental Justice: The Scope and Application of Section 7 of the *Charter*" (1983) 13 *Manitoba Law Journal* 455; Martha Jackman, "The Protection of Welfare Rights Under the *Charter*" (1988) 20 *Ottawa Law Review* 257; Ian Morrison, "Security of the Person and the Person in Need: Section 7 and the Right to Welfare" (1988) 4 *Journal of Law and Social Policy* 1; Ian Johnstone, "Section 7 of the *Charter* and the Right to Welfare" (1988) 46 *University of Toronto Faculty of Law Review* 1; Lucie Lamarche, "La nouvelle loi sur la sécurité du revenu au Québec: quelques réflexions d'actualité" (1991) 21 *Revue de droit de l'Université de Sherbrooke* 335; Teressa Scassa, "Social Welfare and Section 7 of the *Charter*: *Conrad* v. *Halifax (County of)*" (1994) 17 *Dalhousie Law Journal* 187; Martha Jackman, "Poor Rights: Using the *Charter* to Support Social Welfare Claims" (1993) 19 *Queen's Law Journal* 65.

[4] *International Covenant on Economic, Social and Cultural Rights*, GA Res. 2200A (XXI), 21 UN GAOR, (Supp. No. 16), UN Doc. A/6316 (1966), 993 U.N.T.S. 3, Can. T.S. 1976 No. 46 [hereinafter *ICESCR*].

[5] *Convention on the Elimination of All Forms of Discrimination Against Women*, GA Res. 34/180, UN GAOR, 34th Sess., (Supp. No. 46), UN Doc. A/34/46 (1982), Can. T.S. 1982 No. 31 [hereinafter *CEDAW*].

[6] United Nations, *Report of the Fourth World Conference on Women*, Beijing, China, 4–15 September 1995, A/CONF.177/20, 17 October 1995 [hereinafter *Platform for Action*].

[7] *International Covenant on Civil and Political Rights*, GA Res. 2200A (XXI), 21 UN GAOR, (Supp. No. 16) 52, UN Doc. A/6316 (1966), 999 U.N.T.S. 171, Can. T.S. 1976 No. 47 [hereinafter *ICCPR*].

[8] This may seem an obviously foolish reading. However, equalizing down is the approach that was taken by the Government of British Columbia to correcting discrimination after the Court's ruling in the case of *Silano* v. *British Columbia* (1987), 42 D.L.R. (4th) 407, [1987] 5 W.W.R. 739, 16 B.C.L.R. (2d) 113, 29 Admin. L.R. 125, 33 C.R.R. 331 (S.C.). The Court had ruled that the structure for social assistance rates discriminated on the basis of age.

[9] See General Comment No. 3 regarding the interpretation of Article 2(1) in United Nations Committee on Economic, Social and Cultural Rights, *General Comments Nos. 1–4* as reprinted in (1994) 1:1 *International Human Rights Reports* at 8, paragraph 9.

[10] *CEDAW* is a treaty whose subject matter is the subordination of women. Its goal is to eliminate discrimination against women in all its forms, and to advance women. Its goal is not simply to ensure that women and men are treated the same, though that may be a useful means of attacking women's oppression in some circumstances. With respect to economic issues, we believe that *CEDAW* must be read as a whole, with special emphasis on the Articles of Part I and Articles 11 and 14. We note also that General Recommendation No. 19, UN Doc. A/47/38 (1992), on Violence Against Women adopted by the CEDAW Committee in 1992 makes evident that the purpose of *CEDAW* is to bring to an end the subordination of women as a group, and that women's economic inequality

is considered an integral part of this subordination. We note in particular paragraphs 11, 14, 15, and 23.

[11] Lucie Lamarche, "An Historical Review of Social and Economic Rights: A Case for Real Rights" (1995) 15:2&3 *Canadian Woman Studies* 12 at 14.

[12] *Ibid.*

[13] See Philip Alston, "Denial and Neglect," in Richard Reoch, ed., *Human Rights: The New Consensus* (London: Regency House (Humanity), 1994) at 113–14. Alston states that the proposition that economic and social rights should be accorded to every individual is

> ... still almost automatically made subject by decision-makers to an economic calculus which will often culminate in various economically compelling reasons as to why such rights can simply not be recognized. The same sort of process was once applied to certain civil and political rights when it was argued, for example, that giving the vote to women was too costly, that giving the vote to illiterates was not rational because they were inevitably ill-informed, that allowing trade union rights at the expense of industrial harmony was economically ill-advised, that accused persons did not warrant the expense of a fair trial, and that rapid industrialization required unfettered central government control over all forms of political and economic decision-making. Over the past fifty years, all such arguments have been gradually rendered irrelevant by the firm and uncompromising commitment to the relevant values that has been both implicit and explicit in the acceptance of the basic principles of civil and political rights.

> But decision-makers have still not been able to bring themselves to accept the equivalent proposition to the effect that the recognition of economic, social and cultural rights puts the question of whether these rights should be accorded beyond the realm of debate, especially on the grounds of some anticipated negative impact in economic terms. In effect, individual States and the international community as a whole have made a commitment to the realization of those rights, and that commitment must not be read as being contingent upon a demonstration that it is economically or otherwise profitable or rewarding for the Government (or the society as a whole) to accord those rights.

[14] *Supra* note 6. See Chapter IV, section A paragraph 47.

[15] Canada, Secretary of State, *International Covenant on Economic, Social and Cultural Rights: Report of Canada on Articles 10–12, December 1982* (Ottawa: Supply and Services, 1983) [hereinafter *1982 Report of Canada, Articles 10–12*] at 13.

[16] *Ibid.* at 33.

[17] Canada, Human Rights Directorate, Multiculturalism and Citizenship Canada, *International Covenant on Economic, Social and Cultural Rights: Second Report of Canada on Articles 10–15, September 1992* (Ottawa: Supply and Services, 1992) [hereinafter *1992 Second Report of Canada, Articles 10–15*] at 8.

[18] *1982 Report of Canada, Articles 10–12, supra* note 15.

[19] Canada, Secretary of State, *International Covenant on Economic, Social and Cultural Rights: Second Report of Canada on Articles 6–9, December 1987* (Ottawa: Supply and Services, 1988) at 2.

[20] This echoes the federal government's written acknowledgement that s. 36 "commits" both levels of government to, among other things, providing essential services of reasonable quality to all Canadians. *1992 Second Report of Canada, Articles 10–15, supra* note 17 at 2–3.

[21] *Ibid.* at 5.

[22] *Ibid.*

[23] Committee on Economic, Social and Cultural Rights, 8th Session, *Concluding Observations on Report of Canada Concerning the Rights Covered by Articles 10–15 of the International Covenant on Economic, Social and Cultural Rights*, UN Doc. E/C. 12/1993/19; paragraphs 101–5 as reprinted in (1994) 20 *Canadian Human Rights Reporter* C/1.

[24] *Ibid.* paragraph 101.

[25] *Ibid.* paragraphs 110 and 112.

[26] *Ibid.* paragraph 18.

[27] Letter of Bruce Porter on behalf of the Coalition to Philip Alston, Chairperson of the Committee on Economic, Social and Cultural Rights (27 November 1996).

[28] *Ibid.* at 4. Other critical perspectives on the *BIA* and the CHST include Ken Battle and Sherri Torjman, *How Finance Reformed Social Policy* (Ottawa: Caledon Institute of Social Policy, 1995); Canadian Council on Social Development, *Social Policy Beyond the Budget* (Ottawa: Canadian Council on Social Development, April 1995); Canadian Council on Social Development, *Roundtables on the Canada Health and Social Transfer: Final Report* (Ottawa, 1996); Canadian Labour Congress, *Canada: Two Visions — Two Futures: Submission to the Standing Committee on Finance Regarding Bill C-76* (Ottawa, May 1995); Citizens for Public Justice, *Will Ottawa Preserve National Equity?* (Toronto, May 1995); The Council of Canadians, *Danger Ahead: Assessing the Implications of the Canada Health and Social Transfer* (Ottawa, March 1995); Michael Mendelson, *Looking for Mr. Good-Transfer: A Guide to the Canada Health and Social Transfer Negotiations* (Ottawa: Caledon Institute of Social Policy, 1995); Michael Mendelson, *The Provinces' Position: A Second Chance for the Social Security Review?* (Ottawa: Caledon Institute of Social Policy, 1996); National Council of Welfare, *The 1995 Budget and Block Funding: A Report by the National Council of Welfare* (Ottawa: Supply and Services Canada, Spring 1995); Susan Phillips, "The Canada Health and Social Transfer: Fiscal Federalism in Search of a New Vision" in Douglas Brown and Jonathan Rose, eds., *Canada: The State of the Federation 1995* (Kingston: Institute of Intergovernmental Relations, 1995); Paul Steinhauer, *The Canada Health and Social Transfer: A Threat to Health, Development and Future Productivity of Canada's Children and Youth* (Ottawa: Caledon Institute of Social Policy, 1995); and Sherri Torjman and Ken Battle, *Can We Have National Standards?* (Ottawa: Caledon Institute of Social Policy, 1995).

[29] Letter of Philip Alston, Chairperson of the Committee on Economic Social and Cultural Rights, to Ambassador Gerald Shannon, Permanent Representative in the Permanent Mission of Canada to the United Nations Office in Geneva (4 May 1995).

[30] Letter of Philip Alston (December 1996).

[31] The groups impressed upon the Committee the serious implications of the *BIA* for the rights of Canadians under the Covenant. For a discussion of the implications of the Committee's precedent-setting decision that it had the jurisdiction to signal concern about draft legislation and that it could do so between scheduled considerations of reports, see Craig Scott, "Covenant Constitutionalism and the Canada Assistance Plan" (1995) 6 *Constitutional Forum* 79.

[32] Canada, Human Rights Directorate, Multiculturalism and Citizenship Canada, *The International Covenant on Economic, Social and Cultural Rights: Third Report of Canada* (Ottawa: Public Works and Government Services, 1997) at paragraph 83.

[33] Canadian women's NGOs, responding to Canada's third and fourth reports on its compliance with *CEDAW*, submitted in their alternative report that Canada was in contravention of its obligations because of the repeal of CAP and the creation of the CHST. See Canadian Women's NGOs, *Canada: Alternative Report to CEDAW* (Toronto, January 1997).

[34] See *Platform for Action*, *supra* note 6, paragraph 58(c).

[35] *Ibid.* at paragraph 58(g).

[36] See Non-Governmental Organizations from Canada, *Presentation to the Committee on Economic, Social and Cultural Rights, Re: The International Covenant on Economic, Social and Cultural Rights and Proposed Legislation by Canada (Bill C-76) to Eliminate the Canada Assistance Plan (CAP), May 1, 1995* (Ottawa, 1995) at 9.

[37] *The Limburg Principles on the Implementation of the International Covenant on Economic, Social and Cultural Rights*, UN Doc. E/CN.4/1987/17, Annex, as reprinted in (1987) 9 *Human Rights Quarterly* 122 at 131.

[38] United Nations, Committee on Economic, Social and Cultural Rights, *General Comments Nos. 1–4* as reprinted in (1994) 1:1 *International Human Rights Reports* 1 at 8.

[39] *Andrews* v. *Law Society (British Columbia)*, [1989] 1 S.C.R. 143 at 169, [1989] 2 W.W.R. 289, 25 C.C.E.L. 255, 91 N.R. 255, 34 B.C.L.R. (2d) 273, 10 C.H.R.R. D/5719, 36 C.R.R. 193, 56 D.L.R. (4th) 1 [hereinafter *Andrews* cited to S.C.R.].

[40] *Ibid.* at 154.

[41] *R.* v. *Turpin,* [1989] 1 S.C.R. 1296 at 1333, 96 N.R. 115, 34 O.A.C. 115, 48 C.C.C. (3d) 8, 69 C.R. (3d) 97, 39 C.R.R. 306 [hereinafter *Turpin* cited to S.C.R.].

[42] *Slaight Communications Inc.* v. *Davidson*, [1989] 1 S.C.R. 1038 at 1056, 59 D.L.R. (4th) 416 [hereinafter *Slaight* cited to S.C.R.]. Here, Dickson C.J. is quoting from his earlier decision, in dissent, in *Reference Re Public Service Employee Relations Act, Labour Relations Act and Police Officers Collective Bargaining Act*, [1987] 1 S.C.R. 313 at 348, 38 D.L.R. (4th) 161 [hereinafter *Reference Re Public Service Employee Relations Act* cited to S.C.R.].

[43] *Slaight, ibid.* at 1056.

[44] *Ibid.* at 1056–57.

[45] [1990] 1 S.C.R. 190, 103 N.R. 282, 2 W.W.R. 220, 71 Alta. L.R. (2d) 145.

[46] See *Reference Re Public Service Employee Relations Act*, *supra* note 42 at 348–49, and J. Claydon, "International Human Rights Law and the Interpretation of the Canadian Charter of Rights and Freedoms" (1982) 4 *Supreme Court L.R.* 287 at 293.

[47] Matthew Craven, "The Domestic Application of the International Covenant on Economic, Social and Cultural Rights" *Netherlands International Law Review* (1993) 367 at 397–98. The quote from Dickson C.J. to which Matthew Craven refers is drawn from the Supreme Court's decision in *R. v. Keegstra* [1990] 3 S.C.R. 697.

[48] *Supra* note 42.

[49] *Ibid.* at 348.

[50] Anne F. Bayevsky, *International Human Rights Law: Use in Canadian Charter of Rights and Freedoms Litigation* (Toronto: Butterworths, 1992) at 34.

[51] *Supra* note 46 at 287.

[52] C. Lynn Smith and William Black, "Section 15 Equality Rights under the *Charter*: Meaning, Institutional Constraints and a Possible Test" (24 October 1987) [unpublished] at 1.

[53] Canada, Department of Justice, *The Charter in the Context of the International Bill of Rights* (Federal-Provincial-Territorial Conference on Human Rights, September 1983, Document No. 830-130/022, Agenda Item VII(i)(a), 9 August 1983).

[54] Committee on the Elimination of All Forms of Discrimination Against Women, *Summary Record of the 167th Meeting*, U.N. Doc. CEDAW/C/SR.167 (February 1990) at 6.

[55] Discrimination has been defined by the Supreme Court of Canada as a distinction, *whether intentional or not* but based on grounds relating to personal characteristics of the individual or group, which has *the effect* of imposing burdens, obligations, or disadvantages on such individual or group not imposed on others, or which withholds or limits access to opportunities, benefits and advantages available to other members of society. See *Andrews, supra* note 39. This definition is also adopted in subsequent s. 15 decisions of the Court.

[56] For examples of "poor-bashing" and a discussion of this phenomenon, see Kathy Tait, "Joy's reform worth roses" *The [Vancouver] Province* (5 November 1995) A20; "Beware of poor-bashing rhetoric, advocate tells anti-poverty group" *The [Kamloops] Daily News* (29 January 1996) A2; "Speaking Out Against Poor Bashing" *The Long Haul* [Vancouver] (February 1995).

[57] Edward Greenspon, *The [Toronto] Globe and Mail* (17 February 1997) A2. See also: Eric Beauchesne, "Banker would carve up welfare, health systems" *The [Toronto] Star* (19 April 1995) B1; David Frum, "Splitting social welfare bills has only led to waste" *The Financial Post* (25 January 1995) 17; and Margaret Philp, "Ottawa urged to maintain control of welfare spending" *The [Toronto] Globe and Mail* (15 June 1995) A5.

[58] The idea that lack of political power is a criterion for determining which group should receive constitutional protection finds support in the opinion of Wilson J. in *Andrews, supra* note 39 at 152, and its foundation in United States constitutional law is discussed by John Hart Ely in *Democracy and Distrust: A Theory of Judicial Review* (Cambridge, Mass.: Harvard University Press, 1980).

[59] (1991), 70 B.C.L.R. (2d) 325 (S.C.).

[60] *Ibid.* at 344.

[61] *Haig v. Canada* (1992), 9 O.R. (3d) 495, 94 D.L.R. (4th) 1, 16 C.H.R.R. D/226, 57 O.A.C. 272, 10 C.R.R. (2d) 287, 92 C.L.L.C. 17,034.

[62] [1991] 2 S.C.R. 22. In *Tétreault-Gadoury*, extension was simply the result of striking an age restriction. There have been other instances of extension being accomplished by means of striking a restriction or limitation. See also *Schachter* v. *Canada, (Employment and Immigration Commission)*, [1992] 2 S.C.R. 679, 93 D.L.R. (4th) 1, 3 W.D.C.P. (2d) 424, 53 F.T.R. 240 (note), 10 C.R.R. (2d) 1, 139 N.R. 1, 92 C.L.L.C. 14,036 [hereinafter *Schachter*].

[63] Under accepted principles for discrimination analysis, it is not strictly necessary to point to a comparator group within the legislative scheme. Especially where only a particular group needs the protection in question, it is highly appropriate to look beyond the challenged scheme to comprehend the discriminatory dimensions of a given problem. This was recognized in the case of *Brooks* v. *Canada Safeway Ltd.*, [1989] 1 S.C.R. 1219, 26 C.C.E.L. 1, 4 W.W.R. 193, 89 C.L.L.C. 17,012, 94 N.R. 373, 58 Man. R. (2d) 161, 10 C.H.R.R. D/6183, 59 D.L.R. (4th) 321, 45 C.R.R. 115, C.E.B. & P.G.R. 8126, in which it was held that prejudicial treatment because of pregnancy is sex discrimination, notwithstanding that there is no comparator group.

[64] [1992] 3 S.C.R. 813 at 853.

[65] (1992), 112 N.S.R. (2d) 389 (N.S.S.C.) [hereinafter *Sparks (N.S.S.C.)*]; (1993), 101 D.L.R. (4th) 224, 119 N.S.R. (2d) 91, 30 R.P.R. (2d) 146 (N.S.C.A.).

[66] *Sparks (N.S.S.C.)*, *ibid.* at 402.

[67] (1994), 111 D.L.R. 4th 336 (N.S.S.C.).

[68] (1993), 18 C.R.R. (2d) 143 (T.C.C.).

[69] (1994), 121 D.L.R. (4th) 335, 26 Alta. L.R. (3d) 91.

[70] *Symes* v. *Canada* [1993] 4 S.C.R. 695, 1 C.T.C. 40, 19 C.R.R. (2d) 1, 110 D.L.R. (4th) 470, [1994] W.D.F.L. 171; *Thibaudeau* v. *Canada (M.N.R.)*, [1995] 2 S.C.R. 627 at 675–76, [1995] W.D.F.L. 957, [1995] 1 C.T.C. 382, 95 D.T.C. 5273, 12 R.F.L. (4th) 1, 124 D.L.R. (4th) 449, 182 N.R. 1, 29 C.R.R. (2d) 1.

[71] *Reference Re An Act to Amend the Education Act* (1986), 53 O.R. (2d) 513, 25 D.L.R. (4th) 1, 13 OAC 241, 23 C.R.R. 193 (C.A.) per Robins J.A. dissenting on other points. In turn, the opinion of Robins J.A. was cited with approval by the Supreme Court of Canada in *Andrews, supra* note 39 at 171. Regarding the scope of s. 15, the Court said, "In our view, s. 15 read as a whole constitutes a compendious expression of a positive right to equality in both the substance and administration of the law. It is an all-encompassing right governing all legislative action."

[72] See for example *Tétreault-Gadoury* v. *Canada, supra* note 62, and *Schachter, supra* note 62.

[73] See, for example, *Guérin* v. *Canada*, [1984] 2 S.C.R. 335, 13 D.L.R. (4th) 321 (S.C.C.); *Prosper* v. *R.* [1994] 3 S.C.R. 236, 118 D.L.R. (4th), 154 (S.C.C.); *R.* v. *Askov*, [1990] 2 S.C.R. 1199, 75 O.R. (2d) 673, 74 D.L.R. (4th) 355, 113 N.R. 241, 42 O.A.C. 81, 59 C.C.C. (3d) 449, 79 C.R. (3d) 273, 49 C.R.R. 1.

[74] *Andrews, supra* note 39 at 154 per Wilson J.

[75] In some cases, the Supreme Court of Canada has indicated that a degree of deference to the legislature may be warranted in assessing the minimal impairment branch of the s. 1 test, where difficult economic questions are concerned. However, there is a strong argument that a deferential approach should not be applied where the concerns of vulnerable groups are at stake.

[76] *R.* v. *Oakes*, [1986] 1 S.C.R. 103 at 136, 26 D.L.R. (4th) 200, 65 N.R. 87, 14 O.A.C. 335, 24 C.C.C. (3d) 321, 50 C.R. (3d) 1, 19 C.R.R. 308. See also *Benner* v. *Canada (Secretary of State)*, [1997] 1 S.C.R. 358, 143 D.L.R. (3d) 577.

CHAPTER 5

New Directions

Introduction

Women's aspirations to be accorded equal consideration and respect in economic policy matters are not satisfied by the change from the CAP to the CHST. Underlying this attack on the social safety net are the deeply sexist assumptions that women's economic inequality is natural, that women will be looked after inside the family, and that the poverty of women who are not connected to men can be ignored. Women's fight for social programs and services that will support our aspirations for equality, including economic autonomy, must be redoubled. And women must resist fiercely the placement of economic decision making outside the equality rights framework.

In the face of economic decision making that ignores the needs and aspirations of women and treats economic policy as unrelated to the rights of women, women need to be prepared with a new articulation of the meaning of equality. We need to insist on connection, not disconnection. We believe that for women to move forward, connections must be made: between civil and political rights, and economic, social, and cultural rights; between the future of social programs and the future of national unity; between economic policy and Canada's commitments to equality.

Here we suggest some general strategies for approaching our current problems, some ways of using and making political spaces where women can continue to press for the fulfilment of Canada's commitments to equality and for a more generous future for all Canadians.

Courts and Equality Rights

In recent decades, women have made significant legal gains ranging from the attainment of rights to vote and hold office to the removal of explicit barriers to employment opportunities. It has become extremely rare to see legislation that discriminates against women overtly. But these advances towards formal equality do not mean that women have achieved equality in fact. The ongoing challenge is to close the gap between the promise of equality and the realities of women's lives. Government policies have a major role to play. Some legislative choices promote the equality of women. Others do not. Governments in Canada are bound by the *Charter* and by human rights treaties to choose equality-promoting measures.

One of the ways that women have been able to push governments to live up to their equality commitments is by taking them to court, using the *Charter*'s equality rights guarantees. Before the advent of the *Charter*, women took governments to court, using the equality guarantee under the *Canadian Bill of Rights*. From the earliest days of feminist activism, women have been concerned about issues of economic inequality. However, because of shifts in economic policy directions that are extremely threatening to women, there are new and more urgent pressures to ensure that equality rights guarantees are interpreted in ways that respond to concerns about the material conditions of women's lives. Equality rights jurisprudence is at a critical juncture.

Recent s. 15 decisions suggest a tendency for judges to recoil from challenges to legislative schemes that fail to take the needs of disadvantaged groups into account. This tendency can be more pronounced if it is thought that there are social or economic issues at stake.

During a period when governments are having considerable success in their efforts to persuade courts to bob and weave when economic issues come along, and familiar patterns of defeating legal reasoning are repeated, it is reasonable for feminists to ask whether it is worthwhile to continue to invest energy in the courts. Our answer to this question is yes. But our response is positive because of the way we think about strategic litigation. We think of it as one element of a long-term struggle to overcome ideologies of dominance, and to establish understandings of equality that can actually speak to the material conditions of women's inequality.

Litigation can also be a means of protesting against laws, such as the CHST, which have the effect of reinforcing the inequality of women.

In our view, feminists should use all the spaces that are available for feminist advocacy, and should also push for spaces to be created and expanded. Sometimes the courts are a useful place to be because they provide an opening to address an issue of inequality. Other times the opening they provide may be small, but the reason for going there is precisely to object to the smallness of the opening. Clearly, neither the law nor equality discourse were invented with women in mind. Sometimes the courts are a place where this can be illustrated and protested.

Also important to our thinking about the issue of litigation is what is rejected. We reject a conception of litigation as a tool that can accomplish great things in isolation from other strategies. The most important legal victories of the past decade — in cases such as *Brooks*,[1] *Janzen*,[2] and *Morgentaler*[3] — were achieved because they were preceded and accompanied by an enormous swell of activism, which created favourable conditions for litigation. And it is for the same reason that the outcome of those cases was and continues to be culturally significant. Activists have used these cases as elements of broad-based strategies to shift public opinion.

We also reject the naive hope that any one legal case could bring an end to inequality. Sexism, homophobia, racism, anti-Semitism, able-bodyism, and complacency about poverty are values that are so entrenched in the society that the battle against them does not get finally won in a single legal case. No one initiative, whether it be litigation or new legislation, could ever be expected to carry the burden of displacing a powerful ideology. However, a well chosen legal case can make a contribution to a long-term struggle to change attitudes and beliefs.

Nor do we claim that the courts are best suited to the performance of all law-related tasks. One of the compelling reasons for calls for judicial restraint is that most of us actually do want our governments to govern. But what recourse do women have when legislators are not listening? Regarding the *BIA*, and the importance of national standards, women have made their concerns known to government committees, individual politicians, senior government bureaucrats, the media, and international human rights bodies, so far, to little avail. There are times, such as this, when litigation can be useful to open up an alternative forum when other spaces controlled by governments and the media seem to have closed down, even though the ultimate goal is to prompt government action.

It is important to note that there are important ways of influencing the content of rights besides being a plaintiff or a plaintiff's lawyer in a court case. Feminist interventions in cases initiated by others, such as those sponsored by the Women's Legal Education and Action Fund (LEAF) and by other equality rights groups, are an extremely important vehicle for women's participation in litigation. Outside-the-courtroom commentary and activism are important avenues of participation in the shaping of rights. Approving references to feminist scholarship that figure prominently in many Supreme Court of Canada decisions indicate that this kind of commentary from outside the courtroom can also make a difference.

There are strengths, weaknesses, and highly situational strategic considerations associated with each model of litigation involvement. Perhaps the most important role of proactive *Charter* litigation, by which we mean commencing a challenge rather than intervening in a case initiated by others, is that it can be a way of gaining legitimacy and public sympathy for an issue to which elected officials have not been responsive. *Thibaudeau*[4] is a case in point. The issue of discriminatory tax treatment of child support payments had long been the subject of women's movement lobbying efforts, but not of government reform. However, when the tax treatment of child support payments became the subject of a *Charter* challenge, the wheels of legislative reform began to turn, and, interestingly, the momentum was not lost even though the Supreme Court ruled against Suzanne Thibaudeau.

It is also important to note that the *Thibaudeau* challenge consisted not only of the argument advanced by Ms. Thibaudeau and her lawyers. The challenge included legal interventions by LEAF, the Charter Committee on Poverty Issues (CCPI), the National Action Committee on the Status of Women (NAC), and the National Association of Women and the Law (NAWL), feminist writing in academic literature and women's media, and a sustained lobbying effort by women's organizations and individual women, all of which influenced federal government decision makers and the climate of public opinion.

A central characteristic of the proactive litigation model is the tension that exists between the narrower goal of securing a legal outcome that will provide immediate benefits to the claimant, usually an individual, and the broader goal of securing an outcome, including helpful reasons for judgment, which can assist women as a group, both by providing immediate benefits and by pushing the jurisprudence forward in directions favourable to women. This tension can be significantly mitigated by the participation of feminist intervenor groups. The role of the intervenor is precisely to articulate the legal principles on which the case should be decided, in light of the broader impact that it is likely to have. The intervenor group may even define success in terms of the principles adopted by the court, which will be applied as precedent in subsequent cases. The individual plaintiff, on the other hand, acting without broad-based organizational support, may not even be aware of the broader concerns surrounding an issue, even though the outcome of the case stands to have widespread effects.

Another factor, in any litigation, can be the cautious lawyerly disposition that sees any move away from established legal precedent as a threat to legal victory. Whereas lawyers are trained to make legal arguments based on precedent, the challenge of feminist advocacy, quite often, is to take a court in a direction that departs significantly from precedent. The bedrock of feminist advocacy is not only legal precedent; it is also feminist principles. However, the tension between "winning" and "winning the right way" can also be softened if it is recognized that the hope of securing an immediate legal victory is not the only reason for litigating. Even when the prospects of securing a legal victory are poor, litigation can be an effective means of registering serious protest, thereby helping to shift the terms of a debate. Furthermore, the *Charter* is still a relatively new instrument, and there are a lot of areas in which precedent is either very thin or non-existent. This means that there may be a greater requirement and opportunity for the development of effective arguments than is sometimes thought to be the case.

We recommend against decontextualized decisions for or against litigation. Proactive litigation should always be regarded as an option, with the choice to pursue it or not being based on highly situational considerations, such as resource availability and capacity to mount a litigation support campaign among women and in the media. On the other hand, we are strongly of the view that legal interventions to shape the course of equality jurisprudence are crucial. Women do not control which cases get before the courts. Cases that will have widespread effects on women, institutions, and jurisprudence have been, and will continue to be, brought into the courts by various groups and individuals. Women's presence in these cases is essential.

Particularly since 1985 when the equality guarantee of the *Charter* came into force, women have gained considerable experience in using the courts as a forum in which to press women's rights claims. The record shows that the feminist advocacy work of women's rights organizations can have a significant influence on the outcome of legal decisions. Decisions such as *Andrews*[5] strongly reflect the influence of arguments advanced by feminist intervenor groups.

There are other cases in which feminist perspectives have not prevailed. In Supreme Court of Canada *Charter* decisions, the influence of feminist intervenors' arguments is often reflected in dissenting opinions. But, the power of dissenting opinions should not be underestimated. A dissenting opinion can be used to criticize majority decisions and to mobilize public support for an alternative position. The fact that in numerous equality rights decisions, the two women judges on the Supreme Court of Canada have written eloquent dissents has sent a strong public message concerning the gendered character of some key points of disagreement on the Court, and underlined the importance of appointing more women to the bench.

The history of legal decision making shows that, over time, courts can be persuaded to change their minds, reversing earlier decisions that are inconsistent with equality values. One of the reasons that the decision of the Supreme Court of Canada in *Brooks*[6] stands out as such an important victory is that it represented the culmination of a decade-long protest against the Court's earlier holding in *Bliss*[7] that discrimination based on pregnancy is not sex discrimination. Women fought long and hard for this reversal. In *Brooks*, Dickson C.J. said on behalf of a unanimous Supreme Court, "With the benefit of a decade of hindsight and ten years of experience with claims of discrimination and jurisprudence arising therefrom, I am prepared to say that *Bliss* was wrongly decided, or in any event, that *Bliss* would not be decided now as it was decided then."

But the progress of equality struggles is not steady. It is uneven. Looking to the future, there are particular areas of equality rights law that should be the focus of concentrated attention by feminist organizations. The *Charter*'s equality rights guarantees are in danger of being degraded and gutted by arguments advanced in courts by governments, arguments designed to effectively eliminate the right to equal benefit of the law. These arguments involve three basic manoeuvres:

- constructing hurdles that make it impossible for equality rights plaintiffs to prove that legislation that is gender neutral on its face may nonetheless have adverse effects on women (adverse effects are either blamed on extraneous factors such as nature, or adverse effects are ignored);

- erecting a wall between "socio-economic" issues (social justice claims by members of disadvantaged groups) and "rights" issues (claims that seem to fit more easily within a formal equality framework); and

- reducing the burden of proof that governments must meet in order to prove that a *Charter* violation is justified, and therefore permissible under s. 1 of the *Charter*.

Women must resist these government efforts and push equality rights law to accept and understand women's material inequality as a sex discrimination issue. Sustained efforts are needed to displace same treatment, or formal equality, as a normative equality goal. Equality rights analysis must be concerned with eliminating the pattern of unequal results experienced by women.

It has been recognized in equality rights case law that the amelioration of group disadvantage is a goal of s. 15 of the *Charter*. Moreover, courts have repeatedly recognized that discrimination is primarily a question of adverse effects. However, in practice, some claims have failed because the inequality complained of was not seen as being *based on personal characteristics*.

When tested against the problem of the *BIA*, the pitfalls of the requirement that the alleged discrimination be shown to be based on personal characteristics become apparent. We have argued that the *BIA* is discriminatory because it targets poor people for negative treatment, and the *impact* of that negative treatment has *adverse effects* on women, contrary to the sex equality guarantees of the *Charter*, and contrary to Canada's international human rights obligations under *CEDAW*, the *ICESCR* and the *Platform for Action*. The *BIA* removes protections and threatens services on which women are disproportionately reliant. And, although it is clearly possible to reach the conclusion that the *BIA* is discriminatory in that it "treats women differently based on personal characteristics," this formula sounds superficial, individualistic, and biologically reductionist. It can also distract adjudicators so that the potential of the challenged law to contribute to the inequality of the group is not seen.

Concluding that the *BIA* is discriminatory requires inferring adverse treatment from the evidence of adverse effects. The *BIA* has a disproportionate impact on women, and that impact results from a complex interaction of social, economic, and legal factors, including the gendered division of labour and the persistent assumption that women should live in domestic circumstances of economic dependence on men. The *BIA* does, in effect, treat women adversely. Economic inequality is a social consequence of being designated a woman. The *BIA* exacerbates this reality.

In situations of adverse effect discrimination, the "personal characteristics" formula can work, but only if the personal characteristics of women are understood to include the socially constructed indices of inequality that characterize the group, including the economic inequality to which women are subject.

Women must insist upon judicial recognition that lack of economic autonomy is a central reality of women's lives. It is pervasive, persistent, structural, reinforced by legislative choices, and intimately connected to women's lack of power in fora where economic policies are being established. Economic issues are difficult for women to address politically because decision-making processes about economic policy are heavily influenced by those with economic clout, and, increasingly, they are private. Women are excluded from them. This too is indicative of women's unequal status in the society.

Equality rights law took a big step forward when judges on the Supreme Court of Canada decided to endorse adverse effect analysis as appropriate to s. 15. It is a settled principle of equality rights jurisprudence that discrimination is a question of harmful effects, and that an intention to discriminate need not be proven. However, the issue now is actually applying adverse effect analysis to women's group-based circumstances. This issue is the new challenge.

Judges are having a big problem with the issue of causality. Feminist advocacy must expose the weaknesses of a mono-causal theory of discrimination that requires the rights claimant to prove that a challenged law is the sole cause of the inequality complained of. Such a requirement could defeat an equality rights challenge to the *BIA* on the basis that this

140

legislative scheme is not the only cause of women's inequality. However, this is not the claim. The claim, rather, is that the *BIA* worsens conditions for women, in light of a social, legal, and economic context of inequality in which the CAP was especially important to women. Sex equality jurisprudence needs a twentieth century theory of multiple causation that allows women to challenge the various layers of factors that create the economic inequality of the group.

There is more to say about the question of effects. Women need courts to be able to deal with the fact that a given piece of legislation may hurt men and women, and yet still raise a sex equality issue for women, but not for men. Regarding the *BIA*, it is clear that some men are also hurt by the loss of the CAP because they are poor, and further, that some women are economically prosperous. This picture of multiple effects should not be considered a detraction from the validity of the claim that the *BIA* has a disproportionate impact on women.

In a 1992 case dealing with mandatory retirement, Madam Justice L'Heureux-Dubé recognized that a provision may raise gender issues, because of socio-economic patterns, notwithstanding that the provision has the appearance of gender neutrality. She wrote: "Women are penalized, in particular, [by mandatory retirement] because they tend to have lower paying jobs which are less likely to offer pension coverage, and they often interrupt their careers to raise families. (These socio-economic patterns, combined with private and government pension plans which are calculated on years of participation in the work force, in some ways make mandatory retirement at age 65 as much an issue of gender as of age discrimination.)"[8] Similarly, the *BIA* should be understood as a problem of poor people, including poor men, but also as a gender issue.

Women must build on recognitions, such as that of L'Heureux-Dubé J. regarding the impact of mandatory retirement on women, to establish an understanding of adverse effect discrimination that goes beyond the notion that adverse effects are simply a matter of unintended side effects on a minority of the population that can be adequately mitigated by means of a little bit of fine tuning.[9] The narrow focus of much adverse effect analysis means that it cannot properly address or even perceive the systemic problems of women's economic inequality.

As part of the endeavour of protecting equality rights from degradation, women must expose the choices that underlie economic decisions, rather than allowing governments to sustain the myth that just because a decision involves money it does not involve choices. In short, economics must be exposed as politics. The causal link between laws like the *BIA* and women's inequality becomes more visible and less easy for governments to justify, when economic policy is revealed as a product of political choices. Analyzing the political nature of economic policy is a task for which feminist advocacy is exceptionally well suited, as has been demonstrated by the cogency of feminist critiques that challenge the myth that legal reasoning is neutral and therefore not political.

Also central to a feminist agenda for meaningful equality rights must be the matter of judges' tendency to reject claims for distributive justice. From the time of *Bliss*,[10] women have resisted the view that rights are only about removing penalties and not about sharing benefits. However, these efforts must be redoubled because governments are taking benefit schemes away and persistently arguing in litigation that courts should defer to governments in such matters. In turn, this fuels judicial uncertainty about the democratic legitimacy of court involvement in cases where discrimination manifests as material inequality. And yet, judicial abdication of responsibility to deal with the economic dimensions of women's equality rights threatens democratic values in a way that is far more profound than judicial involvement in economic policy, which government lawyers allege is such a danger. Women's capacity to participate as full citizens in Canada's social and political life is vastly diminished if governments can take steps that undermine women's economic autonomy without any fear of judicial review. It is crucial that equality rights jurisprudence be expanded to recognize that, in relation to women's equality aspirations, economic autonomy interests are no less fundamental than liberty interests, and that for women, these interests are actually inseparable from one another.

Finally, for women to pursue this agenda, there is a practical stumbling block that must be removed. Women's participation in the interpretation of the *Charter's* equality rights guarantees has been made possible by the Court Challenges Program. The Court Challenges Program[11] was established by the federal government as a result of concerted lobbying by equality rights groups who pointed out that the equality guarantees of the *Charter* would have little meaning for disadvantaged groups in Canada unless funds were provided that would allow them to actually use their rights and participate in their interpretation.

The Court Challenges Program has provided access to *Charter* rights since 1985. For test cases of national significance, individuals or organizations representing disadvantaged groups can receive $50,000 to cover legal costs for trials, and a further $35,000 for each level of appeal, or for interventions. However, under the contribution agreement between the federal government and the Program, the Program can only fund challenges to federal laws, programs, and policies. No money is available to support challenges to provincial laws or policies through the Program, and no provinces have made similar funds available, with one limited exception.[12]

Health, education, social assistance, and social services are provincial matters because of the constitutional division of powers. As the federal government abandons national standards, and more responsibility for social programs and services is devolved to the provinces, this restriction is increasingly problematic. Women's ability to use their rights to challenge discrimination in the design and provision of social programs and services is barred by the restriction in the mandate of the Court Challenges Program. Now, persuading federal and provincial governments to expand the mandate of the Court Challenges Program is essential so that women and other disadvantaged groups can have access to the use of their equality rights when there is discrimination in provincial laws, programs, and policies.

International Instruments and Fora

As in the domestic sphere, in the international sphere there is also much work to be done. Strategically, women must have dual aspirations: to begin to use international instruments and fora more extensively and effectively now and, simultaneously, to work on shaping them so that they can serve the interests of advancing women's equality better. We believe that Canadian women have not exploited the full potential of international instruments and international fora to advance their claims for equality. But we also believe that the strength of these instruments and the usefulness of the fora must be built by women, and they can only be built by putting concerted and organized energy into them. It is time to devote attention here because Canadian women need to develop a larger, global understanding of the dimensions of women's oppression, need the lever of international human rights law, and need extra-national fora in which to make rights claims.

There are a number of practical reasons for working at the international level now. First, international bodies regularly scrutinize Canada's compliance with its human rights treaty obligations. This provides occasions when attention can be drawn to the gap between Canada's human rights commitments and its performance. For example, the United Nations Development Programme's (UNDP) *Human Development Report 1997* ranks Canada first, as the best country to live in.[13] Canada falls to sixth place, however, when women's access to professional, economic, and political opportunities are taken into account, behind Norway, Sweden, Denmark, Finland, and New Zealand.[14] Even this sixth place ranking must be interpreted. The UNDP points out that no society treats its women as well as its men. So Canada ranks sixth among other countries, all of which treat women less well than men.[15] There is no acceptable justification for the difference in men's and women's conditions in Canada, one of the world's wealthiest and, it claims, most progressive countries.

It should be difficult for Canada to ignore critical observations of UN oversight bodies on its compliance with its treaty obligations, or rulings under UN complaint procedures. While UN bodies cannot force compliance with human rights treaties, Canada is particularly vulnerable to pressure to honour its obligations because in the international arena it holds itself out to other countries as a leader with respect to human rights, and it advocates for respecting treaty commitments.

Secondly, the international arena is fertile ground for activism about women's economic inequality. Globally, the link between being female and being poor is startlingly clear. Seventy percent of the world's women are poor, and women own 1 percent of the world's wealth.[16] Given this global data, it is difficult for UN bodies, interpreting equality commitments, to place women's economic inequality outside their boundaries. Yet UN treaties are still young, and international jurisprudence is still in need of development. Because of this, it is time to build, with women's NGOs from around the world, a feminist interpretation of the *ICESCR*'s guarantees of social and economic rights that will ensure that the diverse and particular dimensions of women's poverty and economic disadvantage are identified, acknowledged, and addressed as an integral part of Covenant commitments.

Similarly, it is important to press for the application of *CEDAW* to economic policy and, in particular, to policies that exacerbate women's poverty and economic inequality, or fail to redress them. And, as we have argued, it is essential for these instruments to be applied together to illuminate fully the nature and range of government obligations with respect to women's economic inequality.

Building these interpretations of the central human rights instruments is important for all women. In Canada, it can make the instruments more useful for women because human rights treaties can be called upon as aids to the interpretation of *Charter* equality rights. Applications of the treaties by UN bodies to the real economic inequality of women can influence the approach to the economic content of domestic guarantees. Using international human rights instruments and the UN system must be viewed as a long-term strategy. It provides women with another political space in which to pursue the development of the feminist and substantive content of rights, and the internationalization of human rights claims can provide assistance in pursuing women's goals, just as strategic *Charter* litigation can.[17]

There is a third reason for looking to the international level. Women are being affected by a global restructuring, corporatist agenda. It is essential to organize against the manifestations and impacts of this inside Canada. But it is also important to organize against the manifestations and impacts of it globally with other women from all parts of the world, and, in particular, to build the strength of human rights treaties and commitments as a platform from which to attack the sexism of this agenda. Human rights activists in Canada, with women prominent among them, have, through years of work, established that human rights laws are of a special nature and are not subject to contracting out by governments, employers, or unions, except by explicit legislative provision. Human rights legislation takes priority over contradictory provisions in ordinary domestic legislation. However, governments are in fact contracting out of international and domestic human rights obligations, by entering into agreements such as NAFTA and the new Multilateral Agreement on Investment (MAI) that diminish the powers of governments to regulate the conduct of corporations, and that permit the erasure of human rights protections and the further exploitation of women's unpaid and underpaid labour. It is important now to identify such agreements as a kind of contracting out that should be understood as impermissible.[18] At the international level, women can address the contradiction between the global, corporatist agenda and women's human rights.[19]

It is important to remember that until recently, violations of women's human rights have not even been recognized as coming within the human rights paradigm. Because women's concerns have been seen to belong to the spheres of the family or culture, spheres where governments should hesitate to interfere, it has been difficult to persuade the members of the UN, the treaty bodies, rapporteurs, and UN officials that human rights should be applied to women's circumstances. Women achieved a breakthrough at the Second World Conference on Human Rights in Vienna in 1993. The *Vienna Declaration and Program of Action* calls for attention to be given to the violation of women's human rights in all UN activities. In particular, women were successful at the Vienna Conference in establishing that violence against women is a form of sex discrimination and that it contravenes human rights standards.[20]

The first strategy of the American-based international women's human rights organizations has been to link women's rights to civil and political rights. Charlotte Bunch notes that it was necessary to dispel the "insidious myth about women's rights ... that they are trivial or secondary to the concerns of life and death."[21] Women were successful in Vienna because they brought forward individual women's stories of torture, mutilation, and abuse, as well as graphic reports of mass rapes, sexual slavery, and executions of women. They proved that far from being trivial, "sexism kills."[22] They proved that women's civil and political rights to life, to security of the person, to freedom from torture and arbitrary detention, are being violated on a massive scale.

It is time, we believe, to make similarly concerted efforts to expose and protest the massive violations of women's economic, social and cultural rights, and to ensure that women's right to equality is understood to embrace the spectrum of civil, political, economic, social, and cultural rights.

However, to use the international instruments and fora effectively and to build them into better tools for advancing equality, women must contend with some practical problems. First of all, using international instruments and fora is not easy. UN human rights bodies do their work in New York and Geneva, their procedures are bureaucratic and technical, and women's groups in Canada do not yet have routine access to information about events and schedules pertinent to their interests. In the Canadian NGO community there is a lack of information about, and experience in using international treaties and the UN system. The best informed NGOs are those that deal with development issues; they are mainly focused on how Canada deals with human rights in other countries. The women's organizations that are focused on women's inequality in Canada still have little expertise in using international instruments and mechanisms.

This problem is not confined to Canada. There are a number of United States–based international women's NGOs that are sophisticated in their knowledge of UN instruments, mechanisms, and how to use them.[23] But, in general, domestic women's NGOs are not.[24] In Canada there is no women's organization specifically devoted to using international instruments and fora to advance Canadian women's interests, and government support for women's participation in this level of rights elaboration and rights claiming has not been sufficient to permit women's NGOs to consolidate expertise and have a consistent presence.[25]

Also, instruments that are of central importance to women, *CEDAW* and the *ICESCR*, have inadequate enforcement mechanisms.[26] Unlike the *ICCPR*, the *Convention Against Torture (CAT)*,[27] and the *Convention on the Elimination of All Forms of Racial Discrimination (CERD)*,[28] neither *CEDAW* nor the *ICESCR* has a complaint procedure attached to it. The *ICCPR* has an Optional Protocol[29] that allows individuals in countries that are signatory to the Covenant and the Protocol to make complaints that their rights have been violated.[30] The same Committee of experts (the Human Rights Committee) that receives periodic reports from States Parties on their compliance adjudicates these complaints. *CERD* permits its oversight Committee to consider complaints from individuals or groups against States Parties that have agreed to this procedure,[31] as does *CAT*.[32] *CAT* also includes a separate inquiry procedure that allows the *CAT* Committee to investigate allegations of systematic violations.[33] However, under *CEDAW* and the *ICESCR*, States Parties are required only to submit reports to the *CEDAW* Committee and the *ICESCR* Committee on their compliance with the treaty obligations.[34]

The failure to provide complaint mechanisms for *CEDAW* and the *ICESCR* has a significant sexist dimension. Inside the UN system, the monitoring and enforcement of women's rights, so far, lack resources and mechanisms comparable to those attached to other human rights instruments. While the *ICCPR* is intended to address the civil and political rights of women as well as men, and the Human Rights Committee has dealt with some important complaints regarding women's loss of citizenship and other rights through marriage, the many dimensions of women's inequality are not the specific focus of the instrument or of the Committee's work. The lack of parallel and adequate enforcement machinery for *CEDAW* accords women's rights a second class status. Also, when 70 percent of the world's poor people are women, the lack of an Optional Protocol for the *ICESCR* means that there is no adequate mechanism to vindicate rights that are crucial to women, and their interests are devalued. Complaint mechanisms for *CEDAW* and the *ICESCR* are essential.

In addition, however, if there were more NGO involvement, the report-reviewing procedure could be much more useful than it currently is. Too often, Canada's own reports on its compliance with the UN instruments are the only source of information that UN oversight bodies have. These reports, written by Canadian governments, are self-congratulatory in the main, and do not provide UN bodies with the alternative information and perspectives necessary to make critical assessments of Canada's performance. At the current time, the UN review procedures are not set up to give NGOs a clear participatory role. This puts women in all countries around the world, not just Canada, in the position of trying to provide information about their conditions to oversight committees through brief written "shadow reports," often without interaction either with their governments, or with the members of the oversight body.

Consequently, there are a number of practical changes for women to press for. First, it must be acknowledged inside the UN system, and by Canada, that women's NGOs can be, and should be, important players when international human rights instruments are being developed and when compliance with them is being monitored. While the instruments are treaties among governments, people are the intended beneficiaries, and women should benefit from them on an equal basis. The human rights treaties can only be given their full vitality if NGOs have access to effective processes for vindicating the rights that are in them.

This means, first of all, pressing for the development of effective Optional Protocols to

CEDAW and the *ICESCR* that will permit women to bring complaints of rights violations into the UN system for adjudication. After the Vienna Conference on Human Rights, at which women pushed for the development of an Optional Protocol to *CEDAW*, the *CEDAW* Committee in 1994 recommended that the Commission on the Status of Women (CSW)[35] begin drafting an optional protocol. This work began at the fortieth session of the CSW in March 1996, continued in 1997 and 1998, and will proceed in 1999, with a goal of implementation in the year 2000.[36] There is currently a document, full of brackets,[37] which is the working draft of the Optional Protocol.[38] Most of the important issues that will determine whether the complaint procedure will be an effective one are as yet unresolved. They include:

- Will groups and organizations be able to make complaints, as well as individuals who are the victims of rights violations? A purely individual complaint procedure will preclude complaints being made by women who lack information, are in danger, illiterate, or poor.

- Will there be, in addition to the complaint procedure, an adequate inquiry procedure that is binding on all signatories that will allow the Committee to investigate allegations of systematic, not just individual, violations, similar to the inquiry procedure for the *CAT*?

- Will all the rights articulated in *CEDAW*, whether they are categorized as civil and political rights, or economic, social, and cultural rights, be subject to the same enforcement procedure? There is the very present danger that rights that are understood to place positive obligations on governments to act, and those that require governments to refrain from acting, will be treated differently by a new Optional Protocol. If such an approach were to prevail, it would serve to perpetuate the damaging perspective that commitments that create obligations for governments to actually do things are not real rights, and to perpetuate those aspects of women's inequality to which such rights are intended to apply. For women, this is a key issue. It will affect whether the Optional Protocol, and *CEDAW*, can be effective instruments for women.

How these central issues are resolved may be determined at the 1999 session of the CSW.

We believe that women should also be concerned about the lack of an Optional Protocol to the *ICESCR*. As we have pointed out, this Covenant contains explicitly articulated rights to economic benefits and protections, the enjoyment of which are fundamental to women's equality. Notwithstanding that an Optional Protocol for the *ICESCR* was also strongly lobbied for at the Vienna Conference on Human Rights in 1993, work on it has not moved steadily forward as it has on the Optional Protocol to *CEDAW*. The longer the *ICESCR* remains without an Optional Protocol, the longer the division of civil and political rights from economic, social, and cultural rights, and the domination of civil and political rights, are maintained. This reinforces the outmoded view that economic policy need not be congruent with human rights.

NGO participation in the review of country reports must be enhanced, which means achieving standing for NGOs to appear before oversight bodies and participate at both the preparatory meetings, at which questions on country reports are prepared, and at the meetings where country reports are presented. NGOs should also have timely access to Canada's reports so that they can prepare commentary and alternative reports for the relevant UN bodies. Without NGO participation, these monitoring and accountability procedures lack usefulness and credibility.

Recently the *ICESCR* Committee has made efforts to make its process more accessible to NGOs. Canadian NGOs have appeared on two occasions before the Committee and have been allowed to make presentations regarding social and economic conditions in Canada that are relevant to the Committee's assessment of Canada's compliance. In May 1993, the Charter Committee on Poverty Issues and the National Anti-Poverty Organization were allowed by the *ICESCR* Committee to make a presentation at the time of Canada presenting its second periodic report concerning the rights covered in Articles 10 to 15 of the *ICESCR*, including the right to an adequate standard of living. The Canadian NGO presence had a marked impact on the *ICESCR* Committee's assessment of Canada's compliance. In its concluding observations on Canada's report, the Committee issued the harshest criticism ever levelled at a developed country because of unacceptable levels of poverty among vulnerable groups, in particular, single mothers.[39]

The subsequent interventions of the coalition with the *ICESCR* Committee to bring to its attention the introduction of the *BIA* are an example of strategic and proactive use of the UN system.

At its January 1997 meeting, the *CEDAW* Committee considered a report regarding improved access for NGOs.[40] Both the *CEDAW* Committee and the *ICESCR* Committee need support and pressure from NGOs to open more space for the participation of NGOs. NGO participation is vital, and women should demand that they be allowed to participate in such a way that the international rights treaties afford some protection from real threats, and the oversight bodies can provide a venue for addressing women's real inequality.

There are other possible kinds of interventions. The CSW can receive communications about systematic violations of the rights of women.[41] The thematic rapporteurs appointed by the Commission on Human Rights can receive information from women about various kinds of violations of human rights.[42] Also women can foster feminist interpretations of human rights treaties by lobbying the Committees to produce general comments on a particular issue, or on principles for interpreting the treaties. For example, the *CEDAW* Committee recently produced a general recommendation on violence against women. General Recommendation No. 19 on gender-based violence is important because violence against women is not expressly mentioned in the text of *CEDAW* itself.[43] Following this precedent, women could encourage the Committee to produce a general recommendation on women's poverty and economic inequality that would incorporate key elements of the *Platform for Action*.

Finally, it is clear that Canadian governments must provide women's groups with the means to participate in the development and vindication of rights at the international level. At other levels where equality commitments have been made in law, such as in human rights legislation and in the *Charter*, governments have recognized that these rights are empty if, for purely monetary reasons, the most disadvantaged people do not have access to the use of them. When Canadian human rights legislation was conceived, commissions were given the power to investigate complaints because the vindication of the right to equality was understood to be in the public interest, and that lack of money should not be a barrier to exercising rights.

Similarly, when s. 15 of the *Charter* was proclaimed in 1985, the federal government was persuaded to ensure that disadvantaged Canadians would have some access to the exercise of their rights through the Court Challenges Program, which provides funds to individuals and groups to engage in the litigation of test cases that have national importance. It is just as important, we believe, that governments, and the federal government in particular, provide funding to women's groups so that they can engage in organized and strategic work at the international level that will allow them to use their treaty-based rights and participate in the development and interpretation of international human rights instruments.

Women's organizations need to begin to incorporate the use of international instruments and fora into the range of tools they deploy for advancing women, to make decisions about when internationalizing a human rights claim is appropriate and strategic, to have a long-term and planned view of this international work, to create coalition-based task forces or networks for organizing international work in Canada, and to demand that funding and other resources are to be available to support the participation of women's NGOs.

A Post-Beijing Commission on Women's Equality

Canada last engaged in a public participatory process to measure the status of women and develop recommendations for change more than a quarter of a century ago when the Royal Commission on the Status of Women did its groundbreaking work. Some aspects of Canadian women's lives have improved since then; some have not. Women's inequality persists, and some of the forms that it takes now are different and differently experienced by diverse groups of women. Women are dealing now with new threats, such as the impacts of globalization, restructuring, and cuts to Canada's social programs and services. Canadian women are experiencing "backlash," the blood-drawing cut of anti-egalitarian policies and ideology. They are facing cuts to, and closures of, the very services and institutions that they created to move women forward — transition houses, day care centres, women's health services, and women's advocacy organizations. These cuts and closures are being justified on the grounds that feminism, like Marxism, is "over"; there is no more need for it — there is no problem of women's inequality still to be solved. Efforts to bring equality to women, the argument runs, have gone overboard, have resulted in unfairness, and in too much government interference with individual liberty. Formal equality must be reasserted; women should now be treated just the same as men, opponents of substantive equality contend.[44]

We believe that it is time for a new and tougher inquiry into women's conditions, for an up-to-date identification of the obstacles to women achieving equality in Canada, and for a new plan that can carry women into a new millennium with confidence. Canadian governments have made commitments to equality at every level of law, and through diverse programs. They belie these commitments when they indulge in anti-egalitarian conduct, and permit anti-egalitarian ideology to infect the Canadian political environment. We believe that Canadian governments have a responsibility to seriously and publicly engage, with the full participation of women, in an examination of their own conduct, and to reformulate policy and practice to reflect their long-standing and deeper commitments.

Though Canada has made new commitments in the *Platform for Action*, there is no mechanism for monitoring government progress in complying with those commitments. The *Platform for Action* identifies as key features of today's sexism the adverse effects on women of restructuring agendas and liberal market economic policies, and the exclusion of women from participation in decision making. In this post-Beijing era, it is essential that governments take stock of women's real conditions as the century closes, abandon outmoded conceptual frameworks, and develop comprehensive, innovative and sophisticated approaches to implementing their equality obligations.

We believe that a Post-Beijing Commission on Women's Equality should be tasked to examine broadly the dimensions of Canadian women's inequality today and the forces that perpetuate it. We also believe that first priority should be given to examining the impact of current economic and social policies on women, and the conformity of these policies with equality commitments. At the Beijing World Conference on Women, the participating nations, including Canada, agreed that governments should "review and modify, with the full and equal participation of women, macroeconomic and social policies with a view to achieving the objectives of the *Platform for Action*." We agree.

It is time to review economic policies, social policies, and human rights commitments together, in light of the importance of economic and social policies to the realization of human rights. It is time to set aside the assumption that economic policy goals can be conceived and pursued in complete isolation from, and complete indifference to, their impact on women. Rather, new economic policy frameworks are needed that can acknowledge that greater equality for women is necessary.

While we do not purport to provide an exhaustive list here, there are many issues that urgently need investigation so that there is a solid basis for the development of new policies that will be suited to Canadian women entering a new century.[45] These include a detailed examination of the impact on women's equality and economic autonomy of the restructuring of social programs, globalization, international trade agreements, the tax system, family-based policies and income testing, and the devolution of increased responsibility for social policy to the provinces. More extensive inquiry is also urgently needed into the implications of women's poverty for *women*, as well as for children, and for society as a whole. Investigation of the current reformulations of social assistance policies and their impact on women is also urgently needed.

It is essential now to engage in a public exercise that will allow us to analyze the policies that are setting women back, and to design new economic policies that can advance women's equality.[46]

We also believe that while other levels of government should also be drawn into the exercise, the federal government has a responsibility to take the lead. A Commission tasked with a review of this kind must be independent from government. Appointments to it must be made not by government alone, but through a negotiated partnership with women's organizations. Only this way will women actually enjoy full and equal participation and will the Commission have the credibility with women necessary to do effective work.[47]

It is clear that there must be a renewed commitment to women's substantive equality, and that a new mechanism is needed to examine, in detail, the impact of social and economic policies on women's equality and to develop equality promoting strategies that match women's needs and aspirations for the twenty-first century.

The Future of Social Programs and "National" Standards

Shrinking Canada's social programs has been a wholly ideological exercise, designed to shift Canadians' expectations and values, to convince us that smaller government is necessary, and that a collective sense of responsibility for everyone's economic security, education, and health is simply outmoded.

But cuts to social programs are not necessary to solve Canada's financial problems. Moreover, we are now in a "post-deficit" era. The "post-deficit" era has been announced by the Liberal government and by economic analysts, with the Liberals promising to divide each billion dollars of surplus among tax cuts, social spending, and paying down Canada's debt.[48] The question now is whether government surpluses will be used to assist the poor or to increase the privileges of the rich, to further widen the gap between rich and poor, or to narrow it. When, even by their own calculations, governments can no longer plead lack of money as the justification for shrinking commitments to social and economic justice, the battle over values will have to be out in the open.[49]

In this post-deficit era, a concerted campaign is needed to challenge the premises of deficit hysteria, to ensure that it is not simply replaced by debt hysteria, and to ensure that women advance. Though deficits have been wiped out with astonishing (and harmful) speed, there remains a fervent commitment among some policy makers to continued fiscal restraint. Some provincial and territorial governments have enacted laws to cap future spending, freeze taxes, or require a balanced budget. In Alberta and Manitoba, deficits are now legally prohibited. In Alberta, the law requires that surpluses be used only to pay down debt. Laws such as these attempt to entrench a permanently inadequate level of social spending, even in times of relative prosperity. When future recessions occur, as they inevitably will, such laws threaten to put Canadians through the trauma of severe cutbacks all over again because they place governments in a fiscal straitjacket. The reality, acknowledged by a vast majority of economists, is that temporary deficits are not always harmful, and indeed can be essential to maintaining a stable economy. Spending restraint during an economic downturn simply aggravates and prolongs recessionary trends by further reducing employment, personal incomes, and consumer demand levels. Besides imposing terrible social costs, a no-deficit policy during recessions is simply bad economic policy. If we are to avoid a repetition of painful budget cutting, Canadians must overcome the unreasonable fear of deficits that has been cultivated in recent years.[50]

In present times, when funds are available for reinvestment in Canadians, governments must focus on redressing the equality deficit that has been exacerbated by recent budgets. We must now ensure that women advance. This means ensuring two things: that money is reallocated to social programs and services, and that social programs and services are designed so that they will actually improve women's conditions.

The change from the CAP to the CHST has not only diminished crucial programs and services that women need. It has also cut off democratic avenues for women to participate in decision making about social programs. The shift to block funding and the removal of conditions on transferred funds are part of a devolutionary strategy that, far from increasing democratic participation in decision making, or increasing the accountability of governments to the public, reduces both.

It is important to remember that debate about the nature of changes that should be made to Canada's social programs was scooped out of the public realm, transformed into a non-debatable issue, and decided by the Liberal government in the context of the 1995 budget. The conclusion is inescapable that this approach was taken in order to characterize cutbacks to social programs and the loss of CAP rights as a simple and indisputable matter of available dollars rather than as a highly political choice of direction with respect to social policy.

As a result of the budget decision to repeal CAP and move to block funding, national standards for social programs, if there are to be any, are now being dealt with by provincial and federal officials and First Ministers in closed door sessions that are all too reminiscent of the Meech Lake Constitutional Conference. This form of decision making lost any credibility with Canadians, as private negotiations among First Ministers as a way of making constitutional change was simply not seen as legitimate.[51]

At their December 1997 meeting, First Ministers announced that they will negotiate a new framework agreement for Canada's social union. The changes to social programs that are occurring now are as significant as any constitutional reform. There are major shifts in allocations of power and responsibility between federal and provincial levels of government. The shape of the nation is being altered. That shape shifting is accompanied by an increasing importance assigned to intergovernmental bodies — working groups, task forces, ministerial conferences — whose decisions affect all Canadians, but whose work is done behind closed doors and without accountability. Power is being shifted, without public agreement, to forums that are, so far, impenetrable.

Executive federalism is an increasing threat to women's participation in decision making.[52] By executive federalism we mean decision making by politicians and government officials that is carried on outside legislative and parliamentary processes among federal, provincial, territorial, and municipal levels of government through ministerial councils and conferences, and intergovernmental working groups and task forces. These meetings are important venues for decision making, and what happens in them is a key, but unacknowledged, form of governance. Intergovernmental meetings are not only the venue into which the matter of developing new national standards for Canada's social programs has been dropped. They are also the venue for decision making on many other matters affecting the equality of women in Canada. We take no exception to intergovernmental consultation and negotiation to arrive at pan-Canadian approaches to particular problems. What is not acceptable is that this form of governance is private. It happens behind closed doors, out of public view. Decisions are taken without public knowledge or input, and delivered as *faits accomplis*.

This is a diminution of democracy, of particular significance to women whose representation on governing bodies is already inadequate, and whose ability to participate in decision making is already curtailed. Women must find new ways to intervene here, to insist on representation, on public access, and on participation. The working out of the future of Canada's social programs, including the question of national standards, cannot be done in closed-door meetings of Ministers and officials.

Nor, however, should women be satisfied with more of the current form of "consultation" by governments. It is not an acceptable form of participation. When women's groups are consulted, governments too often do not provide adequate notice, or adequate resources to conduct the research and policy development that would make consultation meaningful. Sometimes in consultation processes, women are faced with set questions, workbooks with the desired answers built into them, and invitation lists constructed by governments. Too often, the consultation process is a cynical one, and, at the end of the day, what women say is ignored.[53]

Finally, the future of Canada's social programs is also connected to the national unity debate. Quebec's insistence on making autonomous decisions regarding matters within its jurisdiction is being used by the federal government and by other provincial governments as an excuse for having no national standards for social programs and services in the rest of Canada. We reject this reasoning. While a substantial proportion of the Quebec population has expressed its belief that decision making on matters affecting Quebecers should be in the hands of the

Quebec government, no such desire is expressed by the residents of the other provinces. On the contrary, in the rest of Canada, there is a desire for a strong central government,[54] and strong social programs are a key part of Canadian identity. Quebec is not a block to new national standards. The federal government and other provincial governments are. They use Quebec to legitimize a devolutionary strategy that erodes social responsibility at the expense of the poorest people in Canada.

We also believe that the future of Canadian unity is connected to the future of social programs. Canadians, including Quebecers, have a strong investment in Canada's social programs, both as a practical foundation for a shared community life, and as an element of Canadian identity. Quebec voters, who are strong advocates of a progressive "social project" have less incentive to stay in Canada if Canada abandons its commitments to a strong social union. Even if one does not believe, as we do, that the path to national unity lies in respecting Quebec's desire for autonomy in key areas of decision making, it is clear that strengthening social programs is a necessary step. Progressive Quebecers will not vote to stay in a Canada whose social vision they cannot share.

Consequently, we believe that weakening Canada's social programs weakens the ties that bind the diverse regions and peoples of Canada together. The strength of the union depends on the strength of Canada's social programs.

It is essential, then, that the future of Canada's social programs be worked out in a new way. We believe that there are five requirements:

- New national, or common, standards for social programs must be developed;

- The funding formulas that determine the level of transfer payments to the provinces for social programs and services and the level of provincial spending on social programs and services must be developed in a public and accountable forum; and

- A new monitoring body, through which governments are publicly accountable, must be designed to permit public participation in the development of new common standards and to monitor the compliance of governments with them. This body must be accessible, and it must operate in public, so that women's groups, and others, can intervene, and so that Canadians can understand what decisions are being made regarding social programs and services, when, and by whom.

- There must be a means of enforcing common standards and adherence to funding formulas when governments do not comply.

- Quebec must be allowed to choose whether it will participate in this process and comply with new common standards, or whether it will develop its own parallel standards. However, we believe that there is the possibility of a "social partnership" between Quebec and the rest of Canada based on the adoption of a common set of standards for social programs.[55]

The Content of New Standards

Clearly, enforceable standards are essential for health, as well as social assistance. Because we are concerned here principally with the impact of the *BIA* on social assistance and social services, we comment only on the necessary content of new standards in these areas.

In the area of social assistance and social services, new common standards should obligate all governments:

- to provide assistance to any person in need. There should be no limitations or restrictions based on the reasons for need;[56]

- to provide assistance without imposing a residency requirement;[57]

- to meet a standard of adequacy for the level of assistance provided. This standard of adequacy could be set as a percentage of the Statistics Canada Low-Income Cut-Off for an area,[58] or by the cost of a "market basket" of goods and services available in the community.[59] Whatever the methodology, the level of social assistance should "ensure the health, personal security, and dignity of the recipients and their families, as well as their ability to participate as full and equal members in their communities and in Canadian society";[60]

- to provide assistance without imposing work requirements, particularly for caregivers;[61]

- to ensure that there is no discrimination in the design or delivery of programs or services on the grounds of sex, sexual orientation, race, national or ethnic origin, colour, religion, age, mental or physical disability, or other analogous grounds;[62]

- to ensure that programs and services are designed to enhance the equality of all women, fully recognizing their diversity, and to eliminate their social and economic disadvantage;[63]

- to provide a guaranteed right to appeal any decision denying, reducing, restricting or terminating social assistance or a service;[64]

- to ensure that women participate in the design and reform of social programs and services so that they will meet the needs of the women using them, and be accountable to them;[65]

155

- to provide specified social services, including public child care, transition houses, and legal aid for family law matters;

- to ensure that social programs and services realize the commitments made in Canada's human rights treaties, including *CEDAW*, and the *ICESCR*.

Funding Formulas

In addition to standards to govern content and procedural fairness for social programs, there should be a negotiated standard, binding on all levels of government, that will ensure the adequacy of the funding base for social programs in order to conform to s. 36 of the Constitution. When the federal government's financial contributions to social programs are cut unilaterally, or when a provincial government, like Alberta, decides to limit its funding for social assistance when it has no financial need to do so,[66] a general standard giving specific content to the promise of s. 36 is clearly required.

This standard of adequacy for the funding base for social programs should be able to take into account fluctuating needs, because, for example, people's need for social assistance rises and falls depending on the availability of work. Given the nature of this program in particular, the standard should be formulated in such a way as to allow for variations in use. In any case, the standard of adequacy should provide certainty and predictability.

The call of the provinces for stability in the federal government's levels of contributions to social programs should be heeded. The federal government should not be the only party bound, however. The provinces should also be prohibited from allocating social program funding received from the federal government to other purposes, or from allowing social program funding to fall below a reasonable threshold within their own budget allocations.

All of these standards are required in our view in order to meet Canada's commitments to equality.

An Independent Monitoring Body for Social Program and Service Standards

We believe that there should be an independent monitoring body established, first to facilitate public participation in the development of new standards and funding formulas for social programs and services,[67] and secondly to monitor, on an ongoing basis, government compliance with them.[68] Such a body could oversee an open public process of consultation on the development of new standards for social programs and services, seeking input in particular from those non-governmental organizations that represent women and other disadvantaged groups. It could also oversee a parallel public process of consultation on the development of new formulas for funding social programs and social services. The members of the monitoring body could then participate in discussions and negotiations among federal, provincial, and territorial governments leading to the adoption of new standards and funding formulas.

Once new standards and funding formulas are set, the monitoring body would evaluate, on an ongoing basis, compliance with common standards and funding formulas, establishing social indicators for the purpose of evaluating compliance, and compiling statistical and other data relevant to this evaluation. It could also have a role in educating the public and government officials regarding the needs of particular groups. Most important, as a result of its monitoring work, it would identify non-compliance. Individuals and organizations representing disadvantaged groups would have standing to appear before this body to make submissions regarding non-compliance and its effects. The monitoring body would make recommendations to governments and legislative bodies regarding the steps necessary to achieve compliance with common standards.[69]

Enforcing Compliance

Though this public monitoring body would have the capacity to determine that a government was not in compliance with national standards, and to make recommendations regarding what would be necessary to achieve compliance, this process is not likely to be effective unless it is backed up by the threat or reality of financial penalties being imposed. This, of course, has been the strength of the federal spending power as a social policy instrument; it has allowed the federal government to set and enforce national standards. Despite the objections of the provinces and territories, we see no reason to abandon this. We believe that new common standards, once developed, should be adopted by the federal government as amendments to the legislation creating the CHST, and that the federal government, on the recommendation of the monitoring body, should enforce the standards by withholding funds from non-complying governments.

We acknowledge that the procedure we recommend here would not prevent the federal government from repeating its pattern of unilaterally cutting funds to the provinces, despite established funding agreements. It is our hope, however, that the public nature of the process of setting funding formulas, and the increased pressure from the provinces for control, will make it more difficult for the federal government to withdraw from publicly made commitments to established funding formulas.

Quebec

Because commitments to social programs are strong among both the people of Quebec and people in the rest of Canada, Barbara Cameron suggests that the development of a "social partnership" is possible.[70] A social partnership would be based on the development of a common set of standards for social programs,[71] but would "recognize both the sovereignty of Quebec in the area of social programs and a significant role for the federal government in social programs for the rest of Canada."[72] For the rest of Canada, "this would mean a confirmation of the role of the Canadian government in the establishment of 'national norms' or rights without denying the provincial role in the administration and delivery of programs."[73] Responsibility for realization of the standards would rest with the Quebec government for residents of Quebec and with the federal government for residents in the rest of Canada.

With respect to monitoring Quebec's compliance with standards for social programs, it should be free to opt to have its performance scrutinized along with that of other governments, or to establish a parallel mechanism.

For women, the struggle over social programs is a triple one. It is a struggle to regain ground that is being cut away and to improve social programs and services so they can advance women's equality. It is also a struggle, once more, to force crucial decision making out of back rooms and into the public sphere so that women can participate and have a voice. The flimsy principles articulated by the Ministerial Council on Social Policy Reform and Renewal in its *Report to Premiers* cannot be allowed to stand as the framework for Canada's social programs, nor can the process through which they were formulated. Canadian women deserve, and must demand, more. Finally, it is a struggle for a nation that we can believe in because it stands for commonly held values of respect, caring, and equality.

Conclusion

We believe we are at a critical juncture — a defining moment for women. Will women move forward, as Canada's commitments indicate that they should; or will they, as Canada moves into a new millennium, move backwards and reveal that those commitments are hollow?

The biggest threat to women now is economic policy that, at best, ignores women, and, at worst, relies on and exploits women's inequality. The biggest threat is the seductiveness of the idea that economic policy is apolitical and unrelated to the rights of women.

The new challenge for women is to discredit this idea. In every forum women must insist on a social vision that connects social and economic policy to women's right to equality. There can be no equality for women without economic justice and economic autonomy.

Endnotes for Chapter 5

[1] *Brooks* v. *Canada Safeway Ltd.*, [1989] 1 S.C.R. 1219, 59 D.L.R. (4th) 321, C.E.B. & P.G.R. 8126, 26 C.C.E.L. 1, 4 W.W.R. 193, 89 C.L.L.C. 17,012, 94 N.R. 373, 58 Man. R. (2d) 161, 10 C.H.R.R. D/6183, 45 C.R.R. 115 [hereinafter *Brooks*].

[2] *Janzen* v. *Platy Enterprises Ltd.*, [1989] 1 S.C.R. 1252, 59 D.L.R. (4th) 352, 95 N.R. 81, [1989] 4 W.W.R. 39, 58 Man. R. (2d) 1, 89 C.L.L.C. 17,011, 47 C.R.R. 274, 25 C.C.E.L. 1, 10 C.H.R.R. D/6205.

[3] *R.* v. *Morgentaler*, [1988] 1 S.C.R. 30, 44 D.L.R. (4th) 385, 82 N.R. 1, 26 O.A.C. 1, 37 C.C.C. (3d) 449, 62 C.R. (3d) 1, 31 C.R.R. 1.

[4] *Thibaudeau* v. *Canada*, [1994] 2 F.C. 189, [1994] 2 C.T.C. 4, 3 R.F.L. (4th) 153, 167 N.R. 161, 114 D.L.R. (4th) 261, 21 C.R.R. (2d) 35, [1994] W.D.F.L. 812 [hereinafter *Thibaudeau (F.C.A.)* cited to D.L.R.], affirmed *Thibaudeau* v. *Canada (M.N.R.)*, [1995] 2 S.C.R. 627 at 675–76, [1995] W.D.F.L. 957, [1995] 1 C.T.C. 382, 95 D.T.C. 5273, 12 R.F.L. (4th) 1, 124 D.L.R. (4th) 449, 182 N.R. 1, 29 C.R.R. (2d) 1 [hereinafter *Thibaudeau*].

[5] *Andrews* v. *Law Society (British Columbia)*, [1989] 1 S.C.R. 143, [1989] 56 D.L.R. (4th) 1, 91 N.R. 255, [1989] 2 W.W.R. 289, 34 B.C.L.R. (2d) 273, 25 C.C.E.L. 255, 36 C.R.R. 193, 10 C.H.R.R. D/5719.

[6] *Supra* note 1.

[7] *Bliss* v. *Canada (A.G.)*, [1979] 1 S.C.R. 183, 92 D.L.R. (3d) 417, [1978] 6 W.W.R. 711, 23 N.R. 527, 78 C.L.L.C. 14,175 [hereinafter *Bliss*].

[8] *Dickason* v. *University of Alberta*, [1992] 2 S.C.R. 1103 at 1191-1192, 95 D.L.R. (4th) 439, 141 N.R. 1, 6 W.W.R. 385, 4 Alta. L.R. (3d) 193, 127 A.R. 241, 92 C.L.L.C. 17,033 11 C.R.R. (2d) 1, L'Heureux Dubé J. writing in dissent; McLachlin J. concurring.

[9] This approach is inherent in the concept of "reasonable accommodation." For a critique of this idea, see Shelagh Day and Gwen Brodsky, "The Duty to Accommodate: Who Will Benefit?" (1996) 75 *Canadian Bar Review* 433.

[10] *Supra* note 7.

[11] The Court Challenges Program was established in the Department of the Secretary of State in 1978 to assist official language minorities to assert their rights in the courts. In 1982 its mandate was expanded to support litigation clarifying a broadened range of language rights including those set out in s. 23 of the *Charter*. In 1985 there was a major expansion of this Program to permit support to be provided to individuals and groups using s. 15 of the *Charter* to challenge federal laws, programs, and policies. Because of the obvious conflict that would be involved in the government deciding which challenges to its own laws should be funded, the Program moved outside government and was administered at arm's length, first by the Canadian Council on Social Development, then by the Human Rights Centre at the University of Ottawa, and currently by a free-standing non-profit corporation. Decisions regarding the funding of test cases are made by two Panels, a Language Rights Panel and an Equality Rights Panel. The members of the panels are chosen for their language rights or equality rights expertise.

In 1992 the Program was cancelled by the Conservative government then in power, as a "budgetary measure." It was reinstated in 1995 by the newly elected Liberal government. The Program has received accolades from United Nations Committees to whom Canada reports. For example, in 1993 the United Nations Committee on

Economic, Social and Cultural Rights commended Canada for establishing the Court Challenges Program, noted its cancellation, and urged Canada to reinstate the Program and to expand its mandate so that funding could be provided for Charter challenges by disadvantaged Canadians to provincial legislation. See United Nations, Committee on Economic, Social and Cultural Rights, *Concluding Observations on Report of Canada Concerning the Rights Covered by Articles 10–15 of the International Covenant on Economic, Social and Cultural Rights*, UN Doc. E/C. 12/1993/19 as reprinted in (1994) 20 *Canadian Human Rights Reporter* C/1 [hereinafter *Concluding Observations*].

[12] Ontario was the exception. In 1985 it provided financial support for women's equality litigation by giving the Women's Legal Education and Action Fund (LEAF) access to a $1 million fund. However, no other money has been provided.

[13] United Nations Development Programme (UNDP), *Human Development Report 1997* (New York, Oxford, Oxford University Press, 1997) at 40.

[14] *Ibid.* at 39. The UNDP uses three measurements. The human development index (HDI) measures the average achievements in a country in three basic dimensions of human development — longevity, knowledge, and a decent standard of living. The HDI, a composite index, thus contains three variables: life expectancy, educational attainment (adult literacy and combined primary, secondary, and tertiary enrolment) and real GDP per capita. The gender-related development index (GDI) measures achievements in the same dimensions and variables as the HDI does, namely life expectancy, educational attainment, and income, but takes account of inequality in achievement between women and men. The greater the gender disparity in basic human development, the lower a country's GDI compared with its HDI. The GDI is simply the HDI discounted, or adjusted downwards, for gender inequality. The gender empowerment measure (GEM) indicates whether women are able to actively participate in economic and political life. It focuses on participation, measuring gender inequality in key areas of economic and political participation and decision making. It thus differs from the GDI, an indicator of gender inequality in basic capabilities.

[15] For a brief summary of women's inequality compared to men measured worldwide according to these indices in 1997, see "The Global Gender Gap: Measuring Inequalities Between Men and Women," Press Release, United Nations Development Programme, 12 June 1997. In its 1995 Report, the UNDP also noted that in almost every country, women contribute at least as much labour as men but receive a much smaller share of the goods and services produced by total labour. The value of women's unpaid labour is ignored in national and international accounts. Also, the fact that women contribute so much unpaid labour to every country's economy is not taken into account by the UNDP's own human development indices. See *Human Development Report 1995* (New York and Oxford: Oxford University Press, 1995) at 87–98.

[16] United Nations, Statistical Office, *The World's Women, 1970–1990: Trends and Statistics* (New York: United Nations, 1991).

[17] See Andrew Byrnes "Toward More Effective Enforcement of Women's Human Rights Through the Use of International Human Rights Law and Procedures" in Rebecca J. Cook, ed., *Human Rights of Women: National and International Perspectives* (Philadelphia: University of Pennsylvania Press, 1994) [hereinafter "Toward More Effective Enforcement"] 189 at 193.

[18] For critical commentary on these agreements see: Marjorie Griffin Cohen, Presentation to the House of Commons Sub-Committee on International Trade, Trade Disputes and Investment, "The Social and Economic Implications of the Multilateral Agreement on Investment," 26 November 1997; Marjorie Griffin Cohen, *What To Do About Globalization* (Vancouver: Canadian Centre for Policy Alternatives, 1997); Tony Clarke, *Silent Coup: Confronting the Big Business Takeover of Canada* (Toronto: James Lorimer & Co., 1997); Tony Clarke and Maude Barlow, *MAI: The Multilateral Agreement on Investment and the Threat to Canadian Sovereignty* (Toronto: Stoddart, 1997).

[19] Our comments here are confined to the work that women can do internationally that is specifically related to the UN system and the use of human rights instruments. There is another whole sphere of endeavour at the international level, which is related and overlapping, but not at all dependent on UN fora and instruments — the building of an international women's movement and the development of coordinated and supportive political strategies between women of the North and the South. The work that we propose is one part of that larger project. For an account of international feminist alliances being formed to deal specifically with women's social and economic rights, see Joan Grant-Cummings, "Forging a feminist alliance" *Kinesis*, November 1997 at 5.

[20] Donna J. Sullivan, "Women's Human Rights and the 1993 World Conference on Human Rights" (1994) 88:1 *The American Journal of International Law* 152 at 152.

[21] Charlotte Bunch, "Women's Rights as Human Rights: Toward a Re-Vision of Human Rights" (1990) 12 *Human Rights Quarterly* 486 at 488.

[22] *Ibid.* Charlotte Bunch discusses different practical approaches to getting women's rights recognized as human rights. The first approach is linking women's rights to civil and political rights. This is the strategy followed at the Vienna Conference, and indeed it is the principal strategy of the international women's rights movement so far, or at least of the American-based organizations. It is essential to focus attention on the massive violence directed at women around the world, and the strategy has been successful in that it has elicited acknowledgements from governments of this widespread violence and commitments to eradicate it. The weakness of this approach, however, is that it appears to accept the dichotomy between civil and political rights, and economic, social, and cultural rights, and the subordination of economic, social, and cultural rights. It needs to be accompanied by equally forceful strategies to address the sexism inherent in macro-economic policies that take women's inequality for granted, and permit corporations to profit from it.

[23] These include the Centre for Women's Global Leadership, the International Women's Rights Action Watch, the International Human Rights Law Group, and the Women's Environment and Development Organization (WEDO).

[24] Many women's NGOs focused their whole attention at the Beijing World Conference on Women on the NGO Forum, rather than on the Official Conference. Also, many women's NGOs were not allowed to send representatives to the Official Conference to lobby governments because they did not meet the UN's requirements for attendance.

[25] The federal government has provided funds for women to attend some international meetings. Most recently, for example, the federal government provided funding for 40 women to attend the Fourth World Conference on Women in Beijing. It also supplied funds to support the Beijing Facilitating Committee, which provided Canadian women with information about the Conference and facilitated the attendance of NGO representatives. Women's NGO representatives have been included in some Canadian delegations to meetings of the UN Commission on the Status of Women. However, there is no permanent mechanism for women's ongoing participation in the UN process. Arrangements for NGO attendance at UN meetings are ad hoc, often last minute, and government controlled. Women's NGOs need ongoing access to information about Canada's positions on issues of interest to them, so that they can monitor Canada's interventions. Representatives of women's NGOs need training and preparation to be effective in UN fora. New methods of funding and coordinating international work are essential if it is to be effective for women's organizations, and if women are to enjoy genuine participation in this sphere of political life.

[26] The authors acknowledge the research assistance of Gillian Calder on international complaint procedures. Ms. Calder provided a useful summary of UN human rights complaint procedures and the development of an Optional Protocol for *CEDAW* in an unpublished paper entitled, "Women's Rights are Human Rights: The Feasibility of an Optional Protocol to *CEDAW*." The authors gratefully acknowledge access to Ms. Calder's work.

[27] *Convention Against Torture and Other Cruel, Inhuman or Degrading Treatment or Punishment*, adopted 10 December 1984, entered into force 26 June 1987, GA Res. A/RES/39/46, UN GAOR, 39th Sess., (Supp. No. 51), UN Doc. A/39/51, at 197, reprinted in 23 I.L.M. 1027 (1984) [hereinafter *CAT*].

[28] *Convention on the Elimination of All Forms of Racism and Racial Discrimination*, adopted 21 December 1965, entered into force 4 January 1969, UN GA Res. A/RES/2106A (XX) (1969), 660 U.N.T.S. 195, reprinted in 5 I.L.M. (1966) [hereinafter *CERD*].

[29] *Optional Protocol to the International Covenant on Civil and Political Rights*, adopted 16 December 1966, entered into force 23 March 1976, 999 U.N.T.S. 171, reprinted 6 I.L.M. 383 (1967).

[30] Canada is a signatory to both the Covenant and the Optional Protocol. This means that individual Canadians can make complaints to the Human Rights Committee after they have exhausted all domestic remedies.

[31] *CERD, supra* note 28, Article 14 (1). It is interesting to note that although *CERD* was used as a model for the development of *CEDAW*, *CERD* contains a complaint procedure but *CEDAW* does not. The reluctance of States Parties to be bound by complaint procedures is reflected, however, in the fact that, as of 1 September 1996, 148 States Parties had ratified *CERD*, but only 23 had agreed to be bound by Article 14. See *Convention on the Elimination of All Forms of Discrimination Against Women, Including the Elaboration of a Draft Optional Protocol to the Convention: Comparative Summary of Existing Communications and Inquiry Procedures and Practices under International Human Rights Instruments and Under the Charter of the United Nations: Report of the Secretary General*, Commission on the Status of Women, 41st Sess., Agenda Item 5, Paragraph 12, UN Doc. E/CN.6/1997/4 (1997).

[32] Article 22 of *CAT, supra* note 27, provides for a complaint procedure that is similar to that in the Optional Protocol to the *ICCPR*. However, *CAT* allows complaints to be made on behalf of an individual by an NGO, not just by an individual. As of 1 September 1996, 99 States Parties had ratified *CAT*; 36 had declared themselves bound by the complaint procedures in Article 22.

[33] See *ibid.* at Article 20. This inquiry procedure is unique to *CAT*. All States Parties to the Convention are bound by this Article, unless they specifically opt out under Article 28.

[34] The *CEDAW* Committee faces further obstacles to doing its work effectively. By virtue of Article 20, the *CEDAW* Committee has been restricted to meeting for a period of not more than two weeks annually. The Committee cannot possibly carry out even the limited task of reviewing country reports in two weeks a year. It is the only treaty body whose meeting time is restricted by its Convention, and its meeting time is the shortest of all human rights treaty bodies. While the General Assembly has given the *CEDAW* Committee some latitude recently, allowing it to meet in 1996 and 1997 for two three-week sessions, for example, it is obvious that this Committee needs more time, resources, and status in the UN system to do its job effectively. See *Assessing the Status of Women: A Guide to Reporting Under the Convention on the Elimination of All Forms of Discrimination Against Women*, 2d ed. (Minneapolis: International Women's Rights Action Watch, 1996) at 5.

[35] The Commission on the Status of Women (CSW) is a body composed of governmental representatives, unlike the *CEDAW* Committee which is a committee of experts. The CSW prepares recommendations and reports to the Economic and Social Council on the promotion of women's rights in political, economic, social, and educational fields. Established in 1946, it is the primary UN body responsible for women's issues. While the CSW ensures that women's issues are recognized at the UN, the CSW does not have the same powers of other UN bodies. Although the powers of the CSW are limited, as in its inability to take action on complaints, it was actively involved in initiating a United Nations Decade for Women (1976–1985) and in moving the UN from its early emphasis on codifying equal rights for women to a recognition of the economic, cultural, and social realities of women's lives.

[36] *Convention on the Elimination of All Forms of Discrimination Against Women, Including the Elaboration of a Draft Optional Protocol to the Convention,* Commission on the Status of Women, Open-Ended Working Group on the Elaboration of a Draft Optional Protocol to the Convention on the Elimination of All Forms of Discrimination Against Women, 41st Sess., Agenda Item 5, at paragraph 8, UN Doc. E/CN.6/1997 WG/L.3 (1997).

[37] When new instruments are being drafted at the UN, text that is not yet agreed to appears in brackets. The goal in all drafting exercises is to elaborate a text based on a consensus. Text on which consensus has been reached appears without brackets.

[38] *Convention on the Elimination of All Forms of Discrimination Against Women, Including the Elaboration of a Draft Optional Protocol to the Convention, Revised Draft Optional Protocol Submitted by the Chairperson on the Basis of the Compilation Text Contained in the Report of the Commission on the Status of Women on its Forty-First session (E/1997/27) and Proposals made by the Commission at its Forty-Second session,* UN Doc. E/CN.6/1998/WG/L.2 12 March 1998.

[39] See *Concluding Observations, supra* note 11.

[40] *Ways and Means of Expediting the Work of the Committee, CEDAW/C/1997/5,* 6 December 1996.

[41] The CSW can receive communications, and under ECOSOC Resolution 1993/11, the CSW is authorized to make recommendations to the Economic and Social Council on actions that should be taken in response to emerging trends and patterns of discrimination against women. The communications can be confidential or public, and must appear to reveal a consistent pattern of gross and reliably attested injustice against women. See "Toward More Effective Enforcement," *supra* note 17 at 205. See also Sandra Coliver, "United Nations Machineries on Women's Rights: How Might They Better Help Women Whose Rights Are Being Violated?" in Ellen. L. Lutz, Hurst Hannum, and Kathryn J. Burke, eds., *New Directions in Human Rights* (Philadelphia: University of Pennsylvania Press, 1989) 25. *Supra* note 26.

[42] Currently, for example, there is a Special Rapporteur on Violence Against Women. In March of 1994 "in view of the alarming growth in the number of cases of violence against women throughout the world," the Commission on Human Rights adopted resolution 1994/45 in which it decided to appoint the Special Rapporteur on Violence Against Women, with a mandate to collect and analyze comprehensive data and to recommend measures aimed at eliminating violence at the international, national, and regional levels. The mandate is threefold:

1. to collect information on violence against women and its causes and consequences from sources such as governments, treaty bodies, specialized agencies and intergovernmental and non-governmental organizations, and to respond effectively to such information;

2. to recommend measures and ways and means, at the national, regional and international levels, to eliminate violence against women and its causes, and to remedy its consequences; and

3. to work closely with other special rapporteurs, special representatives, working groups and independent experts of the Commission on Human Rights.

Other special rapporteurs on issues relevant for women include those appointed to the following areas: extra judicial, summary or arbitrary executions; torture; the independence and impartiality of the judiciary; jurors, assessors, and the independence of lawyers; religious intolerance; the use of mercenaries; freedom of opinion and expression; racism and racial discrimination and xenophobia; and the sale of children, child prostitution, and pornography.

[43] General Recommendation No. 19, UN Doc. A/47/38 (1992).

[44] A recent media example of this rationalization can be found in Donna LaFramboise's article "You've come a long way, baby ... and for what?" *The [Toronto] Globe and Mail* (26 July 1997) B1. Ms. LaFramboise argues that feminism has already triumphed because bars do not refuse to serve women, book reviewers do not refer to housewives, and it is legal to disseminate birth control information.

[45] Monica Townson, *Women and the Economy: Long-term Policy Research Issues* (Ottawa: Status of Women Canada, 1997).

[46] See Monica Townson, *ibid.* for more detailed descriptions of these issues.

[47] We note that the government's *Federal Plan For Gender Equality* was prepared for the Fourth World Conference on Women without the participation of women's groups. Interestingly, it acknowledges the problems for women that are being created by economic restructuring, including government cuts in spending, but it provides no credible solutions. In many areas, the *Plan* appears to be a catalogue of what government departments are already doing under the rubric of "status of women" initiatives, rather than a plan that can bring change. See *Setting the Stage for the Next Century: The Federal Plan for Gender Equality* (Ottawa: Status of Women Canada, 1995).

[48] See Liberal Party Platform, May 1997.

[49] Alanna Mitchell notes in "Latest poll may give Klein pause" *The [Toronto] Globe and Mail* (28 July 1997) A4, that voters want to know what Klein intends to do now that the deficit has been slayed. She writes that "... in the most prosperous province in Canada — where surpluses have been in the billions of dollars in the past couple of years and the accumulated debt is almost gone — people want to know what Mr. Klein thinks government is actually for. ... The Klein government has made a meal of its determination to extricate the government from as many parts of Albertans' lives as possible. [But the latest Environics poll] speaks of a populace that wants ... a government that won't opt out and leave Darwinian social justice to rule."

[50] We are indebted to Lisa Philipps for her insights about the impact of balanced budget laws on equality goals and the future of social spending. For a full description and analysis of these laws, see Lisa C. Philipps, "The Rise of Balanced Budget Laws in Canada: Legislating Fiscal (Ir)responsibility" (1996) 34:4 *Osgoode Hall Law Journal* 681.

[51] The fact that the First Ministers were all male and all white did not improve their credibility as lone constitution makers with the women of Canada.

[52] There is an increase in executive decision making at other levels of government also, including at the provincial level. Also, access to public decision making by democratically elected representatives is diminished by decisions like that of the Ontario government to abolish local municipal councils in favour of megacity government.

[53] A current example of poor consultation methodology can be found in British Columbia's questionnaire, entitled *B.C.'s Unity Talks*, mailed out to residents in mid-December 1997 (with a required return date of 31 December 1997). The questionnaire asks British Columbia residents to indicate whether they strongly agree, agree, disagree, strongly disagree, or have no opinion about the seven principles of the Calgary Framework. Any additional comments can be included on a separate sheet of paper, though the size of the return envelope does not encourage complex replies. This is a kind of contained, individualized polling that does not allow for full and complex responses from groups that are marginalized because of their lack of representation among elected officials.

[54] See *Rethinking Government 1994: An Overview and Synthesis* (Ottawa, 1994) and *Rethinking Government 1995: Final Report* (Ottawa, 1995).

[55] Barbara Cameron makes this suggestion in "Social Citizenship in a Multinational State: The Social Charter Revisited" (Paper presented to Federal Constitutions in Comparative Perspective, A Conference in Honour of Douglas V. Verney, York University, 1996) [unpublished].

[56] This was the CAP standard of primary importance. It has been repealed under the CHST.

[57] This is the only CAP standard that remains in the CHST.

[58] See Frances Woolley, *Women and the Canada Assistance Plan* (Ottawa: Status of Women Canada, 1995) at 12; and Sherri Torjman and Ken Battle, *Can We Have National Standards?* (Ottawa: Caledon Institute of Social Policy, 1995) at 8.

[59] Isabella Bakker and Janine Brodie, *The New Canada Health and Social Transfer (CHST): The Implications for Women* (Ottawa: Status of Women Canada, 1995) at 34.

[60] Martha Jackman, "Women and the Canada Health and Social Transfer: Ensuring Gender Equality in Federal Welfare Reform" (1995) 8:2 *Canadian Journal of Women and the Law* 371 at 402.

[61] Woolley, *supra* note 58 at 12. The now-repealed CAP standard prohibited requiring recipients of social assistance to work on cost-shared work projects.

[62] Jackman, *supra* note 60 at 402.

[63] See Jackman, *ibid.* at 403, and Woolley, *supra* note 58 at 13.

[64] This CAP standard was repealed by the *BIA*. See Jackman, *ibid.* at 403.

[65] Jackman, *ibid.*

[66] Kevin Taft argues in an op ed article adapted from his new book, *Shredding the Public Interest* (Calgary: University of Alberta Press and Parkland Institute, 1997) that Ralph Klein knew when he became Premier that government spending had already been reduced by the Getty government in which he was a Cabinet Minister to levels at or below the average for Canadian provinces. "In other words, the severe cuts of the Klein government began on budgets that were already relatively low. As the government's own chart shows, the Getty cabinet, for all its bad publicity, fumbled deals and lousy luck, ran the tightest government in Canada. The Klein government has worked hard to rewrite history, portraying Mr. Getty's government as extravagant spenders who drove Alberta to the brink of financial ruin. Playing on the public's memories of the highly subsidized failures of Novatel, Gainers, Magcan and other financial messes, the Klein government has convinced people that costs under Mr. Getty were climbing without restraint." *The [Toronto] Globe and Mail* (8 March 1997) D2. See also the reply by Jim Dinning, *The [Toronto] Globe and Mail* (24 March 1997) A19.

[67] We note that in Australia an external body of experts, called the Commonwealth Grants Commission, sets the levels of equalization payments paid by the central government to the states. Margaret Biggs writes in *Building Blocks for Canada's New Social Union* (Ottawa: Canadian Policy Research Networks Inc., 1996) at 25: "Another unique Australian institution is the Commonwealth Grants Commission, an arm's-length experts' body, which provides an in-depth appraisal of equalization needs. Although the Commission is only advisory, it has over the years developed a high level of expertise and credibility. ... Since the mid-1980s, the Commonwealth has generally taken the Commission's recommendations as the basis for its offer to the states, which they have in turn accepted. ... It serves to help depoliticize these most sensitive of intergovernmental issues and helps put intergovernmental negotiations and public discussion onto a more objective footing."

[68] At the time of the Charlottetown Accord, the New Democratic government in Ontario proposed entrenching in the Constitution a social Charter. In response to Ontario's proposals, a broad coalition of activists and scholars developed a Draft Social Charter, which incorporated economic and social rights set out in the *ICESCR*. The Draft Social Charter had two oversight bodies attached to it, a Social Rights Council and a Social Rights Tribunal. The body that we propose here is modelled on the Social Rights Council set out in the Draft Social Charter. For the complete text of the Draft Social Charter see: Joel Bakan and David Schneiderman, *Social Justice and the Constitution* (Ottawa: Carleton University Press, 1992) at 155.

[69] In order to oversee the process of setting and revising standards and funding formulas, and evaluating compliance, this oversight body would need the powers to:

• hold inquiries and require attendance by individuals, groups or appropriate government officials;

• require that necessary and relevant information, including documents, reports and other materials, be provided by governments;

• require any government to report on matters relevant to compliance;

• receive submissions from groups who have information relevant to government compliance with national standards and funding formulas.

[70] Cameron, *supra* note 55 at 24.

[71] Cameron, *ibid.*, suggests a social Charter.

[72] *Ibid.* at 24.

[73] *Ibid.* at 25.

APPENDIX A

CONSTITUTION ACT, 1982

PART I

CANADIAN CHARTER OF RIGHTS AND FREEDOMS

Guarantee of Rights and Freedoms

1. *The Canadian Charter of Rights and Freedoms* guarantees the rights and freedoms set out in it subject only to such reasonable limits prescribed by law as can be demonstrably justified in a free and democratic society.

Legal Rights

7. Everyone has the right to life, liberty and security of the person and the right not to be deprived thereof except in accordance with the principles of fundamental justice.

Equality Rights

15. (1) Every individual is equal before and under the law and has the right to the equal protection and equal benefit of the law without discrimination and, in particular, without discrimination based on race, national or ethnic origin, colour, religion, sex, age or mental or physical disability.

(2) Subsection (1) does not preclude any law, program or activity that has as its object the amelioration of conditions of disadvantaged individuals or groups including those that are disadvantaged because of race, national or ethnic origin, colour, religion, sex, age or mental or physical disability.

28. Notwithstanding anything in this Charter, the rights and freedoms referred to in it are guaranteed equally to male and female persons.

32. (1) This Charter applies

(a) to the Parliament and government of Canada in respect of all matters within the authority of Parliament including all matters relating to the Yukon Territory and Northwest Territories; and

(b) to the legislature and government of each province in respect of all matters within the authority of the legislature of each province.

(2) Notwithstanding subsection (1), section 15 shall not have effect until three years after this section comes into force.

EQUALIZATION AND REGIONAL DISPARITIES

36. (1) Without altering the legislative authority of Parliament or of the provincial legislatures, or the rights of any of them with respect to the exercise of their legislative authority, Parliament and the legislatures, together with the government of Canada and the provincial governments, are committed to

(*a*) promoting equal opportunities for the well-being of Canadians;

(*b*) furthering economic development to reduce disparity in opportunities; and

(*c*) providing essential public services of reasonable quality to all Canadians.

(2) Parliament and the government of Canada are committed to the principle of making equalization payments to ensure that provincial governments have sufficient revenues to provide reasonably comparable levels of public services at reasonably comparable levels of taxation.

APPENDIX B

THE CONSTITUTION ACT, 1867

VI. Distribution of Legislative Powers

Powers of the Parliament

91. It shall be lawful for the Queen, by and with the Advice and Consent of the Senate and House of Commons, to make Laws for the Peace, Order, and good Government of Canada, in relation to all Matters not coming within the Classes of Subjects by this Act assigned exclusively to the Legislatures of the Provinces; and for greater Certainty, but not so as to restrict the Generality of the foregoing Terms of this Section, it is hereby declared that (notwithstanding anything in this Act) the exclusive Legislative Authority of the Parliament of Canada extends to all Matters coming within the Classes of Subjects next hereinafter enumerated; that is to say,—

1. Repealed.
1A. The Public Debt and Property.
2. The Regulation of Trade and Commerce.
2A. Unemployment insurance.
3. The raising of Money by any Mode or System of Taxation.
4. The borrowing of Money on the Public Credit.
5. Postal Service.
6. The Census and Statistics.
7. Militia, Military and Naval Service, and Defence.
8. The fixing of and providing for the Salaries and Allowances of Civil and other Officers of the Government of Canada.
9. Beacons, Buoys, Lighthouses, and Sable Island.
10. Navigation and Shipping.
11. Quarantine and the Establishment and Maintenance of Marine Hospitals.
12. Sea Coast and Inland Fisheries.
13. Ferries between a Province and any British or Foreign Country or between Two Provinces.
14. Currency and Coinage.
15. Banking, Incorporation of Banks, and the Issue of Paper Money.
16. Savings Banks.
17. Weights and Measures.
18. Bills of Exchange and Promissory Notes.
19. Interest.
20. Legal Tender.
21. Bankruptcy and Insolvency.
22. Patents of Invention and Discovery.
23. Copyrights.
24. Indians, and Lands reserved for the Indians.
25. Naturalization and Aliens.
26. Marriage and Divorce.
27. The Criminal Law, except the Constitution of Courts of Criminal Jurisdiction, but including the Procedure in Criminal Matters.
28. The Establishment, Maintenance, and Management of Penitentiaries.
29. Such Classes of Subjects as are expressly excepted in the Enumeratin of the Classes of Subjects by this Act assigned exclusively to the Legislatures of the Provinces.

And any Matter coming within any of the Classes of Subjects enumerated in this Section shall not be deemed to come within the Class of Matters of a local or private Nature comprised in the Enumeration of the Classes of Subjects by this Act assigned exclusively to the Legislatures of the Provinces.

Exclusive Powers of Provincial Legislatures

92. In each Province the Legislature may exclusively make Laws in relation to Matters coming within the Classes of Subjects next hereinafter enumerated; that is to say,—

1. Repealed.
2. Direct Taxation within the Province in order to the raising of a Revenue for Provincial Purposes.
3. The borrowing of Money on the sole Credit of the Province.
4. The Establishment and Tenure of Provincial Offices and the Appointment and Payment of Provincial Officers.
5. The Management and Sale of the Public Lands belonging to the Province and of the Timber and Wood thereon.
6. The Establishment, Maintenance, and Management of Public and Reformatory Prisons in and for the Province.
7. The Establishment, Maintenance, and Management of Hospitals, Asylums, Charities, and Eleemosynary Institutions in and for the Province, other than Marine Hospitals.
8. Municipal Institutions in the Province.
9. Shop, Saloon, Tavern, Auctioneer, and other Licences in order to the raising of a Revenue for Provincial, Local, or Municipal Purposes.
10. Local Works and Undertakings other than such as are of the following Classes:—
    (*a*) Lines of Steam or other Ships, Railways, Canals, Telegraphs, and other Works and Undertakings connecting the Province with any other or others of the Provinces, or extending beyond the Limits of the Province;
    (*b*) Lines of Steam Ships between the Province and any British or Foreign Country;
    (*c*) Such Works as, although wholly situate within the Province, are before or after their Execution declared by the Parliament of Canada to be for the general Advantage of Canada or for the Advantage of Two or more of the Provinces.
11. The Incorporation of Companies with Provincial Objects.
12. The Solemnization of Marriage in the Province.
13. Property and Civil Rights in the Province.
14. The Administration of Justice in the Province, including the Constitution, Maintenance, and Organization of Provincial Courts, both of Civil and of Criminal Jurisdiction, and including Procedure in Civil Matters in those Courts.
15. The Imposition of Punishment by Fine, Penalty, or Imprisonment for enforcing any Law of the Province made in relation to any Matter coming within any of the Classes of Subjects enumerated in this Section.
16. Generally all Matters of a merely local or private Nature in the Province.

APPENDIX C

Convention on the Elimination of All Forms of Discrimination Against Women

The States Parties to the present Convention,

Noting that the Charter of the United Nations reaffirms faith in fundamental human rights, in the dignity and worth of the human person and in the equal rights of men and women,

Noting that the Universal Declaration of Human Rights affirms the principle of the inadmissibility of discrimination and proclaims that all human beings are born free and equal in dignity and rights and that everyone is entitled to all the rights and freedoms set forth therein, without distinction of any kind including distinction based on sex,

Noting that the States Parties to the International Covenant on Human Rights have the obligation to ensure the equal rights of men and women to enjoy all economic, social, cultural, civil and political rights,

Considering the international conventions concluded under the auspices of the United Nations and the specialized agencies promoting equality of rights of men and women,

Noting also the resolutions, declarations and recommendations adopted by the United Nations and the specialized agencies promoting equality of rights of men and women,

Concerned, however, that despite these various instruments extensive discrimination against women continues to exist,

Recalling that discrimination against women violates the principles of equality of rights and respect for human dignity, is an obstacle to the participation of women, on equal terms with men, in the political, social, economic and cultural life of their countries, hampers the growth of the prosperity of society and the family, and makes more difficult the full development of the potentialities of women in the service of their countries and of humanity,

Concerned that in situations of poverty women have the least access to food, health, education, training and opportunities for employment and other needs,

Convinced that the establishment of the new international economic order based on equity and justice will contribute significantly towards the promotion of equality between men and women,

Emphasizing that the eradication of apartheid, of all forms of racism, racial discrimination, colonialism, neo-colonialism, aggression, foreign occupation and domination and interference in the internal affairs of States is essential to the full enjoyment of the rights of men and women,

Affirming that the strengthening of international peace and security, relaxation of international tension, mutual co-operation among all States irrespective of their social and economic systems, general and complete disarmament and in particular nuclear disarmament under strict and effective international control, the affirmation of the principles of justice, equality and mutual benefit in relations among countries, and the realization of the right of peoples under alien and colonial domination and foreign occupation to self-determination and independence as well as respect for national sovereignty and territorial integrity will promote social progress and development and as a consequence will contribute to the attainment of full equality between men and women,

Convinced that the full and complete development of a country, the welfare of the world and the cause of peace require the maximum participation of women on equal terms with men in all fields,

Bearing in mind the great contribution of women to the welfare of the family and to the development of society, so far not fully recognized, the social significance of maternity and the role of both parents in the family and in the upbringing of children, and aware that the role of women in procreation should not be a basis for discrimination but that the upbringing of children requires a sharing of responsibility between men and women and society as a whole,

Aware that a change in the traditional role of men as well as the role of women in society and in the family is needed to achieve full equality between men and women,

Determined to implement the principles set forth in the Declaration on the Elimination of Discrimination against Women and, for that purpose, to adopt the measures required for the elimination of such discrimination in all its forms and manifestations,

Have agreed on the following:

PART I

Article 1

For the purposes of the present Convention, the term "discrimination against women" shall mean any distinction, exclusion or restriction made on the basis of sex which has the effect or purpose of impairing or nullifying the recognition, enjoyment or exercise by women, irrespective of their marital status, on a basis of equality of men and women, of human rights and fundamental freedoms in the political, economic, social, cultural, civil or any other field.

Article 2

States Parties condemn discrimination against women in all its forms, agree to pursue by all appropriate means and without delay a policy of eliminating discrimination against women and, to this end, undertake:

(a) To embody the principle of the equality of men and women in their national constitutions or other appropriate legislation if not yet incorporated therein and to ensure, through law and other appropriate means, the practical realization of this principle;

(b) To adopt appropriate legislative and other measures, including sanctions where appropriate, prohibiting all discrimination against women;

(c) To establish legal protection of the rights of women on an equal basis with men and to ensure through competent national tribunals and other public institutions the effective protection of women against any act of discrimination;

(d) To refrain from engaging in any act or practice of discrimination against women and to ensure that public authorities and institutions shall act in conformity with this obligation;

(e) To take all appropriate measures to eliminate discrimination against women by any person, organization or enterprise;

(f) To take all appropriate measures, including legislation, to modify or abolish existing laws, regulations, customs and practices which constitute discrimination against women;

(g) To repeal all national penal provisions which constitute discrimination against women.

Article 3

States Parties shall take in all fields, in particular in the political, social, economic and cultural fields, all appropriate measures, including legislation, to ensure the full development and advancement of women , for the purpose of guaranteeing them the exercise and enjoyment of human rights and fundamental freedoms on a basis of equality with men.

Article 4

1. Adoption by States Parties of temporary special measures aimed at accelerating de facto equality between men and women shall not be considered discrimination as defined in the present Convention, but shall in no way entail as a consequence the maintenance of unequal or separate standards; these measures shall be discontinued when the objectives of equality of opportunity and treatment have been achieved.

2. Adoption by States Parties of special measures, including those measures contained in the present Convention, aimed at protecting maternity shall not be considered discriminatory.

Article 5

States Parties shall take all appropriate measures:

(a) To modify the social and cultural patterns of conduct of men and women, with a view to achieving the elimination of prejudices and customary and all other practices which are based on the idea of the inferiority or the superiority of either of the sexes or on stereotyped roles for men and women;

(b) To ensure that family education includes a proper understanding of maternity as a social function and the recognition of the common responsibility of men and women in the upbringing and development of their children, it being understood that the interest of the children is the primordial consideration in all cases.

Article 6

States Parties shall take all appropriate measures, including legislation, to suppress all forms of traffic in women and exploitation of prostitution of women.

PART II

Article 7

States Parties shall take all appropriate measures to eliminate discrimination against women in the political and public life of the country and, in particular, shall ensure to women, on equal terms with men, the right:

(a) To vote in all elections and public referenda and to be eligible for election to all publicly elected bodies;

(b) To participate in the formulation of government policy and the implementation thereof and to hold public office and perform all public functions at all levels of government;

(c) To participate in non-governmental organizations and associations concerned with the public and political life of the country.

Article 8

States Parties shall take all appropriate measures to ensure to women, on equal terms with men and without any discrimination, the opportunity to represent their Governments at the international level and to participate in the work of international organizations.

Article 9

1. States Parties shall grant women equal rights with men to acquire, change or retain their nationality. They shall ensure in particular that neither marriage to an alien nor change of nationality by the husband during marriage shall automatically change the nationality of the wife, render her stateless or force upon her the nationality of the husband.

2. States Parties shall grant women equal rights with men with respect to the nationality of their children.

PART III

Article 10

States Parties shall take all appropriate measures to eliminate discrimination against women in order to ensure to them equal rights with men in the field of education and in particular to ensure, on a basis of equality of men and women:

(a) The same conditions for career and vocational guidance, for access to studies and for the achievement of diplomas in educational establishments of all categories in rural as well as in urban areas; this equality shall be ensured in pre-school, general, technical, professional and higher technical education, as well as in all types of vocational training;

(b) Access to the same curricula, the same examinations, teaching staff with qualifications of the same standard and school premises and equipment of the same quality;

(c) The elimination of any stereotyped concept of the roles of men and women at all levels and in all forms of education by encouraging coeducation and other types of education which will help to achieve this aim and, in particular, by the revision of textbooks and school programmes and the adaptation of teaching methods;

(d) The same opportunities to benefit from scholarships and other study grants;

(e) The same opportunities for access to programmes of continuing education, including adult and functional literacy programmes, particulary those aimed at reducing, at the earliest possible time, any gap in education existing between men and women;

(f) The reduction of female student drop-out rates and the organization of programmes for girls and women who have left school prematurely;

(g) The same opportunities to participate actively in sports and physical education;

(h) Access to specific educational information to help to ensure the health and well-being of families, including information and advice on family planning.

Article 11

1. States Parties shall take all appropriate measures to eliminate discrimination against women in the field of employment in order to ensure, on a basis of equality of men and women, the same rights, in particular:

(a) The right to work as an inalienable right of all human beings;

(b) The right to the same employment opportunities, including the application of the same criteria for selection in matters of employment;

(c) The right to free choice of profession and employment, the right to promotion, job security and all benefits and conditions of service and the right to receive vocational training and retraining, including apprenticeships, advanced vocational training and recurrent training;

(d) The right to equal remuneration, including benefits, and to equal treatment in respect of work of equal value, as well as equality of treatment in the evaluation of the quality of work;

(e) The right to social security, particularly in cases of retirement, unemployment, sickness, invalidity and old age and other incapacity to work, as well as the right to paid leave;

(f) The right to protection of health and to safety in working conditions, including the safeguarding of the function of reproduction.

2.	In order to prevent discrimination against women on the grounds of marriage or maternity and to ensure their effective right to work, States Parties shall take appropriate measures:

(a) To prohibit, subject to the imposition of sanctions, dismissal on the grounds of pregnancy or of maternity leave and discrimination in dismissals on the basis of marital status;

(b) To introduce maternity leave with pay or with comparable social benefits without loss of former employment, seniority or social allowances;

(c) To encourage the provision of the necessary supporting social services to enable parents to combine family obligations with work responsibilities and participation in public life, in particular through promoting the establishment and development of a network of child-care facilities;

(d) To provide special protection to women during pregnancy in types of work proved to be harmful to them.

3.	Protective legislation relating to matters covered in this article shall be reviewed periodically in the light of scientific and technological knowledge and shall be revised, repealed or extended as necessary.

Article 12

1.	States Parties shall take all appropriate measures to eliminate discrimination against women in the field of health care in order to ensure, on a basis of equality of men and women, access to health care services, including those related to family planning.

2.	Notwithstanding the provisions of paragraph 1 of this article, States Parties shall ensure to women appropriate services in connection with pregnancy, confinement and the post-natal period, granting free services where necessary, as well as adequate nutrition during pregnancy and lactation.

Article 13

States Parties shall take all appropriate measures to eliminate discrimination against women in other areas of economic and social life in order to ensure, on a basis of equality of men and women, the same rights, in particular:

(a) The right to family benefits;

(b) The right to bank loans, mortgages and other forms of financial credit;

(c) The right to participate in recreational activities, sports and all aspects of cultural life.

Article 14

1.	States Parties shall take into account the particular problems faced by rural women and the significant roles which rural women play in the economic survival of their families, including their work in the non-monetized sectors of the economy, and shall take all appropriate measures to ensure the application of the provisions of the present Convention to women in rural areas.

2.	States Parties shall take all appropriate measures to eliminate discrimination against women in rural areas in order to ensure, on a basis of equality of men and women, that they participate in and benefit from rural development and, in particular, shall ensure to such women the right:

(a) To participate in the elaboration and implementation of development planning at all levels;

(b) To have access to adequate health care facilities, including information, counselling and services in family planning;

(c) To benefit directly from social security programmes;

(d) To obtain all types of training and education, formal and non-formal, including that relating to functional literacy, as well as, inter alia, the benefit of all community and extension services, in order to increase their technical proficiency;

(e) To organize self-help groups and co-operatives in order to obtain equal access to economic opportunities through employment or self employment;

(f) To participate in all community activities;

(g) To have access to agricultural credit and loans, marketing facilities, appropriate technology and equal treatment in land and agrarian reform as well as in land resettlement schemes;

(h) To enjoy adequate living conditions, particularly in relation to housing, sanitation, electricity and water supply, transport and communications.

PART IV

Article 15

1. States Parties shall accord to women equality with men before the law.

2. States Parties shall accord to women, in civil matters, a legal capacity identical to that of men and the same opportunities to exercise that capacity. In particular, they shall give women equal rights to conclude contracts and to administer property and shall treat them equally in all stages of procedure in courts and tribunals.

3. States Parties agree that all contracts and all other private instruments of any kind with a legal effect which is directed at restricting the legal capacity of women shall be deemed null and void.

4. States Parties shall accord to men and women the same rights with regard to the law relating to the movement of persons and the freedom to choose their residence and domicile.

Article 16

1. States Parties shall take all appropriate measures to eliminate discrimination against women in all matters relating to marriage and family relations and in particular shall ensure, on a basis of equality of men and women:

(a) The same right to enter into marriage;

(b) The same right freely to choose a spouse and to enter into marriage only with their free and full consent;

(c) The same rights and responsibilities during marriage and at its dissolution;

(d) The same rights and responsibilities as parents, irrespective of their marital status, in matters relating to their children; in all cases the interests of the children shall be paramount;

(e) The same rights to decide freely and responsibly on the number and spacing of their children and to have access to the information, education and means to enable them to exercise these rights;

(f) The same rights and responsibilities with regard to guardianship, wardship, trusteeship and adoption of children, or similar institutions where these concepts exist in national legislation; in all cases the interests of the children shall be paramount;

(g) The same personal rights as husband and wife, including the right to choose a family name, a profession and an occupation;

(h) The same rights for both spouses in respect of the ownership, acquisition, management, administration, enjoyment and disposition of property, whether free of charge or for a valuable consideration.

2. The betrothal and the marriage of a child shall have no legal effect, and all necessary action, including legislation, shall be taken to specify a minimum age for marriage and to make the registration of marriages in an official registry compulsory.

Article 17

1.   For the purpose of considering the progress made in the implementation of the present Convention, there shall be established a Committee on the Elimination of Discrimination against Women (hereinafter referred to as the Committee) consisting, at the time of entry into force of the Convention, of eighteen and, after ratification of or accession to the Convention by the thirty-fifth State Party, of twenty-three experts of high moral standing and competence in the field covered by the Convention. The experts shall be elected by States Parties from among their nationals and shall serve in their personal capacity, consideration being given to equitable geographical distribution and to the representation of the different forms of civilization as well as the principal legal systems.

2.   The members of the Committee shall be elected by secret ballot from a list of persons nominated by States Parties. Each State Party may nominate one person from among its own nationals.

3.   The initial election shall be held six months after the date of the entry into force of the present Convention. At least three months before the date of each election the Secretary-General of the United Nations shall address a letter to the States Parties inviting them to submit their nominations within two months. The Secretary-General shall prepare a list in alphabetical order of all persons thus nominated, indicating the States Parties which have nominated them, and shall submit it to the States Parties.

4.   Elections of the members of the Committee shall be held at a meeting of States Parties convened by the Secretary-General at United Nations Headquarters. At that meeting, for which two thirds of the States Parties shall constitute a quorum, the persons elected to the Committee shall be those nominees who obtain the largest number of votes and an absolute majority of the votes of the representatives of States Parties present and voting.

5.   The members of the Committee shall be elected for a term of four years. However, the terms of nine of the members elected at the first election shall expire at the end of two years; immediately after the first election the names of these nine members shall be chosen by lot by the Chairman of the Committee.

6.   The election of the five additional members of the Committee shall be held in accordance with the provisions of paragraphs 2, 3 and 4 of this article, following the thirty-fifth ratification or accession. The terms of two of the additional members elected on this occasion shall expire at the end of two years, the names of these two members having been chosen by lot by the Chairman of the Committee.

7.   For the filling of casual vacancies, the State Party whose expert has ceased to function as a member of the Committee shall appoint another expert from among its nationals, subject to the approval of the Committee.

8.   The members of the Committee shall, with the approval of the General Assembly, receive emoluments from United Nations resources on such terms and conditions as the Assembly may decide, having regard to the importance of the Committee's responsibilities.

9.   The Secretary-General of the United Nations shall provide the necessary staff and facilities for the effective performance of the functions of the Committee under the present Convention.

Article 18

1.   States Parties undertake to submit to the Secretary-General of the United Nations, for consideration by the Committee, a report on the legislative, judicial, administrative or other measures which they have adopted to give effect to the provisions of the present Convention and on the progress made in this respect:

(a) Within one year after the entry into force for the State concerned;

(b) Thereafter at least every four years and further whenever the Committee so requests.

2.   Reports may indicate factors and difficulties affecting the degree of fulfilment of obligations under the present Convention.

Article 19

1. The Committee shall adopt its own rules of procedure.

2. The Committee shall elect its officers for a term of two years.

Article 20

1. The Committee shall normally meet for a period of not more than two weeks annually in order to consider the reports submitted in accordance with article 18 of the present Convention.

2. The meetings of the Committee shall normally be held at United Nations Headquarters or at any other convenient place as determined by the Committee.

Article 21

1. The Committee shall, through the Economic and Social Council, report annually to the General Assembly of the United Nations on its activities and may make suggestions and general recommendations based on the examination of reports and information received from the States Parties. Such suggestions and general recommendations shall be included in the report of the Committee together with comments, if any, from States Parties.

2. The Secretary-General of the United Nations shall transmit the reports of the Committee to the Commission on the Status of Women for its information.

Article 22

The specialized agencies shall be entitled to be represented at the consideration of the implementation of such provisions of the present Convention as fall within the scope of their activities. The Committee may invite the specialized agencies to submit reports on the implementation of the Convention in areas falling within the scope of their activities.

PART VI

Article 23

Nothing in the present Convention shall affect any provisions that are more conducive to the achievement of equality between men and women which may be contained:

(a) In the legislation of a State Party; or

(b) In any other international convention, treaty or agreement in force for that State.

Article 24

States Parties undertake to adopt all necessary measures at the national level aimed at achieving the full realization of the rights recognized in the present Convention.

Article 25

1. The present Convention shall be open for signature by all States.

2. The Secretary-General of the United Nations is designated as the depositary of the present Convention.

3. The present Convention is subject to ratification. Instruments of ratification shall be deposited with the Secretary-General of the United Nations.

4. The present Convention shall be open to accession by all States. Accession shall be effected by the deposit of an instrument of accession with the Secretary-General of the United Nations.

Article 26

1. A request for the revision of the present Convention may be made at any time by any State Party by means of a notification in writing addressed to the Secretary-General of the United Nations.

2. The General Assembly of the United Nations shall decide upon the steps, if any, to be taken in respect of such a request.

Article 27

1. The present Convention shall enter into force on the thirtieth day after the date of deposit with the Secretary-General of the United Nations of the twentieth instrument of ratification or accession.

2. For each State ratifying the present Convention or acceding to it after the deposit of the twentieth instrument of ratification or accession, the Convention shall enter into force on the thirtieth day after the date of the deposit of its own instrument of ratification or accession.

Article 28

1. The Secretary-General of the United Nations shall receive and circulate to all States the text of reservations made by States at the time of ratification or accession.

2. A reservation incompatible with the object and purpose of the present Convention shall not be permitted.

3. Reservations may be withdrawn at any time by notification to this effect addressed to the Secretary-General of the United Nations, who shall then inform all States thereof. Such notification shall take effect on the date on which it is received.

Article 29

1. Any dispute between two or more States Parties concerning the interpretation or application of the present Convention which is not settled by negotiation shall, at the request of one of them, be submitted to arbitration. If within six months from the date of the request for arbitration the parties are unable to agree on the organization of the arbitration, any one of those parties may refer the dispute to the International Court of Justice by request in conformity with the Statute of the Court.

2. Each State Party may at the time of signature or ratification of the present Convention or accession thereto declare that it does not consider itself bound by paragraph 1 of this article. The other States Parties shall not be bound by that paragraph with respect to any State Party which has made such a reservation.

3. Any State Party which has made a reservation in accordance with paragraph 2 of this article may at any time withdraw that reservation by notification to the Secretary-General of the United Nations.

Article 30

The present Convention, the Arabic, Chinese, English, French, Russian and Spanish texts of which are equally authentic, shall be deposited with the Secretary-General of the United Nations.

IN WITNESS WHEREOF the undersigned, duly authorized, have signed the present Convention.

APPENDIX D

International Covenant on Economic, Social and Cultural Rights

THE STATES PARTIES TO THE PRESENT COVENANT,

Considering that, in accordance with the principles proclaimed in the Charter of the United Nations, recognition of the inherent dignity and of the equal and inalienable rights of all members of the human family is the foundation of freedom, justice and peace in the world,

Recognizing that these rights derive from the inherent dignity of the human person,

Recognizing that, in accordance with the Universal Declaration of Human Rights, the ideal of free human beings enjoying freedom from fear and want can only be achieved if conditions are created whereby everyone may enjoy his economic, social and cultural rights, as well as his civil and political rights,

Considering the obligation of States under the Charter of the United Nations to promote universal respect for, and observance of, human rights and freedoms,

Realizing that the individual, having duties to other individuals and to the community to which he belongs, is under a responsibility to strive for the promotion and observance of the rights recognized in the present Covenant,

Agree upon the following articles:

PART I

Article 1

1. All peoples have the right of self-determination. By virtue of that right they freely determine their political status and freely pursue their economic, social and cultural development.

2. All peoples may, for their own ends, freely dispose of their natural wealth and resources without prejudice to any obligations arising out of international economic co-operation, based upon the principle of mutual benefit, and international law. In no case may a people be deprived of its own means of subsistence.

3. The States Parties to the present Covenant, including those having responsibility for the administration of Non-Self-Governing and Trust Territories, shall promote the realization of the right of self-determination, and shall respect that right, in conformity with the provisions of the Charter of the United Nations.

PART II

Article 2

1. Each State Party to the present Covenant undertakes to take steps, individually and through international assistance and co-operation, especially economic and technical, to the maximum of its available resources, with a view to achieving progressively the full realization of the rights recognized in the present Covenant by all appropriate means, including particularly the adoption of legislative measures.

2. The States Parties to the present Covenant undertake to guarantee that the rights enunciated in the present Covenant will be exercised without discrimination of any kind as to race, colour, sex, language, religion, political or other opinion, national or social origin, property, birth or other status.

3. Developing countries, with due regard to human rights and their national economy, may determine to what extent they would guarantee the economic rights recognized in the present Covenant to non-nationals.

Article 3

The States Parties to the present Covenant undertake to ensure the equal right of men and women to the enjoyment of all economic, social and cultural rights set forth in the present Covenant.

Article 4

The States Parties to the present Covenant recognize that, in the enjoyment of those rights provided by the State in conformity with the present Covenant, the State may subject such rights only to such limitations as are determined by law only in so far as this may be compatible with the nature of these rights and solely for the purpose of promoting the general welfare in a democratic society.

Article 5

1.   Nothing in the present Covenant may be interpreted as implying for any State, group or person any right to engage in any activity or to perform any act aimed at the destruction of any of the rights or freedoms recognized herein, or at their limitation to a greater extent than is provided for in the present Covenant.

2.   No restriction upon or derogation from any of the fundamental human rights recognized or existing in any country in virtue of law, conventions, regulations or custom shall be admitted on the pretext that the present Covenant does not recognize such rights or that it recognizes them to a lesser extent.

PART III

Article 6

1.   The States Parties to the present Covenant recognize the right to work, which includes the right of everyone to the opportunity to gain his living by work which he freely chooses or accepts, and will take appropriate steps to safeguard this right.

2.   The steps to be taken by a State Party to the present Covenant to achieve the full realization of this right shall include technical and vocational guidance and training programmes, policies and techniques to achieve steady economic, social and cultural development and full and productive employment under conditions safeguarding fundamental political and economic freedoms to the individual.

Article 7

The States Parties to the present Covenant recognize the right of everyone to the enjoyment of just and favourable conditions of work which ensure, in particular:

(a) Remuneration which provides all workers, as a minimum, with:
(i) Fair wages and equal remuneration for work of equal value without distinction of any kind, in particular women being guaranteed conditions of work not inferior to those enjoyed by men, with equal pay for equal work;
(ii) A decent living for themselves and their families in accordance with the provisions of the present Covenant;

(b) Safe and healthy working conditions;

(c) Equal opportunity for everyone to be promoted in his employment to an appropriate higher level, subject to no considerations other than those of seniority and competence;

(d) Rest, leisure and reasonable limitation of working hours and periodic holidays with pay, as well as remuneration for public holidays.

Article 8

1. The States Parties to the present Covenant undertake to ensure:

(*a*) The right of everyone to form trade unions and join the trade union of his choice, subject only to the rules of the organization concerned, for the promotion and protection of his economic and social interests. No restrictions may be placed on the exercise of this right other than those prescribed by law and which are necessary in a democratic society in the interests of national security or public order or for the protection of the rights and freedoms of others;

(*b*) The right of trade unions to establish national federations or confederations and the right of the latter to form or join international trade-union organizations;

(*c*) The right of trade unions to function freely subject to no limitations other than those prescribed by law and which are necessary in a democratic society in the interests of national security or public order or for the protection of the rights and freedoms of others;

(*d*) The right to strike, provided that it is exercised in conformity with the laws of the particular country.

2. This article shall not prevent the imposition of lawful restrictions on the exercise of these rights by members of the armed forces or of the police or of the administration of the State.

3. Nothing in this article shall authorize States Parties to the International Labour Organisation Convention of 1948 concerning Freedom of Association and Protection of the Right to Organize to take legislative measures which would prejudice, or apply the law in such a manner as would prejudice, the guarantees provided for in that Convention.

Article 9

The States Parties to the present Covenant recognize the right of everyone to social security, including social insurance.

Article 10

The States Parties to the present Covenant recognize that:

1. The widest possible protection and assistance should be accorded to the family, which is the natural and fundamental group unit of society, particularly for its establishment and while it is responsible for the care and education of dependent children. Marriage must be entered into with the free consent of the intending spouses.

2. Special protection should be accorded to mothers during a reasonable period before and after childbirth. During such period working mothers should be accorded paid leave or leave with adequate social security benefits.

3. Special measures of protection and assistance should be taken on behalf of all children and young persons without any discrimination for reasons of parentage or other conditions. Children and young persons should be protected from economic and social exploitation. Their employment in work harmful to their morals or health or dangerous to life or likely to hamper their normal development should be punishable by law. States should also set age limits below which the paid employment of child labour should be prohibited and punishable by law.

Article 11

1. The States Parties to the present Covenant recognize the right of everyone to an adequate standard of living for himself and his family, including adequate food, clothing and housing, and to the continuous improvement of living conditions. The States Parties will

take appropriate steps to ensure the realization of this right, recognizing to this effect the essential importance of international co-operation based on free consent.

2. The States Parties to the present Covenant, recognizing the fundamental right of everyone to be free from hunger, shall take, individually and through international co-operation, the measures, including specific programmes, which are needed:

(*a*) To improve methods of production, conservation and distribution of food by making full use of technical and scientific knowledge, by disseminating knowledge of the principles of nutrition and by developing or reforming agrarian systems in such a way as to achieve the most efficient development and utilization of natural resources;

(*b*) Taking into account the problems of both food-importing and food-exporting countries, to ensure an equitable distribution of world food supplies in relation to need.

Article 12

1. The States Parties to the present Covenant recognize the right of everyone to the enjoyment of the highest attainable standard of physical and mental health.

2. The steps to be taken by the States Parties to the present Covenant to achieve the full realization of this right shall include those necessary for:

(*a*) The provision for the reduction of the stillbirth-rate and of infant mortality and for the healthy development of the child;

(*b*) The improvement of all aspects of environmental and industrial hygiene;

(*c*) The prevention, treatment and control of epidemic, endemic, occupational and other diseases;

(*d*) The creation of conditions which would assure to all medical service and medical attention in the event of sickness.

Article 13

1. The States Parties to the present Covenant recognize the right of everyone to education. They agree that education shall be directed to the full development of the human personality and the sense of its dignity, and shall strengthen the respect for human rights and fundamental freedoms. They further agree that education shall enable all persons to participate effectively in a free society, promote understanding, tolerance and friendship among all nations and all racial, ethnic or religious groups, and further the activities of the United Nations for the maintenance of peace.

2. The States Parties to the present Covenant recognize that, with a view to achieving the full realization of this right:

(*a*) Primary education shall be compulsory and available free to all;

(*b*) Secondary education in its different forms, including technical and vocational secondary education, shall be made generally available and accessible to all by every appropriate means, and in particular by the progressive introduction of free education;

(*c*) Higher education shall be made equally accessible to all, on the basis of capacity, by every appropriate means, and in particular by the progressive introduction of free education;

(*d*) Fundamental education shall be encouraged or intensified as far as possible for those persons who have not received or completed the whole period of their primary education;

(*e*) The development of a system of schools at all levels shall be actively pursued, an adequate fellowship system shall be established, and the material conditions of teaching staff shall be continuously improved.

3.   The States Parties to the present Covenant undertake to have respect for the liberty of parents and, when applicable, legal guardians to choose for their children schools, other than those established by the public authorities, which conform to such minimum educational standards as may be laid down or approved by the State and to ensure the religious and moral education of their children in conformity with their own convictions.

4.   No part of this article shall be construed so as to interfere with the liberty of individuals and bodies to establish and direct educational institutions, subject always to the observance of the principles set forth in paragraph 1 of this article and to the requirement that the education given in such institutions shall conform to such minimum standards as may be laid down by the State.

Article 14

Each State Party to the present Covenant which, at the time of becoming a Party, has not been able to secure in its metropolitan territory or other territories under its jurisdiction compulsory primary education, free of charge, undertakes, within two years, to work out and adopt a detailed plan of action for the progressive implementation, within a reasonable number of years, to be fixed in the plan, of the principle of compulsory education free of charge for all.

Article 15

1.   The States Parties to the present Covenant recognize the right of everyone:
   (*a*) To take part in cultural life;
   (*b*) To enjoy the benefits of scientific progress and its applications;
   (*c*) To benefit from the protection of the moral and material interests resulting from any scientific, literary or artistic production of which he is the author.

2.   The steps to be taken by the States Parties to the present Covenant to achieve the full realization of this right shall include those necessary for the conservation, the development and the diffusion of science and culture.

3.   The States Parties to the present Covenant undertake to respect the freedom indispensable for scientific research and creative activity.

4.   The States Parties to the present Covenant recognize the benefits to be derived from the encouragement and development of international contacts and co-operation in the scientific and cultural fields.

PART IV

Article 16

1.   The States Parties to the present Covenant undertake to submit in conformity with this part of the Covenant reports on the measures which they have adopted and the progress made in achieving the observance of the rights recognized herein.

2.   (*a*) All reports shall be submitted to the Secretary-General of the United Nations, who shall transmit copies to the Economic and Social Council for consideration in accordance with the provisions of the present Covenant;

(*b*) The Secretary-General of the United Nations shall also transmit to the specialized agencies copies of the reports, or any relevant parts therefrom, from States Parties to the present Covenant which are also members of these specialized agencies in so far as these reports, or parts therefrom, relate to any matters which fall within the responsibilities of the said agencies in accordance with their constitutional instruments.

Article 17

1. The States Parties to the present Covenant shall furnish their reports in stages, in accordance with a programme to be established by the Economic and Social Council within one year of the entry into force of the present Covenant after consultation with the States Parties and the specialized agencies concerned.
2. Reports may indicate factors and difficulties affecting the degree of fulfilment of obligations under the present Covenant.
3. Where relevant information has previously been furnished to the United Nations or to any specialized agency by any State Party to the present Covenant, it will not be necessary to reproduce that information, but a precise reference to the information so furnished will suffice.

Article 18

Pursuant to its responsibilities under the Charter of the United Nations in the field of human rights and fundamental freedoms, the Economic and Social Council may make arrangements with the specialized agencies in respect of their reporting to it on the progress made in achieving the observance of the provisions of the present Covenant falling within the scope of their activities. These reports may include particulars of decisions and recommendations on such implementation adopted by their competent organs.

Article 19

The Economic and Social Council may transmit to the Commission on Human Rights for study and general recommendation or, as appropriate, for information the reports concerning human rights submitted by States in accordance with articles 16 and 17, and those concerning human rights submitted by the specialized agencies in accordance with article 18.

Article 20

The States Parties to the present Covenant and the specialized agencies concerned may submit comments to the Economic and Social Council on any general recommendation under article 19 or reference to such general recommendation in any report of the Commission on Human Rights or any documentation referred to therein.

Article 21

The Economic and Social Council may submit from time to time to the General Assembly reports with recommendations of a general nature and a summary of the information received from the States Parties to the present Covenant and the specialized agencies on the measures taken and the progress made in achieving general observance of the rights recognized in the present Covenant.

Article 22

The Economic and Social Council may bring to the attention of other organs of the United Nations, their subsidiary organs and specialized agencies concerned with furnishing technical assistance any matters arising out of the reports referred to in this part of the present Covenant which may assist such bodies in deciding, each within its field of competence, on the advisability of international measures likely to contribute to the effective progressive implementation of the present Covenant.

Article 23

The States Parties to the present Covenant agree that international action for the achievement of the rights recognized in the present Covenant includes such methods as the conclusion of conventions, the adoption of recommendations, the furnishing of technical assistance and the holding of regional meetings and technical meetings for the purpose of consultation and study organized in conjunction with the Governments concerned.

Article 24

Nothing in the present Covenant shall be interpreted as impairing the provisions of the Charter of the United Nations and of the constitutions of the specialized agencies which define the respective responsibilities of the various organs of the United Nations and of the specialized agencies in regard to the matters dealt with in the present Covenant.

Article 25

Nothing in the present Covenant shall be interpreted as impairing the inherent right of all peoples to enjoy and utilize fully and freely their natural wealth and resources.

PART V

Article 26

1.   The present Covenant is open for signature by any State Member of the United Nations or member of any of its specialized agencies, by any State Party to the Statute of the International Court of Justice, and by any other State which has been invited by the General Assembly of the United Nations to become a party to the present Covenant.
2.   The present Covenant is subject to ratification. Instruments of ratification shall be deposited with the Secretary-General of the United Nations.
3.   The present Covenant shall be open to accession by any State referred to in paragraph 1 of this article.
4.   Accession shall be effected by the deposit of an instrument of accession with the Secretary-General of the United Nations.
5.   The Secretary-General of the United Nations shall inform all States which have signed the present Covenant or acceded to it of the deposit of each instrument of ratification or accession.

Article 27

1.   The present Covenant shall enter into force three months after the date of the deposit with the Secretary-General of the United Nations of the thirty-fifth instrument of ratification or instrument of accession.

2.   For each State ratifying the present Covenant or acceding to it after the deposit of the thirty-fifth instrument of ratification or instrument of accession, the present Covenant shall enter into force three months after the date of the deposit of its own instrument of ratification or instrument of accession.

Article 28

The provisions of the present Covenant shall extend to all parts of federal States without any limitations or exceptions.

Article 29

1.   Any State Party to the present Covenant may propose an amendment and file it with the Secretary-General of the United Nations. The Secretary-General shall thereupon communicate any proposed amendments to the States Parties to the present Covenant with a request that they notify him whether they favour a conference of States Parties for the purpose of considering and voting upon the proposals. In the event that at least one third of the States Parties favours such a conference, the Secretary-General shall convene the conference under the auspices of the United Nations. Any amendment adopted by a majority of the States Parties present and voting at the conference shall be submitted to the General Assembly of the United Nations for approval.

2.   Amendments shall come into force when they have been approved by the General Assembly of the United Nations and accepted by a two-thirds majority of the States Parties to the present Covenant in accordance with their respective constitutional processes.

3.   When amendments come into force they shall be binding on those States Parties which have accepted them, other States Parties still being bound by the provisions of the present Covenant and any earlier amendment which they have accepted.

Article 30

Irrespective of the notifications made under article 26, paragraph 5, the Secretary-General of the United Nations shall inform all States referred to in paragraph 1 of the same article of the following particulars:

(*a*) Signatures, ratifications and accessions under article 26;

(*b*) The date of the entry into force of the present Covenant under article 27 and the date of the entry into force of any amendments under article 29.

Article 31

1.   The present Covenant, of which the Chinese, English, French, Russian and Spanish texts are equally authentic, shall be deposited in the archives of the United Nations.

2.   The Secretary-General of the United Nations shall transmit certified copies of the present Covenant to all States referred to in article 26.

The Beijing Declaration
and
The Platform for Action

Fourth World Conference on Women
Beijing, China
4-15 September 1995

STRATEGIC OBJECTIVES
AND ACTIONS

45. In each critical area of concern, the problem is diagnosed and strategic objectives are proposed with concrete actions to be taken by various actors in order to achieve those objectives. The strategic objectives are derived from the critical areas of concern and specific actions to be taken to achieve them cut across the boundaries of equality, development and peace - the goals of the Nairobi Forward-looking Strategies for the Advancement of Women - and reflect their interdependence. The objectives and actions are interlinked, of high priority and mutually reinforcing. The Platform for Action is intended to improve the situation of all women, without exception, who often face similar barriers, while special attention should be given to groups that are the most disadvantaged.

46. The Platform for Action recognizes that women face barriers to full equality and advancement because of such factors as their race, age, language, ethnicity, culture, religion or disability, because they are indigenous women or because of other status. Many women encounter specific obstacles related to their family status, particularly as single parents; and to their socio-economic status, including their living conditions in rural, isolated or impoverished areas. Additional barriers also exist for refugee women, other displaced women, including internally displaced women as well as for immigrant women and migrant women, including women migrant workers. Many women are also particularly affected by environmental disasters, serious and infectious diseases and various forms of violence against women.

A. Women and poverty

47. More than 1 billion people in the world today, the great majority of whom are women, live in unacceptable conditions of poverty, mostly in the developing countries. Poverty has various causes, including structural ones. Poverty is a complex, multidimensional problem, with origins in both the national and international domains. The globalization of the world's economy and the deepening interdependence among nations present challenges and opportunities for sustained economic growth and development, as well as risks and uncertainties for the future of the world economy. The uncertain global economic climate has been accompanied by economic restructuring as well as, in a certain number of countries, persistent, unmanageable levels of external debt and structural adjustment programmes. In addition, all types of conflict, dis-

placement of people and environmental degradation have undermined the capacity of Governments to meet the basic needs of their populations. Transformations in the world economy are profoundly changing the parameters of social development in all countries. One significant trend has been the increased poverty of women, the extent of which varies from region to region. The gender disparities in economic power-sharing are also an important contributing factor to the poverty of women. Migration and consequent changes in family structures have placed additional burdens on women, especially those who provide for several dependants. Macroeconomic policies need rethinking and reformulation to address such trends. These policies focus almost exclusively on the formal sector. They also tend to impede the initiatives of women and fail to consider the differential impact on women and men. The application of gender analysis to a wide range of policies and programmes is therefore critical to poverty reduction strategies. In order to eradicate poverty and achieve sustainable development, women and men must participate fully and equally in the formulation of macroeconomic and social policies and strategies for the eradication of poverty. The eradication of poverty cannot be accomplished through anti-poverty programmes alone but will require democratic participation and changes in economic structures in order to ensure access for all women to resources, opportunities and public services. Poverty has various manifestations, including lack of income and productive resources sufficient to ensure a sustainable livelihood; hunger and malnutrition; ill health; limited or lack of access to education and other basic services; increasing morbidity and mortality from illness; homelessness and inadequate housing; unsafe environments; and social discrimination and exclusion. It is also characterized by lack of participation in decision-making and in civil, social and cultural life. It occurs in all countries - as mass poverty in many developing countries and as pockets of poverty amidst wealth in developed countries. Poverty may be caused by an economic recession that results in loss of livelihood or by disaster or conflict. There is also the poverty of low-wage workers and the utter destitution of people who fall outside family support systems, social institutions and safety nets.

48. In the past decade the number of women living in poverty has increased disproportionately to the number of men, particularly in the developing countries. The feminization of poverty has also recently become a significant problem in the countries with economies in transition as a short-term consequence of the process of political, economic and social transformation. In addition to economic factors, the rigidity of socially ascribed gender roles and women's limited access to power, education, training and productive resources as well as other emerging factors that may lead to insecurity for families are also responsible. The failure to adequately mainstream a gender perspective in all economic analysis and planning and to address the structural causes of poverty is also a contributing factor.

49. Women contribute to the economy and to combating poverty through both remunerated and unremunerated work at home, in the community and in the workplace. The empowerment of women is a critical factor in the eradication of poverty.

50. While poverty affects households as a whole, because of the gender division of labour and responsibilities for household welfare, women bear a disproportionate burden, attempting to manage household consumption and production

under conditions of increasing scarcity. Poverty is particularly acute for women living in rural households.

51. Women's poverty is directly related to the absence of economic opportunities and autonomy, lack of access to economic resources, including credit, land ownership and inheritance, lack of access to education and support services and their minimal participation in the decision-making process. Poverty can also force women into situations in which they are vulnerable to sexual exploitation.

52. In too many countries, social welfare systems do not take sufficient account of the specific conditions of women living in poverty, and there is a tendency to scale back the services provided by such systems. The risk of falling into poverty is greater for women than for men, particularly in old age, where social security systems are based on the principle of continuous remunerated employment. In some cases, women do not fulfil this requirement because of interruptions in their work, due to the unbalanced distribution of remunerated and unremunerated work. Moreover, older women also face greater obstacles to labour-market re-entry.

53. In many developed countries, where the level of general education and professional training of women and men are similar and where systems of protection against discrimination are available, in some sectors the economic transformations of the past decade have strongly increased either the unemployment of women or the precarious nature of their employment. The proportion of women among the poor has consequently increased. In countries with a high level of school enrolment of girls, those who leave the educational system the earliest, without any qualification, are among the most vulnerable in the labour market.

54. In countries with economies in transition and in other countries undergoing fundamental political, economic and social transformations, these transformations have often led to a reduction in women's income or to women being deprived of income.

55. Particularly in developing countries, the productive capacity of women should be increased through access to capital, resources, credit, land, technology, information, technical assistance and training so as to raise their income and improve nutrition, education, health care and status within the household. The release of women's productive potential is pivotal to breaking the cycle of poverty so that women can share fully in the benefits of development and in the products of their own labour.

56. Sustainable development and economic growth that is both sustained and sustainable are possible only through improving the economic, social, political, legal and cultural status of women. Equitable social development that recognizes empowering the poor, particularly women, to utilize environmental resources sustainably is a necessary foundation for sustainable development.

57. The success of policies and measures aimed at supporting or strengthening the promotion of gender equality and the improvement of the status of women should be based on the integration of the gender perspective in general policies relating to all spheres of society as well as the implementation of positive measures with adequate institutional and financial support at all levels.

F. Women and the economy

150. There are considerable differences in women's and men's access to and opportunities to exert power over economic structures in their societies. In most parts of the world, women are virtually absent from or are poorly represented in economic decision-making, including the formulation of financial, monetary, commercial and other economic policies, as well as tax systems and rules governing pay. Since it is often within the framework of such policies that individual men and women make their decisions, *inter alia,* on how to divide their time between remunerated and unremunerated work, the actual development of these economic structures and policies has a direct impact on women's and men's access to economic resources, their economic power and consequently the extent of equality between them at the individual and family levels as well as in society as a whole.

151. In many regions, women's participation in remunerated work in the formal and non-formal labour market has increased significantly and has changed during the past decade. While women continue to work in agriculture and fisheries, they have also become increasingly involved in micro, small and medium-sized enterprises and, in some cases, have become more dominant in the expanding informal sector. Due to, *inter alia,* difficult economic situations and a lack of bargaining power resulting from gender inequality, many women have been forced to accept low pay and poor working conditions and thus have often become preferred workers. On the other hand, women have entered the workforce increasingly by choice when they have become aware of and demanded their rights. Some have succeeded in entering and advancing in the workplace and improving their pay and working conditions. However, women have been particularly affected by the economic situation and restructuring processes, which have changed the nature of employment and, in some cases, have led to a loss of jobs, even for professional and skilled women. In addition, many women have entered the informal sector owing to the lack of other opportunities. Women's participation and gender concerns are still largely absent from and should be integrated in the policy formulation process of the multilateral institutions that define the terms and, in cooperation with Governments, set the goals of structural adjustment programmes, loans and grants.

152. Discrimination in education and training, hiring and remuneration, promotion and horizontal mobility practices, as well as inflexible working conditions, lack of access to productive resources and inadequate sharing of family responsibilities, combined with a lack of or insufficient services such as child care, continue to restrict employment, economic, professional and other opportunities and mobility for women and make their involvement stressful. Moreover, attitudinal obstacles inhibit women's participation in developing economic policy and in some regions restrict the access of women and girls to education and training for economic management.

153. Women's share in the labour force continues to rise and almost everywhere women are working more outside the household, although there has not been a parallel lightening of responsibility for unremunerated work in the household and community. Women's income is becoming increasingly necessary to households of all types. In some regions, there has been a growth in women's entrepreneurship and other self-reliant activities, particularly in the

informal sector. In many countries, women are the majority of workers in non-standard work, such as temporary, casual, multiple part-time, contract and home-based employment.

154. Women migrant workers, including domestic workers, contribute to the economy of the sending country through their remittances and also to the economy of the receiving country through their participation in the labour force. However, in many receiving countries, migrant women experience higher levels of unemployment compared with both non-migrant workers and male migrant workers.

155. Insufficient attention to gender analysis has meant that women's contributions and concerns remain too often ignored in economic structures, such as financial markets and institutions, labour markets, economics as an academic discipline, economic and social infrastructure, taxation and social security systems, as well as in families and households. As a result, many policies and programmes may continue to contribute to inequalities between women and men. Where progress has been made in integrating gender perspectives, programme and policy effectiveness has also been enhanced.

156. Although many women have advanced in economic structures, for the majority of women, particularly those who face additional barriers, continuing obstacles have hindered their ability to achieve economic autonomy and to ensure sustainable livelihoods for themselves and their dependants. Women are active in a variety of economic areas, which they often combine, ranging from wage labour and subsistence farming and fishing to the informal sector. However, legal and customary barriers to ownership of or access to land, natural resources, capital, credit, technology and other means of production, as well as wage differentials, contribute to impeding the economic progress of women. Women contribute to development not only through remunerated work but also through a great deal of unremunerated work. On the one hand, women participate in the production of goods and services for the market and household consumption, in agriculture, food production or family enterprises. Though included in the United Nations System of National Accounts and therefore in international standards for labour statistics, this unremunerated work - particularly that related to agriculture - is often undervalued and under-recorded. On the other hand, women still also perform the great majority of unremunerated domestic work and community work, such as caring for children and older persons, preparing food for the family, protecting the environment and providing voluntary assistance to vulnerable and disadvantaged individuals and groups. This work is often not measured in quantitative terms and is not valued in national accounts. Women's contribution to development is seriously underestimated, and thus its social recognition is limited. The full visibility of the type, extent and distribution of this unremunerated work will also contribute to a better sharing of responsibilities.

157. Although some new employment opportunities have been created for women as a result of the globalization of the economy, there are also trends that have exacerbated inequalities between women and men. At the same time, globalization, including economic integration, can create pressures on the employment situation of women to adjust to new circumstances and to find new sources of employment as patterns of trade change. More analysis needs to be done of the impact of globalization on women's economic status.

158. These trends have been characterized by low wages, little or no labour standards protection, poor working conditions, particularly with regard to women's occupational health and safety, low skill levels, and a lack of job security and

social security, in both the formal and informal sectors. Women's unemployment is a serious and increasing problem in many countries and sectors. Young workers in the informal and rural sectors and migrant female workers remain the least protected by labour and immigration laws. Women, particularly those who are heads of households with young children, are limited in their employment opportunities for reasons that include inflexible working conditions and inadequate sharing, by men and by society, of family responsibilities.

159. In countries that are undergoing fundamental political, economic and social transformation, the skills of women, if better utilized, could constitute a major contribution to the economic life of their respective countries. Their input should continue to be developed and supported and their potential further realized.

160. Lack of employment in the private sector and reductions in public services and public service jobs have affected women disproportionately. In some countries, women take on more unpaid work, such as the care of children and those who are ill or elderly, compensating for lost household income, particularly when public services are not available. In many cases, employment creation strategies have not paid sufficient attention to occupations and sectors where women predominate; nor have they adequately promoted the access of women to those occupations and sectors that are traditionally male.

161. For those women in paid work, many experience obstacles that prevent them from achieving their potential. While some are increasingly found in lower levels of management, attitudinal discrimination often prevents them from being promoted further. The experience of sexual harassment is an affront to a worker's dignity and prevents women from making a contribution commensurate with their abilities. The lack of a family-friendly work environment, including a lack of appropriate and affordable child care, and inflexible working hours further prevent women from achieving their full potential.

162. In the private sector, including transnational and national enterprises, women are largely absent from management and policy levels, denoting discriminatory hiring and promotion policies and practices. The unfavourable work environment as well as the limited number of employment opportunities available have led many women to seek alternatives. Women have increasingly become self-employed and owners and managers of micro, small and medium-scale enterprises. The expansion of the informal sector, in many countries, and of self-organized and independent enterprises is in large part due to women, whose collaborative, self-help and traditional practices and initiatives in production and trade represent a vital economic resource. When they gain access to and control over capital, credit and other resources, technology and training, women can increase production, marketing and income for sustainable development.

163. Taking into account the fact that continuing inequalities and noticeable progress coexist, rethinking employment policies is necessary in order to integrate the gender perspective and to draw attention to a wider range of opportunities as well as to address any negative gender implications of current patterns of work and employment. To realize fully equality between women and men in their contribution to the economy, active efforts are required for equal recognition and appreciation of the influence that the work, experience, knowledge and values of both women and men have in society.

164. In addressing the economic potential and independence of women, Governments and other actors should promote an active and visible policy of mainstreaming a gender perspective in all policies and programmes so that before decisions are taken, an analysis is made of the effects on women and men, respectively.

REFERENCES

I   CASES CITED

Alden v. *Gagliardi et al*, [1973] S.C.R. 199, 30 D.L.R. (3d) 760, [1973] 2 W.W.R. 92.

Andrews v. *Law Society (British Columbia)*, [1989] 1 S.C.R. 143, [1989] 56 D.L.R. (4th) 1, 91 N.R. 255, [1989] 2 W.W.R. 289, 34 B.C.L.R. (2d) 273, 25 C.C.E.L. 255, 36 C.R.R. 193, 10 C.H.R.R. D/5719.

Benner v. *Canada (Secretary of State)*, [1997] 1 S.C.R. 358, 143 D.L.R. (4th) 577, 208 N.R. 81.

Bliss v. *Canada (A.G.)*, [1979] 1 S.C.R. 183, 92 D.L.R. (3d) 417, [1978] 6 W.W.R. 711, 23 N.R. 527, 78 C.L.L.C. 14,175.

Brooks v. *Canada Safeway Ltd.*, [1989] 1 S.C.R. 1219, 59 D.L.R. (4th) 321, 94 N.R. 373, [1989] 4 W.W.R. 193, 58 Man. R. (2d) 161, 26 C.C.E.L. 1, 89 C.L.L.C. 17,012, 45 C.R.R. 115, 10 C.H.R.R. D/6183.

Canada (A.G.) v. *Lavell*, [1974] S.C.R. 1349, (1973) 38 D.L.R. (3d) 481, 7 C.N.L.C. 236, 23 C.R.N.S. 197, 11 R.F.L. 333.

Canada (Treasury Board) v. *Robichaud*, [1987] 2 S.C.R. 84, 40 D.L.R. (4th) 577, 75 N.R. 303, 87 C.L.L.C. 17,025, 8 C.H.R.R. D/4326.

Canadian National Railway Co. v. *Canada (Human Rights Commission)*, [1987] 1 S.C.R. 1114, 40 D.L.R. (4th) 193, 76 N.R. 161, 27 Admin. L.R. 172, 87 C.L.L.C. 17,022, 8 C.H.R.R. D/4210.

Colfer v. *Ottawa Police Commission* (1979), (Ont. Bd. of Inq.) [unreported].

Dandridge v. *Williams*, 90 S. Ct. 1153 (1970).

Dartmouth/Halifax County Regional Housing Authority v. *Sparks* (1993), 119 N.S.R. (2d) 91, 101 D.L.R. (4th) 224, 30 R.P.R. (2d) 146, 330 A.P.R. 91, 1 D.R.P.L. 462 (C.A.).

Dickason v. *University of Alberta*, [1992] 2 S.C.R. 1103, 95 D.L.R. (4th) 439, 141 N.R. 1, 6 W.W.R. 385, 4 Alta. L.R. (3d) 193, 127 A.R. 241, 92 C.L.L.C. 17,033, 11 C.R.R. (2d) 1.

Egan v. *Canada*, [1995] 2 S.C.R. 513, 124 D.L.R. (4th) 609, 182 N.R. 161, 12 R.F.L. (4th) 201, 95 C.L.L.C. 210-025, W.D.F.L. 981, C.E.B. & P.G.R. 8216, 29 C.R.R. (2d) 79, 96 F.T.R. 80 (note).

Eldridge v. *British Columbia (A.G.)* (1995), 125 D.L.R. (4th) 323 (1995) 59 B.C.A.C. 254, 7 B.C.L.R. (3d) 156, [1995] 1 W.W.R. 50, 96 B.C.A.C., reversed [1997] 3 S.C.R. 624, 151 D.L.R. (4th) 577, 218 N.R. 161, 624, [1998] 1 W.W.R. 50, 96 B.C.A.C. 81, 38 B.C.L.R. (3d) 1.

Federated Anti-Poverty Groups of B.C. v. *British Columbia (A.G.)* (1991), 70 B.C.L.R. (2d) 325, B.C.W.L.D. 1571, W.D.F.L. 710 (S.C.).

Finlay v. *Canada (Minister of Finance)*, [1986] 2 S.C.R. 607, 33 D.L.R. (4th) 321, 71 N.R. 338, [1987] 1 W.W.R. 603, 23 Admin. L.R. 197, 17 C.P.C. (2d) 289.

Finlay v. *Canada (Minister of Finance)*, [1993] 1 S.C.R. 1080, 101 D.L.R. (4th) 567, 150 N.R. 81, 63 F.T.R. 99 (note), 2 D.M.P.L. 203.

Guérin v. *Canada,* [1984] 2 S.C.R. 335, 13 D.L.R. (4th) 321, 55 N.R. 161, [1984] 6 W.W.R. 481, [1985] C.N.L.R. 120.

Haig v. *Canada* (1992), 9 O.R. (3d) 495, 94 D.L.R. (4th) 1, 57 O.A.C. 272, 92 C.L.L.C. 17,034, 10 C.R.R. (2d) 287.

Huck v. *Canadian Odeon Theatres Ltd.*, (1985) 18 D.L.R. 4th 93, [1985] 3 W.W.R. 717, 39 Sask. 81, 6 C.H.R.R. D/2682, leave to appeal to S.C.C. refused (1985), 18 D.L.R. (4th) 93 (note).

International Fund for Animal Welfare v. *Canada (Minister of Fisheries & Oceans)*, [1989] 1 F.C. 335, (1988), 83 N.R. 303, 45 C.C.C. (3d) 457, 35 C.R.R. 359 (F.C.A.).

Janzen v. *Platy Enterprises Ltd.*, [1989] 1 S.C.R. 1252, 59 D.L.R. (4th) 352, 95 N.R. 81, [1989] 4 W.W.R. 39, 58 Man. R. (2d) 1, 89 C.L.L.C. 17,011, 47 C.R.R. 274, 25 C.C.E.L. 1, 10 C.H.R.R. D/6205.

Masse v. *Ontario (Minister of Community and Social Services)*, [1996] 134 D.L.R. (4th) 20, 35 C.R.R. (2d) 44, 89 O.A.C. 81, 40 Admin. L.R. (2d) 87, leave to appeal refused [1996] S.C.C.A. No. 373.

McKinney v. *University of Guelph*, [1990] 3 S.C.R. 229, 76 D.L.R. (4th) 545, 118 N.R. 1, 45 O.A.C. 1, 91 C.L.L.C. 17,004, 2 C.R.R. (2d) 1 13 C.H.R.R. D/171.

Mia v. *British Columbia (Medical Services Commission)* (1985), 17 D.L.R. (4th) 385, 61 B.C.L.R. 273, 15 Admin. L.R. 265, 16 C.R.R. 233 (B.C.S.C.).

Miron v. *Trudel*, [1995] 2 S.C.R. 418, 23 O.R. (3d) 160, 124 D.L.R. (4th) 693, 181 N.R. 253, 29 C.R.R. (2d) 189, [1995] I.L.R. 1-3185, 10 M.V.R. (3d) 151, 13 R.F.L. (4th) 1.

M.(R.H.) v. *H.(S.S.)* (1994), 121 D.L.R. (4th) 335, 26 Alta. L.R. (3d) 91 (Alta. Q.B.).

Moge v. *Moge,* [1992] 3 S.C.R. 813, 99 D.L.R. (4th) 456, 145 N.R. 1, [1993] 1 W.W.R. 481, 81 Man. R. (2d) 161, 43 R.F.L. (3d) 345.

Ontario (Human Rights Commission) and O'Malley v. *Simpsons Sears,* [1985] 2 S.C.R. 536, 23 D.L.R. (4th) 321, 64 N.R. 161, 12 O.A.C. 241, 17 Admin. L.R. 89, 9 C.C.E.L. 185, 86 C.L.L.C. 17,022, 7 C.H.R.R. D/3102.

Prosper v. *R.*, [1994] 3 S.C.R. 236, 118 D.L.R. (4th) 154, 172 N.R. 161, 92 C.C.C. (3d) 353.

RJR MacDonald Inc. v. *Canada (A.G.)*, [1995] 3 S.C.R. 199, 33 C.R. (4th) 85, 6 M.V.R. (3d) 181, 127 D.L.R. (4th) 1, 100 C.C.C. (3d) 449, 62 C.P.R. (3d) 417.

R. v. *Askov,* [1990] 2 S.C.R. 1199, 75 O.R. (2d) 673, 74 D.L.R. (4th) 355, 113 N.R. 241, 42 O.A.C. 81, 59 C.C.C. (3d) 449, 79 C.R. (3d) 273, 49 C.R.R. 1.

R. v. *Big M Drug Mart Ltd.,* [1985] 1. S.C.R. 295, 18 D.L.R. (4th) 321, 58 N.R. 81, [1985] 3 W.W.R. 481, 37 Alta. L.R. (2d) 97, 60 A.R. 161, 18 C.C.C. (3d) 385, 85 C.L.L.C. 14,023, 13 C.R.R. 64.

R. v. *Brydges*, [1990] 1 S.C.R. 190, 103 N.R. 282, 2 W.W.R. 220, 71 Alta. L.R. (2d) 145.

R. v. *Drybones*, [1970] S.C.R. 282, 9 D.L.R. (3d) 473, (1969) 71 W.W.R. 161, [1970] 3 C.C.C. 355, 6 C.N.L.C. 273, 10 C.R.N.S. 334.

R. v. *Keegstra*, [1990] 3 S.C.R. 697, 117 N.R. 1, [1991] 2 W.W.R. 1, 77 Alta. L.R. (2d) 193, 114 A.R. 81, 61 C.C.C. (3d) 1, I.C.R. (4th) 129.

R. v. *Morgentaler*, [1988] 1 S.C.R. 30, 44 D.L.R. (4th) 385, 82 N.R.1, 26 O.A.C., 37 C.C.C. (3d) 449, 62 C.R. (3d) 1, 31 C.R.R. 1.

R. v. *Nguyen (sub nom R.* v. *Hess)*, [1990] 2 S.C.R. 906, 119 N.R. 353, [1990] 6 W.W.R. 289, 73 Man. R. (2d) 1, 46 O.A.C. 13, 59 C.C.C. (3d) 161, 79 C.R. (3d) 332, 50 C.R.R. 71.

R. v. *Oakes*, [1986] 1 S.C.R. 103, 26 D.L.R. (4th) 200, 65 N.R. 87, 14 O.A.C. 335, 24 C.C.C. (3d) 321, 50 C.R. (3d) 1, 19 C.R.R. 308.

R. v. *Rehberg* (1994), 111 D.L.R. (4th) 336, 127 N.S.R. (2d) 331, 19 C.R.R. (2d) 242, W.D.F.L. 3787 (N.S.S.C.T.D.).

R. v. *Swain*, [1991] 1 S.C.R. 933, 125 N.R. 1, 47 O.A.C. 81, 63 C.C.C. (3d) 481, 5 C.R. (4th) 253, 3 C.R.R. (2d) 1.

R. v. *Turpin*, [1989] 1 S.C.R. 1296, 96 N.R. 115, 34 O.A.C. 115, 48 C.C.C. (3d) 8, 69 C.R. (3d) 97, 39 C.R.R. 306.

Reference Re An Act to Amend the Education Act (1986), 53 O.R. (2d) 513, 25 D.L.R. (4th) 1, 13 O.A.C. 241, 23 C.R.R. 193, (C.A.).

Reference Re Canada Assistance Plan (B.C.), [1991] 2 S.C.R. 525, 83 D.L.R. (4th) 297, 127 N.R. 161, [1991] 6 W.W.R. 1, 1 B.C.A.C. 241, 58 B.C.L.R. (2d) 1, 1 Admin. L.R. (2d) 1, 36 C.R.R. 305.

Reference Re Public Service Employee Relations Act, Labour Relations Act and Police Officers Collective Bargaining Act, [1987] 1 S.C.R. 313, 38 D.L.R. (4th) 161, 74 N.R. 99, [1987] 3 W.W.R. 577, 51 Alta. L.R. (2d) 97, 78 A.R. 1, 87 C.L.L.C. 14,021, 28 C.R.R. 305.

Rosenberg v. *Canada (A.G.)* (1995), 25 O.R. (3d) 612, 127 D.L.R. (4th) 738, appeal to Ont. C.A. heard 19 October 1997.

Schachter v. *Canada (Employment & Immigration Commission)*, [1992] 2 S.C.R. 679, 93 D.L.R. (4th) 1, 139 N.R. 1, 92 C.L.L.C. 14,036, 10 C.R.R. (2d) 1.

Schaff v. *R.* (1993), 18 C.R.R. (2d) 143, [1993] 2 C.T.C. 2695 (T.C.C.).

Silano v. *British Columbia* (1987), 42 D.L.R. (4th) 407, [1987] 5 W.W.R. 739, 16 B.C.L.R. (2d) 113, 29 Admin. L.R. 125, 33 C.R.R. 331 (S.C.).

Singh v. *Canada (Minister of Employment and Immigration)*, [1985] 1 S.C.R. 177, 17 D.L.R. (4th) 422, 58 N.R. 1, 12 Admin. L. R. 137, 14 C.R.R. 13

Singh v. *Security and Investigation Services Ltd.* (1977) (Ont. Bd. Inq.) [unreported].

Slaight Communications Inc. v. *Davidson*, [1989] 1 S.C.R. 1038, 59 D.L.R. (4th) 416, 93 N.R. 183, 26 C.C.E.L. 85, 89 C.L.L.C. 14,031, 40 C.R.R. 100.

Symes v. *Canada*, [1989] 3 F.C. 59, 25 T.T.R. 306, 40 C.R.R. 278, 1 C.T.C. 476, (F.C.T.D.), reversed [1991] 3 F.C. 507, 127 N.R. 348, 7 C.R.R. (2d) 333, 2 C.T.C. 1, 91 D.T.C. 5386 (F.C.A.) affirmed [1993] 4 S.C.R. 695, 110 D.L.R. (4th) 470, 161 N.R. 243, 19 C.R.R. (2d) 1, [1994] 1 C.T.C. 40, 94 D.T.C. 6001, [1994] W.D.F.L. 171.

Tétreault-Gadoury v. *Canada (Employment & Immigration Commission)*, [1991] 2 S.C.R. 22, 81 D.L.R. (4th) 358, 126 N.R. 1, 50 Admin. L.R. 1, 36 C.C.E.L. 117, 91 C.L.L.C. 14,023, 4 C.R.R. (2d) 12.

Tharp v. *Lornex Mining Corp. Ltd.* (1975), Dec. No. 57 (B.C. Bd. of Inq.) [unreported].

Thibaudeau v. *Canada,* [1994] 2 F.C. 189, 114 D.L.R. (4th) 261, 167 N.R. 161, 21 C.R.R. (2d) 35, [1994] 2 C.T.C. 4, 3 R.F.L. (4th) 153, W.D.F.L. 812 (F.C.A.); affirmed [1995] 2 S.C.R. 627, 124 D.L.R. (4th) 449, 182 N.R. 1, 95 D.T.C. 5273, 12 R.F.L. (4th) 1, 1 C.T.C. 382, 29 C.R.R. (2d) 1.

Vriend v. *Alberta (A.G.)* (1996), 132 D.L.R. (4th) 595, 5 W.W.R. 617, 37 Alta. L.R. (3d) 364, 181 A.R. 16, 18 C.C.E.L. (2d) 1 (Alta. C.A.); reserved [1998] S.C.J. No. 29.

Winnipeg School Division No. 1 v. *Craton*, [1985] 2 S.C.R. 150, 21 D.L.R. (4th) 1, 61 N.R. 241, [1985] 6 W.W.R. 166, 38 Man. R. (2d) 1, 15 Admin. L.R. 177, 8 C.C.E.L. 105, 85 C.L.L.C. 17,010, 6 C.H.R.R. D/3014.

Winterhaven Stables Ltd. v. *Canada (A.G.)* (1988), 53 D.L.R. (4th) 413, [1989] 1 W.W.R. 193, 62 Alta. L.R. (2d) 266, 91 A.R. 114, [1989] 1 C.T.C. 16. (Alta. C.A.).

II   KEY LEGISLATION AND REGULATIONS CITED

The Budget Implementation Act, 1995, S.C. 1995, c. 17.

Canada Assistance Plan Act, R.S.C. 1985, c. C-1.

Canada Assistance Plan Regulations, C.R.C. 1978, c. 382.

Canadian Bill of Rights, S.C. 1960, c. 44, reprinted in R.S.C. 1985, App. III.

Canadian Charter of Rights and Freedoms, Part I of the *Constitution Act, 1982,* being Schedule B to the *Canada Act 1982* (U.K.), 1982, c. 11.

Constitution Act, 1982, s. 36.

Constitution Act, 1867.

Federal-Provincial Fiscal Arrangements Act, R.S.C. 1985, c. F-8.

III   INTERNATIONAL INSTRUMENTS CITED

Charter of the United Nations, 26 June 1945, Can. T.S. 1945 No. 7, 59 Stat. 1031, 145 U.K.F.S. 805, art. 2(7).

Convention Against Torture and Other Cruel, Inhuman or Degrading Treatment or Punishment, GA Res. A/RES/39/46, UN GAOR, 39th Sess., (Supp. No. 51), UN Doc. A/39/51 (1986), Can. T.S. 1987 No. 36.

Convention on the Elimination of All Forms of Discrimination Against Women, GA Res. 34/180, UN GAOR, 34th Sess., (Supp. No. 46), UN Doc. A/34/46 (1982), Can. T.S. 1982 No. 31.

Convention on the Elimination of All Forms of Racial Discrimination, UN GA Res. A/RES/2106A (XX) (1969), 660 U.N.T.S. 195, Can T.S. 1970 No. 28.

Convention on the Rights of the Child, GA Res. 44/25, UN GAOR, 44th Sess., (Supp. No. 49), UN Doc. A/44/49 (1989).

International Covenant on Civil and Political Rights, GA Res. 2200A (XXI), 21 UN GAOR, (Supp. No. 16) 52, UN Doc. A/6316 (1966), 999 U.N.T.S. 171, Can. T.S. 1976 No. 47.

International Covenant on Economic, Social and Cultural Rights, GA Res. 2200A (XXI), 21 UN GAOR, (Supp. No. 16), UN Doc. A/6316 (1966), 993 U.N.T.S. 3, Can. T.S. 1976 No. 46.

Optional Protocol to International Covenant on Civil and Political Rights, GA Res. 2200A (XXI), 21 UN GAOR, (Supp. No. 16) 59, UN Doc. A6316 (1966), 999 U.N.T.S. 302, Can. T.S. 1976 No. 47.

Universal Declaration of Human Rights, GA Res. 217A (III), UN Doc. A/810 (1948).

Vienna Convention on the Law of Treaties, 1155 U.N.T.S. 331, Can. T.S. 1980 No. 37.

IV   UNITED NATIONS DOCUMENTS CITED

United Nations, Commission on Human Rights, *Limburg Principles on the Implementation of the International Covenant on Economic, Social and Cultural Rights*, UN Doc. E/CN.4/1987/17, Annex; reproduced in (1987) 9 *Human Rights Quarterly* 122.

United Nations, Commission on the Status of Women, Open-Ended Working Group on the Elaboration of a Draft Optional Protocol to the Convention on the Elimination of All Forms of Discrimination Against Women, *Revised Draft Optional Protocol Submitted on the Basis of Compilation Text Contained in UN Doc. E/CN.6/1997/WG/L.1 and Proposals Made at the Forty-First Session of the Commission (Part I)*, 41st Sess., Agenda Item 5, UN Doc. E/CN.6/1997/WG/L.3 (1997).

United Nations, Commission on the Status of Women, Open-Ended Working Group on the Elaboration of a Draft Optional Protocol to the Convention on the Elimination of All Forms of Discrimination Against Women, *Revised Draft Optional Protocol Submitted on the Basis of Compilation Text Contained in UN Doc. E/CN.6/1997/WG/L.1 and Proposals Made at the Forty-First Session of the Commission (Part II)*, 41st Sess., Agenda Item 5, UN Doc. E/CN.6/1997/WG/L.3/Add.1 (1997).

United Nations, Commission on the Status of Women, Open-Ended Working Group on the Elaboration of a Draft Optional Protocol to the Convention on the Elimination of All Forms of Discrimination Against Women, *Revised Draft Optional Protocol Submitted by Chairperson on the Basis of Compilation Text Contained in in the Report of the Commission on the Status of Women on its Forty-First Session (E/1997/27) and Proposals made by the Commssion at its Forty-Second Session*, UN Doc. E/CN.6/1998/WG/L.2 12 March 1998.

United Nations, Commission on the Status of Women, *Convention on the Elimination of All Forms of Discrimination Against Women, Including the Elaboration of a Draft Optional Protocol to the Convention: Comparative Summary of Existing Communications and Inquiry Procedures and Practices under International Human Rights Instruments and Under the Charter of the United Nations: Report of the Secretary General*, 41st Sess., Agenda Item 5, Para. 12, UN Doc. E/CN.6/1997/4 (1997).

United Nations, Committee on Economic, Social and Cultural Rights, General Comments Nos. 1–4 as reprinted in (1994) 1:1 *International Human Rights Reports* 1.

United Nations, Committee on Economic, Social and Cultural Rights, *Concluding Observations on Report of Canada Concerning the Rights Covered by Articles 10–15 of the International Covenant on Economic, Social and Cultural Rights*, UN Doc. E/C. 12/1993/19 as reprinted in (1994) 20 *Canadian Human Rights Reporter* C/1.

United Nations, Committee on the Elimination of All Forms of Discrimination Against Women, *Ways and Means of Expediting the Work of the Committee,* UN Doc. CEDAW/C/1997/5, (6 December 1996).

United Nations, Committee on the Elimination of Discrimination Against Women, General Recommendation No. 19, UN Doc. A/47/38 (1992).

United Nations, General Assembly, *Declaration on International Economic Co-operation, in Particular the Revitalization of Economic Growth and Development of the Developing Countries*, GA Res. S-18/13, UN GAOR, 18th Spec. Sess., (Supp. 2), UN Doc. A/S-18/15 (1990).

United Nations, General Assembly, *Implementation of the Nairobi Forward-Looking Strategies for the Advancement of Women*, GA Res. 49/161, UN GAOR, 49th Sess. (1994).

United Nations, General Assembly, *Toward Full Integration of Persons with Disabilities into Society: A Continuing World Programme of Action,* GA Res. 47/88, UN GAOR, 47th Sess., (Supp. No. 49), UN Doc. A/47/49 (1992).

United Nations, General Assembly, *Toward Full Integration of Persons with Disabilities into Society: A Continuing World Programme of Action,* GA Res. 48/99, UN GAOR, 48th Sess. (Supp. No. 49), UN Doc. A/48/49 (1993).

United Nations, General Assembly, *World Program of Action Concerning Disabled Persons*, GA Res. 37/52, 37/53, A/37/351/Add.1, Add.1/Corr.1, Annex, GAOR, 37th Sess. (1982).

United Nations, *Compilation of General Comments and General Recommendations Adopted by Human Rights Treaty Bodies*, UN Doc. HRI/GEN/1, 4 September 1992.

United Nations Declaration on the Rights of the Child, GA Res. 1386 (XIV), UN GAOR, 14th Sess. (1959).

United Nations Declaration on the Rights of Disabled Persons, GA Res. 3447 (XXX), UN GAOR, 30th Sess. (1975).

United Nations Declaration on Social Progress and Development, GA Res. 2542 (XXIV), UN GAOR, 24th Sess. (1969).

United Nations, *Report of the Fourth World Conference on Women, Beijing, China, 4–15 September 1995*, A/CONF.177/20, 17 October 1995 (*Platform for Action*).

United Nations, Statistical Office, *The World's Women, 1970–1990: Trends and Statistics* (New York: United Nations, 1991).

V SELECTED BIBLIOGRAPHY OF BOOKS, ARTICLES, REPORTS

Abner, Erika J., *Equality Rights in the Context of Distributive Legislation* (Toronto: Ministry of Social Services Review Committee, May 1987).

Abner, Erika, J., *The Merits of the Use of Constitutional Litigation to Unravel the Fabric of the Feminization of Poverty in Canada* (LL.M. Thesis, York University, 1990).

Abner, Erika, J., Mary Jane Mossman and Elizabeth Pickett, "No More than Simple Justice: Assessing the Royal Commission Report on Women, Poverty and the Family" (1990) 22 *Ottawa Law Review* 573.

Addario, Lisa, "The Tax Treatment of Child Support Payments" (1994) 14 *Jurisfemme* 1.

Agarwal, Bina, "The Gender and Environmental Debate: Lessons from India" (1992) 18 *Feminist Studies* 119.

Alston, Philip, "Denial and Neglect" in Richard Reoch, ed., *Human Rights: The New Consensus* (London: Regency House (Humanity), 1994).

Alston, Philip, ed., *The Best Interests of the Child: Reconciling Culture and Human Rights* (Oxford: Clarendon Press, 1994).

Alston, Philip, and Gerard Quinn, "The Nature and Scope of States Parties' Obligations Under the *International Covenant on Economic, Social and Cultural Rights*" (1987) 9 *Human Rights Quarterly* 156.

Anton, Thomas J., "Scandinavian Realism" (1995) 20 *Journal of Health Politics, Policy and Law* 739.

Armstrong, Pat, "The Feminization of the Labour Force: Harmonizing Down in a Global Economy" in Isabella Bakker, ed., *Rethinking Restructuring: Gender and Change in Canada* (Toronto: University of Toronto Press, 1996) 29.

Armstrong, Pat, and Hugh Armstrong, "Beyond Sexless Class and Classless Sex: Towards Feminist Marxism" in R. Hamilton and M. Barrett, eds., *The Politics of Diversity* (Montreal: Book Center, 1986).

Armstrong, Pat, and Hugh Armstrong, *The Double Ghetto: Canadian Women and Their Segregated Work* (Toronto: McClelland and Stewart, 1984).

Axworthy, Lloyd, "Barlow has it backwards" *The [Toronto] Globe and Mail* (17 April 1994) A16.

Bakan, Abigail B., and Davia K. Stasiulis, "Structural Adjustment, Citizenship and Foreign Domestic Labour: The Canadian Case" in Isabella Bakker, ed., *Rethinking Restructuring: Gender and Change in Canada* (Toronto: University of Toronto Press, 1996) 217.

Bakan, Joel, and David Schneiderman, *Social Justice and the Constitution: Perspectives on a Social Union for Canada* (Ottawa: Carleton University Press, 1992).

Bakker, Isabella, "Gender Relations, Macroeconomics and Structural Change in the OECD in the 1980s" (Paper presented at the "Out of the Margins" conference, Amsterdam, 1993) [unpublished].

Bakker, Isabella, "Introduction: The Gendered Foundations of Restructuring in Canada" in Isabella Bakker, ed., *Rethinking Restructuring: Gender and Change in Canada* (Toronto: University of Toronto Press, 1996) 3.

Bakker, Isabella, "Macroeconomics Through a Feminist Lens" in Isabella Bakker, *Economic Equality* (Ottawa: Status of Women Canada, 1994).

Bakker, Isabella, "The Politics of Scarcity: Deficits and the Debt" in Michael Whittington and Glen Williams, eds., *Canadian Politics in the 1990s*, 3rd ed. (Toronto: Nelson, 1990).

Bakker, Isabella, ed., *Rethinking Restructuring: Gender and Change in Canada* (Toronto: University of Toronto Press, 1996).

Bakker, Isabella, *The Strategic Silence: Gender and Economic Policy* (London: Zed Books / The North-South Institute, 1994).

Bakker, Isabella, "Women's Employment in Comparative Perspective" in Jane Jenson et al., eds., *The Feminization of the Labour Force: Paradoxes and Promises* (Oxford: Polity Press, 1988).

Bakker, Isabella, and Janine Brodie, *The New Canada Health and Social Transfer (CHST): The Implications for Women* (Ottawa: Status of Women Canada, 1995).

Ball, Carlos A., "The Making of a Transnational Capitalist Society: The Court of Justice, Social Policy, and Individual Rights Under the European Community's Legal Order" (1996) 37 *Harvard International Law Journal* 307.

Banting, Keith, "Who 'R' Us?" in Thomas J. Courchene and Thomas A. Wilson, eds., *The 1995 Federal Budget: Retrospect and Prospect* (Kingston, Ont.: John Deutsch Institute for the Study of Economic Policy, Queen's University, 1995).

Banting, Keith, et al., eds., *The Future of Fiscal Federalism* (Kingston, Ont: School of Policy Studies, Queen's University, 1994).

Banting, Keith, and Ken Battle, eds., *A New Social Vision for Canada: Perspectives on the Federal Discussion Paper on Social Security Reform* (Kingston, Ont.: School of Policy Studies, Queen's University, 1994).

Barlow, Maude, and David Robinson, "How the Liberals are unravelling the social safety net" *The [Toronto] Globe and Mail* (11 April 1995) A21.

Bashevkin, Sylvia, "Free Trade and Canadian Feminism: The Case of the National Action Committee on the Status of Women" (1989) 15 *Canadian Public Policy* 363.

Battle, Ken, *Constitutional Reform by Stealth* (Ottawa: Caledon Institute of Social Policy, 1995).

Battle, Ken, *The National Child Benefit: Best Thing Since Medicare or New Poor Law?* (Ottawa: Caledon Institute of Social Policy, 1997).

Battle, Ken, and Leon Muszynski, *One Way to Fight Child Poverty* (Ottawa: Caledon Institute of Social Policy, 1995).

Battle, Ken, and Sherri Torjman, *Federal Social Programs: Setting the Record Straight* (Ottawa: Caledon Institute of Social Policy, 1993).

Battle, Ken, and Sherri Torjman, *How Finance Reformed Social Policy* (Ottawa: Caledon Institute of Social Policy, 1995).

Battle, Ken, and Sherri Torjman, *The Welfare Wall: Reforming the Welfare and Tax Systems* (Ottawa: Caledon Institute of Social Policy, 1993).

Bayefsky, Anne F., "General Approaches to the Domestic Application of Women's International Human Rights Law" in Rebecca J. Cook, ed., *Human Rights of Women: National and International Perspectives* (Philadelphia: University of Pennsylvania, 1994).

Bayefsky, Anne F., "International Human Rights Law in Canadian Courts" in William Kaplan and Don McRae, eds., *Law, Policy and International Justice* (Montreal: McGill-Queen's University Press, 1993).

Bayefsky, Anne F., *International Human Rights Law: Use in Canadian Charter of Rights and Freedoms Litigation* (Toronto: Butterworths, 1992).

Bayefsky, Anne F., "The Principle of Equality or Non-Discrimination in International Law" (1990) 11 *Human Rights Law Journal* 1.

Bayefsky, Anne F., "The United Nations Human Rights Treaties: Facing the Implementation Crisis" (1996) 15 *Windsor Yearbook of Access to Justice*, 189.

Beatty, David, "The Canadian Conception of Equality" (1996) 46 *University of Toronto Law Journal* 349.

Beatty, Jim, "Budget cuts will slice services in some areas" *The [Vancouver] Sun* (1 November 1996) A5c.

Beauchesne, Eric, "Banker would carve up welfare, health systems" *The [Toronto] Star* (19 April 1995) B1.

Begin, Patricia, and Abdou Saouab, *Homelessness in Canada*. rev. ed. (Ottawa: Library of Parliament, Research Branch, 1992).

Bellemare, Diane, and Lise Poulin-Simon, *What is the Real Cost of Unemployment in Canada* (Ottawa: Canadian Centre for Policy Alternatives, 1994).

Bellett, Gerry, "Federal budget 'didn't cut enough'" *The [Vancouver] Sun* (11 March 1995) A4.

Beneria, Lourdes, and Shelley Feldman, eds., *Unequal Burden: Economic Crisis, Persistent Poverty, and Women's Work* (Boulder, Colo.: Westview Press, 1992).

Beneria, Lourdes, and Martha Roldan, "Introduction and Theoretical Framework" in L. Beneria and M. Roldan, *The Crossroads of Class and Gender* (Chicago: University of Chicago Press, 1987).

Berg, Brad, "Fumbling Toward Equality: Promise and Peril in *Egan*" (1995) 5 *National Journal of Constitutional Law* 263.

Bergeron, Suzanne, "The Nation as a Gendered Subject of Macroeconomics" in Isabella Bakker, ed., *Rethinking Restructuring: Gender and Change in Canada* (Toronto: University of Toronto Press, 1996) 111.

Bernier, Gerard, and David Irwin, "Fiscal Federalism: The Politics of Intergovernmental Transfers" in G. Bernier and D. Irwin, *New Trends in Canadian Federalism* (Peterborough: Broadview Press, 1995).

Besharov, Douglas J., "The Feminization of Poverty: Has Legal Services Failed to Respond?" (1990) 24 *Clearinghouse Review* 218.

"Beware of poor-bashing rhetoric, advocate tells anti-poverty group" *The [Kamloops] Daily News* (29 January 1996) A2.

Biddle, Tony, *'Doesn't Anyone Want to Question What's Going on Here?' Understanding Deficit Mania: An Illustrated Guide* (Toronto: Perfect World Productions and LIFT, 1996).

Margaret Biggs, *Building Blocks for Canada's New Social Union* (Ottawa: Canadian Policy Research Networks, 1996).

Binion, Gayle, "Human Rights: A Feminist Perspective" (1995) 17 *Human Rights Quarterly* 509.

Bird, Richard, "Federal-Provincial Fiscal Transfers in Canada: Retrospect and Prospect" (1987) 35 *Canadian Tax Journal* 118.

Black, William, "The Charter of Rights and Freedoms and Positive Obligations" in William Kaplan and Donald McRae, eds., *Law, Policy, and International Justice* (Kingston, Ont.: McGill-Queen's University Press, 1993).

Black, William, and Lynn Smith, "The Equality Rights" in Gerald Beaudoin and Errol Mendes, eds., *The Canadian Charter of Rights and Freedoms* (Ottawa: Carswell, 1996).

Blackwell, Richard, and James Walker, "Block funding to replace transfer payments" *The Financial Post* (28 February 1995) B6.

Blake, Raymond, and Jeff Keshen, *Social Welfare Policy in Canada: Historical Readings* (Toronto: Copp Clark Ltd., 1995).

Blank, Rebecca, and Alan Blinder, "Macroeconomics, Income Distribution, and Poverty" in S. Danziger and D. Weinberg, eds., *Fighting Poverty: What Works and What Does Not* (Cambridge, Mass.: Harvard University Press, 1986).

Blau, Francine, and Marianne Ferber, *The Economics of Women, Men and Work* (Englewood Cliffs, N.J.: Prentice Hall, 1986).

Boadway, Robin, "The Implications of the Budget for Fiscal Federalism" in Thomas J. Courchene and Thomas A. Wilson, eds., *The 1995 Federal Budget: Retrospect and Prospect* (Kingston, Ont.: John Deutsch Institute for the Study of Economic Policy, Queen's University, 1995).

Boadway, Robin, and Paul Hobson, *Intergovernmental Fiscal Relations in Canada* (Toronto: Canadian Tax Foundation, 1993).

Boadway, Robin, and Frank Flatters, "Federal-Provincial Fiscal Relations Revisited: Some Consequences of Recent Constitutional and Policy Developments" in M. McMillan, ed., *Provincial Public Finances: Plaudits, Problems, and Prospects,* v. 2, Canadian Tax Paper n. 91 (Toronto: Canadian Tax Foundation, 1991).

Brackman, H., et al., "Wedded to the Welfare State: Women Against Reaganite Retrenchment" in Jane Jenson et al., eds., *Feminization of the Labour Force* (Cambridge, Mass.: Polity Press, 1988).

British Columbia, *A Financial Plan for British Columbia: Protecting Medicare and Education* (Victoria: Queen's Printer, 1996).

British Columbia, *Children, Families and the Social Safety Net. British Columbia Premier's Forum: New Opportunities for Working and Living* (Background Paper: 3) (Victoria: Office of the Premier, Social Program Renewal Secretariat, 1994).

"B.C. to abolish welfare rule" *The [Toronto] Globe and Mail* (6 March 1997) A1, A14.

Broad, Dave, "Globalization versus Labour" (1995) 36 *Canadian Review of Social Policy* 75.

Brodie, Janine, *Politics on the Boundaries: Restructuring and the Canadian Women's Movement* (North York: Robarts Centre for Canadian Studies, 1994).

Brodie, Janine, ed., *Women and Canadian Public Policy* (Toronto: Hartcourt Brace, 1995).

Brodsky, Gwen, and Shelagh Day, *Charter Equality Rights For Women: One Step Forward or Two Steps Back?* (Ottawa: Canadian Advisory Council on the Status of Women, 1989).

Bryden, Joan, "Battle to save Canada's social programs not over" *The [Vancouver] Sun* (13 March 1995) A4.

Bunch, Charlotte, "Women's Rights as Human Rights: Toward a Re-Vision of Human Rights" (1990) 12 *Human Rights Quarterly* 486.

Bunting, Annie, "Theorizing Women's Cultural Diversity in Feminist International Human Rights Strategies" (1993) 20 *Canadian Journal of Law and Society* 6.

Burgess, Michael, "Introduction: Competing Perspectives of Canadian Federalism" in Michael Burgess, ed., *Canadian Federalism: Past, Present and Future* (New York: Leicester University Press, 1990).

Burt, Sandra, "What's Fair? Changing Feminist Perceptions of Justice in English Canada" (1992) 12 *Windsor Yearbook of Access to Justice* 337.

Byrnes, Andrew, "Toward More Effective Enforcement of Women's Human Rights Through the Use of International Human Rights Law and Procedures" in Rebecca J. Cook, ed., *Human Rights of Women: National and International Perspectives* (Philadelphia: University of Pennsylvania Press, 1994).

Calder, Gillian, "Women's Rights Are Human Rights: The Feasibility of an Optional Protocol to CEDAW" [unpublished].

Cameron, Barbara, "Social Citizenship in a Multinational State: The Social Charter Revisited" (Paper presented to Federal Constitutions in Comparative Perspective: A Conference In Honour of Douglas V. Verney, York University 1996) [unpublished].

Cameron, David, "Comments" *Roundtables on the Canada Health and Social Transfer: Final Report* (Ottawa: Canadian Council on Social Development, 1996) 137.

Cameron, Duncan, "Freedom" (June 1995) *Canadian Forum* 5.

Cameron, Duncan, *The Impoverishment of Canada: Notes for a presentation before the House of Commons Standing Committee on Finance* (Ottawa: Canadian Centre for Policy Alternatives, 1995).

Camp, Dalton, "CHST minus EPF and CAP just has to equal LESS" *The [Toronto] Star* (1 March 1995) A21.

"Canada assistance cuts cause 'grave concerns'" *The [Vancouver] Sun* (5 May 1995) A14.

Canada, *Canada's Economic and Fiscal Challenges: A Graphical Exposition* by David Dodge (Ottawa: Department of Finance, 1994).

Canada, *Canada's National Report to the United Nations for the Fourth World Conference on Women* (Ottawa: Queen's Printer, 1995).

Canada, *The Charter in the Context of the International Bill of Rights*, (Federal-Provincial-Territorial Conference on Human Rights, September 1983, Document No. 830-130/022, Agenda Item VII(i)(a), 9 August 1983).

Canada, *Child Care and Development: A Supplementary Paper* (Ottawa: Queen's Printer, 1994).

Canada, *Creating a Healthy Fiscal Climate: An Economic and Fiscal Update* (Ottawa: Queen's Printer, 1994).

Canada, *Employment Development Services: A Supplementary Paper* (Ottawa: Queen's Printer, 1994).

Canada, *Federal Transfers to the Provinces* (Ottawa: Department of Finance, 1992).

Canada, *Getting Government Right: A Progress Report* (Ottawa: Supply and Services, Privy Council Office Canada, 1996).

Canada, *Improving Social Security in Canada: The Context of Reform, A Supplementary Paper* (Ottawa: Queen's Printer, 1994).

Canada, *Improving Social Security in Canada: A Discussion Paper* (Ottawa: Queen's Printer, 1994).

Canada, *Income Security for Children: A Supplementary Paper* (Ottawa: Queen's Printer, 1994).

Canada, *International Covenant on Economic, Social and Cultural Rights: Report of Canada on Articles 10–12, December 1982* (Ottawa: Supply and Services, 1983).

Canada, *International Covenant on Economic, Social and Cultural Rights: Second Report of Canada on Articles 6–9, December 1987* (Ottawa: Queen's Printer, 1987).

Canada, *International Covenant on Economic, Social and Cultural Rights: Second Report of Canada on Articles 10–15, September 1992* (Ottawa: Supply and Services, 1992).

Canada, *International Covenant on Economic, Social and Cultural Rights: Third Report of Canada* (Ottawa: Public Works and Government Services, 1997).

Canada, *A New Framework for Economic Policy* (Ottawa: Queen's Printer, 1994).

Canada, *Ministerial Council on Social Policy Reform and Renewal: Report to Premiers* (Ottawa: Canadian Intergovernmental Conference Secretariat, December 1995).

Canada, *The 1995 Budget and Block Funding* (Ottawa: Supply and Services Canada, 1995).

Canada, *Persons with Disabilities: A Supplementary Paper* (Ottawa: Queen's Printer, 1994).

Canada, *Reforming the Canada Assistance Plan: A Supplementary Paper* (Ottawa: Queen's Printer, 1994).

Canada, *Report on the United Nations World Conference on Human Rights, Vienna (1993)* (Ottawa: External Affairs and International Trade Canada).

Canada, *Responsive Institutions for a Modern Canada* (Ottawa: Supply and Services Canada, 1991).

Canada, *Social Security in Canada: Background Facts* (Ottawa: Human Resources Development Canada, 1994).

Canada, Standing Committee on Health and Welfare, Social Affairs, Seniors and the Status of Women, *Canada's Children: Investing in our Future: Report of the Sub-Committe on Poverty of the Standing Committee on Health and Welfare, Social Affairs, Seniors and the Status of Women* (Ottawa: Supply and Services Canada, 1991) (Chair: Barbara Green).

"Canadian women closing wage gap" *The [Toronto] Globe and Mail* (23 July 1997) A6.

Canadian Advisory Council on the Status of Women, *Planning Our Future: Do We Have to Be Poor?* (Ottawa, 1986).

Canadian Advisory Council on the Status of Women, *Research Notes: The Social Security Review and Its Implications for Women* (Ottawa, 1994).

Canadian Advisory Council on the Status of Women, *The Tax Treatment of Child Support: Preferred Policy Options* (Ottawa, 1994).

Canadian Advisory Council on the Status of Women, *Women and Social Security Reform.* (Presentation to the House of Commons Standing Committee on Human Resources Development, 27 October 1994).

Canadian Advisory Council on the Status of Women, *Work in Progress: Tracking Women's Equality in Canada* (Ottawa, 1994).

Canadian Centre for Policy Alternatives, "Liberals' New Blueprint for Future Focuses on Cutbacks, Not Job Creation" (1994) Special Issue *Monitor* 1.

Canadian Centre for Policy Alternatives, *The 1997 Alternative Federal Budget: Framework in Brief* (Ottawa, 1997).

Canadian Centre for Policy Alternatives, "Social Policy Review Ignores Alternatives" (November 1994) 1 *Monitor* 1.

Canadian Council on Social Development, *Canada's Social Programs Are in Trouble* (Ottawa, 1990).

Canadian Council on Social Development, *Roundtables on the Canada Health and Social Transfer: Final Report* (Ottawa, 1996).

Canadian Council on Social Development, *Social Policy Beyond the Budget* (Ottawa, 1995).

Canadian Council on Social Development, Communiqué, "Study Shows Poor Families Losing Market Share" (Ottawa, 18 March 1997).

Canadian Labour Congress, *Canada: Two Visions — Two Futures: Submission to the Standing Committee on Finance Regarding Bill C-76* (Ottawa, May 1995).

Canadian Labour Congress, *We're Out for Justice* (Ottawa: Canadian Labour Congress, Spring 1997).

Canadian Labour Congress, "Women Workers and the Recession" (Ottawa, June 1993).

Canadian Women's NGOs, *Canada: Alternative Report to CEDAW* (Toronto, January 1997).

Cárdenas, Cuauhtémoc, "Free Trade, the Environment, and the Need for a Social Charter" (1992) 15:1 *Loyola of Los Angeles International and Comparative Law Journal* 71.

Carluccio, Teresa, *Tax Expenditures for Social Policy: A Study of the Federal Child Tax Benefit System* (LL.M. Thesis, University of Toronto, 1993).

Carr, Andrea, "Don't blame the poor for working moms' plight" *Surrey/North Delta Now* (23 March 1994) A20.

Carruthers, Errlee, "Prosecuting Women for Welfare Fraud in Ontario: Implications for Equality" (1995) 11 *Journal of Law and Social Policy* 241.

Carty, Linda, ed., *And Still We Rise: Feminist Political Mobilization in Contemporary Canada* (Toronto: Women's Press, 1993).

Casper, Lynne, Sara S. McLanahan and Irwin Garfinkel, "The Gender Poverty Gap — What We Can Learn From Other Countries" (1994) 59 *American Sociological Review* 594.

Certosimo, Matthew, "Does Canada Need a Social Charter?" (1992) 15 *Dalhousie Law Journal* 568.

Certosimo, Matthew, "A Social Charter Within Reach" (1992) 2 *National Journal of Constitutional Law* 249.

Charter Committee on Poverty Issues, *Bill C-76 and the Human Rights of the Poor: Notes for a Presentation Before the Standing Committee on Finance by the Charter Committee on Poverty Issues* (Ottawa: Charter Committee on Poverty Issues/National Anti-Poverty Organization, 1995).

Charter Committee on Poverty Issues, National Anti-Poverty Organization and the National Action Committee on the Status of Women, *Re: The International Covenant on Economic, Social and Cultural Rights and Proposed Legislation by Canada (Bill C-76) to Eliminate the Canada Assistance Plan (CAP) – Presentation to the Committee on Economic, Social and Cultural Rights by Non-Governmental Organizations from Canada, May 1, 1995* (Ottawa, 1995).

Charter Committee on Poverty Issues, *The Right to an Adequate Standard of Living in a Land of Plenty: Submission of the National Anti-Poverty Organization and the Charter Committee on Poverty Issues to the Committee on Economic, Social and Cultural Rights* (Ottawa: Charter Committee on Poverty Issues/National Anti-Poverty Organization, 17 May 1993).

Charter Committee on Poverty Issues, *Symes v. R.*, Court file No. 22659 (Supreme Court of Canada) *Factum of the Intervenor, Charter Committee on Poverty Issues*, February, 1993.

Child Poverty Action Group et al., Joint Statement, *Paying for Canada: Perspectives on Public Finance and National Programs* (Toronto: Social Planning Council of Metropolitan Toronto, 1994).

Chorney, Harold, et al., *"The Deficit Made Me Do It!" The Myths About Government Debt* (Ottawa: Canadian Centre for Policy Alternatives, May 1992).

Choudhry, Sujit, "The Enforcement of the *Canada Health Act*" (1996) 41 *McGill Law Journal* 461.

"Chrétien, Clark warming to each other" *The [Toronto] Globe and Mail* (7 March 1997) A7.

Chunn, Dorothy, "Regulating the Poor in Ontario: From Police Courts to Family Courts" in Tina Loo and Lorna R. MacLean, eds., *Historical Perspectives on Law and Society in Canada* (Toronto: Copp Clark Longman, 1994).

Citizens for Public Justice, *Will Ottawa Preserve National Equity?* (Toronto, May 1995).

Clark, Chris, and Susan Carter, "Unravelling the Social Safety Net" (1995) 18:3&4 *Perception* 27.

Clarke, Tony, *Silent Coup: Confronting the Big Business Takeover of Canada* (Toronto: James Lorimer & Co., 1997).

Clarke, Tony, and Maude Barlow, *MAI: The Multilateral Agreement on Investment and the Threat to Canadian Sovereignty* (Toronto: Stoddart, 1997).

Claydon, J., "International Human Rights Law and the Interpretation of the Canadian Charter of Rights and Freedoms," (1982) 4 *Supreme Court Law Review* 287

Claydon, John, "The Use of International Human Rights Law to Interpret Canada's Charter of Rights and Freedoms" (1987) 2 *Connecticut Journal of International Law* 349.

Cohen, Marjorie Griffin, *What To Do About Globalization* (Vancouver: Canadian Centre for Policy Alternatives, 1997).

Cohen, Marjorie Griffin, *Women and Economic Structures: A Feminist Perspective on the Canadian Economy* (Ottawa: Canadian Centre for Policy Alternatives, 1991).

Cohen, Marjorie, "New International Trade Agreements: Their Reactionary Role in Creating Markets and Retarding Social Welfare" in Isabella Bakker, ed., *Rethinking Restructuring: Gender and Change in Canada* (Toronto: University of Toronto Press, 1996) 187.

Cohen, Marjorie, "Democracy and Trade Agreements: Challenges for Disadvantaged Women, Minorities and States" in R. Boyer and D. Drache, eds., *Markets Against States: The Limits of Globalization* (London: Routledge, 1996)

Coliver, Sandra, "United Nations Machineries on Women's Rights: How Might They Better Help Women Whose Rights Are Being Violated?" in E. L. Lutz et al., eds., *New Directions in Human Rights* (Philadelphia: University of Pennsylvania Press, 1989).

Commonwealth Secretariat, *A Commonwealth Vision for Women Towards the Year 2000: The Commonwealth Plan of Action on Gender and Development 1995*, Executive Summary (1995).

Cook, Rebecca J., "Human Rights and Reproductive Self-Determination" (1995) 44 *The American University Law Review* 976.

Cook, Rebecca J., ed., *Human Rights of Women: National and International Perspectives* (Philadelphia: University of Pennsylvania Press, 1994).

Cook, Rebecca J., "State Accountability Under the Convention on the Elimination of All Forms of Discrimination Against Women" in Rebecca Cook, ed., *Human Rights of Women: National and International Perspectives* (Philadelphia: University of Pennsylvania Press, 1994).

Cook, Rebecca J., "State Responsibility for Violations of Women's Human Rights" (1994) 7 *Harvard Human Rights Journal* 125.

Cook, Rebecca J., "Women's International Human Rights Law: The Way Forward" (1993) 15 *Human Rights Quarterly* 230.

Cook, Rebecca J., and Valerie Oosterveld, "A Select Bibliography on Women's Human Rights" (1995) 44 *American University Law Review* 1429.

Coote, Belinda, "The Trade Trap: Poverty and the Global Commodity Markets" (1992) 8(2) *International Insights* 103.

Cotter, Brent, "Enforcing the Human Rights of the Poor" in J. Tarnopolsky et al., eds, *Discrimination in the Law and the Administration of Justice* (Ottawa: Canadian Institute for the Administration of Justice, 1993).

The Council of Canadians, *Danger Ahead: Assessing the Implications of the Canada Health and Social Transfer* (Ottawa, March 1995).

Council of Canadians with Disabilities, *Initial Comments on a Social Audit* (Winnipeg, 1996).

Council of Canadians with Disabilities, *Justiciable Standards Re: Social Assistance and Services* (Winnipeg, 1996).

Courchene, Thomas J., *ACCESS: A Convention on the Canadian Economic and Social Systems* (Toronto: Government of Ontario, 1996).

Courchene, Thomas J., "The Federal-Provincial Dimension of the Budget: Two Cheers for the CHST" in Thomas J. Courchene and Thomas A. Wilson, eds., *The 1995 Federal Budget: Retrospect and Prospect* (Kingston, Ont.: John Deutsch Institute for the Study of Economic Policy, Queen's University, 1995).

Courchene, Thomas J., *Redistributing Money and Power: A Guide to the Canada Health and Social Transfer* (Toronto: C.D. Howe Institute, 1995).

Courchene, Thomas J., and Thomas A. Wilson, eds., *The 1995 Federal Budget: Retrospect and Prospect* (Kingston, Ont.: John Deutsch Institute for the Study of Economic Policy, Queen's University, 1995).

Cousineau, Jean-Michel, et al., *Delivering the Goods: The Federal-Provincial Division of Spending Powers* (Toronto: C.D. Howe Institute, 1992).

Crane, David, "Budget breeds new kind of government" *The [Toronto] Star* (1 March 1995) A19.

Craven, Matthew, "The Domestic Application of the *International Covenant on Economic, Social and Cultural Rights*" (1993) *Netherlands International Law Review* 367.

Dale, Patricia, *Women and Jobs: The Impact of Federal Government Employment Strategies on Women* (Ottawa: Canadian Advisory Council on the Status of Women, 1980).

Dale, Jennifer, and Peggy Foster, *Feminists and State Welfare* (London: Routledge & Kegan Paul, 1986).

Danaher, Kevin, and Muhammad Yunus, *50 Years is Enough: The Case Against the World Bank and the International Monetary Fund* (Boston: South End Press, 1994).

Danziger, Sheldon, et al., "Work and Welfare and Determinants of Female Poverty and Household Headship" (1982) 97 *Quarterly Journal of Economics* 519.

Day, Shelagh, "Constitutional Reform: Canada's Equality Crisis" in David Schneiderman, ed., *Conversations Among Friends — Entre Amies: Proceedings of an Interdisciplinary Conference on Women and Constitutional Reform* (Edmonton: University of Alberta, Centre for Constitutional Studies, 1991).

Day, Shelagh, and Gwen Brodsky, "The Duty to Accommodate: Who Will Benefit?" (1996) 75 *Canadian Bar Review* 433.

des Rosiers, Nathalie, and Bruce Feldthusen, "Discretion in Social Assistance Legislation" (1992) 8 *Journal of Law and Social Policy* 204.

Dieng, Adama, ed., "Economic, Social and Cultural Rights and the Role of Lawyers" (1995) Special Issue *International Commission of Jurists — The Review* 7.

Dion, Stéphane, "Canada has to change, but so do federalists in Quebec" *Canadian NewsDisc* (25 November 1995) B5.

Doern, Bruce, ed., *The Politics of Economic Policy* (Toronto: University of Toronto Press, 1985).

Dohnal, Jerry, "Structural Adjustment Programs: a Violation of Rights" (1994) 1 *Australian Journal of Human Rights* 57.

Donnelly, Maureen, "The Disparate Impact of Pension Reform on Women" (1993) 6 *Canadian Journal of Women and the Law* 419.

Donner, Laura A., "Gender Bias in Drafting International Discrimination Conventions: The 1979 Women's Convention Compared with the 1965 Racial Convention" (1994) 24 *California Western International Law Journal* 241.

Dooley, Martin D., "Women, Children and Poverty in Canada" in *Economic Equality Workshop: Summary of Proceedings* (Ottawa: Status of Women Canada, 1993).

Drache, Daniel, and Andrew Ranachan, eds., *Warm Heart Cold Country: Fiscal and Social Policy Reform in Canada* (Ottawa: Caledon Institute of Social Policy, 1995).

Drumbl, Mark Anthony, "Exploring the Constitutional Limits to Workfare and Learnfare" (1994) 10 *Journal of Law and Social Policy* 107.

Drummond, Alison, *The Social Charter: Evolution of the Concept in Recent Constitutional Negotiations* (Toronto: Ontario Legislative Library, Legislative Research Service, 1992).

Echenberg, H., *Notes on the Federal Government's Proposals for Reform of the Social Services Component of the Canada Assistance Plan* (Ottawa: Canadian Advisory Council on the Status of Women, 1994).

Echenberg, Havi, *A Social Charter for Canada?* (Toronto: C.D. Howe Institute, 1992).

Echenberg, Havi, and Bruce Porter, "The Case for Social and Economic Rights" (1989) 6 *Canadian Housing* 26.

Echenberg, Havi, and Bruce Porter, "Poverty Stops Equality: Equality Stops Poverty: The Case for Social and Economic Rights" in Ryszard Cholewinsky, ed., *Human Rights in Canada: Into the 1990s and Beyond* (Ottawa: Human Rights Research and Education Centre, 1990) 1.

Economic Commission for Latin America and the Caribbean, "Human Rights in Latin America and the Caribbean: Growth with Equity," in Richard Reoch, ed., *Human Rights: The New Consensus* (London: Regency House (Humanity), 1994).

Economic Council of Canada, *The New Face of Poverty: Income Security Needs of Canadian Families* (Ottawa, 1992).

Ecumenical Coalition for Economic Justice, "Women Bear the Brunt of Economic Restructuring" (December 1992) 3 *Economic Justice Report* 1.

Ehrenreich, Barbara, and Frances Fox Piven, "The Feminization of Poverty: When the 'Family-Wage System' Breaks Down" (1984) 31 *Dissent* 162.

Eichler, Margrit, "The Limits of Family Law Reform, or the Privatization of Female and Child Poverty" (1990) 7 *Canadian Family Law Quarterly* 9.

Einhorn, Barbara, "Can Cinderella Become a Citizen?" in B. Einhorn, *Cinderella Goes to Market: Citizenship, Gender and Women's Movements in East Central Europe* (London: Verso, 1993).

Einhorn, Barbara, "The 'Woman Question': The Legacy of State Socialism" in B. Einhorn, *Cinderella Goes to Market: Citizenship, Gender and Women's Movements in East Central Europe* (London: Verso, 1993).

EKOS Research Associates Inc., *Rethinking Government 1994: An Overview and Synthesis* (Ottawa, 1994)

EKOS Research Associates Inc., *Rethinking Government 1995: Final Report* (Ottawa, 1995).

"Election-minded Chrétien comes to B.C. bearing gifts," *The [Vancouver] Sun* (7 March, 1997) A1.

Ellsworth, Randall, et al., "Poverty Law in Ontario: The Year in Review" (1993) 9 *Journal of Law and Social Policy* 1.

Ellsworth, Randall, et al., "Poverty Law in Ontario: The Year in Review" (1994) 10 *Journal of Law and Social Policy* 1.

Ellsworth, Randall, and Ian Morrison, "Poverty Law in Ontario: The Year in Review" (1992) 8 *Journal of Law and Social Policy* 1.

Ellsworth, Randall, and Ian Morrison, "Poverty Law in Ontario: The Year in Review" (1991) 7 *Journal of Law and Social Policy* 1.

Elson, Diane, "From Survival Strategies to Transformation Strategies: Women's Needs and Structural Adjustment" in Lourdes Beneria and Shelly Feldman, eds., *Unequal Burden: Economic Crisis, Persistent Poverty, and Women's Work* (Boulder, Colo.: Westview Press, 1992).

Elson, Diane, "Gender-Aware Analysis and Development Economics" (1993) 5 *Journal of International Development* 237.

Ely, John Hart, *Democracy and Distrust: A Theory of Judicial Review* (Cambridge, Mass.: Harvard University Press, 1980).

End Legislated Poverty, "Speaking Out Against Poor Bashing" *The Long Haul* [*Vancouver*] (February 1995) supplement.

Engle, Karen, *Women and the Market: Collapsing Distinctions in International Law* (Toronto: Faculty of Law, 1994).

Evans, Patricia M., "From Workfare to the Social Contract: Implications for Canada of Recent U.S. Welfare Reforms" (1993) 9 *Canadian Public Policy* 54.

Evans, Patricia M., "The Sexual Division of Poverty: The Consequences of Gendered Caring" in Carol Baines et al., eds., *Women's Caring: Feminist Perspectives on Social Welfare* (Toronto: McClelland and Stewart, 1991).

Evans, Patricia M., "Single Mothers and Ontario's Welfare Policy: Restructuring the Debate" in Janine Brodie, ed., *Women and Canadian Public Policy* (Toronto: Harcourt Brace, 1995).

Evans, Patricia M., "Work Incentives and the Single Mother: Dilemmas of Reform" (1988) 14 *Canadian Public Policy* 125.

Evatt, Elizabeth, "Eliminating Discrimination Against Women: The Impact of the UN Convention" (1991) 18 *Melbourne University Law Review* 435.

Fainer, Andrew, *Social Assistance, Equality and Section 15 of the Charter.* (LL.M. Thesis, York University, 1993).

Feldman, Shelley, "Crises, Poverty and Gender Inequality: Current Themes and Issues" in L. Beneria and S. Feldman, eds., *Unequal Burden: Economic Crisis, Persistent Poverty, and Women's Work* (Boulder, Colo.: Westview Press, 1992).

Fellegi, Ivan, "StatsCan measures income, not 'poverty'" *The [Montreal] Gazette* (17 September 1997) B3.

Ferber, Marianne, and Julie Nelson, eds., *Beyond Economic Man: Feminist Theory and Economics* (Chicago: University of Chicago Press, 1993).

Ferguson, Derek, "Funding changes would hurt poor, Coalition says" *The [Toronto] Star* (8 February 1995) A10.

Ferguson, Derek, "Legislation gives cabinet control over safety net" *The [Toronto] Star* (25 March 1995) A3.

Ferguson, Derek, "Liberal block funding scheme dooms safety net, critics say" *The [Toronto] Star* (27 May 1995) B4.

Fineman, Martha L., "Images of Mothers in Poverty Discourses" (1991) *Duke Law Journal* 274.

Finkelstein, Neil, and Russell Cohen, "Suggestions for the Decentralization of Canada" (1996) 75 *Canadian Bar Review* 251.

Finnie, Ross, "Women, Men and the Economic Consequences of Divorce: Evidence from Canadian Longitudinal Data" (1993) 30 *Canadian Review of Sociology and Anthropology* 205.

Fisher, John, "The Impact of the Supreme Court Decision in *Egan* v. *Canada* Upon Claims for the Equal Recognition of Same-Sex Relationships" (1997) [unpublished].

Folbre, Nancy, "Feminist Theory and Political Economy" in N. Folbre, *Who Pays for the Kids? Gender and the Structures of Constraint* (London: Routledge, 1994).

Forsythe, David P., Book Review of *International Cooperation for Social Justice: Global and Regional Protection of Economic/Social Rights* by A. Glenn Mower (1986) 8:3 *Human Rights Quarterly* 540.

Fraser, Nancy, and Linda Gordon, "A Genealogy of Dependency: Tracing a Keyword of the U.S. Welfare State" (1994) 19 *Signs* 309.

Fréchette, Jean-Denis, *Federal Provincial Fiscal Arrangements* (Ottawa: Library of Parliament, Research Branch, 1990).

Freeman, Marsha A., "Measuring Equality: A Comparative Perspective on Women's Legal Capacity and Constitutional Rights in Five Commonwealth Countries" (1989–90) 5 *Berkeley Women's Law Journal* 110.

Frum, David, "Splitting social welfare bills has only led to waste" *The Financial Post* (25 January 1995) 17.

Fudge, Judy, "The Privatization of the Costs of Social Reproduction: Some Recent *Charter* Cases" (1989) 3 *Canadian Journal of Women and the Law* 246.

Fudge, Judy, "What Do We Mean by Law and Social Transformation?" (1990) 5 *Canadian Journal of Law and Society* 47.

Fulcher, Ted J.E., "Using a Contextual Methodology to Accommodate Equality Protections Along with the Other Objectives of Government: 'Not the Right Answer, Stupid. The Best Answer'" (1996) 34 *Alberta Law Review* 416.

Gabriel, Christina, and Laura MacDonald, "NAFTA and Economic Restructuring: Some Gender and Race Implications" in Isabella Bakker, ed., *Rethinking Restructuring: Gender and Changes in Canada* (Toronto: University of Toronto Press, 1996) 165.

Galaway, Burt, and Joe Hudson, eds., *Community Economic Development: Perspectives on Research and Policy* (Toronto: Thompson Educational Publishing, 1994).

Garpenby, Peter, "Health Care Reform in Sweden in the 1990s: Local Pluralism versus National Coordination" (1995) 20:3 *Journal of Health Politics, Policy and Law* 695.

Gavigan, Shelley, "Poverty Law and Poor People: The Place of Gender and Class in Clinic Practice" (1995) 11 *Journal of Law and Social Policy* 165.

Ghalam, Nancy Z., *Women in the Workplace*, 2d ed. (Ottawa: Statistics Canada, 1993), cat. no. 71-534E.

Gibson, Gordon, "So little time for, so much opposition to, a Canada with a future" *The [Vancouver] Sun* (10 February 1995) A23.

Glendinning, Caroline, "Losing Ground: Social Policy and Disabled People in Great Britain, 1980-90" (1991) 6 *Disability, Handicap & Society* 3.

Goggin, Janice M., "The Health Care State in Global Perspective" (1995) 20:3 *Journal of Health Politics, Policy and Law* 783.

Gold, Steven, "Issues Raised by the New Federalism" (1996) 74 *National Tax Journal* 273.

Goldberg, Gertrude, and Eleanor Kremen, eds. *The Feminization of Poverty: Only in America?* (New York: Praeger, 1990).

Gomez, Mario, "Social Economic Rights and Human Rights Commissions" (1995) 17 *Human Rights Quarterly* 155.

Goyette, Linda, "The Liberals abandon a Canadian way of speaking" *The [Edmonton] Journal* (2 April 1996) A14.

Grabb, Edward, *Theories of Social Inequality: Classical and Contemporary Perspectives,* 3d ed. (Toronto: Harcourt Brace, 1996).

Grady, Patrick, et al., *Redefining Social Security* (Kingston, Ont.: School of Policy Studies, Queen's University 1995).

Graycar, Regina, "Legal Categories and Women's Work: Explorations for a Cross-Doctrinal Feminist Jurisprudence" (1994) 7 *Canadian Journal of Women and the Law* 34.

Grewal, Inderpal, and Caren Kaplan, "Introduction: Transnational Feminist Practices and Questions of Postmodernity" in I. Grewal and C. Kaplan, eds., *Scattered Hegemonies* (Minnesota: University of Minnesota Press, 1994).

Griffin, Kevin, "Anti-poverty groups plan complaint to UN" *The [Vancouver] Sun* (28 April 1995) B2.

Gross, Bertram, "Book Review: Civilization and Work" (1994) 16 *Human Rights Quarterly* 757.

Guest, Dennis, *The Emergence of Social Security in Canada* (Vancouver: University of British Columbia Press, 1980).

Gunderson, Morley, et al., *Women and Labour Market Poverty* (Ottawa: Canadian Advisory Council on the Status of Women, 1990).

Gwyn, Richard, "Era of 'special interest' dies on chopping block" *The [Toronto] Star* (1 March 1995) A21.

Gwyn, Richard, "Martin's budget will create a new kind of Canada" *The [Toronto] Star* (26 February 1995) E3.

Gwyn, Richard, "Ottawa is fading away along with the old Canada" *The [Toronto] Star* (5 February 1995) C3.

Haddow, Rodney S., *Poverty Reform in Canada, 1958–1978: State and Class Influences on Policy Making* (Montreal: McGill-Queen's University Press, 1993).

Haq, Mahbub Ul, *New Imperatives of Human Security: Barbara Ward Lecture 1994* (Mexico City: Society for International Development 21st World Conference, 1994).

Harcourt, Wendy, "The Globalisation of the Economy" (1994) 2 *Focus on Gender* 6.

Harder, Sandra, *Women in Canada: Socio-Economic Status and Other Contemporary Issues* (Ottawa: Library of Parliament, Research Branch, 1992).

Harder, Sandra, *Economic Restructuring in Canada: Developing a Gender-Sensitive Analytic Framework* (Ottawa: Status of Women Canada, 1992).

Harrington, Michael, "The New Gradgrinds" (1984) 31 *Dissent* 171.

Hasson, Reuben, "What's Your Favourite Right? The Charter and Income Maintenance Legislation" (1989) 5 *Journal of Law and Social Policy* 1.

Hathaway, James C. "Poverty Law and Equality Rights: Preliminary Reflections" (1985) 1 *Journal of Law and Social Policy* 455.

Head, Tina, "Strategic Approaches and Specific Measures for the Exercise of Citizenship Rights by Persons with Disabilities" in *The Will to Act for Canadians with Disabilities: Research Papers* (Ottawa: Federal Task Force on Disability Issues, Human Resources Development Canada, 1996).

Helleiner, Gerald K., *Poverty in the South: Northern Responsibilities — and a Role for Canada* (Guelph, Ont.: Centre for International Programs, University of Guelph, 1995).

Himes, James R., ed., *Implementing the Convention on the Rights of the Child: Resource Mobilization in Low Income Countries* (The Hague: Martinus Nijhoff, 1995).

Hodge, Gerald J.F., *Incomes, Low Incomes and Welfare in the West, 1980–1990* (Saskatoon: Western Institute for Public Policy, 1993).

Hogg, Peter, *Constitutional Law of Canada,* 3d ed. (Toronto: Carswell, 1993)

Hogg, Roy, and Jack Mintz, eds., *Who Pays the Piper? Canada's Social Policy* (Kingston: John Deutsch Institute for the Study of Economic Policy, Queen's University, 1994).

Hossfeld, Karen, "'Their Logic Against Them': Contradictions in Sex, Race, and Class in Silicon Valley" in K. Ward, ed., *Women Workers and Global Restructuring* (Ithaca, N.Y.: I.L.R. Press, 1990).

Howse, Robert, "Another Rights Revolution? The *Charter* and the Reform of Social Regulation in Canada." in Judith Maxwell, et al., eds., *Redefining Social Security* (Kingston: School of Policy Studies, Queen's University, 1995).

Hughes, Karen, et al., "Public Attitudes Toward Budget Cuts in Alberta: Biting the Bullet or Feeling the Pain?" (1996) 22 *Canadian Public Policy* 268.

Hughes, Mark, "Middle Class Windfalls and the Poverty of the Welfare State" (1991) 10 *Philanthropy* 3.

Hum, Derek, "The Working Poor, the Canada Assistance Plan, and Provincial Responses in Income Supplementation" in Jacqueline Ismael, ed., *Canadian Social Welfare Policy, Federal and Provincial Dimensions* (Montreal: Institute of Public Administration of Canada, 1985).

Hume, Stephen, "Why it's best to exclude the right from any deficit-fighting arsenal" *The [Vancouver] Sun* (22 February 1995) A13.

Ibrahim, Youseff, "Norwegian welfare leads world" *The [Toronto] Globe and Mail* (18 December 1996) A8.

Institute of Intergovernmental Relations, *Approaches to National Standards in Federal Systems: A Research Report* (Kingston: Institute of Intergovernmental Relations, Queen's University, 1991).

International Women's Rights Action Watch, *Assessing the Status of Women: A Guide to Reporting Under the Convention on the Elimination of All Forms of Discrimination Against Women,* 2d ed. (Minneapolis, 1996).

Ismael, Jacqueline S., ed., *Canadian Social Welfare Policy: Federal and Provincial Dimensions* (Kingston: McGill-Queen's University Press, 1985).

Ismael, Jacqueline S., and Yves Vaillancourt, eds., *Privatization and Provincial Social Services in Canada* (Edmonton: University of Alberta Press, 1988).

Jackman, Martha, "The Cabinet and the Constitution: Participatory Rights and *Charter* Interests: *Manicom* v. *County of Oxford*" (1990) 35 *McGill Law Journal* 943.

Jackman, Martha, "Constitutional Contact with the Disparities in the World: Poverty as a Prohibited Ground of Discrimination under the Canadian *Charter* and Human Rights Law" (1994) 2 *Review of Constitutional Studies* 76.

Jackman, Martha, "Le 'nouveau partage des pouvoirs' : l'efficacité ou l'équité?" (1991) 23 *Ottawa Law Review* 421.

Jackman, Martha, "Poor Rights: Using the *Charter* to Support Social Welfare Claims" (1993) 19 *Queen's Law Journal* 65.

Jackman, Martha, "The Protection of Welfare Rights Under the *Charter*" (1988) 20 *Ottawa Law Review* 257.

Jackman, Martha, "The Regulation of Private Health Care Under the *Canada Health Act* and the Canadian *Charter*" (1995) 6 *Constitutional Forum* 54.

Jackman, Martha, "The Right to Participate in Health Care and Health Resource Allocation Decisions Under Section 7 of the Canadian *Charter*" (1995) 4 *Health Law Review* 3.

Jackman, Martha, "Women and the Canada Health and Social Transfer: Ensuring Gender Equality in Federal Welfare Reform" (1995) 8:2 *Canadian Journal of Women and the Law* 371.

Jackman, Martha, "Women, Poverty and Welfare Reform: Can the *Charter* Make a Difference?" in *Les femmes et le droit criminel : Actes de la Conférence* (Moncton: Comité femmes et droit, École de droit, Université de Moncton, 1996) 15.

Jackson, Chris, "Measuring and Valuing: Households' Unpaid Work" (Autumn 1996) *Canadian Social Trends* 25.

Janisch, Hudson, "Case Comment: *National Anti-Poverty Organization* v. *Canada*" (1989) 32 *Administrative Law Review* 60.

Jennissen, T., "The Federal Social Security Review: A Gender Sensitive Critique" in J. Pulkingham and G. Ternowetsky, eds., *Remaking Canadian Social Policy: Social Security in the Late 1990's* (Halifax: Fernwood Press Publishing, 1996) 238.

Jenson, Jane, and Ruth Kantrow, "Labor Market and Family Policy in France: An Intersecting Complex for Dealing with Poverty" in Gertrude Goldberg and Eleanor Kremen, eds., *The Feminization of Poverty: Only in America?* (New York: Praeger, 1990).

Johnson, Andrew F., "Federal Policies and the Privatization of Provincial Social Services" in Jacqueline S. Ismael and Yves Vaillancourt, eds., *Privatization and Provincial Social Services in Canada: Policy, Administration and Service Delivery* (Edmonton: University of Alberta Press, 1988).

Johnsrude, Larry, "Alberta's raw deal called no surprise" *The [Edmonton] Journal* (14 June 1996) A6.

Johnstone, Ian, "Section 7 of the *Charter* and the Right to Welfare" (1988) 46 *University of Toronto Faculty of Law Review* 1.

Kabeer, Naila, "Cultural Dopes or Rational Fools? Women and Labour Supply in the Bangladesh Garment Industry" (1991) *The European Journal of Development Research* 133.

Kabeer, Naila, and John Humphrey, "Neo-liberalism, Gender, and the Limits of the Market" in Christopher Colclough and James Manor, eds., *States or Markets? Neo-liberalism and the Development Policy Debate* (Oxford University Press, 1993).

Kamerman, Sheila, "Women, Children, and Poverty: Public Policies and Female-Headed Families in Industrialized Countries" in Barbara Gelpi et al., eds., *Women and Poverty* (Chicago: University of Chicago Press, 1986).

Keene, Judith, "Discrimination in the Provision of Government Services and s. 15 of the *Charter*: Making the Best of the Judgments in *Egan, Thibaudeau* and *Miron*" (1995) 11 *Journal of Law and Social Policy* 107.

Kentridge, Sydney, "Bill of Rights — The South African Experiment" (1996) 19:4 *Law Quarterly Review* 237.

Kerr, Donna, *The Economic Situation of Women Over 55, Present and Projected* (Edmonton: Alberta Advisory Council on Women's Issues, 1994).

Kerr, Joanna, ed., *Ours by Right — Women's Rights as Human Rights* (Ottawa: North-South Institute, 1993).

Kerr, Joanna, *Report from the Expert Group Meeting on Women and Global Restructuring* (Ottawa: North-South Institute, 1994).

Kilfoil, Valerie, *Casual Labour — A Women's Issue* (Fredericton: Women Together/Ensemble, 1994).

Kohler, Thomas C., "Lessons from the Social Charter: State, Corporation, and the Meaning of Subsidiarity" (1993) 43:3 *University of Toronto Law Journal* 607.

Ku, Charlotte, "A Feminist Approach to International Relations: an Emerging Concept of Concurrent Identities" (1992) *Canadian Council of International Law* 91.

Künnemann, Rolf, "A Coherent Approach to Human Rights" (1995) 17 *Human Rights Quarterly* 323.

Ladd, Helen, and Fred Doolittle, "Which Level of Government Should Assist the Poor?" (1982) 35 *National Tax Journal* 523.

LaFramboise, Donna, "You've come a long way baby ... and for what? *The [Toronto] Globe and Mail* (26 July 1997) B1.

Lamarche, Lucie, "An Historical Review of Social and Economic Rights: A Case for Real Rights" (1995) 15:2&3 *Canadian Woman Studies* 12.

Lamarche, Lucie, "Le débat sur les droits sociaux au Canada : respecte-t-il la juridicité de ces droits? in Joel Bakan and David Schneiderman, eds., *Social Justice and the Constitution: Perspectives on a Social Union for Canada* (Ottawa: Carleton University Press, 1992).

Lamarche, Lucie, "Le droit international des droits économiques de la personne et le quart monde occidental: A-t-on parlé pour ne rien dire?" in *L'actualité de la Déclaration universelle des droits de l'homme – Cahier des communications du Colloque du 10 décembre 1993* (Montréal: Commission des droits de la personne du Québec, Départment des sciences juridiques de l'U.Q.A.M. et Société québécoise de droit international, 1993).

Lamarche, Lucie, "La nouvelle loi sur la securité du revenu au Québec: quelques réflexions d'actualité" (1991) 21 *Revue de droit de l'Université de Sherbrooke* 335.

LaSelva, Samuel, "Federalism as a Way of Life: Reflections on the Canadian Experiment" (1993) 26 *Canadian Journal of Political Science* 219.

Latella, Matthew, "Rethinking Groupism: An Alternative to the Postmodern Strategy" (1994) 3 *Dalhousie Journal of Legal Studies* 137.

Leach, Belinda, "Behind Closed Doors: Homework Policy and Lost Possibilities for Change" in Isabella Bakker, ed., *Rethinking Restructuring: Gender and Change in Canada* (Toronto: University of Toronto Press, 1996) 203.

League for Social Reconstruction, *Social Planning for Canada* (Toronto: University of Toronto Press, 1975).

LeBoeuf, Jacques, "The Economics of Federalism and the Proper Scope of the Federal Commerce Power" (1994) 3 *San Diego Law Review* 555.

Lefebour, Patricia, "Same Sex Spousal Recognition in Ontario: Declarations and Denials: a Class Perspective" (1993) 9 *Journal of Law and Social Policy* 272.

Lero, Donna S., and Karen L. Johnson, *110 Canadian Statistics on Work and Family* (Ottawa: Canadian Advisory Council on the Status of Women, 1994).

Lero, Donna S., et al, *Canadian National Child Care Study: Introductory Report* (Ottawa: Statistics Canada; Health and Welfare Canada, 1992), cat. no. 89-526E.

Leslie, Peter, *National Citizenship and Provincial Communities: A Review of Canadian Fiscal Federalism* (Kingston: Institute of Intergovernmental Relations, 1988).

Lessard, Hester, "Creation Stories: Social Rights and Canada's Social Contract" in Joel Bakan and David Schneiderman, eds., *Social Justice and the Canadian Constitution: Perspectives on a Social Union for Canada* (Ottawa: Carleton University Press, 1992).

Lessard, Hester, "Relationship, Particularity and Change: Reflections on *R.* v. *Morgentaler* and Feminist Approaches to Liberty" (1991) 36(2) *McGill Law Journal* 263.

Liberal Party of Canada, Press Release, "Liberals Will Strengthen Health Care Funding" (28 April 1997).

Lipovenko, Dorothy, "Elderly women at risk: Report" *The [Toronto] Globe and Mail* (5 December 1996) A1.

Little, Bruce, "When the big shift in spending took place" *The [Toronto] Globe and Mail* (20 November) A6.

Low Income Tax Relief Working Group of the Fair Tax Commission, *Working Group Report: Low Income Tax Relief* (Toronto: Fair Tax Commission, 1992).

Lowenberger, Lois, et al., "Welfare: Women, Poverty and the *Charter*" (1985) 1 *Journal of Law and Social Policy* 42.

MacBride-King, Judith L., *Work and Family: Employment Challenge of the '90s* (Ottawa: Conference Board of Canada, 1990).

MacDonald, Martha, "Economic Restructuring and Gender in Canada: Feminist Policy Initiatives" (1995) 23:11 *World Development* 2005.

Marks, Susan, "Nightmare and Noble Dream: The 1993 World Conference on Human Rights" (1994) 53 *The Cambridge Law Journal* 54.

Martin, Dianne L., "Passing the Buck: Prosecution of Welfare Fraud: Preservation of Stereotypes" (1992) 12 *Windsor Yearbook of Access to Justice* 52.

Martin, Paul, "A New Framework for Economic Policy" (Presentation to the House of Commons Standing Committee on Finance, Ottawa 1994).

Maslove, Allan M., *National Goals and the Federal Role in Health Care* (Ottawa: National Forum on Health, 1995).

McArthur, Jack, "Transfer payments cover less and less" *The [Toronto] Star* (27 September 1993) D2.

McCallum, Sandra K., Case Comment on *Reference Re: Canada Assistance Plan* (1991) 45 *Administrative Law Review* 80.

McCarthy, Shawn, "Budget bill hits poor, Liberal MP charges" *The [Toronto] Star* (6 June 1995) A9.

McCarthy, Shawn, "Cuts keep programs alive: Martin" *The [Toronto] Star* (1 March 1995) A10.

McConnell, M.L., "The Relationship Between Theories about Women and Theories about International Law" (1992) *Canadian Council of International Law* 68.

McDowell, Linda, "Life Without Father and Ford: The New Gender Order of Post-Fordism" (1991) 16 *Trans. Institute British Geography* 400.

McFarland, Joan, "Combining Economic and Social Policy through Work and Welfare: The Impact on Women" (Paper presented to the Economic Equity Workshop, Status of Women Canada, Ottawa, 1993).

McGilly, Frank, *An Introduction to Canada's Public Social Services: Understanding Income and Health Programs* (Toronto: McClelland & Stewart, 1995).

McInnes, Craig, "B.C. to abolish welfare rule: Ottawa agrees to pay sixty million for dropping of controversial residency requirement" *The [Toronto] Globe and Mail* (6 March 1997) A1.

McQuaig, Linda, *Shooting the Hippo: Death by Deficit and Other Canadian Myths* (Toronto: Viking, 1995).

Mendelson, Michael, "Establishing a Social Investment Framework" in *Roundtables on the Canada Health and Social Transfer* (Ottawa: Canadian Council on Social Development, 1996) 129.

Mendelson, Michael, *Looking for Mr. Good-Transfer: A Guide to the Canada Health and Social Transfer Negotiations* (Ottawa: Caledon Institute of Social Policy, 1995).

Mendelson, Michael, *The Provinces' Position: A Second Chance for the Social Security Review?* (Ottawa: Caledon Institute of Social Policy, 1996).

Miller, Dorothy, "Feminist Theory and Social Policy or Why is Welfare So Hard to Reform?" (1985) 12 *Journal of Sociology and Social Welfare* 664.

Mimoto, H., and P. Cross, "The Growth of the Federal Debt" (1991) 3:1 *Canadian Economic Observer* 1.

Minow, Martha, "The Welfare of Single Mothers and Their Children" (1994) 26:3 *Connecticut Law Review* 817.

Mitchell, Alanna, "Latest poll may give Klein pause" *The [Toronto] Globe and Mail* (28 July 1997) A4.

Mitter, Swasi, "On Organising Women in Casualized Work: A Global Overview" in Sheila Rowbotham and Swasti Mitter, eds., *Dignity and Daily Bread: New Forms of Economic Organising Among Poor Women in the Third World and First* (London: Routledge, 1994).

Moghadam, Valentine, "An Overview of Global Employment and Unemployment in a Gender Perspective" (Paper for UNU/WIDER Conference on the Politics and Economics of Global Employment, 17 June, 1994, draft).

Moore, Sarah, "Social Policy: Nothing Positive from the Court of Justice" (1996) 21:2 *European Law Review* 156.

Morrison, Ian, *Beyond Cost-Sharing: The Canada Assistance Plan and National Welfare Standards.* (Toronto: Clinic Resource Office, 1994).

Morrison, Ian, "Poverty Law and the Charter: The Year in Review" (1990) 6 *Journal of Law and Social Policy* 1.

Morrison, Ian, "Security of the Person and the Person in Need: Section Seven of the *Charter* and the Right to Welfare" (1988) 4 *Journal of Law and Social Policy* 1.

Morrison, Ian, and G. Pearce, "Under the Axe: Social Assistance in Ontario in 1995" (1995) 11 *Journal of Law and Social Policy* 1.

Morrissette, France. "Le droit à l'égalité de la *Charte* appliqué à certain programmes sociaux fédéraux" (1991) 22 *Revue générale de droit* 509.

Morton, Mary, "Dividing the Wealth, Sharing the Poverty: The (Re)Formation of 'Family' Law in Ontario" (1988) 25 *Canadian Review of Sociology and Anthropology* 254.

Moser, Caroline, "Gender Planning in the Third World: Meeting Practical and Strategic Gender Needs" (1989) 17 *World Development* 1799.

Moser, Caroline, "Towards an Emancipation Approach: The Political Agenda of Women's Organizations" in C. Moser, *Gender Planning and Development* (London: Routledge, 1993).

Mosher, Janet, "The Harms of Dichotomy: Access to Welfare Benefits as a Case in Point" (1991) 9 *Canadian Journal of Family Law* 97.

Mossman, Mary Jane, "Constitutional Reform and the Feminization of Poverty" in David Schneiderman, ed., *Conversations Among Friends – Entre Amies: Proceedings of an Interdisciplinary Conference on Women and Constitutional Reform* (Edmonton: University of Alberta, Centre for Constitutional Studies, 1991).

Mossman, Mary Jane, and Morag MacLean, "Family Law and Social Assistance Programs: Rethinking Equality" in Patricia Evans and Gerda Wekerle, eds., *Rethinking the Welfare State: Women and the Canadian Experience* (Toronto: University of Toronto Press, 1997).

Motula, Ziyad, "Socio-Economic Rights, Federalism, and the Courts: Comparative Lessons in South Africa" (1995) 112 *South African Law Journal* 63.

Mullan, David J., "Canada Assistance Plan: Denying Legitimate Expectation a Fair Start?" (1993) 7 *Administrative Law Reports (2d)* 269.

National Action Committee on the Status of Women, *Submission of the National Action Committee on the Status of Women to the House of Commons Standing Committee on Finance Regarding Bill C-76* (Toronto, 1995).

National Anti-Poverty Organization, *An Analysis of the Federal Discussion Paper on Social Programs* (Ottawa, 1994).

National Anti-Poverty Organization, *Monitoring the Impacts on Social Assistance Recipients of Welfare Cuts and Changes: An Update* (Ottawa, March 1997).

National Anti-Poverty Organization, *Monitoring the Impacts on Social Assistance of Welfare Cuts and Changes: An Overview* (Ottawa, 1996).

National Anti-Poverty Organization, *NAPO's Response to the Federal Discussion Paper "Improving Social Security in Canada"* (Ottawa, 1995).

National Anti-Poverty Organization, "The 1997 Federal Budget ... Much Ado About Nothing?" (1997) 57 *NAPO News* 1.

National Anti-Poverty Organization, *Poverty in Canada: Some Facts and Figures* (Ottawa, March 1995).

National Anti-Poverty Organization, *Striking a Better Balance: A Summary of NAPO's Position on C-91* (Ottawa, March 1997).

National Anti-Poverty Organization, *30 Million Good Reasons to Have National Standards for Welfare — an Action Guide from N.A.P.O.* (Ottawa, 1995).

National Association of Women and the Law, *Background Paper in Support of Tax Resolutions: NAWL 1991 Biennial Conference: The Feminization of Poverty, February 1991* (Ottawa, 1991).

National Association of Women and the Law, *The Federal Social Security Reform: Taking Gender into Account: Submission to the Standing Committee on Human Resources Development and to the Federal Department of Human Resources Development* (Ottawa, 1994).

National Association of Women and the Law, *The 1995 Federal Pre-Budget Consultations: Taking Gender Into Account* (Ottawa, 1994).

National Council of Welfare, *The Canada Assistance Plan: No Time for Cuts* (Ottawa: Supply and Services Canada, 1991).

National Council of Welfare, *Legal Aid and the Poor* (Ottawa: Supply and Services Canada, 1995).

National Council of Welfare, *The 1995 Budget and Block Funding*: A Report by the National Council of Welfare (Ottawa: Supply and Services Canada, 1995).

National Council of Welfare, *Poverty Profile, 1995*: A Report by the National Council of Welfare (Ottawa: Supply and Services Canada, 1997).

National Council of Welfare, *Welfare Income 1994* (Ottawa: Supply and Services Canada, 1996).

National Council of Welfare, *Welfare Income 1995* (Ottawa: Supply and Services Canada, 1997).

National Council of Welfare, *Women and Poverty Revisited: A Report* (Ottawa: Supply and Services Canada, 1990).

Nelson, Julie, *Feminism, Objectivity and Economics* (New York: Routledge, 1996).

Nelson, Julie, "Gender, Metaphor and the Definition of Economics" (1992) 8 *Economics and Philosophy* 103.

Nixon, P.G., "The Welfare State North: Early Developments in Inuit Income Security" (1990) 25 *Journal of Canadian Studies* 144.

Norris, Alexander, "Commentators split over outcome of first-ministers' meeting" *The [Montreal] Gazette* (27 June 1996) B3.

Oderkirk, Jillian, "Old Age Security" (Spring 1996) *Canadian Social Trends* 3, Cat. no. 11-008E.

Olsen, Frances, "The Family and the Market: a Study of Ideology and Legal Reform" (1983) 96 *Harvard Law Review* 1497.

Ontario Association of Interval and Transition Houses (OAITH), Submission to the UN Special Rapporteur on Violence Against Women, *Home Truth: Exposing the False Face of Equality and Security Rights For Abused Women in Canada* (Toronto: OAITH, November 1996).

Ontario, *The Protection of Social and Economic Rights: A Comparative Study* (Toronto: Attorney General, Constitutional Law and Policy Division, 1991).

Organisation for Economic Cooperation and Development, *The OECD Jobs Study: Facts, Analysis, Strategies* (Paris, 1994).

Orloff, Ann, "Gender and the Social Rights of Citizenship: The Comparative Analysis of Gender Relations and Welfare States" (1993) 58 *American Sociological Review* 303.

Orton, Helena, "Section 15, Benefits, Programs and Other Benefits at Law: The Interpretation of Section 15 of the *Charter* Since *Andrews*" (1990) 19 *Manitoba Law Journal* 288.

Parashar, Archana, "Essentialism or Pluralism: The Future of Legal Feminism" (1993) 6 *Canadian Journal of Women and the Law* 328.

Parker, David, "Resources and Child Rights: An Economic Perspective" in James Himes, ed., *Implementing the Convention on the Rights of the Child: Resource Mobilization in Low Income Countries* (The Hague: Martinus Nijhogg, 1995).

Parker, Stephen, "The Best Interests of the Child: Principles and Problems" in Philip Alston, ed., *The Best Interests of the Child: Reconciling Culture and Human Rights* (Oxford: Clarendon Press, 1994).

Parliamentary Task Force on Federal-Provincial Fiscal Arrangements, *Fiscal Federalism in Canada* (Ottawa: Supply and Social Services, 1981).

Pask, Diane, "Gender Bias and Child Support: Sharing the Poverty?" (1993) 10 *Canadian Family Law Quarterly* 33.

Pask, Diane, et al., *Women, the Law and the Economy* (Toronto: Butterworths, 1985).

Pearce, Diana, and Kelley Ellsworth, "Welfare and Women's Poverty: Reform or Reinforcement" (1990) 16 *Journal of Legislation* 141.

Pearson, Lester B., *Federalism for the Future: A Statement of Policy by the Government of Canada* (Ottawa: Government of Canada, 1968).

Pennar, Karen, "Are Block Grants the Answer?" *Business Week* (3 April 1995) 89.

Peters, Julie, and Andrea Wolper, eds., *Women's Rights, Human Rights: International Feminist Perspectives* (New York: Routledge, 1995).

Peterson, Janice, "The Feminization of Poverty" (1987) 21 *Journal of Economic Issues* 329.

Peterson, Paul E., and Mark Rom, *Welfare Magnets: A New Case for a National Standard* (Washington, D.C.: The Brookings Institution, 1990).

Petter, Andrew, "Federalism and the Myth of the Federal Spending Power" (1989) 68 *Canadian Bar Review* 449.

Philipps, Lisa, "Discursive Deficits: A Feminist Perspective on the Power of Technical Knowledge in Fiscal Law and Policy" (1996) 11:1 *Canadian Journal of Law and Society* 141.

Philipps, Lisa, "The Rise of Balanced Budget Laws in Canada: Legislating Fiscal (Ir)responsibility" (1996) 34:4 *Osgoode Hall Law Journal* 681.

Philipps, Lisa, "Tax Law: Equality Rights: *Thibaudeau v. Canada*" (1995) 74 *Canadian Bar Review* 668.

Philipps, Lisa, "Tax Policy and the Gendered Distribution of Wealth" in Isabella Bakker, ed., *Rethinking Restructuring: Gender and Change in Canada* (Toronto: University of Toronto Press, 1996) 141.

Philipps, Lisa, and Margot Young, "Sex, Tax and the *Charter*: A Review of *Thibaudeau v. Canada*" (1995) 2 *Review of Constitutional Studies* 221.

Phillips, Susan, "The Canada Health and Social Transfer: Fiscal Federalism in Search of a New Vision" in Douglas Brown and Jonathan Rose, eds., *Canada: The State of the Federation 1995* (Kingston: Institute of Intergovernmental Relations, 1995) 65.

Phipps, Shelley, "International Perspectives on Income Support for Families with Children" (Presentation to the Canadian Employment Research Forum Workshop on Income Support, Ottawa, 24 September 1993) [unpublished].

Picot, Garnett, and John Myles, "Children in Low-Income Families" (August 1996) *Canadian Social Trends* 15.

Pilkington, Marilyn, "The *Canadian Charter of Rights and Freedoms*: Impact on Economic Policy and Economic Liberty Regarding Women in Employment" (1988) 17 *Manitoba Law Journal* 267.

Piven, Frances Fox, "Poorhouse Politics" (1995) 59 *The Progressive* 22.

Pollak, Nancy, *Critical Choices, Turbulent Times: A Community Workbook on Social Programs* (Vancouver: School of Social Work, University of British Columbia, 1994).

Porter, Bruce, "The Uninvited Guests: Reflections on the Brief History of Poor People Seeking their Rightful Place in Equality Jurisprudence" in Canadian Bar Association, ed., *Roads to Equality: Continuing Legal Education Program, 1994 Annual Meeting, vol. 3.* (Ottawa: Canadian Bar Association, 1994).

Pothier, Diane, "M'Aider, Mayday: Section 15 of the *Charter* in Distress" (1996) 6 *National Journal of Constitutional Law* 295.

Pothier, Diane, "The Sounds of Silence: *Charter* Application When the Legislature Declines to Speak" (1996) 7 *Constitutional Forum* 113.

Pulkingham, Jane, "Private Troubles, Private Solutions: Poverty Among Divorced Women and the Politics of Support Enforcement and Child Custody Determination" (1994) 9 *Canadian Journal of Law and Society* 73.

Pulkingham, Jane, and Gordon Ternowetsky, eds., *Remaking Canadian Social Policy: Social Security in the Late 1990s* (Halifax: Fernwood Press, 1996).

Pulkingham, Jane, Gordon Ternowetsky and David Hay "The New Canada Child Tax Benefit: Eradicating Poverty or Victimizing the Poorest?" (1997) 4:1 *The Monitor*.

Quigley, John, and Daniel Rubinfeld, "Federalism and Reductions in the Federal Budget" (1996) 74 *National Tax Journal* 289.

Rathgeber, Eva, "WID, WAD, GAD: Trends in Research and Practice" (1990) 24 *The Journal of Developing Areas* 489.

Razack, Sherene, "Using Law for Social Change: Historical Perspectives" (1992) 17 *Queen's Law Journal* 31.

Reform Party of Canada, *A Fresh Start for Canadians*, (Ottawa: Reform Party of Canada, 1996).

Reoch, Richard, ed. *Human Rights: The New Consensus* (London: Regency House (Humanity), 1994).

Rich, Michael J., *Federal Policy Making and the Poor: National Goals, Local Choices, and Distributional Outcomes* (Princeton: Princeton University Press, 1993).

Rioux, Marcia, "The CHST: From Pathology to Social Investment" *Roundtables on the Canada Health and Social Transfer* (Ottawa: Canadian Council on Social Development, 1996) 141.

Robertson, Robert, "The Right to Food — Canada's Broken Covenant" (1989-90) 6 *Canadian Human Rights Yearbook* 185.

Rocher, Francois, and Miriam Smith, eds., *New Trends in Canadian Federalism* (Peterborough: Broadview Press, 1995).

Rochman, Paula, "Working for Welfare: A Response to the Social Assistance Review Committee" (1989) 5 *Journal of Law and Social Policy* 198.

Rosenbluth, Gideon, "The Political Economy of Deficit-Phobia" in Gideon Rosenbluth and Robert Allen, eds., *False Promises: The Failure of Conservative Economics* (Vancouver: New Star Books, 1992).

Ross, David P. *The Canadian Fact Book on Poverty* (Ottawa: Canadian Council on Social Development, 1994).

Rubin, Edward L., and Malcolm Feeley, "Federalism: Some Notes on a National Neurosis" (1994) 41:4 *U.C.L.A. Law Review* 903.

Rutwind, Stan, "A Cap on C.A.P." (1991) 3 *Constitutional Forum* 38.

Ryder, Bruce, "*Egan* v. *Canada*: Equality Deferred, Again" (1996) 4 *Canadian Labour and Employment Law Journal* 101.

Sarvasy, Wendy, and Judith Van Allen, "Fighting the Feminization of Poverty: Socialist-Feminist Analysis and Strategy" (1984) 16 *Review of Radical Political Economics* 89.

Savage, John, "Two Canadas: The Devolution Debate" (Address to the Empire Club, Toronto, 15 October 1996) [unpublished].

Scassa, Teresa, "Social Welfare and Section 7 of the *Charter*: *Conrad* v. *Halifax (County of)*" (1994) 17 *Dalhousie Law Journal* 187.

Schneiderman, David, "The Constitutional Politics of Poverty" in Joel Bakan and David Schneiderman, eds., *Social Justice and the Canadian Constitution: Perspectives on a Social Union for Canada* (Ottawa: Carleton University Press, 1992).

Schneiderman, David, ed., *Conversations Among Friends — Entre Amies: Proceedings of an Interdisciplinary*

Conference on Women and Constitutional Reform (Edmonton: University of Alberta, Centre for Constitutional Studies, 1991).

"School boards mount campaign on child poverty" *The [Toronto] Globe and Mail* (24 March 1997) A4.

Schwartz, Bryan, "A New Federal Role in Building the Social Safety Net for Disabled Persons" (1994) 22 *Manitoba Law Journal* 395.

Scott, Craig, "Covenant Constitutionalism and the Canada Assistance Plan" (1995) 6 *Constitutional Forum* 79.

Scott, Craig, "The Interdependence and Permeability of Human Rights Norms: Towards a Partial Fusion of the International Covenants on Human Rights" (1989) 27 *Osgoode Hall Law Journal* 768.

Scott, Craig, and Patrick Macklem, "Constitutional Ropes of Sand or Justiciable Guarantees? Social Rights in a New South African Constitution" (1992) 141:1 *University of Pennsylvania Law Review* 1.

Scott, K., *Women and Welfare State Restructuring: Inventory of Canadian Income Security and Employment-Related Initiatives* (North York: Centre for Research on Work and Society, York University, 1995).

Scott, Katherine, and Clarence Lochhead, *Are Women Catching Up in the Earnings Race?* (Ottawa: Canadian Council on Social Development, 1997).

Sealey-Burke, Jacqueline, "The Role of Maintenance Enforcement in Female Poverty: A Barbadian Perspective" (LL.M. Thesis, York University, 1989) (Ottawa: National Library of Canada, 1990).

Sen, Amartya, "Gender and Cooperative Conflicts" in Irene Tinker, ed., *Persistent Inequalities: Women and World Development"* (New York: Oxford University Press, 1990).

Shewchuk, Tara Rayne, "Regulation of Pre-Conception Agreements: A Synthesis of Individual Rights and Community Values" (1993) 1 *Health Law Journal* 147.

Shime, Pamela, "AIDS and Poverty Law: Inaction, Indifference and Ignorance" (1994) 10 *Journal of Law and Social Policy* 155.

Shone, Margaret A., "Health, Poverty and the Elderly: Can the Courts Make a Difference?" (1991) 29 *Alberta Law Review* 839.

Siegel, Richard L., "Socioeconomic Human Rights: Past and Future" (1985) 7:3 *Human Rights Quarterly* 255.

Skrypnek, Berna, and Jane Fast, "Trends in Canadian Women's Labour Force Behavior: Implications for Government and Corporate Policy" (Paper presented at the Economic Equality Workshop, Status of Women Canada, Ottawa, 29–30 November, 1993).

Smart, Stephen, "A Step Towards Workfare: The Supports to Employment Program and Sole Support Mothers" (1989) 6 *Journal of Law and Social Policy* 226.

Smith, Lynn C., and William Black, "Section 15 Equality Rights under the *Charter*: Meaning, Institutional Constraints and a Possible Test" (24 October 1987) [unpublished].

Social Planning Council of Winnipeg, *Standards for Social Assistance, Health and Health Care and Post-Secondary Education* (Winnipeg: Social Planning Council of Winnipeg, 1996).

Somerville, Janet, "CPJ sounds warning about Bill C-76" *Catholic New Times* (28 May 1995) 9.

Sossin, Lorne, "Redistributing Democracy: An Inquiry into Authority, Discretion and the Possibility of Engagement in the Welfare State" (1994) 26 *Ottawa Law Review* 1.

Stairs, Felicite, "Sole Support Mothers and Opportunity Planning in the Thomson Report" (1989) 5 *Journal of Law and Social Policy* 165.

Standing, Guy, "Global Feminization Through Flexible Labor" (1989) 17 *World Development* 1077.

Stark, Barbara, "International Human Rights Law, Feminist Jurisprudence, and Nietzche's 'Eternal Return': Turning the Wheel" (1996) 19 *Harvard Women's Law Journal* 169.

Statistics Canada, *Crossing the Low Income Line: Survey of Labour and Income Dynamics* (Ottawa: Statistics Canada, 1997), cat. no. 97-11.

Statistics Canada, *Schooling, Work and Related Activities, Income, Expenses and Mobility* (Ottawa: Industry, Science and Technology, 1993).

Statistics Canada, *Women in Canada: A Statistical Report*, 3d ed., (Ottawa: Industry, 1995).

Status of Women Canada, *Economic Equality Workshop: Papers on Economic Equality* (Ottawa, 1994).

Status of Women Canada, *Economic Equality Workshop: Summary of Proceedings* (Ottawa, 1994).

Status of Women Canada, *Living Without Fear — Everyone's Goal, Every Woman's Right* (Ottawa, 1991).

Status of Women Canada, National Consultation with Women's Groups on Social Security Reform with task team representatives of Human Resources Development Canada, Verbatim Report (Ottawa: Status of Women Canada, 3 December 1994).

Status of Women Canada, National Consultation with Women's Groups on Social Security Reform with Lloyd Axworthy, Verbatim Report (Ottawa: Status of Women Canada, 5 December 1994).

Status of Women Canada, *Setting the Stage for the Next Century: The Federal Plan for Gender Equality* (Ottawa, 1995)

Steenkamp, Anton J. "The South African Constitution of 1993 and the Bill of Rights: An Evaluation in Light of International Human Rights Norms" (1995) 17 *Human Rights Quarterly* 101.

Steinhauer, Paul, *The Canada Health and Social Transfer: A Threat to Health, Development and Future Productivity of Canada's Children and Youth* (Ottawa: Caledon Institute of Social Policy, 1995).

Stevenson, Garth, "Federalism and Intergovernmental Relations" in Michael Whittington and Glen Williams, eds., *Canadian Politics in the 1990s*, 3d ed. (Toronto: Nelson Canada, 1995).

Stychin, Carl, "Novel Concepts: A Comment on *Egan and Nesbit* v. *R.*" (1995) 6 *Constitutional Forum* 101.

Sullivan, Donna J., "Women's Human Rights and the 1993 World Conference on Human Rights" (1994) 88:1 *The American Journal of International Law* 152.

Taft, Kevin, *Shredding the Public Interest* (Calgary: University of Alberta Press and the Parkland Institute, 1997).

Tait, Kathy, "Joy's reform worth roses" *The [Vancouver] Province* (5 November 1995) A20.

Thiessen, Gordon, "My way to a better life for all, by the Governor of the Central Bank" *The [Vancouver] Sun* (20 January 1996).

Thompson-Harry, Karen, "Report of the Social Assistance Review Committee: Transitions" (1989–1990) 3 *Canadian Journal of Women and the Law* 673.

Tibbetts, Janice, "Albertans tell Klein to trim debt" *The [Vancouver] Sun* (16 April 1996) A7.

Tibbetts, Janice, "Klein Promises to Put Heart Back in Government" *The [Vancouver] Sun* (2 January 1996) A4.

Timms, H. Grant., "Social Welfare Programs under Pressure: The Role of Legal Clinics as Facilitators of Poverty Law Reform Activities" (1993) 9 *Journal of Law and Social Policy* 116.

Toope, Stephen, "The Convention on the Rights of the Child: Implications for Canada" in Michael Freeman, ed., *Children's Rights: A Comparative Perspective* (Aldershot: Dartmouth, 1996).

Torjman, Sherri, *The Let-Them-Eat-Cake Law* (Ottawa: Caledon Institute of Social Policy, 1995).

Torjman, Sherri, "Is C.A.P. in Need of Assistance?" in K. Banting and Ken Battle, eds., *A New Social Vision for Canada: Perspectives on the Federal Discussion Paper on Social Security Reform* (Kingston: School of Policy Studies, Queen's University, 1994).

Torjman, Sherri, and Ken Battle, *Can We Have National Standards?* (Ottawa: Caledon Institute of Social Policy, 1995).

Townson, Monica, *Independent Means: A Canadian Woman's Guide to Pensions and a Secure Financial Future* (Toronto: MacMillan, 1997)

Townson, Monica, *Non-Standard Work: The Implications for Pension Policy and Retirement Readiness* (Paper prepared for the Women's Bureau, Ottawa: Human Resources Development Canada, 1996) [unpublished].

Trakman, Leon, "The Demise of Positive Liberty? *Native Women's Association of Canada* v. *Canada*" (1995) 6 *Constitutional Forum* 71.

Trakman, Leon, "Section 15: Equality? Where?" (1995) 6 *Constitutional Forum* 112.

Trimble, Linda, "Federalism, the Feminization of Poverty and the Constitution" in David Schneiderman, ed., *Conversations Among Friends — Entre Amies: Proceedings of an Interdisciplinary Conference on Women and Constitutional Reform* (Edmonton: University of Alberta, Centre for Constitutional Studies, 1991).

Trudeau, Pierre Elliott, *The Constitution and the People of Canada: An Approach to the Objectives of Confederation, the Rights of People and the Institutions of Government* (Ottawa: Government of Canada, 1969).

Turkington, Sheilagh, "A Proposal to Amend the Ontario Human Rights Code: Recognizing Povertyism" (1993) 9 *Journal of Law and Social Policy* 134.

Turner, Joanne, and Francis Turner, *Canadian Social Welfare* (Scarborough: Allyn and Bacon, 1995).

"UN gives low ranking to Canada for its record on child poverty, suicide" *The [Vancouver] Sun* (12 June 1996) B8.

Ursel, Jane, *Private Lives, Public Policy: 100 Years of State Intervention in the Family* (Toronto: Women's Press, 1992).

Usher, Dan, *The Uneasy Case for Equalization Payments* (Vancouver: Fraser Institute, 1995).

Valverde, Mariana, "Moral Capital" 9 *Canadian Journal of Law and Society* 213.

Vandamme, Francois, "The Revision of the European Social Charter" (1994) 133:5&6 *International Labour Review* 635.

Vickers, Jill, "Why Should Women Care About Federalism" in Douglas M. Brown and Janet Hiebert, eds., *Canada: The State of the Federation 1994* (Ottawa: Institute of Intergovernmental Relations, 1994).

Ward, Kathryn, ed., *Women Workers and Global Restructuring* (Ithaca, N.Y.: ILR Press, 1990).

Waring, Marilyn, *If Women Counted: A New Feminist Economics* (San Francisco: Harper and Row, 1988).

Wells, Paul, "'Group of 22' offers proposal for fixing Canadian federalism" *The [Montreal] Gazette* (2 May 1996) A12.

West, Guida, "The National Welfare Rights Movement: The Social Protest of Poor Women" (1983) 6 *Harvard Women's Law Journal* 325.

West, Robin, "Reconstructing Liberty" (1992) 59 *Tennessee Law Review* 441.

Weston, David, "Gainful Employment" *Nanaimo Times* (25 June 1996) A7.

White, Lucie, "No Exit: Rethinking 'Welfare Dependency' From a Different Ground" (1993) 81 *The Georgetown Law Journal* 1961.

White, Walter, et al., *Introduction to Canadian Politics and Government*, 6th ed. (Toronto: Harcourt Brace, 1994).

Whyte, John D., "Fundamental Justice: The Scope and Application of Section 7 of the *Charter*" (1983) 13 *Manitoba Law Journal* 455.

Wilkins, Russell, *Special Study on the Socially and Economically Disadvantaged, produced for the Health Promotion Studies Unit, Health and Welfare Canada, 1988*.

Williams, Lucy, "The Ideology of Division: Behavior Modification Welfare Reform Proposals" (1992) 102 *The Yale Law Journal* 719.

Windsor, Hugh, "Reflections on a Golden Age" *The [Toronto] Globe and Mail* (16 July 1995) D3.

Wintemute, Robert, "Discrimination Against Same-Sex Couples: Section 15(1) and 1 of the *Charter: Egan* v. *Canada*" (1995) 74 *The Canadian Bar Review* 682.

Wolfe, David, "The Politics of the Deficit" in Bruce Doern, ed., *The Politics of Economic Policy* (Toronto: University of Toronto Press, 1985).

Wolfson, Michael, "Comments" in *Roundtables on the Canada Health and Social Transfer: Final Report* (Ottawa: Canadian Council on Social Development, 1996) 151.

The Women's Caucus Statement: The World Summit for Social Development (February 10, 1994).

Woolley, Frances, *Women and the Canada Assistance Plan* (Ottawa: Status of Women Canada, 1995).

Wright, Michael, "Women, Work and Welfare: The Thomson Report and Beyond" (1989) 5 *Journal of Law and Social Policy* 227.

Wright, Shelley, "Economic Rights and Social Justice: A Feminist Analysis of Some International Human Rights Conventions" (1992) 12 *Australian Yearbook of International Law* 241.

Wright, Shelley, "Economic Rights, Social Justice and the State: A Feminist Reappraisal" in Dorinda Dallmeyer, ed., *Reconceiving Reality: Women and International Law* (Washington: American Society of International Law, 1993).

Wright, Shelley, "Women and the Global Economic Order: A Feminist Perspective" (1995) 10 *American University Journal of International Law and Policy* 861.

Yaffe, Barbara, "Financially-strapped Ottawa views B.C. as a cash cow" *The [Vancouver] Sun* (22 June 1996) A3.

Yalnizyan, Armine, "Budget 1995: Open Intentions, Hidden Costs" (1995) 13 *Social Infopac* 1.

Yalnizyan, Armine, *Defining Social Security: Defining Ourselves: Why We Need to Change Our Thinking Before It's Too Late* (Ottawa: Canadian Centre for Policy Alternatives, 1993).

Yeatman, Anna, "Voice and Representation in the Politics of Difference" in Sneja Gunew and Anna Yeatman, eds., *Feminism and the Politics of Difference* (Halifax: Fernwood Publishing, 1993).

Young, Claire F.L., "(In)visible Inequalities: Women, Tax and Poverty" (1995) 27 *Ottawa Law Review* 99.

Young, Claire, "It's All in the Family: Child Support, Tax and *Thibaudeau*" (1995) 6 *Constitutional Forum* 107.

Young, Claire, "Taxing Times for Women" (1994) 11:3 *SPARC News* 15.

Young, Margot, "Starving in the Shadow of the Law" (1994) 5 *Constitutional Forum* 31.

Zweibel, Ellen, "Women and Poverty Revisited: A Report by the National Council of Welfare" (1990) 22 *Ottawa Law Review* 761.

RESEARCH REPORTS FUNDED BY STATUS OF WOMEN CANADA ON THE CANADA HEALTH AND SOCIAL TRANSFER (CHST) AND ITS IMPACT ON WOMEN

Benefiting Canada's Children: Perspectives on Gender and Social Responsibility
(Des prestations pour les enfants du Canada : perspectives sur l'égalité des sexes et la responsabilité sociale)
Christa Freiler and Judy Cerny
Child Poverty Action Group

Qui donnera les soins? Les incidences du virage ambulatoire et des mesures d'économie sociale sur les femmes du Québec
(Who Will Be Responsible for Providing Care? The Impact of the Move Toward More Ambulatory Care and of Social Economic Policies on Quebec Women)
Association féminine d'éducation et d'action sociale (AFÉAS), Denyse Côté, Éric Gagnon, Claude Gilbert, Nancy Guberman, Francine Saillant, Nicole Thivierge and Marielle Tremblay

Women and the CHST: A Profile of Women Receiving Social Assistance, 1994
(Les femmes et le TCSPS : profil des femmes à l'assistance sociale en 1994)
Katherine Scott
Centre for International Statistics, Canadian Council on Social Development

Women and the Equality Deficit: The Impact of Restructuring Canada's Social Programs
(Les femmes et le déficit en matière d'égalité : l'incidence de la restructuration des programmes sociaux du Canada)
Shelagh Day and Gwen Brodsky
Day, Brodsky and Associates

The Impact of Block Funding on Women with Disabilities
(L'incidence du financement global sur les femmes ayant un handicap)
Shirley Masuda
DAWN Canada

Women's Support, Women's Work: Child Care in an Era of Deficit Reduction, Devolution, Downsizing and Deregulation
(Le soutien aux femmes, le travail des femmes et la garde d'enfants à l'ère de la réduction du déficit, du transfert des responsabilités, de la réduction de la taille de l'État et de la déréglementation)
Gillian Doherty, Martha Friendly and Mab Oloman
Doherty Inc.

RESEARCH REPORTS FUNDED BY STATUS OF WOMEN CANADA ON WOMEN'S ACCESS TO JUSTICE

A Complex Web: Access to Justice for Abused Immigrant Women in New Brunswick
(Une toile complexe : l'accès au système de justice pour les femmes immigrantes victimes de violence au Nouveau-Brunswick)
Baukje Miedema and Sandra Wachholz

Lesbian Struggles for Human Rights in Canada (not published)
(La lutte des lesbiennes pour la reconnaissance de leurs droits fondamentaux au Canada) (non publié)
Ann Robinson and Sandra Kirby

L'accès à la justice pour des victimes de harcèlement sexuel : l'impact de la décision *Béliveau-St-Jacques* sur les droits des travailleuses à l'indemnisation pour les dommages
(Access to Justice for Sexual Harassment Victims: The Impact of *Béliveau St-Jacques* on Female Workers' Right to Damages)
Katherine Lippel and Diane Demers

Getting a Foot in the Door: Women, Civil Legal Aid and Access to Justice
(Un pied dans la porte : les femmes, l'aide juridique en matière civile et l'accès à la justice)
Lisa Adario
National Association of Women and the Law

Family Mediation in Canada: Implications for Women's Equality
(La médiation familiale au Canada : ses implications pour l'égalité des femmes)
Sandra A. Goundry, Yvonne Peters and Rosalind Currie
Equality Matters! Consulting

Status of Women Canada Policy Research Fund

Title: _____

We Value Your Feedback

Your comments and suggestions can help us make sure our publications are useful. If you have a moment, please answer and return the following questionnaire. Thank you for your time.

(5 = extremely useful)
(1 = not very useful)

1. Was the report useful to you?   5 4 3 2 1

    a)   Which part of the report did you find most helpful?

    _____

    _____

    b)   How could it have been more helpful?
    Comments:_____

    _____

    _____

    _____

2. How did you use the report? As a tool in:

    Policy development   ☐   Policy research ☐   Advocacy ☐

    Other:_____

    _____

3. Are you affiliated with:

    Women's Organization   ☐   Federal Government   ☐

    Other Non-Governmental   Provincial/Territorial Government ☐
    Organization   ☐
                                     Municipal Government   ☐

    University/College   ☐

    Other:_____

    _____

Please return this questionnaire by mail or fax to:
   Status of Women Canada
   Research Directorate
   360 Albert Street
   Suite 700
   Ottawa, Ontario K1A 1C3   Fax: (613) 957-3359